VOICES OF
COLDITZ

VOICES OF COLDITZ

HANDWRITTEN ACCOUNT BY ALLIED OFFICERS INSIDE OFLAG IV-C

Transcribed and edited by Peter Clay from
the original Second World War compilation
by Lieutenant William A. 'Dopey' Millar
and Lieutenant J. E. R. 'Jerry' Wood

FONTHILL

Fonthill Media Limited
Fonthill Media LLC
www.fonthillmedia.com
office@fonthillmedia.com

First published in the United Kingdom
and the United States of America 2014

British Library Cataloguing in Publication Data:
A catalogue record for this book is available from the British Library

ISBN 978-1-78155-249-0

Typeset in 10pt on 13pt Minion Pro
Printed and bound in England

CONTENTS

EDITORIAL NOTE

The Colditz YMCA Wartime Log is 240mm high by 170mm wide and extends to 150 numbered pages with six unnumbered preliminary pages. A few pages are blank and the reason for this is unknown, but it may have been that these pages were left for unknown officers to make their entries—entries which never occurred. Some other pages are faint to the extent that they are barely legible. In some cases these were written in pencil, in other cases the quality of the original ink was poor and has faded away. All of the completed pages are reproduced in this book, some much fainter than others. Pages 139 to 142 (two complete leaves) are missing from the Wartime Log.

A selection of pages is also included in the colour section, and this provides a better visual representation of the Wartime Log.

The reproduction of the faint pages has been extremely challenging and the reader is asked to be forbearing. This problem was compounded by the fact that the original is not completely 'squared' into a correct rectangular shape due to imprecise guillotining when the blank book was manufactured in Switzerland. It will also be seen that the red line at the top of each page was also not completely horizontal. To make life even more challenging, many writers used every space possible to cram in their text, with writing often going right up to the edge—from the gutter to the fore-edge. Therefore, when scanned, some black or dark edges occasionally appear on the pages. Where this has occurred these have been left, and no attempt has been made to 'clean' them up.

When the 1945-46 incomplete transcription was published as *Detour* in 1946, additional colour and black and white illustrations were added—mostly made up of head and shoulder portraitures, 29 of which have been included. These have been included in the colour section in this edition, but it should be emphasized that these were from *Detour* only, and do not appear in the original Wartime Log. A few other contemporary and modern photographs are also included in this edition.

INTRODUCTION

1. COLDITZ CASTLE—OFLAG IVC

Perched imposingly on top of the highest point of a small town in eastern Germany, Colditz Castle was built originally in 1014 as a hunting lodge for the kings of Saxony. As a focal point of various battles and sieges, the castle has suffered serious damage at many times over the centuries and was completely destroyed in the fifteenth century during the Hussite wars. By 1800 it had become a prison, and then a mental hospital in 1828. The Second World War saw its transition once again to a German prison camp for the duration of the conflict. Initially Colditz was used as a transit camp for Polish prisoners after the fall of Poland in 1939. In November 1940 the first British prisoners arrived, soon to be joined by comrades from various other allied countries.

Colditz Prison, or Oflag IVC as it was known by the Nazis, was chosen as the place of incarceration for the most important and most notorious escapers among allied officers. The castle walls were thought initially by the Germans to be totally secure. Hermann Goering visited the castle himself and declared that escape was an impossibility, yet the cunning, ingenuity and sheer persistence of the prisoners showed otherwise.

By the end of the war there had been 120 escapes. Although most men were recaptured, thirty-one made 'home runs' to their own countries, which is a high rate of success for prisoners isolated in a very secure prison fortress in Saxony.

The Red Cross organization was instrumental in maintaining the morale and health of allied prisoners in German prison camps. Regular deliveries of parcels contained various items of food including jam and chocolate, as well as clothing, gramophone records other goods to make life tolerable for the interned men. In 1943 the international YMCA produced blank Wartime Log books for inclusion in the parcels.

Delivery of Red Cross parcels was made possible because of the Geneva Convention, to which Germany was a signatory, and evidently the guards in Colditz adhered to its rules. This is illustrated by the fact that at times with the help of the parcels, the prisoners were fed better than their captors and enjoyed such luxuries as chocolate, while the Germans went without, even though they inspected the parcels before handing them to their prisoners, but respected their rights.

In researching the story of Colditz and comparing it with the savage brutality of wartime events in other parts of Europe, particularly in the prison camps and especially the concentration camps of Germany, one is struck by the fact that treatment of prisoners in Colditz was relatively humane. The allied officers and men, many of whom were young and rebellious, amused themselves on occasion by annoying the guards or 'goon-baiting' and even dropping water bombs on them without suffering serious or violent consequences in retaliation. One might say that on both sides in general there was a degree of mutual gentlemanly respect. However, it was still the duty of every officer to attempt to escape, and the duty of every guard to shoot any fleeing prisoner to prevent him from gaining freedom.

2. HOW THIS MANUSCRIPT WAS DISCOVERED

Growing up in the Channel Island of Guernsey in the nineteen-fifties and sixties, I was keenly aware of the history of the Second World War, partly because I attended a boys' school where we trained in an Army Cadet Corps, and where war comics were traded and read with avid enthusiasm. The Channel Islands were the only part of the British Isles occupied by the Germans during the war. Mr Churchill had other priorities, so the allies did not attempt to recapture the islands.

In 1939, because of the outbreak of war and the impending enemy occupation, my mother, who was a teenage girl at the time, was evacuated from the island and sent on a ship to Canada for the duration of the war. Soon after she arrived in Canada, she met the man who was to become my father. He was a Canadian teacher and elocution coach who joined the army in order to serve his country. Leaving Canada for the expedition to Europe, he kept my mother's home address in Guernsey with him as he entered the war, serving as a Captain in the Canadian Army.

After the 1945 fall of Berlin— the final victory when Russian, American, French and British troops entered the city and brought an end to the tyranny of Hitler—the armistice was signed and weary troops made their way home from Europe. The mission was accomplished, so the Canadian Army prepared to make their way westward to the coast for destinations in Britain and finally back to Canada. My father was demobilized in England where he worked for a period after the war as entertainment manager for Butlin's Holiday Camps in Filey and other locations. My mother, who returned once again to Guernsey from Canada, received a telegram from him, and they married soon after.

Because of his military duties, my father was one of the later Canadian soldiers to leave Europe. Many years afterwards he showed me the souvenirs he brought back from the war, including a German gold watch that he obtained by trading his cigarette rations, a hand-crafted cigarette box with a maple leaf on the lid, a Zeiss German movie camera, and finally, a very well-worn book which I shall describe in more detail.

Captain Carl Clay.

One day as Captain Carl Clay supervised the clean-up of Canadian army quarters, he came across a somewhat battered log book in an empty locker in the Officers' Mess. The book had a hardbound light brown coarse cloth cover and a large maple leaf printed on the front, and above the maple leaf were the words 'A Wartime Log'. Inside were 150 pages, each numbered in red at the top. Inside the back cover in red type were the words 'Printed by Atar S.A., Geneva 1943'. Every page was covered with small hand-written stories, poems and illustrations, as if each writer had tried to cram as much information as possible onto his assigned pages. Seeing that there were interesting accounts written in the book, my father brought it back with him and subsequently kept it in a drawer in his bedroom for many years. He did not seem to know much about it, and never really read it to my knowledge.

When I reached my teens and was more interested in war stories, I attempted to read some of the book, but because of the small size of the writing, different styles of penmanship and the fact that some accounts were written in French, this was not an easy task, so I read only a few. However, I could tell from the more easily legible pages that they contained fascinating first-hand experiences of allied officers, signed and dated by each man. Years later, sometime in the 1980s, when I had become an adult, my father who was advancing in years, gave the book to me to keep with a view possibly to publishing the material, which he thought had never seen the light of day and would be lost forever if I could not arrange somehow for its publication.

I began the task of transcribing the book, page by page. Inside the front cover were two large loose sheets of paper containing a numbered list of all the writers with their names, signatures, ranks, units and home addresses. On another loose sheet was a typewritten description and small illustration of Mike Sinclair, a British officer who was killed in an escape attempt from a German prison camp.

As I progressed through the pages, painstakingly copying every word onto my computer, I began to notice a pattern. Although the stories were of various battles, bombings and prisons escapes, at the end of every account was the writer's name, rank and unit, dated at a specific time in 1944, many with the words 'Oflag IVC' or 'Colditz'.

Then I began to realize that the whole book was handwritten inside the walls of the famous German castle that had been converted into a prisoner of war camp to house the most important officers and prolific escapers among the allied prisoners captured by the Germans.

This book was indeed significant.

I decided to continue with the daunting task of working through all the pages, because of the historical value of the work. In my research I shared part of one of the stories with a Colditz expert in England. To my utter amazement, he recognized the text as being part of a book called *Detour*, which was published under the auspices of the Red Cross, and supported by high-ranking British dignitaries in 1946. At first I did not understand how this was possible. My father brought the original handwritten document from a locker in the Officers' Mess in 1945 and kept it in a drawer until about 1985. In order to discover more, I located and purchased a copy of *Detour* from a used bookseller in the South of England.

After further research I eventually deduced what had transpired; by the summer of 1943, the International YMCA has started sending to prison camps blank bound log books in which to write stories, paste photographs and sketch scenes. It was thought that these memoirs would be worth keeping after the war. Inside Colditz, in a project initiated by Lieutenant William A. 'Dusty' Millar and continued by another Canadian Engineer Lieutenant, J. E. R. Wood, referred to in some of the hand-written accounts as 'Jerry', the two Canadian officers passed around the blank book in which fellow prisoners were asked to write short, poignant personal accounts of events at any time during the war. Millar was killed during an escape attempt in 1944, but Wood kept the project going, and after liberation he took the original work to the Red Cross for publication. This was received well, and Wood's project gained support and inclusions from many allied dignitaries and high-ranking figures in the Commonwealth countries. Illustrations of officers were included, as were a few handwritten accounts from two other log books.

Because of the obvious shortages of paper and other materials at the end of the war, the manuscript for *Detour* was taken to various places in order to have the book produced and printed. The British Army of the Rhine became involved and enlisted the assistance of plate-makers in Antwerp and a civilian printing company in Hamburg. An industrious Private Judy Cleveland in the Canadian Women's Army Corps typed out the pages in 1945.

After the war was over, Lieutenant Wood returned to Canada. In 1947 he was asked to make a presentation at the Empire Club in Toronto, detailing his wartime experience and how *Detour* came to be. The following excerpts are taken directly from his speech:

> We learned about the Geneva Convention and Red Cross parcels. Ridiculous as it sounds, none of us had ever read the Geneva Convention, and few, if any, of us knew the score on parcels.
>
> The Red Cross aimed at getting one parcel to each P.O.W. each week. All the parcels went to a Central International Red Cross Pool at Geneva. They were then dispatched to German distribution centres. One might get a British, Canadian, American or New Zealand parcel. It made for variety.
>
> In addition, the Red Cross aimed at 50 cigarettes per man per week. This was augmented by private parcels from home. In the case of the Canadians, we had thousands. Very handy they were, too, for trading with the German guards for food and other things we needed.
>
> Uniforms, greatcoats, boots, blankets, etc. came to us through Red Cross channels as did Y.M.C.A. sports equipment, and plenty of it!
>
> Shortly after our arrival at Oflag IVC the International Y.M.C.A. sent each of us Canadians

a grand diary with a large maple leaf on the front. It had nice white pages to write on and buff coloured ones for sketching.

The late Lt. Bill Miller, Royal Canadian Engineers, of Edmonton, the Canadian 'Escape King', hit upon the idea of having the boys write short, punchy incidents of their military and prison career. I asked Bill if he minded if I did the same. He said: "By all means go ahead. The more the merrier!" That was the start of *Detour*.

A brilliant young English artist, a Mortar Officer by trade, by the name of Lt. John Watton, did the seventy odd pastel portraits and cartoons in the book. The Red Cross sent him the drawing materials.

By the end of the war we had quite a collection of incidents covering battle, prison and escape. A Dutchman in the R.A.F. said: "Why not publish it for the benefit of the Red Cross?" The boys unanimously thought that was a swell idea.

The Americans liberated us on April 15, 1945. Four days later we flew to England.

Being a Canadian I contacted our Canadian Red Cross through Lord Bennett, who was Chairman of the London Committee. He sent me to Col. R. W. Frost, the Overseas Commissioner. The Colonel thought the idea a good one and passed me to the Hon. Vincent Massey and to Canadian Military Headquarters. All threw in their weight, including the British Ministry of Information. The Right Hon. Sir Stafford Cripps guided us through a maze of detail.

The British and Australian Red Cross Societies agreed to join the Canadians in financing the production of 100,000 copies. V.J. Day came so we reduced it to 50,000. Ultimate paper restrictions reduced us to 16,000 copies.

These negotiations took two months. We fiddled away two more trying to get paper. It was now September. Then a Toronto Engineer, Colonel Mickey MacDonald, dropped into the little hole–in–the–wall in Cancross House that I called my office, and suggested I go over to Army Headquarters in Holland. He was sure the 'boys' could do something. They did.

Lt. Col. John Craig, M.B.E., also of Toronto, lined up the deal. The type for the script would be set up in the 1 Cdn. Mobile Printing Section, R.C.A.S.C. at Army H.Q. Then the British boys would take over. A German firm in Hamburg would print the 32 plates in four colours and the monocolour ones; the boys at Field Marshal Montgomery's H.Q., British Army of the Rhine would do the binding, while Canadian Movement Control would get it back to England.

Those English boys were simply terrific. "Of course, old boy, we'll do the job for you". Then a few minutes later: "Just what do you want us to do for you, old boy?" That is co–operation at its best. Answer: "Yes!" And then find a way to do it.

It was now November. I returned to England. The publisher had quit because he could not control the production in Germany. Then just to cheer matters up we found that the wangle we were going to get our paper on went sour.

However, we finally got off the mark in Hamburg in January, 1946. Within four months we had the production job complete. The printing was finished in May. The type was set up by the Canadians in Holland. The Hamburg Germans did the printing; the Rhine Army boys the binding; while the R.C.A.F. flew the completed job back to England in the spare space in the 'mail can'! The paper came from England, the photo plates from Antwerp, gold for the lettering from The Northern Miner in Toronto. A young English parachutist 'Saboteur' and ex-P.O.W., Capt.

Peter Baker, M.C., acted as publisher with his Falcon Press. He was silly enough to be captured behind the lines skulking around in civilian clothes.

I made six trips to the Continent, most of them by air, and clocked up 10,000 miles in a jeep rattling about Northern Europe, coordinating all this nonsense. We called it the "Pony Express".

3,000 copies went to Australia, 3,500 to Canada, and the rest to Britain.

The Rhine Army boys bound some deluxe copies in Morocco leather; one in blue for the King, the rest were in brown for Mr. Churchill, Mr. Atlee, the Dominion Prime Ministers and High Commissioners, Field Marshal the Lord Chetwood, who headed the Red Cross, Field Marshal Alexander, Field Marshal Montgomery, and General Crerar.

The P.O.W. side was only one of many Red Cross Departments, but their parcels kept us in one piece. From the bottom of our hearts we say "Thank you!"

As explained by Wood in his own words, the logistical challenges in producing any publication immediately after the war were formidable, but *Detour* had support from the very top and was the first book about Colditz.

At some point between typing out the pages, copying the illustrations, making plates and producing the final printed and bound version, the original handwritten document containing the bulk of the material was left behind in the locker in an Officers' Mess. It was possibly simply discarded because it seemed to have no further use. The information had been copied for printing, so there may have been no point in keeping it. My father, unaware of the whole story, picked it up and saved it for posterity. In leaving it to me, he presented me with a larger undertaking than I imagined, as I grappled with the task of bringing the original book to life in a form in which the reader can gain as close an understanding as possible of the time, effort and memories that were poured into the pages of that wartime log by the prisoners of Colditz.

I have spent countless hours over many years reading, deciphering and typing every story, checking each word, number, rank and comma. *Detour* was useful for comparing texts, so I took the liberty of borrowing the last two paragraphs of page 138 from that book as the lines were missing from my original. I also deferred gratefully to *Detour* for certain portions of the French tales. However, there were many discrepancies between the original log and the *Detour* version, including missing lines and incorrect words. This is entirely understandable given the circumstances under which it was reproduced. Even one of the illustrations in *Detour* is a slightly altered tracing of the original.

Although most of the stories contained in the following pages were printed in 1946, others were excluded, presumably omitted by the editor for reasons of space. Ten stories from the original log were not included in *Detour* so to the best of my knowledge the poem at the beginning, and the stories commencing in the logbook on pages 10, 11, 27, 30, 32, 52, 69, 111 and 130 have never been read. They have sat unpublished since they were written seventy years ago. There are also illustrations here that have never seen the light of day before; the signature on two of them is that of Seni, whose name does not appear on most lists of prisoners of Colditz, so is something of an enigma. The only name I have found with any similarity is that of the French Major General Arsene-Marie-Paul Vauthier who arrived at

Colditz in 1945. He could have been nicknamed 'Seni' but whether he or somebody else penned the sketches is unknown.

My goal in presenting this book is to bring to the reader the text in a form as close as possible to the original, so that a sense may be perceived of how this log was written, and perhaps what it must have felt like to be an incarcerated allied officer.

There are accounts by four of the 'Prominente', the important prisoners of war who were incarcerated in Colditz partly because of their potential use as hostages during later negotiations with the British and their allies. The four were General Bór-Komorowski who led the Warsaw Uprising, Captain the Earl of Hopetoun who was the son of the Viceroy of India, Lieutenant Max de Hamel and Captain Michael Alexander. After a foiled escape attempt together, all the Prominente were removed from Colditz towards the end of the war when Hitler gave orders to have them executed. However, a German officer, realizing that his own chances during post-war law trials would be improved if he liberated the Prominente instead of killing them, released them to the advancing American troops as Germany surrendered.

The standard of literacy in this wartime log is generally high, as would be expected from officers, with a matter-of-fact, unemotional style that one would anticipate from trained military men. When reading this, one feels the sense of resolve, determination and spirit that these men exhibited, in their fantastically daring escapes and simple will to live and fight another day.

VOICES OF COLDITZ
THE YMCA NOTEBOOK FROM
OFLAG IVC

To Those who have Governed Us.

This time they died with a cynical smile
A few twisted thoughts and a muttered word,
"Peace in our Time" was the slogan they'd heard
While hysterical crowds were shouting "Sieg Heil".
They knew you'd bungled and would bungle more
But were too tired for anger, too hopeless
To worry about the grim bloodiness
Of the war that followed "War to end War".
Remember they died strong in conviction
That "Peace Everlasting" is only fiction :
But think no less of them for that blast you,
Remember those men your smugness slew
Died with a shrug and a lop-sided grin
Paying the price of your Party's sin.

May — 1944

A WARTIME LOG

A REMEMBRANCE

FROM HOME

THROUGH THE CANADIAN Y. M. C. A.

Published by
THE WAR PRISONERS' AID OF THE Y. M. C. A.
37 Quai Wilson
GENEVA — SWITZERLAND

The Wartime Log notebook has six un-numbered pages at the front. The text below was written on un-numbered page 2. This is followed by un-numbered page 3 which is the title page.

To Those Who Have Governed Us

This time they died with a cynical smile
A few twisted thoughts a muttered word,
"Peace in our time" was the slogan they'd heard
While hysterical crowds were shouting "Sieg Heil"
They know you'd bungled and would bungle more
But were too tired for anger, too hopeless
To worry about the grim bloodiness
Of the war that followed "War to end War".
Remember they died strong in conviction
That "Peace Everlasting" is only a fiction;
But think no less of them for that blast you,
Remember those men your smugness slew
Died with a shrug and a lopsided grin
Paying the price of your Party's sin

May 1944
(*Pat Ferguson*)
Un-numbered page 4.

Colditz '42

Some birds sing a strain in joy
Others a song of sorrow
One is merry: the other sad
Yet neither heeds the morrow.

Each strikes a poise of beauty
Within its range of feeling
One is merry: the other sad
Yet neither is revealing.

Each bird sings quite differently
Unmindful of the weather
One is merry: the other sad
Yet both must live together.

Alan C.

Some birds sing a strain in joy
Other a song of sorrow
One is merry: the other sad
Yet neither heeds the morrow.

Each strikes a poise of beauty
Within its range of feeling
One is merry: the other sad
Yet neither is revealing.

Each bird sings quite differently
Unmindful of the weather
One is merry: the other sad
Yet both must live together.

1. MIKE SINCLAIR—KILLED SEPT. 25 1944 WHILE ATTEMPTING TO ESCAPE

Mike came from an Ulster family living in England. He was at school at Winchester, went up to Cambridge, and joined the 60th just before the war. He fought at Calais, was taken prisoner, was sent to Laufen and then to Poland. There he made his first escape, in which he crossed frontiers of the General Government, Slovakia, Hungary, Yugoslavia, and was caught getting into Bulgaria. He tried to escape on the way back through Czecho-Slovakia, was recaptured, held for a time by the Gestapo, and finally sent on here two and a half years ago.

Since then his life has been practically one attempt after another to escape. On different occasions he has got as far as Cologne, the Swiss Frontier, the Dutch Frontier. You know better than any congregation in the world what that means. About a hundred of you have got right away from a camp once, only about twenty more than once—let alone near a frontier—and this is the 'escapers' camp.

He didn't usually take foolhardy risks, but when he went with others and risks were unavoidable he took his full share—and more. You remember his escape as Franz Josef (Mike was wounded in an attempt to get a party out. He was disguised as the sergeant major of the guard company). And in his last and riskiest attempt he went alone. Whenever the story of escaping in this war is written, Mike Sinclair's name will be there, high up on the list. And he deserves it because he had qualities that really, ultimately matter.

When he'd made his mind up on a thing he was absolutely determined to carry it through. He made mistakes, as we all do, but he learnt from them and he had a conscience about them. Most people's reaction to failure is to wipe it out of their memories and be comfortable. Mike's reaction was NOT to forget it—and at times it made him very depressed—but to go on trying till he'd made up for it. That is the kind of character that really matters in a soldier—the kind of quality that made Wellington and Sir John Moore great.

On at least two occasions while he was here he made escapes that any soldier would be proud of. When he and Jack Best went through the wire in the orchard, the scheme—and it was largely Mike's scheme—was about the most brilliant there's been here. It came off, so we took it for granted, vbut it was a grand piece of work. The other occasion, was his earlier Franz Josef escape, when he was nearly killed by a guard losing his head. Mike took the lead in the preparations and the escape itself—he spent three months on it. With 2 or 3 people it was a 'certainty' with the members he agreed to include—well, not likely to succeed. At one stage in the escape it was clear to Mike that to get the main body out was going to be much more dangerous and difficult job than expected, but that by forgetting about them he and Lance could walk out and get clear away. That's a testing moment for a man's character, and we know how unhesitatingly he chose the unselfish way.

Finally, Mike was a believing Christian, and one who'd known suffering and turned it to use. That's why, although his death is a tragedy for his parents, it isn't just a wasteful tragedy of a life. We say in our Creed that we believe in the Resurrection of the dead, and we KNOW that Christ's promises are sure. Mike was the kind of man who wouldn't be confident about himself, but we who knew him know that he is all right, and that he's met up with his younger brother, who fell at Anzio, and the countless others who in their country's service have gone before us on the way that leads through death, but comes out in a brighter eternal world.

MIKE SINCLAIR

Killed Sept. 25 1944 while attempting to escape.

—came from an Ulster family living in England. He was at school at Winchester, went up to Cambridge, joined the 60th just before the war. He fought at Calais, was taken prisoner, was sent to Laufen, and to Poland. There he made his first escape, in which he crossed the frontiers of the General Government, Slovagy, Jugo-Slavia, and was caught getting into Bulgaria. He tried to escape on the way back through Slovakia, was recaptured, held for a time by the Gestapo, and finally sent on here two and a half years —. Since then his life has been practically one attempt after another to escape. On different occasions he has got as far as Cologne, the Swiss Frontier, the Dutch Frontier. You know better than any congregation in the world what that means. About a hundred of you have got right away from a prison, only about twenty more than once — let alone near a frontier — and this is the 'escapers of—

He takes—self take foolhardy risks, but when he went with others and risks were unavoidable he pull share — and more. You remember his escape as Franz Josef [Mike was wounded in an attempt at a party out. He was disguised as the sergeant-major of the guard company] And on his last attempt he went alone. Wherever the story of escaping in this war is written, Mike Sinclair be there, high up on the list. And he deserves it because he had qualities that really, ultimately mattered. When he'd made his mind up on a thing he was absolutely determined to carry it through. He made—this, as we all do, but he learnt from them and he had a conscience about them. Most people's action to failure is to wipe it out of their memories and be comfortable. Mike's reaction was to—right it — and at times it made him very depressed — but to go on trying till he'd made up for it. That's the kind of character that really matters in a soldier — the kind of quality that made Wellington and John Moore great.

On at least two occasions while he was here he made escapes that any soldier would be proud—when he and Jack Best went through the wire in the Orchard, the scheme — and it was largely he's scheme — was about the most brilliant there's been here. It came off, so we took it for—ted, but it was a grand piece of work. The other occasion was on his earlier 'Franz Jos—escape, when he was nearly killed by a guard losing his head. Mike took the lead in the preparation—the escape itself — he spent three months on it. With 2 or 3 people it was a certainty, with th—whom he agreed to include — well not likely to succeed. At one stage in the escape it was clear to—to get the whole body out was going to be a much more dangerous and difficult job than expected, but th—getting about three he and Lance could walk out and get clear away. That's a testing moment for—his character, and we know how unhesitatingly he chose the unselfish way.

Finally, Mike was a believing Christian, and one who'd known suffering and turned it to use. That's why, altho' his death is a tragedy for his parents, it isn't just a wasteful tragedy of a life. We say in our Creed that we believe in the Resurrection of the dead. We know that Christ's promises are sure. Mike was the kind of man who wouldn't be confident about himself, but we who knew him know that he is all right, and that he has met up with his younger brother, who fell at Anzio, and the countless others who in country's service have gone before us on the way that leads through death, but comes in a brighter eternal world.

———————

...ellent German + my complete silence at all times we had a simple journey travelling ... except for a few hours walking during both nights.
On our return to Colditz we were told that one or other or both of us had accidentally ... alarm bell on the terrace + so summoned to goon to witness our escape.
                                John W. Best   17-12-44

Escaping is one of the most exciting things you can do + it is certainly the most exciting thing I have done. On February 23rd 1944 Mike Sinclair had a carefully prepared scheme + I was lucky enough to be going to accompany him. Many hours had been spent stooging, from points of vantage, watching the 'goons' on guard to note any loop holes, however small. At last we had been noted + it seemed a first class show for two men if the conditions were right for starting.

We had just had a last hot meal eaten in haste + we were already dressed in our best 'civvies' brought out from hides; papers + money on us also a brief case with food + change of socks. Our shoes were muffled with socks pulled over the top + dark balaclava was covering our heads except for our eyes. Two bars had already been cut in the window + a trestle pushed up against it so that we could be pushed out easily. A 60ft rope was ready anchored + the brief case + stout rope tied on to the free end. Mike was lying on the table arms + legs straight out + the wire cutters tied to him ; the two window bar benders standing by + some one else was ready to feed him out. The controller was at another window watching + listening for the 'go' signal on the observation post 2 stories higher. There was a net work of stooges bringing reports of the routine movements of the guards; an extra complication was caused by a workman + sentry doing a repair just outside the room! There was even our artist settled at the back taking it all in. The whole room was dead silent, but you could feel prophecy throbbing with excitement + my heart was going 19 to the dozen as any second now we were off.

"Go!" The bars are bent, the rope thrown out + Mike pushed out feet first through the bars. Some trouble with the wire cutters getting jammed, but he is ready just before the all out; I lie down ready on the operating table + out I go. The first drop is just 25ft onto the terrace. Mike is disentangling the rope + I throw the end over the balustrade so that the stout rope + brief case jerk off + so save us untying them. Mike goes off first + I follow him very quickly as I hear the door from the terrace into the guard room unlocked! We lie flat close under the wall + I have the stout rope + brief case in my hands. The 60ft rope disappears up like a streak of lightening. We stay motionless about 3 minutes; it seems an age. I can watch a goon placidly pacing his beat. We are off again — a short dash across the orchard — Mike goes to the wire + starts cutting at the side of the sentry box that I have run to. On the terrace I see a goon looking at the window we have just left!

Many! goes Mike first out on the wire; the goon on the terrace turns round + looks straight at us. I try to tell Mike, but daren't make too much noise + I fail to contact Mike. The goon on duty goes does not hear a thing. The terrace goon looks back at the window. Mike does second + third cuts with the terrace goon hearing each one, but miraculously seeing nothing. Mike now crawls through the wire + fastens the rope + drops over. I follow through the wire, + lie on top of the wall + start patching up the hole in the wire. "Hullo!" shouts the goon on the terrace. I don't wait, but drop over, only 15 or so to tell Mike the situation. We are on a very steep slope covered in barbed wire. We keep close under the wall + go as fast as we can; slipping, sliding + tearing our clothes. In about 20 secs we are on a path + immediately cut a large hole through the barbed wire, we are through like a flash + slide down into the back yard of a cottage. An old woman rushes to her window to see what it is all about. All is quiet back at the castle. We hastily brush ourselves, walk out + away.

We are very lucky outside after an exciting start. We have to sew up the holes torn by the barbed wire in our clothes, threading a needle by the light of a cigarette end is not easy, but we are presentable at last. 46 hours later we are caught by the civil police at Kerve, 25 miles from the Dutch frontier. There + while

3. THE RED FOX (MIKE SINCLAIR)

Escaping is one of the most exciting things you can do and it is certainly the most exciting thing I have done. On February 23rd 1944 Mike Sinclair had a carefully prepared scheme and I was lucky enough to be going to accompany him. Many hours had been spent 'stooging' from points of vantage and watching the 'Goons' on guard to note any loop holes, however small. At last one had been noted and it seemed a first class show for two men if the conditions were right for starting.

We had just had a last hot meal eaten in haste and we were already dressed in our best 'civis' brought out from hides; papers and money on us also a brief case with food and a change of socks. Our shoes were muffled with socks pulled over the top and dark balaclavas covering our heads except for our eyes. Two bars had already been cut on the window and a trestle pushed up against it so that we could be pushed out easily. A 60 ft rope was already anchored and the brief case and short rope tied on to the free end. Mike was lying on the table, arms and legs straight out and the wire cutters tied to his leg, the two window bar benders standing by and someone else was ready to feed the rope out. The controller was at another window watching and listening for the 'Go' signal from the observation post 2 stories higher. There was a network of 'stooges' bringing in reports of the routine movements of the guards; an extra complication was by a workman and sentry doing a repair just outside the room! There was even our artist sitting at the back taking it all in. The whole room was dead silent, but you could feel the atmosphere throbbing with excitement and my heart was going 19 to the dozen as any second now we were off.

Go!! The bars are bent, the rope thrown out and Mike pushed out feet first through the bars. He has some trouble with the wire cutters getting jammed, but he is ready just before the rope is all out. I lie down ready on the operating table and out I go. The first chap is just over 25 ft onto the terrace. Mike is disentangling the rope and I throw the end over the ballustrade and note that the short rope and brief case jerk off and so save us untying them. Mike goes over first and I follow him very quickly as I hear the door from the terrace into the guard house being unlocked! We lie flat close under the wall and I have the short rope and brief case in my hands. The 60ft rope disappears up like a streak of lightning. We stay motionless for about 3 minutes; it seems like an age. I can watch a goon placidly pacing his feet. We are off again—a short dash across the orchard—Mike goes to the wire and starts cutting to the side of the sentry box that I have run to. On the terrace I see a Goon looking back at the window we have just left!

Twang! goes Mike's first cut on the wire; the goon on the terrace turns round and looks straight at us. I try to tell Mike, but daren't make too much noise and I fail to contact Mike. The Goon on sentry go does not hear a thing. The terrace Goon looks back at the window. Mike does his second and third cuts with the terrace Goon hearing each one, but miraculously seeing nothing. Mike now crawls through the wire, fastens the rope and drops over. I follow through the wire, lie on top of the wall and start patching up the hole in the wire. "Hullo!" shouts the Goon on the terrace. I don't wait, but drop over, only 15' or so and tell Mike the situation. We are on a very steep slope covered in barbed wire. We keep close under the wall and go as fast as we can; slipping, sliding and tearing our clothes. In about 20 yds we are on a path and immediately cut a large hole through the final wire; we are through like a flash and slide down into the back yard of a cottage. An old woman rushes to her window to see what it is all about. All is quiet back at the castle. We hastily brush ourselves, walk out and away.

We are very lucky outside after an exciting start. We have to sew up the holes torn by the barbed wire in our clothes, threading a needle by the light of a cigarette end is not easy, but we are presentable at last. 46 hours later we are caught by the civil police at Reine, 25 miles from the Dutch frontier. Thanks to Mike's excellent German and my complete silence at all times we had a simple journey travelling by train except for a few hours walking during both nights.

On our return to Colditz we were told that one or other or both of us had accidentally pressed the alarm bell on the terrace and so summoned the Goon to witness our escape.

John W. Best, Fl/Lt. R.A.F.   17-12-44

Page 4 of the notebook is blank except for the single word 'Wings' written at the top left next to the printed number 4.

5.   SOUTH OF ENGLAND—AUGUST 1940

It was Sunday noon on a hot summer day. As we drove into Edenbridge on the conclusion of our recce, the streets were almost empty and the warm peaceful drowsiness of a Kent village good to look upon. The wail of the air-raid siren—at once mournful and strident—seemed particularly discordant in that lovely scene.

But that it was necessary none could doubt because this was during the Battle of Britain. Even as we climbed out of our car we heard shouts of "There they are!" from people running out of houses, into the streets, to see the first of the regular afternoon shows. And as I looked up, following their gaze, into that cloudless sky with its hot sun blazing down, I saw an unforgettable sight.

Right above me, at no great height, a large, closely packed formation of two-motored German bombers was droning its seemingly slow and implacable way towards London. The thought of their capacity for destruction cut sharply across my appreciation of the glint of sunlight upon their glistening wings.

I was acutely aware of the vast power behind these determined attempts upon the chief stronghold of fair-dealing and freedom. The skill and dash of those charged with the parrying of these continuous heavy blows inspired me with confidence indeed, but I could not help being oppressed by the comparison between the importance of the issue and the slenderness of the numerical resources of Fighter Command.

But I need not have worried. As I looked I saw, some thousand yards behind the bombers, the flash of a section of our fighters diving on their tails and simply eating up the distance between them.

The leading fighter closed the gap. There was a sharp rattle above the drone of the motors—the noise of an eight-gun Spitfire. The nearest bomber turned on its back and plummetted to the ground. Two and then a third white parachute blossomed against the background of the blue sky. The other two fighters joined the action.

My vague fears were stilled.

C.C. I. Merritt, Lt. Col.

6. LEST WE FORGET!

In November 1941 I was living 'incognito' in a certain town in Poland. My hosts at this particular time had a flat near the outskirts of the town. One bright, cold morning I was having breakfast when seven shattering explosions shook the town. "Friendly planes," exclaimed my host, "Come on." We bundled ourselves into coats and rushed out into the street.

I shall never forget the sight that met our eyes. The streets were crowded with people of every age and hundreds more were pouring from their houses. Many were pointing and gazing at the sky, most were hurrying towards the centre of the town. My host grabbed me and rushed me through the melee till we reached the tram terminus, where people fought to get on the vehicles. At last we got on and bought tickets "to the bombs."

Everywhere people, thousands of them it seemed, were moving rapidly in the same direction. At last we got out near a small square, 500 yards from the station. The crowds were very thick, but I could see several ruined houses, some dead horses, ambulances, stretchers, quite a lot of dead, dying or wounded people and masses of broken glass. As each ambulance drove away the throng burst into delirious cheering. "Why are they cheering?" I asked. "They have come to see the Germans who have been hacked up by the bombs," was the reply. "Some are dead, others will have much pain and may be mutilated for life. It is good."

"But were they all Germans who got hit?" I asked again. My host shrugged. "The majority I suppose, were our people, but if twenty Germans were killed today, it is worth while."

"It is worth while." That is what Poland thinks today. The Polish armies have long since disappeared, but the people carry on the war. In the concentration camps and prisons, in the gangs of forced labour, or face to face with the firing squads, they remain true to their ally, England. Will England remain true to them?

Grismond Davies-Scourfield, Lt. 60th Rifles   Nov 12th 1943

7. AN EVACUATION INCIDENT—FRANCE MAY 1940

'They don't seem to want him up at Hdqrs and we can't find no prisoners' cage, Sir.' The German Oberleutnant looked disconsolate and resigned as he stood between the pair of immaculate Welsh Guardsmen. 'All right Sergeant,' I said, 'you leave him here: I'll look after

South of England - August 1940

It was Sunday noon on a hot summer day. As we drove to Edenbridge on the conclusion of our recce, the streets were almost empty and the warm peaceful drowsiness of a Kent village was good to look upon. The wail of the air-raid siren — at once mournful and strident - seemed particularly discordant in that lovely scene.

But that it was necessary none could doubt because this was during the Battle of Britain. Even as we climbed out of our car we heard shouts of "There they are"! from people running out of houses, into the streets, to see the first of the regular afternoon shows. And as I looked up, following them, to that cloudless sky with its hot sun blazing down, I saw an unforgettable sight.

Right above me, at no great height, a large, closely packed formation of two-motored German Bombers was droning its seemingly slow and implacable way towards London. The sight of their capacity for destruction cut sharply across my appreciation of the glint of the sunlight upon their glistening wings.

I was acutely aware of the vast power behind these determined attempts upon the chief stronghold of fair-dealing and freedom. The skill and dash of these changed with the parrying of these dastardous heavy blows inspired me with confidence indeed, but I could not help being oppressed by the comparison between the importance of the one and the slenderness of the numerical resources of Fighter Command.

But I need not have worried. As I looked I saw, some thousand yards behind the bombers, the flash of a section of our fighters being on their tails and simply eating up the distance between.

The leading fighter closed the gap. There was a sharp rattle above the drone of the motors — the voice of an eight-gun Spitfire. The rearmost bomber turned on its back and plummetted to the ground and then a third white parachute blossomed against the background of blue sky. The other two fighters joined the action.

Lest we forget!

In November 1941 I was living 'incognito' in a certain town in Poland. My hosts at this particular time had a flat near the outskirts of the town. One bright, cold morning I was having breakfast when seven shattering explosions shook the town. "Friendly planes," exclaimed my host, "Come on." We bundled ourselves into coats and rushed out into the street.

I shall never forget the sight that met our eyes. The streets were crowded with people of every age and hundreds more were pouring from their houses. Many were pointing and gazing at the sky, most were hurrying towards the centre of the town. My host grabbed me and rushed me through the mêlée till we reached the tram terminus, where people fought to get on the vehicles. At last we got on and bought tickets "to the bombs."

Everywhere people, thousands of them it seemed, were moving rapidly in the same direction. At last we got out near a small square 500 yards from the station. The crowds were very thick, but I could see several ruined houses, some dead horses, ambulances, stretchers, quite a lot of dead, dying or wounded people and masses of broken glass. As each ambulance drove away the throng burst into delirious cheering. "Why are they cheering?" I asked. "They have come to see the Germans who have been hacked up by the bombs," was the reply. "Some are dead, others will have much pain and may be mutilated for life. It is good." "But were they all Germans who got hit?" I asked again. My host shrugged. "The majority, I suppose, were our people, but if twenty Germans were killed today, it is worth while."

"It is worth while." That is what Poland thinks today. The Polish armies have long since disappeared, but the people carry on the war. In the concentration camps and prisons, in the gangs of forced labour, or face to face with the firing squad, they remain true to their ally, England. Will England remain true to them?

Grismond Davies-Scourfield.

Lt. 60th Rifles.

'They don't seem to want him up at Hdqrs & we can't find no prisoners' cage, Sir'. The German Oberleutnant looked disconsolate & resigned as he stood between the pair of immaculate Welsh Guardsmen. 'All right Sergeant', said, 'you leave him here: I'll look after him'. Yes, I thought, I'll take him back home: he might one day serve as a swop for one of our chaps cast by fate for a thankless rôle in the Dunkirk rearguard.

The beach at La Panne on May 30 1940, where this conversation took place, was a strange sight. Gone were the holiday makers, the deck-chairs & the jolly sun-browned children. Their places had been taken by remnant of the B.E.F – tired men rather dazed by the cataclysm that had swept them there.

I had been told to unload a small Dutch coasting vessel that had arrived with 4000 cases of rations for the rearguard, to load her up with a many men as she could take, & then to sail back home. As the tide came in the men were working up to their waists in the water passing the cases from hand to hand: sixteen hours non-stop saw the last of the cases above high-water mark and we sailed on the morning de-five hundred and twentyone men loaded into a space for thirty-five hundred & twenty tired soaked but happy men – and the oberleutnant & at least was dry!

Twelve hours on a misty sea brought us unmolested to Margate. I visited the oberleutnant twice during the voyage. The first time he told me all about Mr Hitler's plans & about his fiancée in Hannover & I gave him a bottle of stout to lighten his burdens: on the second occasion I found both him & his guard asleep: so I left them.

From Margate pier the 520 dishevelled rabble sang their way to the station. They would have sung their way home if the Ladies of Margate had not stuffed them with tea, buns, chocolate & cake. But I still had my oberleutnant. Got a guard for him & we made our way separately to the railway station. One feels rather stupid taking an oberleutnant for a walk in Margate in wartime. Try it & you will find that the Margate urchins are unbelievably curious. I crossed the road to continue alone on the opposite footpath away from the little crowd that followed, 'Coo', they said, 'es a reel live German Coo, lumme!' But English urchins, as I say, are inquisitive. I had gone a few hundred yards or so when a diminutive grubby little nipper ran across the road and, touching his cap, looked up at me, 'Did catch 'im, Sir?' he said, pointing to my oberleutnant.

Miles Reid.
Maj.

him.' Yes, I thought, I'll take him back home: he might one day serve as a swap for one of our chaps cast by fate for a thankless role in the Dunkirk rearguard.

The beach at La Panne on May 30 1940, where this conversation took place, was a strange sight. Gone were the holiday makers, the deck-chairs and the jolly sun-browned children. Their place had been taken by remnants of the B.E.F.—tired men rather dazed by the cataclysm that had swept them there.

I had been told to unload a small Dutch coasting vessel that had arrived with 4,000 cases of rations for the rearguard, to load her up with as many men as she could take, and then to sail back home. As the tide came in the men were working up to their waists in the water passing the cases from hand to hand: sixteen hours non-stop saw the last of the cases above high-water mark and we sailed on the morning tide—five hundred and twenty one men loaded into a space for thirty—five hundred and twenty tired soaked but happy men—and the Oberleutnant: he at least was dry!

Twelve hours on a misty sea brought us unmolested to Margate. I visited the Oberleutnant twice during the voyage. The first time he told me all about Mr. Hitler's plans and about his fiancée in Hanover, and I gave him a bottle of stout to lighten up his burdens: on the second occasion I found both him and his guard asleep: so I left them.

From Margate Pier the 520 dishevelled rabble sang their way to the station: they would have sung their way home if the ladies of Margate had not stuffed them with tea, buns, chocolate and cake. But I still had my Oberleutnant. I got a guard for him and we made our way separately to the railway station. One feels rather stupid taking an Oberleutnant for a walk in Margate in wartime. Try it and you will find that the Margate urchins are unbelievably curious! I crossed the road to continue alone on the opposite footpath away from the little crowd that followed. 'Coo!' they said' 'e's a reel live German—coo, lumme!' But English urchins, as I say, are inquisitive. I had gone a few hundred yards or so when a diminutive grubby little nipper ran across the road and, touching his cap, looked up at me. 'Didjer catch 'im, Sir!?' he said, pointing to my Oberleutnant.

Miles Reid, Maj.

13. X. 1943.
Oflag IV. C

8. EICHSTÄTT—30TH JUNE, 1943, 12.10 P.M.

After many "fittings" and "rehearsals" our party was ready for the "opening performance." The "plot" was short and simple; namely to walk out of our prison in daylight as a German General and his staff. My "part" was that of the General.

After the finishing touches had been given us by our "dressers" we set out for the gate. As we approached I shouted to the sentry in a raucous voice to open the gate. He responded immediately by shouting to the N.C.O. of the guard.

We continued to "act" standing in front of the gate, examining a large plan of the camp which we had prepared and discussing it. It seemed to me an age, but soon an N.C.O.

appeared, running, and began to open the gate. I shouted at him to hurry up and was delighted to see his hand shaking visibly as he inserted the key in the lock.

The gate opened, the German heels clicked and we passed through but the "show" had to go on as there was a second gate. Again we discussed a proposed extension to our prison and re-examined our "property," the plan. The discussion seemed endless. At last I got my "cue" and we walked up some steps to the next gate. The sentry produced the key, one of my staff opened the gate and we passed through.

We were outside, we were free!

The "opening performance" had been a success.

W. M. Broomhall
Lt. Col. R.E.

9. "TOURNAI" (BELGIUM)—MAY, 1940

We'd been doing the rear-guard for the withdrawal over the line of the canal at Grammont. Our orders had been to hold the positions until 1145 hours and then pull out as fast as we could to an R.V. in a small village behind the line of the Schelde one or two kilometers south of Tournai. As the withdrawal had been completed in the small hours of the morning, a detachment of the 4/7th D.G.s, who were following close behind us and my own company provided the only visible movement on the road at this time. Periodically the stillness of the early summer afternoon was rended by the droning of aircraft, swelling in volume as they thundered overhead somewhat to our left. Then somewhere ahead of us the powerful whine of aircraft gave place to dull detonations, growing louder as we drew nearer to a thick pall of smoke, which stretched out like a screen across our front. The screaming whistle whistle of falling bombs intermingled with explosions, and above the bank of grey-black smoke we could see the flashing of innumerable wings, with their black crosses standing out, like something grim and evil, as they wheeled and banked, returning, like flashes of sun in a mirror, to dive into the billowing smoke, to the accompaniment of the chatter of machine guns. Then gracefully they lifted up out of the dirty smoke and swung off back in the direction from which they'd come.

I now told my driver to speed up, as I thought it best to get through this town of ruins and desolation, sections of which appeared either smoldering or burning furiously, marks of this latest or a previous raid. As we approached the first heap of ruins of what had been Tournai, we were forced to slow down, by a long stream of overturned farm-carts, cars, handcarts and perambulators, with various house-hold goods and chattels scattered over all. The draught animals lay for the most part in their tracks, occasionally a horse or horses with cart slewed out behind them, lying on their backs with their legs sticking up in the air. Dotted about amongst all this—and on the sides of the road—lay, still, lifeless, forms of men women and children. I say lifeless, I hope they were. I could only bring myself to stop at one place, where a woman and three children lay huddled together in the middle of a cross-roads. They had been machine-gunned. From the position of the lifeless bodies it looked as if they'd been

After many "fittings" and "rehearsals" our party
was ready for the "opening performance". The "p[lot]
was short and simple; namely to walk out of [the]
prison in daylight as a German General and [his]
staff. My "part" was that of the General.
After the finishing touches had been given us by
our "dressers" we set out for the gate. As we
approached I shouted to the sentry in a raucou[s]
voice to open the gate. He responded immediate[ly]
by shouting to the N.C.O. of the guard.
We continued our "act" standing in front of the g[ate]
examining a large plan of the camp which we
had prepared and discussing it.   It seemed
to me an age, but soon an N.C.O. appeared,
running, and began to open the gate. I shouted a[t]
him to hurry up and was delighted to see his
hand shaking visibly as he inserted the key in the lo[ck]
The gate opened, German heels clicked and we
passed through but the "show" had to go on as there [was]
a second gate. Again we discussed a proposed
extension to our prison and re-examined our "prop[s]
the plan. The discussion seemed endless. At last
I got my "cue" and we walked up some steps t[o]
the next gate. The sentry produced the key, o[ne]
of my staff opened the gate and we passed thro[ugh]
We were outside, we were free,
The "opening performance" had been a success,

                    W. A. Brooksb[ank]

We'd been doing the rear-guard for the withdrawal over the line of the canal at Grammont. Our orders had been to hold the positions until 1145 hours & then pull out as fast as we could to an R.V. in a small village behind the line of the Schelde one or two kilometers south of Tournai. As the withdrawal had been completed in the small hours of the morning, a detachment of the 4/7th D.G's, who were following close behind us & my own company provided the only visible movement on the road at this time. Periodically the stillness of the early summer afternoon was rended by the droning of aircraft, swelling in volume as they thundered overhead somewhat to our left. Then somewhere ahead of us the powerful whine of aircraft gave place to dull detonations, growing louder as we drew nearer to a thick pall of smoke, which stretched out like a screen across our front. The screaming whistle whistle of falling bombs intermingled with explosions and above the bank of grey-black smoke we could see the flashing of innumerable wings, with their black crosses standing out, like something grim & evil, as they wheeled & banked, returning, like flashes of sun in a mirror, to dive into the billowing smoke, to the accompaniment of the chatter of machine guns. Then gracefully they lifted up out of the dirty smoke & swung off back in the direction from which they'd come. I now told my driver to speed up, as I thought it best to get through this town of ruins & desolation, sections of which appeared either smouldering or burning furiously, marks of this latest or a previous raid. As we approached the first heap of ruins of what had been Tournai, we were forced to slow down, by a long stream of overturned farm-carts, cars, handcarts & perambulators, with various house-hold goods & chattels scattered over all. The draught animals lay for the most part in their tracks, occasionally a horse or horses with cart skewed out behind them, lying on their backs with their legs sticking up in the air. Dotted about amongst all this - and on the sides of the road-lay, still, lifeless, forms of men women and children. I say lifeless, I hope they all were. I could only bring myself to stop at one place, where a woman and three children lay huddled together in the middle of a cross-roads. They had been machine-gunned. From the position of the lifeless bodies it looked as if they'd been running for shelter in the ditch. The only military target I saw amidst all this carnage & destruction, were four trucks at the far side of the town, which had apparently been struck by an incendiary & burnt out. It appeared as if the raid had just been too late to get this last block of the withdrawing column, all but these four trucks. The term "error of judgement" would have to be very elastic indeed to cover this attack on a refugee column, in circumstances, where the aircraft were indisputably the unmolested masters of that area, with a clear summer's day giving them unhampered visibility, insofar as they could pay sufficient attention to the target to line it up on their sights & machine-gun it. This may of course be explained by the new theory of total war, as introduced into Poland & Holland not long prior to this incident. The exponents of this theory probably reccommend the destruction of a Refugee column as the ideal way of impeding the progress of the enemy armed forces.

J. Penman   Lieut

C.H. & l Highl...

running for shelter in the ditch. The only military target I saw amidst all this carnage and destruction, were four trucks at the far side of the town, which had apparently been struck by an incendiary and burnt out. It appeared as if the raid had just been too late to get this last block of the withdrawing column, all but these four trucks.

The term "Error of judgement" would have to be very elastic indeed to cover this attack on a refugee column, in circumstances where the aircraft were undisputedly the unmolested masters of that area, with a clear summer's day giving them unhampered visibility, insofar as they could pay sufficient attention to the target to line it up on their sights and machine-gun it. This may of course be explained by the new theory of total war, as introduced into Poland and Holland not long prior to this incident. The exponents of this theory probably recommend the destruction of a refugee column as the ideal way of impeding the progress of the enemy armed forces.

J. Penman, Lieut.
Argyle and Sutherland Highlanders.

10. FROM CAKE TINS TO . . . . . . ?

Early one morning, shortly after the recrudescence of the World War in 1939, and as a result of an urgent telephone message from the W.O., two officers—a Major and a Capt—set off on a secret mission to Reading.

On arrival at Reading they proceeded to the works of Messrs. Huntley and Palmer where one of the principals was awaiting them. The two officers were escorted round that part of the factory devoted to the manufacture of cake and biscuit tins. In these articles the officers took a great deal of interest and, eventually—after all types had been inspected and after much discussion—a particular cake tin was selected.

The representative of H. & P. seemed to be very puzzled and intrigued by the strange behaviour of the military gentlemen—more so when he was asked if he could supply 250,000 of the cake tins within 3 weeks. He agreed that this could be done, but could not conceal his curiosity as to the purpose for which they were required. His curiosity was not satisfied, but the reader of this—if there is one—will be luckier.

First, a little explanation is required. Before the war the Military Authorities had spent a great deal of time and thought in devising an Anti-Tank mine. Eventually they designed what they considered a perfect mine, and even went to the expense of producing one or two which—rumour has it—were kept under glass cases at Chatham!!

This mine was built like a watch and with as much precision. It was beautifully machined and nothing was spared to make it a high grade article—which it was. Unfortunately, in war time mines do not serve their purpose under glass cases, however beautiful they may be; and they are required in millions—not in ones and two's!

When the blue prints of the mine were sent out, the manufacturers held up their hands in horror! It was not a practicable proposition to make them in vast numbers, and that is why a cake tin, filled with explosive, and with a strengthened lid and cheap fuse, is now the standard A/TK mine in the British Army!!

E. L. Rash, Lt. Col.

23.11.43—

11.   RHINELAND 01.20 HRS—7/6/42

"There go the flares, Navigator.

"Funny there's another lot away to starboard.

"There's the mouth of the Ruhr anyway, that lot must be Essen.

"Yes, I'm altering course now to———"

"Aircraft to port!"

I looked up in time to see it about fifty yards away on the port bow. As it flashed across my windscreen I saw the silhouette of a Wellington's tail, into which my starboard wing crashed a moment later.

My veneer of self-confidence vanished. That so carefully nursed belief that I would always get away with it dissolved in the momentary clutch of despair, as the aircraft remorselessly and uncontrollably rolled over into a spiral dive. This is it at long last, I thought.

It is impossible in such circumstances to judge the length of time available. You can only do what is necessary, meanwhile reflecting whether or not the process will end abruptly before completion. It was necessary to bail out through the roof, an exit which is not recommended owing to the risk of hitting things on the way. It is better, however than not bailing out at all.

The wind was overwhelming in its force as it tore me out of the cockpit, then everything clicked into oblivion, as my head hit the tail. I came to, rotating slowly and struggled to retrieve the threads of thought. Once again I was waiting for the abrupt end, which I knew must now be very near, while with horrible deliberation, made worse by semi-consciousness and a broken shoulder, I groped for the rip cord. I found something, and pulled it with a force verging on the desperate.

Nothing happened. It was very dark and I felt myself a self-contained body, detached in space and waiting to die, when suddenly there was a jerk and once again I knew that I had got away with it.

About then ten other men ended—abruptly.

W. McD. Morison,

F/Lt. R.A.F.

Early one morning, shortly after the recrudescence of the World War in 1939, as a result of an urgent telephone message the W.O., two officers - a major & a Capt - set off on a secret mis to Reading.

On arrival at Reading they proceeded to the works of Messrs Huntley & Palmer where one of the principals was awaiting them.

The two officers were escorted round that part of the facto devoted to the manufacture of cake & biscuit tins. In these article the officers took a great deal of interest and, eventually - aft all types had been inspected and after much discussion - a particular cake tin was selected.

The representative of H. & P. seemed to be very puzzled and intrigued by the strange behaviour of the military gentlemen more so when he was asked if he could supply 250,000 o the cake tins within 3 weeks. He agreed that this could be done but could not conceal his curiosity as to the purpose for which they were required. His curiosity wa not satisfied, but the reader of this - if there is one - will be luckier.

First, a little explanation is required. Before the war th military authorities had spent a great deal of time & thought in devising an Anti-Tank mine. Eventually they designed wha they considered the perfect mine, & even went to the expense of producing one or two which - rumour had it - were kep under glass cases at Chatham!

This mine was built like a watch & with as much precision. It was beautifully machined and nothing was spared to make a high grade article - which it was. Unfortunately, in war mines do not serve their purpose under glass cases, howe beautiful they may be; and they are required in millions - no in one's and two's!

When the blue prints of the mine were sent out the manufactu held up their hands in horror! It was not a practicable proposi to make them in vast numbers, and that is why a cake tin, fill with explosive, and with a strengthened lid and cheap fuze, is

" There go the flares, navigator.

" Funny there's another lot away to starboard.

"There's the mouth of the Ruhr anyway, that lot must be Essen

" Yes, I'm altering course now to - - - - "

" Aircraft to port!"

I looked up in time to see it about fifty yards away on the port bow. As it flashed across my windscreen I saw the silhouette of a Wellington's tail, into which my starboard wing crashed a moment later.

My veneer of self-confidence vanished. That so carefully nursed belief that I would always get away with it, dissolved in the momentary clutch of despair, as the aircraft remorselessly and uncontrollably rolled over into a spiral dive. This is it at long last, I thought.

It is impossible in such circumstances to judge the length of time available. You can only do what is necessary, meanwhile reflecting whether or not the process will end abruptly before completion. It was necessary to bail out through the roof, an exit which is not recommended owing to the risk of hitting things on the way. It is better, however, than not bailing out at all.

The wind was overwhelming in its force as it tore me out of the cockpit, then everything clicked into oblivion as my head hit the tail. I came to rotating slowly and struggled to retrieve the threads of thought. Once again I was waiting for the abrupt end which I knew must now be very near, while with horrible deliberation, made worse by semi consciousness and a broken shoulder, I groped for the rip cord. I found something, and pulled it with a force verging on the desperate.

Nothing happened. It was very dark and I felt myself a self-contained body, detached in space and waiting to die, when suddenly there was a jerk and once again I knew that I had got away with it.

About then ten other men ended — abruptly.

W. M^cS. Morison
F/Lt. R.A.F.

Le vendredi 13 août 1943, à minuit 35, la sirène réveillait brusquement les prisonniers de guerre blessés et malades à l'hôpital 207 de Milan. Les alertes précédentes, assez peu nombreuses, d'ailleurs, n'avaient été que rarement suivies du bombardement de la ville par quelques dizaines d'avions alliés. Cependant, la descente aux abris s'effectua comme d'habitude, dans l'ordre et le calme, les grands malades étant transportés sur des brancards par les "orderlies" britanniques. Un peu avant une heure du matin, nous entendîmes les premières bombes et le tir de la D.C.A. italienne. Il nous semblait que le bombardement était, cette fois, très sérieux, et effectué par un nombre d'avions considérable. Vers une heure cinq une violente explosion nous fit sursauter, toutes les vitres des portes et soupiraux de l'abri se brisèrent, blessant légèrement quelques prisonniers. Quelques deux ou trois minutes après une seconde explosion ébranla les murs de la cave servant d'abri et le plafond s'écroula avec un bruit effroyable ensevelissant une vingtaine d'officiers et d'orderlies. Je fus plaqué au sol et je sentis les gravats et les pierres s'abattre sur moi. J'avais, heureusement, la tête et partie du corps sous un banc ce qui me permit de respirer et de ne pas être broyé par les pierres. Au bout de quelques minutes, les secours s'organisèrent et les prisonniers valides commencèrent à délivrer leurs camarades ensevelis sous les décombres. Les sauveteurs, que les soldats italiens n'aidèrent en aucune façon, se dépensèrent sans compter, au milieu d'une fumée opaque, au bruit des bombes qui tombaient de tous côtés, à la lueur rouge des incendies et s'attendant à chaque instant, à être écrasés sous les ruines de l'hôpital qui menaçait de s'écrouler. Je fus délivré au bout de trois heures d'efforts et certains de mes camarades ne purent être dégagés qu'à l'aube. Le bilan de la catastrophe se soldait par 10 morts, dont 7 officiers britanniques, français et américains et 3 orderlies néo-zélandais, et quelques blessés. La bombe qui avait causé l'effondrement des quatre étages de l'hôpital sur notre abri était une bombe à souffle de grande puissance et était tombée à environ une trentaine de mètres du bâtiment. Plusieurs usines qui se trouvaient à quelques centaines de mètres de l'hôpital avaient été détruites et brûlèrent jusqu'au matin. Avec une quinzaine de nos camarades je fus transporté dans la matinée au centre des Mutilés de Milan qui devait être évacué le jour même par les blessés italiens qui s'y trouvaient. La première nuit se passa bien mais la nuit suivante eut lieu un bombardement extrêmement violent. Notre hôpital fut atteint par une bombe explosive et une bombe incendiaire. La nuit suivante, au cours d'un raid non moins important que le précédent, cinq bombes éclatèrent sur l'hôpital qui fut en grande partie détruit. Grâce à Dieu, l'abri où nous avions été descendus ne fut pas touché et le lendemain matin nous étions recueillis en l'hôpital de Baggio, dans un des faubourgs de Milan, où quelques jours après, nous rejoignîmes le gros de nos camarades à l'hôpital de Bergame.

Oflag IV C, le 3 novembre 1943. Lochard lieutenant corps franc d'...

12. BOMBARDEMENT DE MILAN* (AOÛT 1943)

On Friday the 13th of August 1943 at 0035 hours, the siren suddenly woke up the wounded and sick prisoners of war in Hospital 207 in Milan. Previous alerts, which were rather infrequent, had only rarely been followed by a bombardment of the city by dozens of allied aircraft. However, as usual, we made our way down to the shelters, in a calm orderly fashion, with serious cases transported on stretchers by British orderlies. A little before 0100 hours we heard the first bombs and the return fire of Italian anti-aircraft guns. It seemed to us that the bombing was very serious this time, and carried out by a considerable number of aircraft.

At about 0105 hours a violent explosion shook the whole place and shattered all the panes of glass, causing wounds to some of the prisoners. Then about two or three minutes later a second explosion cracked the walls of the cellar where we were sheltering and the ceiling collapsed with a hideous noise, burying a score of officers an orderlies.

I was pinned to the ground and I could feel pieces of plaster and stones falling on me. Fortunately my head and part of my body were under a bench, so I was able to breathe and not become buried by the rocks. After several minutes, help was organised and able-bodied prisoners began to free their comrades from the rubble. The rescuers, to whom the Italian soldiers gave no assistance at all, worked tirelessly in the midst of a thick cloud of smoke and the deafening sound of bombs falling all around, with the red glow of fire lighting the whole scene, expecting at any moment that they could all be crushed under the ruins of the hospital, which threatened to collapse.

I got out after about three hours of effort, while some of my comrades were not rescued until dawn. The tally of the catastrophe included ten dead soldiers, of which seven were British, French and American officers, and three New Zealand orderlies, plus numerous wounded.

The bomb which caused the collapse of the four stories of the hospital on our shelter was a powerful block-buster that had fallen about thirty metres from our building. Several factories, situated a few hundred metres from the hospital, were destroyed and the ruins burned until morning.

With about fifteen of my comrades I was transported during the morning to the centre of the ruins of Milan, from where all the wounded were to be evacuated. The first night there went well, but the following night there was another extremely violent bombardment. Our hospital was hit by a high explosive bomb and by an incendiary. On the next night again, during a heavy air-raid, five bombs hit the hospital which was now almost completely destroyed. By the grace of God the shelter in which we had taken refuge was not touched, and the morning after we were evacuated to the hospital in Boggio, in a one of the suburbs of Milan. From there a few days later we set out to join the main body of our comrades in the hospital at Bergamo.

Oflag IVC 3rd November 1943
Ecochard, Lieutenant, Corps France d'Afrique

* *Bombardment of Milan*

13. "DIEPPE"—19/8/42

We landed at 0445 hours in the first wave. To give you an idea of why we got to our point of capture you must know some of the facts of our landing.

Companies were split up because of landing from different craft on different parts of the beach. The fire power coming down on us was extremely heavy and casualties high. Consequently communication broke down and neither sections, platoons or Company could get together. The sea wall was too high and under too heavy fire to cross and by 0700 hours we realized this.

Having a small party of 4 men and 1 Sgt with me we began making our way along the wall. No pleasant task, but better than sitting and being pounded. After travelling about 500 yards we came upon a low spot in the wall and some cover afforded by part of the dock. A very short dash at the end of this cover brought us to the first corner of the town and the promenade which ran the length of the front.

We were immediately forced to ground by fire from a post under whose observation we had stumbled. Our refuge was a shop window. Suddenly the noise of an approaching vehicle made us look up to see a German lorry slowly approaching. As it passed we all noticed, at the same moment, I guess, that it was full of troops because we fired simultaneously. One troop survived and the lorry wound up in another shop window. Our ammo was practically expended by now so we began our way back. This was not to be however as our route had been blocked since coming in. We remained there until the force from the beach surrendered and marched up. I'm glad those Germans didn't know we were out of ammo, Jerry or it may have been hot.

Bill Scott, Lieut.

14. EICHSTÄTT—3RD JUNE 43

At about 9.45 pm. we were on our way up the 'groove' for the last time. During 3 years of unsuccessful tunnelling I'd often had serious doubts that this moment would ever arrive, and the progress of this particular tunnel had certainly been no exception to the rule. I had also often idly thought what it would feel like, but it certainly didn't live up to expectation, and romance was singularly lacking. Much more immediate problems drove everything else out of mind—wondering who or what in the whole complicated plan was most likely to break down, and coming to the regretful conclusion it was me, how ridiculously overdressed I was, if I took off my hat should I ever find it again, and how to stop the iron spike stuck in my shirt and trousers from skewering me.

Apart from two large rocks which had been defying the laws of gravity and then suddenly gave up the unequal struggle, the whole process of breaking went so exactly according to plan, it seemed too good to be true. But having scrambled out and crossed the open stretch

We landed at 0445 hours in the first wave.
To give you an idea of why we got to our
point of capture you must know some
of the facts of our landing.

Companies were split up because of
landing from different craft on different
parts of the beach. The fire power
coming down on us was extremely heavy
and casualties high. Consequently communications
broke down and neither sections, platoons or
company could get together. The sea wall
was too high & under too heavy fire to
cross and by 0700 hours we realized this.
Taking a small party of 4 men and 1 Sgt with
me we began making our way along the
wall. No pleasant task but better than sitting
and being pounded. After travelling about
100 yds we came upon a low spot in the
wall and some cover afforded by part of the deep.
A very short dash at the end of this [?] overall brought
us to the first corner of the town beyond the
promenade which ran the length of the front.
We were immediately forced to ground by fire from a
post under whose observation we had stumbled.
Our refuge was a shop window. Suddenly the noise
of an approaching vehicle made us look up to see
a German lorry slowly approaching. As it passed we
all noticed at the same moment & guessed that it was
full of troops because we fired simultaneously. On
observing & the lorry wound up in another shop
window. Our ammo was practically expended by now
so we began our way back. This was not to be
however as our route had been blocked, since coming in
We remained there until the force from the beach surrendered
and marched up. I'm glad these Germans didn't know we were out of
ammo, sorry or it may have been hot.   Bill Scott

At about 9.45 pm we were on our way up the 'groove' for the last time.   During 3 years of unsuccessful tunnelling I'd often had serious doubts that this moment would ever arrive, & the progress of this particular tunnel had certainly been no exception to the rule.   I had also often idly thought what it would feel like, but it certainly didn't live up to expectation, & romance was singularly lacking. Much more immediate problems drove everything else out of mind — wondering who or what in the whole complicated plan was most likely to break down, & coming to the regretful conclusion it was me, how rediculously overdressed I was, if I took off my hat I should ever find it again, and how to stop the iron spike stuck under my shirt & trousers from skewering me.

Apart from two large rocks which had been defying the laws of gravity & then suddenly gave up the unequal struggle, the whole process of breaking went so exactly according to plan, it seemed too good to be true.   But having scrambled out & crossed the open stretch in safety, in spite of it being a fine calm evening instead of blowing a half gale, confidence flowed slowly back.

Making the hole in the fence took an unconscionable time, but at last the signal for the general evacuation could be sent, much to every ones relief, judged by the remarks overheard from the windows of Block 2. In a surprisingly short space of time, heavy breathing, grunts — the swishing of grass announced the arrival of the next two out.   A few seconds later we were on our way up the hillside, reeling out the guide string on the way, and eventually arrived sweating & heaving at the top.

Just before crossing the skyline, I took what I fondly hoped would be the last look at the 'camp.'   It was now quite dark & the orderly lines of perimeter lights with the occasional flash of a search light made quite a picturesque sight.   And here I must admit a pleasant feeling of satisfaction.   Whatever happened now, the gentleman who so unwisely said tunnelling here was 'gang unmöglich', had never been more wrong.

W.A. Weldon
Capt.
Royal Horse Artillery.

The dusty road down to the Ventrivos was crammed with
traffic; staff cars Greek & British, trucks carrying 2- or pulling 25-
pounders, trucks groaning under a tenfold load, motor buses, motor
cycles, & those fantastic Greek steam tractors towing a most
improbable selection of guns.   On a trunk road in peacetime this catholic convoy might have covered five miles in
an hour; but here, with dive bombers & Me 110's sweeping
on every 10 minutes & leaving always more twisted &
screaming hazards on that twisted & screaming road, progress
was barely perceptible.   And I waited for my squadron,
tried to help the column round the first & worst hairpin
bend on the road up from the south bank of the river, where
many trucks & all the buses had to take the corner in two
instalments.   There was no great difficulty till a large
Greek bus came along, with a harassed driver & a vast
accumulation of blankets & clothes. Try as he might, this
driver could not, after taking the first bite at the corner &
slipping back for the second, persuade his bus to do more than
shiver at the prospect & expire   I suggested trying bottom gear
instead of top, but he did it understand my very rudimentary Greek,
& I eased him out & brought his bus round into the straight. He
was reluctant to take charge again; & I don't blame him: never
once, he said, had he driven a car of any kind.
          He got in again; but I was glad, for his sake &
anyone else's, to see him aim his charge in a series of
purposeful jerks for a vacant stretch of ditch, leap out, & take up
a less care-worn post of passenger in the truck behind. Day by

in safety, in spite of it being a fine calm evening instead of blowing a half gale, confidence flowed slowly back.

Making the hole in the fence took an unconscionable time, but at last the signal for the general evacuation could be sent, much to everyone's relief, judged by the remarks overheard from the windows of Block 2. In a surprisingly short space of time, heavy breathing, grunts and the swishing of grass announced the arrival of the next two out. A few seconds later we were on our way up the hillside, reeling out the guide string on the way, and eventually arrived sweating and heaving at the top.

Just before crossing the skyline, I took what I fondly hoped would be the last look at the camp. It was now quite dark and the orderly lines of perimeter lights with the occasional flash of a search light made quite a picturesque sight. And here I must admit a pleasant feeling of satisfaction. Whatever happened now, the gentleman who so unwisely said tunnelling was "ganz unmöglich," had never been more wrong.

F. W. C. Weldon
Capt. Royal Horse Artillery

15. GRAVENA—APRIL 15 1941

The dusty road down to the Ventrios was crammed with traffic: staff cars Greek and British trucks carrying 2 or pulling 25-pounders, trucks groaning under a tenfold load, motor buses, motor bicycles and those fantastic Greek steam tractors towing a most improbable selection of guns. On a trunk road in peace-time this catholic convoy might have covered five miles in the hour; but here, with dive bombers and ME110's sweeping over every 10 minutes and leaving always more twisted and screaming hazards on that twisted and screaming road, progress was barely perceptible.

As I waited for my squadron, I tried to help the column round the first and worst hairpin bend on the road up from the south bank of the river, where many trucks and all the buses had to take the corner in two instalments. There was no great difficulty till a large Greek bus came along, with a harassed driver and a vast accumulation of blankets and clothes. Try as he might, this driver could not, after taking the first bite at the corner and slipping back for a second, persuade his bus to do more than quiver at the prospect and expire. I suggested trying bottom gear instead of top, but he didn't understand my very rudimentary Greek, so I eased him out and brought his bus round into the straight. He was reluctant to take charge again: and I don't blame him: never before, he said, had he driven a car of any kind.

He got in again: but I was glad for his sake and everyone else's, to see him aim his charge in a series of purposeful jerks for a vacant stretch of ditch, leap out, and take up the less care-worn post of passenger in the truck behind.

J. L. Pumphrey 2/Lt.
(The Northumberland Hussars.)

16. VIENNA—MAY 13 1941—12.15 P.M.

"Wien, Wien, nur du allein, Stadt meiner Träume auf ewig sein." ["*Vienna, Vienna, only you alone will be the city of my dreams forever*"]. Footsore and hungry and gently humming Strauss' waltz I arrived in the middle of Vienna. It was a very dejected "Kriegie" that walked into the public call box to look up the address of the American Consulate, but a very contented one. Forgotten were the agony of the last six days of continuous walking without food, of the 300 kilometres between Regensburg and Vienna. What were raw feet and stomach cramps compared with a safe haven only a few blocks away? Just a 20 Mark note enough to get some medical attention, a good meal, some beer and then a ticket to the Hungarian frontier 60 kilometres distant. I had no map of the frontier but what were frontiers to me? I could have crossed any of them for in a few hours I would be rested and fed!!

A taxi driver tells me the street I have dreamed of for 6 days. I am met in the entrance by an old woman housekeeper.

"Sind Sie Amerikaner?"

"Jawohl," I answer, "I have come to pay my respects to the Consul."

"He's not in at present. Come back in an hour and a half."

The time goes by rapidly enough and I reappear. I meet a German girl secretary who asks me my business and for my passport etc. I say my baggage is at the station and I just want to pay my compliments.

"What colour is your passport and visa?" she asks. "Brown and green" I reply. She seems satisfied and shows me into an ante-room. Lifes and New York Herald Tribunes are on the table—what a treat after 1 year of the "Volkischer Beobachter." 10 minutes later I am ushered into the Consul's office.

"Sir, I am an escaped British officer caught in France with the 51st Highland Division. I have escaped from Leipzig—I have worn my feet out and I am terribly hungry. You must help me. I don't want you to give me a passport or hide me in your buildings. All I want is a 20 mark note to help me over the frontier."

He looks at me suspiciously. What thoughts pass through his mind? A stoolpigeon? Shall I risk my diplomatic career by one act of foolishness? It may all be a blind. After 15 seconds he replies.

"No" he says, "You have made a mistake; this is not the place to get help. Get out and forget you ever came here." Stunned I hear these words.

"But just a little money that's all I need—surely"......

"This is under diplomatic privilege and it would be".....

I can't hear the rest. The tears well up into my eyes and my throat chokes.

"It's no use" he is saying. "They'll get you in the end, they always do."

I find myself in the street again. "Himmelhoch jauchzend, zum Tode betrubt". ["*From the top of the world to the depths of despair*"].

A.M. Allan 2/Lt.,
Q. O. Cameron Highlanders.

"Wien, Wien nur du allein, Stadt meiner Träume auf ewig sein". Footsore and hungry and gently humming Strauss' waltz I arrived in the middle of Vienna. It was a very dejected "Kriegie" that walked into a public call box to look up the address of the American Consulate, but a very contented one. Forgotten were the agony of the past six days of continuous walking without food, of 300 kilometres between Regensburg and Vienna What were raw feet and stomach cramps compared with a safe haven only a few blocks away? Just a 20 Mark note enough to get some medical attention, a good meal some beer and then a ticket to the Hungarian frontier 60 kilometres distant I had no map of the frontier but what were frontiers to me? I could have crossed any of them for in a few hours I would be rested and fed!!

A taxi driver tells me the street I have dreamed of for 6 days. I am met in the entrance by an old woman house keeper.
"Sind Sie Amerikaner"?
"Jawohl" I answer; "I have come to pay my respects to the Consul".
"He's not in at present, Come back in an hour and a half."
The time goes rapidly enough and I reappear. I meet a German girl secretary who asks me my business and for my passport etc. I say my baggage is at the station and I just want to pay my compliments.
"What colour is your passport and visa"? she asks. "Brown and Green" I reply She seems satisfied and shows me into an ante-room. Lifes and New York Herald tribunes are on the table - What a treat after 1 year of the "Völkischer Beobachter", 10 minutes later I am ushered into the Consuls office.
"Sir, I am an escaped British officer caught in France with the 51st Highland Division. I have escaped from Leipzig - I have worn my feet out and I am terribly hungry. You must help me - I don't want you to give me a passport or hide me in your buildings. All I want is a 20 mark note to help me over the frontier".
He looks at me suspiciously: What thoughts pass through his mind?
A stoolpigeon? Shall I risk my diplomatic career by one act of foolishness? It may be all a blind. After 15 seconds he replies.
"No" he says, "You have made a mistake; This is not the place to get help Get out and forget you ever came here." Stunned I hear these words.
"But just a little money that's all I need - Surely"......
"This is under diplomatic privilege and it would be".....
I can't hear the rest. The tears well up into my eyes and my throat chokes
"It's no use" he is saying "They'll get you in the end, they always do.
I find myself in the street again." Himmelhoch jauchzend, zum Tode betrübt

Jerry, here goes for that b—y story I promised you some time ago. Our Bn, after
much cursing, digging & wearing out of boot leather, finished up with the job of helping
guard the Rethymo aerodrome which is situated on the narrow coastal strip on the north of
the island. The force in this area consisted of two A.I.F. Bns, both of which were in rather poor fighting
condition after their Greek show, & two Greek Bns that were not too keen. Our positions were on the hills
overlooking the coastal strip which is about 500 yds wide & we had a front of roughly one mile.
At 8 oclock on the morning of May 20th, 1941 the first signs of the expected attack appeared in
the shape of about a dozen Junker 52s flying low over the ocean & heading straight for us. Everyone
took to earth in a hurry but it was a false alarm as the planes turned off & headed for Canea
which is the main harbour & near which is the biggest 'drome on the Island. These planes were all towing
one to four gliders & made rather a novel sight. This first flight was closely followed by another
couple of groups towing gliders & then at about 15 minute intervals larger, gliderless, flights were seen
mostly turning off for Canea but a few turning West to the only other drome on the Island at Heraklion.
This went on till about 3 oclock when we were bombed for an hour, at the end of which an armada of
Junkers, about 140 strong, & escorted by 40 or 50 ME 109s & 110s, hove in sight. Flying in perfect
formation they made for the shore line to the right of our positions &, on reaching the coastal
strip, turned sharp East & commenced to spill their cargoes right along in front of us. The first
planes unloaded slightly wide of our right flank & the last ones just clear of our left flank.
Their timing & judgement was excellent but a slight cross wind drifted some of the chutes, & therefore
men, right onto our positions — which was bad luck for the load. A paratroop attack is no time for
sight seeing, but busy as we all were pumping up lead, I think everyone there managed to snatch a look
or two while yanking the old bolt back. A couple of hundred planes about 300 feet up, the air full
of multi-coloured parachutes, planes crashing right & left, ourselves pumping lead up just as fast
as we could, the planes shooting plenty back — all packed into about ten minutes. Our fire was paying
good dividends in the shape of crashing planes & limp bodies — I saw seven or eight planes heading earthwards
in a hurry — two of them crashed 50 yards from me & made a hell of a mess. As the paratroops neared
the ground their tommy-guns were used to spray lead at us but didn't do much good against the old 303 &
the bayonet was used to good effect to clean up anything landing on top of us. Some chutes were caught on
the wings & tails & the people hanging in the straps must have had a most unpleasant ride back to
Greece — or perhaps a swim in the Med. The Junkers 52 which crashed near me unloaded 6 bodies
from about 60 ft up — three had chutes which opened satisfactorily but three of them must have
been trying to fly — they hopped out without chutes & hit the deck pretty hard. Later on, when
things quietened down, I had the job of burying these six & the crew of three who stayed on board.
Another '52 crashed into the ocean — just one big splash & she was gone. On top of these
crashes we saw quite a few planes must have failed to reach Greece as some of them were
well on fire before leaving us. Although we could see some of the effects of our fire we
were all surprised at the number of men still harnessed into their chutes when we started
here to do some burying, & judging from what I saw in our area I would say that close on
300 were dead, or near enough, before hitting the ground & another 200 killed soon after
landing. Add to this another couple of hundred killed in the ten days between the landing &
when we packed in & it makes about 900 killed out of a landing force of approx.
1800. We also had 200 prisoners & quite a number of their wounded. Our own casualties
were roughly 100 killed, 300 wounded & the rest in the bag. By sundown on the day of
the landing we had the coastal strip in front of us cleaned up & the remaining
paratroops were split into two groups — one on each of our flanks. These groups
could not be attacked in daylight — their air support was too hot — & so we had to have
them at night, & house to house fighting in the dark is no joke, believe me. After ten days
whose night shows the enemy were reinforced with troops, guns & tanks from Ptolemi &, as the
rest of the island was in the bag, we were ordered to pack in — & here I am.

J.R. Moffatt Lt
2/1 Bn A.I.F.

This is the sad ending of an otherwise successful escape. Finally, after being refused help by the American Consulate, tired and hungry, he gave up and turned himself in to a police station. See Brief Biographies of Contributors at the end of this book.

17. CRETE, MAY 1941

Well Jerry, here goes for that b–y story I promised you some time ago. Our bn, after much cursing, digging and wearing out of boot leather, finished up with the job of helping defend the Rethymno aerodrome which is situated on the narrow coastal strip on the north of the island. The force in this area consisted of two A.I.F. bns, both of which were in rather poor fighting condition after their Greek show, and two Greek bns that were not too keen. Our positions were on the hillsides overlooking the coastal strip which is about 500 yds wide and we had a front of roughly one mile.

At ten o'clock on the morning of May 20th, 1941 the first signs of an expected attack appeared in the shape of about a dozen Junker 52's flying low over the ocean and heading straight for us. Everyone went to earth in a hurry but it was a false alarm as the planes turned off and headed for Canea, which is the main harbour and near which is the biggest 'drome on the island. These planes were all towing from one to four gliders and made rather a novel sight.

This first flight was closely followed by another couple of groups towing gliders and then at about 15 minute intervals larger, gliderless flights were seen mostly turning off for Canea but a few turning west to the only other 'drome on the island at Hearakleon. This went on until about 3 o'clock when we were bombed for an hour, at the end of which an armada of Junkers, about 140 strong, and escorted by 40 or 50 ME109's and 110's, hove in sight. Flying in perfect formation they made for the shoreline to the right of our positions and on reaching the coastal strip, turned sharp east and commenced to spill their cargoes right along in front of us.

The first planes unloaded slightly wide of our right flank and the last ones just clear of our left flank. Their timing and judgement was excellent but a slight cross wind drifted some of the chutes, and their load right into our positions—which was bad luck for the load. A paratroop attack is no time for sight seeing, but busy as we all were pumping up lead, I think everyone there managed to snatch a look while yanking the old bolt back. A couple of hundred planes, about 300 feet up, the air just full of multi-coloured parachutes, planes crashing right and left, ourselves pumping lead up just as fast as we could, the planes shooting plenty back—all packed into about ten minutes. Our fire was paying good dividends in the shape of crashing planes and limp bodies—I saw seven or eight planes heading earthwards in a hurry—two of them crashed 50 yards from me and made a hell of a mess.

As the paratroops neared the ground their tommy-guns were used to spray lead at us but didn't do much good against the old 303, and the bayonet was used to good effect to clean up anything landing on top of us. Some chutes were caught up on wings and tails and the people hanging in the straps must have had a most unpleasant ride back to Greece—or perhaps a swim in the Med. The Junkers 52 which crashed near me unloaded 6 bodies from about 60 feet up—three had chutes which opened satisfactorily but three of them must have been trying to fly—they hopped out without chutes and hit the deck pretty hard. Later on, when things quietened down, had the job of burying these 6 and the crew of three who stayed on board. Another '52 crashed into the ocean—just one big splash and she was gone. On top of the crashes we saw quite a few planes must have failed to reach Greece as some of them were well on fire before leaving us.

Although we could see some of the effects of our fire we were all surprised at the number of men still harnessed into their chutes when we started in to do some burying, and judging from what I saw in our area I would say that close on 500 were dead, or near enough, before hitting the ground and another 200 killed soon after landing. Add to this another couple of hundred killed in the ten days between the landing and when we packed in and it makes about 900 killed out of a landing force of approx 1800. We also had 200 prisoners and quite a number of their wounded. Our own casualties were roughly 100 killed, 300 wounded and the rest in the bag. By sundown on the day of the landing we had the coastal strip in front of us cleaned up and the remaining paratroops were split into two groups—one on each side of our flanks. These groups could not be attacked in daylight—their air support was too hot—and so we had to hammer them at night, and house to house fighting in the dark is no joke, believe me. After ten days of these night shows the enemy were reinforced with troops guns and tanks from Maleme and as the rest of the island was in the bag, we were ordered to pack in—and here I am.

J. R. Millett Lt.,
2/n Bn A.I.F.

18.   THE NORTH SEA—JANUARY 1940

The night was very still as the submarine slowly made her way towards the island of H. The only sound came from the exhaust of the diesels, and to the O.O.W. on the bridge it seemed as if they must be heard many miles away. He felt sure that any enemy vessel would hear him, before he could see them; but it was up to him to sight them first, as the reverse meant certain destruction, especially when so close to the enemy shore.

Down below all was quiet. 2/3 of the crew were asleep, the remainder on watch. The helmsman was studiously watching the compass, the messenger was brewing some cocoa, whilst the stokers and L.T.O. were tending the diesels, dynamos and batteries.

Suddenly the bark of the klaxon woke everyone from their slumbers. The messenger rushed to the panel and opened the vents; the helmsman left the wheel and put the hydroplanes 'hard-a-dive'; the stokers stopped the engines, whilst the L.T.O. went 'Full Ahead' on the motors. A rush of air followed as the tanks emptied, then only the whir of the motors and the barest minimum of orders broke the silence.

The Captain, straight from his bunk, was already in the control room. "What is it No. 1?" he asks. "A large minesweeping trawler on the starboard beam, Sir. Coming this way. The moon is right behind her." With a bit of luck and a bright moon it might be possible to carry out a submerged attack. "Where is she now?" The captain asked the Ardre operator. "Green 60

e night was very still as the Submarine slowly made her way towards the
H. The only sound came from the exhaust of the Diesels, and to the O.O.W. on t
idge it seemed as if they must be heard many miles away. He felt sure that any
ny vessel would hear him, before he could see them; but it was up to him to see
n first, as the reverse meant certain destruction, especially when so close to t
ny shore.   Down below all was quiet. ⅔ of the crew were asleep
remainder on watch. The helmsman was studiously watching the compass,
essenger was brewing some cocoa, whilst the Stokers & L.T.O. were tending the
namos & batteries.   Suddenly the bark of the Klaxon woke everyone from their sl
e messenger rushed to the panel & opened the Vents; the helmsman left the wheel and p
droplanes 'Hard-a-dive'; the stokers stopped the engines, whilst the L.T.O went 'Full Ahead'
motors. A rush of air followed as the tanks emptied, then only the whirr of the m
the barest minimum of orders broke the silence.

 The Captain, straight from his bunk, was already in the Control Room. "What is it,
asks. "A large minesweeping trawler on the Starboard beam, Sir. Coming this way. T
is right behind her." With a bit of luck and a bright moon it might be possible to carr
a submerged attack. "Where is she now?" The Capt; asked the Asdic Operator. "G
wing aft, Sir. Otherwise all clear." "Very good. Port 10. ½ Speed together. Bring 1 & 2 t
 ready."   After a few minutes run he asked for another bearing. "Red 80.
y good — Midships — Steady — Slow both — 30 feet". Slowly the needles of the depth gaug
e from 60' to 30'. "Up periscope!" A good all round sweep was followed by a clos
uiny of the Target. "Perfect! We're 60° on her starboard bow. Range 800"
d 12 knots. What's the D.A?" "19°, sir" came the reply from the navigator
ood. Stand by the tubes!"   Everyone was alert — on edge — waiting for th
al order.   "Stand by .... Fire!" A dull thud shook the S/m as th
rpedoes left the tubes. But this was no place to hang around.
ull Speed together. Starboard 20. 60 feet". The Captain gave the order
ietly and wandered to the Chart Table. A few seconds silence — t
oud report — the S/m shivered and shook, but nobody minded — t
Torpedo had found its mark and there was one less vessel
guard the German Coast.

R. M. Harvey

Lieutenant - Commander

France 1940. We were doing a recce survey of the old Fort at Doullens
where an underground H Q was to be built. Detached from our RE un—
2 subalterns were temporary members of the local A.M.P.C. Mess. The A.M.—
—lonel had served his country gallantly in the last War but he didn—
the Sappers and he spent his time telling the Sapper Subalterns a—
—bout it. He felt that as a Colonel, a V.C. and Mess President, he wa—
pretty strong ground and he was, though, Well! its another stor—
—t it was he who lost his temper in the end

Later the Sappers moved into the Fort in force, we were a Tunnelling
company, and with a sigh of relief we got down to mining. We ha—
—got again and military ceremonial died away. The two subaltern—
were back in their own mess and quite casually told their O.C—
their arguments in the AMPC mess. The O.C was a major. He h—
—en mining all over the World for 25 years & had served through—
—e last War. He was big and we called him Jumbo and like—
never forgot.

Two weeks later he was sitting in his office when an urgent phone ca—
—me through from AMPC H.Q. It was the Colonel. An infernal machine
—opped by parachute, had fallen on the railway line — would the Sapp—
—me and deal with it. Now the Major had been an expert on booby-tra—
the last War, he wanted a bit of excitement and he didn't want t—
—terfere with the job. So he put on his hat and away he went & deal—
th the matter himself

By the time he arrived at the scene the news had got around and a—
—ggish crowd had gathered at a respectable distance from a white—
—ect on the line. They were a shade worried but the Colonel, he knew—
—t what his position was all the time, said he had sent for the—
—d everything would be perfectly all right. When the Major arrived—
—lonel assured him it was a mine and that the Major's first duty—
—s to remove it from the line. Well one never wastes time with th—
—t of thing and the Major soon left the crowd and walked forward
—ickly — a lone figure—toward the white object. When he got within—
—rds of it he saw at once that the white part was indeed a para—
—t that the mine was not a mine but a wireless set. Now the Maj—
—ld merely have shouted this information back to the crowd but h—
—am he remembered and he also recalled the Colonel's last orde—
—t it away from the line" So he shouted — "I may have to run—
—" and sure enough he picked up the mine and ran as har—
—s he could. But the crowd took a poor view because he ran in the
—rong direction and that was straight towards them. Now the
—lonel, did I say he knew his place all the time, was still
—tty nippy on his pins and when the crowd scattered he—
—th them and not in the rear of them. But he was no match—
—e Major. Well there is really no more to it. The Colonel show—
—e pleasure when he heard that it was just a wireless set,
—pecially as the Major was a Sapper, who was obviously try—
—t to laugh and the silly crowd was standing around grinning
But the two Subalterns were pleased. I was one of them.

Douglas J. Rogers
Capt. R.E

growing aft, Sir. Otherwise all clear." "Very good. Port 10. Half speed together. Bring 1 and 2 tubes to the ready." After a few minutes run he asked for another bearing. "Red 80, Sir." "Very good. Midships. Steady. Slow both. 30 feet." Slowly the needle of the depth gauge rose from 60' to 30'. "Up periscope!" A good all round sweep was followed by a close scrutiny of the target. "Perfect! We're 60 degrees on her starboard bow. Range 800 yards, speed 12 knots. What's the D.A.?" "18 degrees Sir." Came the reply from the navigator. "Good. Stand by the tubes." Everyone was alert. On edge. Waiting for the fatal order. "Stand by . . . . fire!"

A dull thud shook the submarine as the torpedoes left the tubes. But this was no place to hang around. "Full speed together. Starboard 20. 60 feet." The captain gave the orders quietly and wandered to the chart table. A few seconds silence—then a loud report—the s/m shivered and shook, but nobody minded. The torpedo had found its mark and there was one less vessel to guard the German coast.

L. W. Harvey
Lieutenant Commander,
Royal Navy

19. THE INFERNAL MACHINE—FRANCE 1940

France 1940. We were doing a recce survey of the old fort at Doullens where an underground HQ was to be built. Detached from our RE unit two Subalterns were temporary members of the local A.M.P.C. mess. The A.M.P.C. Colonel had served his country gallantly in the last war but he didn't like Sappers and he spent his time telling the Sapper Subalterns all about it. He felt that as a Colonel, a V.C. and a Mess President, he was on pretty strong ground and he was though. Well! It's another story but it was he who lost his temper in the end.

Later the Sappers moved into the fort in force. We were a tunnelling company, and with a sigh of relief we got down to mining. We had a job again and military ceremonial died away. The two Subalterns were back in their own Mess and quite casually told their O.C. of their arguments in the A.M.P.C. Mess. The O.C. was a Major. He had been mining all over the world for 25 years and had served through the last war. He was big and we called him Jumbo, and like one who never forgot.

Two weeks later he was sitting in his office when an urgent phone call came though from A.M.P.C. H.Q. It was the Colonel. An infernal machine, dropped by parachute, had fallen on the railway line—would the Sappers come and deal with it. Now the Major had been an expert on booby traps in the last war, he wanted a bit of excitement and he didn't want to interfere with the job. So he put on his hat and away he went to deal with the matter himself.

By the time he arrived at the scene the news had got around and a biggish crowd had gathered as a respectable distance from a white object on the line. They were a shade worried, but the Colonel, he knew just what his position was all the time, said he had sent for the R.E.'s and everything would be perfectly all right. When the Major arrived the Colonel assured him it was a mine and that the Major's first duty was to remove it from the line. Well one never wastes time with that sort of thing and the Major soon left the crowd and walked forward quickly—a lone figure—toward the white object. When he got within 10 yards of it he saw at once that the white part was indeed a parachute but the mine was not a mine but a wireless set. Now the Major could merely have shouted this information back to the crowd but once again he remembered and he also recalled the Colonel's last order—"Get it away from the line." So he shouted:—"I may have to run for it." And sure enough he picked up the mine and ran as hard as he could. But the crowd took a poor view because he ran in the wrong direction and that was straight towards them. Now the Colonel, did I say he knew his place all the time, was still pretty nippy on his pins and when the crowd scattered he was with them and not in the rear of them. But he was no match for the Major. Well there is really no more to it. The Colonel showed no pleasure when he heard that it was just a wireless set, especially as the Major was a Sapper, who was obviously trying not to laugh and the silly crowd was standing around grinning. But the two Subalterns were pleased. I was one of them.

Douglas J. Rogers,
Capt. R.E.

20.   A ROUND IN THE GREECE INCIDENT

"I" Report No. 51. 6th April, 1941, 1000 hours
Twelve German Divisions, (2 armoured, 10 infantry) crossed the Yugo-Slav frontier yesterday. They appear to be heading towards Florina, where all bridges have been 'blown'.

"I" Report No. 52. 6th April, 1941, 1800 hours:—The Germans have occupied Florina where the bridges were NOT, repeat NOT 'blown'.

There were but 2 British divisions and 1 armoured Bde. in Greece but we were confident, and more would arrive. Next morning at first light, from a Field O.P. which was very close to that of a medium regiment, the movement of the Enemy M.T. became visible. Being out of 25 pdr range, I walked across to see the O.P.O. of the Mediums.

All the previous afternoon he had been busy with his maps and Artillery Board, silently registering the conspicuous points on the Florina Plain, and this morning the line and range to the various targets had been corrected to comply with the local weather conditions. He was mildly excited, as one column of large German troop carriers was approaching a cross roads which he had registered at almost the extreme range of his guns. Seeing me, he said, (optimistically I thought), "If they stop at that cross roads they're for it" and turning to his signaller, sent "2 Troop Target Bare, 1 round gun fire, report when ready".

The excitement became infectious and while eagerly watching the approaching column which I expected would soon be disturbed, I imagined the actions at his gun positions— G.P.O.s giving their orders, clearly and carefully; Sergeants briskly stirring their teams who needed no goad; Nos. 4 loading; "Set" from No. 2; "Ready" from the gun layers; and the suspense awaiting the order which would start our war in Greece—"Battery ready" came over the phone.

"I" Report No. 51. 6th, April, 1941., 1000 hours:-

Twelve German Divisions (2 armoured, 10 infantry) crossed the Yugo-Slav frontier yesterday. They appear to be heading towards Florina, where all bridges have been "blown".

"I" report No. 52 6th April, 1800 hours:- The Germans have occupied Florina where the bridges were NOT repeat NOT "blown".

There were but 2 British divisions and 1 armoured Bde. in Greece, but we were confident, and more would arrive.

Next morning at first light, from a Field O.P. which was very close to that of a Medium regiment, the movement of Enemy M.T. became visible, and being out of 25 pdr. range, I walked across to see the O.P.O. of the Mediums.

All the previous afternoon he had been busy with his maps & Artillery Board, registering the conspicuous points on the Florina plain, and this morning the line & range of the various targets had been corrected to comply with the local weather conditions.

He was mildly excited when I arrived, as one column of large German troop carriers was approaching a cross roads which he had registered at almost the extreme range of his guns. Seeing me, he said, optimistically, I thought, "If they stop at that cross roads there for it", and turning to his signaller sent, "2 Troop Target Beer, 1 round gunfire, report when ready."

The excitement became infectious, and, while eagerly watching the approaching column which I expected would soon be disturbed, I imagined the actions at his gun position: No 1's giving their orders, clearly & carefully; Sergeants busily stirring their teams who needed no goad; No 4 loading; "Set" from No 2; "Ready" from the gun layers: and then the suspense awaiting the order which would start our war in Greece — "Battery Ready" came over the phone.

Meanwhile, like a dark grey caterpillar on a great green lawn, the column advanced, and, to our agreeable astonishment stopped about the cross roads, apparently in doubt as to which road to take.

Four large tracked vehicles stopped at a cross roads is a good target, and a direct hit could be expected in about 10 rounds of observed shooting, but with prediction who could say.

"Fire" ordered the O.P.O. quietly to the telephonist, and I pressed my stop watch.

The time of flight at the range was 38 seconds.

I fidgeted with my glasses, and watched the target: would they move before the welcome arrived. Ten seconds - a dull roar - followed immediately by the thunderous whirl of 8 times 75 pounds overhead...

Thirtysix seconds, (It had seemed an eternity, but they had not moved.) I broke my glasses and the next instant a puff of dust and smoke appeared, as if by magic, where the nearest enemy lorry had been.

A direct hit first round! And by absolute prediction!!...

The other 7 were only "in the area" but who cared.

"5 Rounds Gunfire!" shouted the O.P.O., and I returned to my own O.P. "watch the tactical situation and send back information".

The war was on.

A day I shall not forget in a hurry as it landed me in gefangenschaft where I have since resided. I was in a night bomber squadron, but owing to the invasion of Norway & our almost complete lack of long-range day bombers, we were called up to operate in daylight.

A German heavy cruiser (later identified as the Karlsruhe) had been damaged in early morning hours by our navy, but owing to heavy seas & bad visibility had made a hell escape. We were ordered to locate & destroy her. After a stinking trip across the North - the 12 of us arrived over the south coast of Norway & opening up into a wide vic of sections commenced a sweep. I was a little worried about our formation as, operating over enemy territory with heavy, & consequently slow aircraft, we ran every chance of meeting fighters. However we carried on, & after about two hours sweeping we sighted the enemy lying in Kristiansand harbour. What very shortly proved to be a costly mistake was made here as our leader ordered us into sections astern, aircraft astern which presented a long line of single bombers to the enemy, anyone of which could be engaged without assistance from another & it also cut down our firepower to a bare minimum.

Opening our bomb doors we fused our bombs & commenced our run up. The picture is & will forever be clear in my mind; a cloudless sky, height 12,000 feet, airspeed ___ miles per hour, the cruiser appearing as a small grey sliver of steel dashing headlong for the open sea & pumping up AA for all she was worth. Leading the last section of three I was just coming onto the target when lo & behold enemy fighters, six ME 109's. Needless to say I attached my section & in less time than it takes to put it in writing my No 3 aircraft was shot down in flames & all hands were lost. My No 2 & I managed to weather the storm up, bombed, & as I did a turn to the west I saw a direct hit scored just forward of the funnel. But I had very little time to observe as I was unable to catch up the rest of the formation owing to their increased speed & the heavy & accurate attacks of the enemy.

Being completely unable to hold them off having neither the speed nor the firepower I came down to sea level, that at least protected our belly. The two of us had only just arrived here & got properly formed up when No 2 simply exploded in mid air in a mass of flames & in the twinkling of an eye had disappeared forever under the cold grey surface of the sea. I was about ready to throw in the towel then & there as with all my section except myself shot down, one of my gunners killed, the rest of us all hit & bullets & cannon shells simply raining in from all directions, we were a gone goose. But one doesn't surrender in ten & fight on we did.

After about 3/4 of an hour of concentrated hell my starboard engine took fire & I was forced to turn north & try & make the Norwegian coast. On the run in, the Jerries sensing we were cold meat threw caution to the winds & attacked recklessly right up to 20 yards. It was a bad mistake on their part as we still had a certain sting in the tail in the form of two Vickers K's. By simply heroic work my remaining rear gunner downed three of them in quick succession with the result the remainder held off to a more respectable distance. Just as we were approaching the shore, a well placed burst brought us crashing down in flames in the sea. By the

Meanwhile, like a dark grey caterpillar on a great green lawn, the column advanced, and to our agreeable astonishment it stopped about the cross-roads, apparently in doubt as to which road to take. Four large tracked vehicles stopped at a cross-roads is a good target, and a direct hit could be expected in about 10 rounds of observed shooting, but with pure prediction who could say?

"Fire", ordered the O.P.O. quietly to the telephonist, and I pressed my stop watch. The time of flight at the range was 38 seconds. I fidgeted with my glasses and watched the target: would they move before our welcome arrived. Ten seconds—a dull roar—followed immediately by the thunderous whirl of 8 times 75 pounds overhead . . .

Thirty-six seconds (it had seemed an eternity, but they had not moved). I brought up my glasses and the next instant a puff of dust and smoke appeared, as if by magic, where the nearest enemy lorry had been.

A direct hit first round! And by absolute prediction!!.. The other seven were only "in the area" but who cared.

"5 rounds gun fire!" shouted the O.P.O. and I returned to my own O.P. to "watch the tactical situation and send back information".

The war was on.

D. A. Crawford,
Capt. A.I.F.

21. SOUTH NORWAY—APRIL 12/40

A day I shall not forget in a hurry as it landed me in Gefangenshaft where I have since resided. I was in a night bomber squadron, but owing to the invasion of Norway and our almost complete lack of long range day bombers, we were called up to operate in daylight.

A German heavy cruiser (later identified as the Karlsruhe) had been damaged in the early morning hours by our navy, but owing to heavy seas and bad visibility had made good her escape. We were ordered to locate and destroy her. After a sticky trip across the North Sea the 12 of us arrived over the south coast of Norway and opening up into a wide vie of sections commenced a sweep. I was a little worried about our formation as operating over enemy territory with heavy and consequently slow aircraft, we ran every chance of meeting fighters. However we carried on, and after about two hours sweeping we sighted our quarry lying in Kristiansand harbour. What very shortly proved to be a costly mistake was made here as our leader ordered us into sections astern, aircraft astern which presented a long line of single bombers to the enemy, anyone of which could be engaged without assistance from another, and it also cut down our firepower to a bare minimum.

Opening our bomb doors we fused our bombs and commenced our run up. The picture is still and will forever be clear in my mind, a cloudless sky, height 12,000 feet, airspeed 180 miles per hour, the cruiser appearing as a small grey sliver of steel dashing headlong for the open sea and pumping up AA for all she was worth. Leading the last section of three I was just coming onto the target, when low and behold enemy fighters, six ME109's. Needless to say was shot down in flames and all hands were lost. My No. 2 and I managed to weather the storm, ran up, bombed and as I did a turn to the West I saw a direct hit scored just forward of the funnel. But I had very little time to observe as I was unable to catch up the rest of the formation owing to their increased speed and the heavy and accurate attacks of the enemy.

Being completely unable to hold them off having neither the speed nor the firepower I came down to sea level, that at least protected our belly. The two of us had only just arrived there and got properly formed up when No. 2 simply exploded in mid air in a mass of flames and in the twinkling of an eye had disappeared forever under the cold grey surface of the sea. I was just about ready to throw in the towel then and there as with all my section except myself shot down, one of my gunners killed, the rest of us all hit and bullets and cannon shells simply raining in from all directions, we were a gone goose. But one doesn't surrender in the air, and fight on we did.

After about ¾ of an hour of concentrated hell my starboard engine took fire and I was forced to turn North and try and make the Norwegian coast. On the run in, the Jerries figuring we were cold meat threw caution to the wind and attacked recklessly right up to 20 yards. It was a bad mistake on their part as we still had a certain sting in the tail in the form of two Vickers K's.

By simply heroic work my remaining rear gunner bounced three of them in quick succession with the result the remainder held off to a more respectable distance. Just as we were approaching the shore, a well placed burst brought us crashing down in flames in the sea. By the grace of God and a lot of luck we in the aircraft who were alive as we were shot down all emerged alive and kicking from what had a few seconds before been an aircraft.

Well, there it is Jerry, you will no doubt think it just one big moan. Probably it is, but one does hate like hell to be as thoroughly thrashed as we were, and have practically no means of fighting back.

F/Lt. Donaldson RAF

23. DOVER—DUNKIRQUE PATROL

Coaled and provisioned, "Jasper" (anti-submarine trawler) left Harwich in company with her sister ship "Amethyst"; it was A.M. 26th May '40, the grey sea calm bearing a slight haze. Night found us off Dover with orders to patrol in the vicinity of the N. Goodwin lightship: other than the hissing noise of destroyers at high speed passing close and the rumbling of guns on the French coast nothing of interest happened. The following morning saw more activity in the shape of eight Men of War converging on Dover—signals were decoded and one was informed that various groups of ships were assembling for evacuation duties; what an armada it was to be.

In the meantime we had been ordered to extend our patrol along the lane between Dover and Dunkirque acting as covering force for the evacuation craft, anti-submarine and anti "E" boat patrol. The time had come for lifebelts to be worn at all times, hands to sleep or rest

grace of God & a lot of luck we in the aircraft who were alive as we were shot down all emerged alive & kicking from what had a few seconds before been an aircraft.

Well, there it is Jerry, you will no doubt think it just one big ... probably it is, but one does hate like hell to be as thoroughly thrashed as ... hell, & have practically no means of fighting back.

F/LT. Donaldson R.A.F.

blankets. A destroyer minus her steam exhaust pipe comes limping along, an escort vessel just a mass of twisted iron from her bridge aft returns slowly in tow of a tug; weather now misty, sea still calm – here comes a little drifter out of the mist, comes alongside for a compass course to Dover (lost his bearings & has no chart!) – there's a minefield close at hand & so one can't be too careful – soldiers of all nationalities are packed onboard this queue little vessel, infact almost to the top of his funnel. the mist now lifting, now see a "Jerry" two engined jot heavily smoking & diving to-wards the sea; over our R.T. comes the frantic S.O.S call from some trawler skipper, calling for fighter support is being heavily attacked from the air; his voice comes through quick, clear & high then tragic silence before finishing his reply now looking at two minesweepers on our beam; water spouts very close to them & quickly move in our direction, thank H... that high level bombing is very poor. Night routine is a ... of challenging all craft & avoiding collision; planes drone overhead & guns continue to thunder on the French side. Daybreak sees an ocean of wreckage, spars, boxes, boats etc – we ordered to sink a British trawler (heavily damaged) – proceed in her direction but ordered to return after half an hour (destroys herself). It is now ... 30th & there are many gaps in the traffic lanes, evacuation drawing to a close what appear to be a fall of shot near an 'Isle of Wight ferry boat in tow of a tug demands investigation – on closing we find everything in order, infact the crew of the ferry boat are kicking a sort of football about on deck. A fair sized transport passes with large painted words on ships side, we read "Dunkirque Ferry" & some Scottish football score. Sunday finds very little traffic abroad, we are ordered to return to anchor off Dover. Turn in about 11. P.M – a good nights rest after six days patrol, Pushedon to Harwich at daybreak next day; thank God for a fair wind & calm seas throughout these operations – so much depended on these brave small craft.

J. Crisp. Bosn. R.N.

coaled & provisioned, "Jasper" (anti-submarine trawler) left Harwich in comp
with her sister ship "Amethyst"; it was A.M. 26th May '40. the
sea calm wearing a slight haze; Night found us off Dover wi
orders to patrol in the vicinity of the N. Goodwin lightships
other than the hissing noise of destroyers at high speed passi
close & the rumbling of guns on the French coast nothin
of interest happened. the following morning saw more activity
in the shape of light men of war converging on Dover - signal
were decoded & one was informed that various groups of shi
were assembling for evacuation duties; what an Armada it w
to be. In the meantime we had been ordered to extend our
patrol along the lane between Dover & Dunkirque acting
covering force for the evacuation craft, anti-submarine &
anti 'E' boat patrol. the time had come for lifebelts to be w
at all times, hands to sleep or rest on deck between wat
close range weapons within reach of all, the 4" gun at al
times manned by two crew "progy & charge" ready on the tray.
Subby & I, the only officers took turns at kipping near the
binnacle on the upper bridge. Each day & night now
brought something of lively interest. What an amazing day
scene, like a "Spithead Review" of all the small craft in the
world - the sea was litterly covered with hundreds of sm
craft of all sizes & description slowly wending their way
to-wards the French coast, with destroyers & other fast men
war passing them at high speed. What a collection, sl
destroyers, escort vessels, minesweepers, trawlers, motor boats, op
boats in tow, lifeboats, pleasure craft, thames barges in tow
tugs, ferryboats, dutch barges, transports of all types + the
majority manned by amateur sailors; a regatta that was to
go down in history, covering itself with glory, the means
of bringing back 350,000 men to England! At times sm
forces of English bombers escorted by fighters roared high
overhead while three coastal patrol types flew low keep
a continuous patrol along the lane of ships. No risks we
now taken, whenever our operator contacted what was co
to be reliable we immediately hoisted warning flags "about t
drop depth charges & then went in to attack with a
"pattern" of five 300lb charges; this was executed at our t
speed of ten knots, consequently it shook the little ship
up now & again, upsetting the dynamo & putting the set out
order for about ten minutes. After an attack the gun was tr
on the position of the expected resurfacing of the submarine
wreck never came our way, only dead fish & the bloated
body of some unfortunate seaman. Several craft were now
returning overloaded with tired grimy looking men, still
smiling & with sufficient spirit to wave us a cheer; man

on deck between watches, close range weapons within reach of all, the 4" gun at all times manned by two crew "progy and charge" ready on the tray.

Subby and I, the only officers took turns at kipping near the binnacle on the upper bridge. Each day and night now brought something of lively interest. What an amazing daybreak scene, like a "Spithead Review" of all the small craft in the world—the sea was literally covered with hundreds of small craft of all sizes and description slowly wending their way towards the French coast, with destroyers and other fast men of war passing them at high speed. What a collection, sloops, destroyers, escort vessels, minesweepers, trawlers, motor boats, open boats in tow, life boats, pleasure craft, Thames barges in tow of tugs, ferryboats, dutch barges, transports of all types and the majority manned by amateur sailors; a regatta that was to go down in history, covering itself with glory, the means of bringing back 350,000 men to England. At times small forces of English bombers escorted by fighters roared high overhead while three coastal patrol types flew low keeping a continuous patrol along the lane of ships.

No risks were now taken. Whenever our operator contacted what was or appeared to be reliable we immediately hoisted warning flags "about to drop depth charges and then went in to attack with a "pattern" of five, 300 lb charges; this was executed at out top speed of ten knots, consequently it shook the little ship up now and again, upsetting the dynamo and putting the set out of order for about ten minutes. After an attack the gun was trained on the position of the expected surfacing of the submarine—luck never came our way, only dead fish and the bloated body of some unfortunate seaman. Several craft were now returning overloaded with tired grimy looking men, still smiling and with sufficient spirit to wave us a cheer; many were without clothes but kept warm by being wrapped in [*original text continued on page 22 of diary*] blankets. A destroyer minus her steam exhaust pipe came limping along, an escort vessel just a mass of twisted iron from her bridge aft returns slowly in tow of a tug; weather now misty, sea still calm—here comes a little drifter out of the mist, comes alongside for a compass bearing course to Dover (lost her bearings and has no chart!)—there's a minefield close at hand and so one can't be too careful—soldiers of all nationalities are packed onboard this game little vessel, in fact almost to the top of his funnel. The mist keeps lifting, now see a "Jerry" two engined job heavily smoking and diving to-wards the sea; over our R.T. comes the frantic S.O.S. call from some trawler Skipper, calling for fighter support, is being heavily attacked from the air; his voice comes through quick, clear and high then tragic silence before finishing his report.

Now looking at two minesweepers on our beam; water spouts rise very close to them and quickly move in our direction, thank the Lord high level bombing is very poor. Night routine is a policy of challenging all craft and avoiding collision; planes drone overhead and guns continue to thunder on the French side.

Daybreak sees an ocean of wreckage, spars, boxes, boats, etc—we are ordered to sink a Sister trawler (heavily damaged)—proceed in her direction but ordered to return after half an hour (destroys herself). It is now the 30th and there are many gaps in the traffic lanes, evacuation drawing to a close. What appears to be a fall of shot near an Isle of Wight ferry boat in tow of a tug demands investigation—on closing we find everything in order, in fact the crew of the ferry boat are kicking a sort of football about on deck. A fair sized transport passes with large painted words on her ships side, we read "Dunkirque Ferry" and some Scottish football score!

Sunday finds little traffic abroad, we are ordered to return and anchor off Dover. Turn in about 11pm—a good night's rest after six days patrol. Pushed on to Harwich at daybreak next day, thank God for a fair wind and calm seas throughout those operations—so much depended on those brave small craft.

J. Chrisp, Bos'n. R. N.

24. TO BE PUT DOWN AS AN EXPERIMENT "DIEPPE"

Impossible to continue the fight. Enough blood has been spilt already in a hopeless effort to gain the heights of the town. All possible retreat has been cut off from the sea. The deadly accurate aim of the Jerry's artillery has cut down our last chance of getting back across the Channel.—We have to give up, not even with the satisfaction of an accomplished duty . . .

We are driven off the bloody beaches to reassemble in the yard of Dieppe's hospital. From there we are marched off through the streets of the town towards "Envermeux" 10 kilometres south.—Always I'll remember this march. The poor sad-faced French people would assemble in small groups along the streets, tears running down their cheeks would tell of how anxious they were to see better days for their liberation.

At "Envermeux" we are separated from the men and locked up in the village church. There an old white-headed priest is waiting for us in order to give us all the comfort he can offer, which consists of a handful of straw to each. He is very surprised to see how well the French Canadians can speak his own language.

"Pourquoi", dit-il, etes vous venues. Il vous attendaient depuis trois semaines?—Pourquoi! ai-je repondu, Pourquoi! Nous le saurons après la guerre!—Peut-être.*

Colditz Novembre/43
A. R. Marchand Lieut, Fus. Mont Royal.

* *"Why", said he, "have you come?" They have been waiting for you for three weeks?—"Why," I replied, "Why! We will know after the war!—Perhaps".*

25. "APPEL" 1942 EICHSTÄTT OFLAG VII B GERMANY

The Earl of Hopetoun, Capt., Lothian and Borders Yeomanry

"Officers will wear overcoats properly buttoned up, when on Appel. The reading of books on Appel is forbidden and will be punished. By order of Oberst-Leutnant Blätterbau, Oflag VIIB"

Have you heard the latest notice? Who the hell does he think we are?

To be put down as an experiment &c ?

Impossible to continue the fight. Enough
blood has been spilled already, in hopeless eff
to gain the heights of the town. All possible retre
has been cut from the sea. The deadly accurate aim of the Terry's artillery has cut down
our last chance of getting back across the
channel. – We have to give up, not even with
the satisfaction of an accomplished duty ... –
We are driven off the bloody beaches to re-
semble in the yard of Dieppe's hospital. – From
there we are marched off through the streets of
the town towards "Envermeu" 10 kilometer
south. – Always I'll remember this march
the poor sad faced French people would
assemble in small groups along the streets
with tears running down their cheeks would tell of how
anxious they were to see better days for their liber-
tion. – At "Envermeu" we are separated from them
and locked up in the village church. There an old white
headed priest is waiting for us in order to give us all
the comfort he can offer, which consist of a hand full
of straw to each of us. – He is very surprise to see how
well the French Canadians can speak his own langu-
Pourquoi, dit-il êtes-vous venus. Il vous attendaient de pu
rois semaines? – Pourquoi! ai-je répondre, Pourqu
vous le saurons après la guerre! – Peut-être

Coldetz November /43.   A. R. Marchand Lie
                                     Fus mont Royal.

Officers will wear overcoats properly buttoned up, when on appel. The reading of books on appel is forbidden & will be punished.   By order of Oberst. Lieutenant Blätterbau. Oflag VII B "

Have you heard the latest notice? Who the hell does he think we are?

Appel 9. am. Bugle has blown. Very few overcoats in evidence. Nearly all have a book or a newspaper. The companies fall in, the Sentries and inspecting officer arrive for the count. Suddenly someone laughs, loudly, deliberately and offensively. "Ha Ha Ha. Oh. boys look at that. "Achtung" the commandant.

" Come on down you old bastard. Don't stand there on the bank with your legs apart. We're waiting "   " wot'yer Blätters, old bag. Paper, evening paper, all the winners and prices. Boots, filthy pictures. " — Roars of applause as he majestically approaches the parade. Some of the Sentries are tittering. They've been in the fighting. The Oberst. Lieutenant never heard a bullet in his life. — "Parade 'Shun!" (British orders, and therefore obeyed) — Stand at ease — Blätters takes the Salute with a click of his podgy legs and walks threateningly towards the leading ranks. " Blimey. He's inspecting us. Yoo-hoo Blätters, you old Sod. How are we looking "   An awful roar is heard, necks are craned. "what's up?"   "He's cursing someone for not looking at him. The f — r. he's put him in arrest "Erchen! You bastard. Nach dem krieg. Mind your own business"   "Look out, here is is"   Terry P. has carefully removed his overcoat and draped it over his shoulders. He takes out a huge volume, stands in the front rank & reads. Deadly Silence. Blätters Speechless. Suddenly like a roll of distant thunder it comes " So. Was haben wir hier. Ein Britisch Offizier, ja. " Silence. Louder " Ein Britishe Offize - r - i - E -"R " all in chorus " JA "   " Ruhe! Sind Sie Schweine, oder offiziere ? " chorus " Dolmetscher! Interpreter! Speak English you f — r, J. P. has his name taken & his book confiscated   the inspection continues. The opposition grows less & less subtle & more & more outerous. The Sentries are enjoying it hugely. Every now & then there is an ugly rumble of abuse above the banter as Blätters once again rises to the fly. and gives an exhibition of german vocal fury, which is the best that we have ever heard, and we've heard a good deal in our 3 years in Germany. & continue the parade is in an uproar. I think Blätterbau is beginning to realise we don't like him. He expresses his intention of leaving the parade ground. There is much saluting & heel clicking from his junior officers, which is loudly applauded & Blätters gives up the unequal struggle & leaves amid & yells of derision. His junior officer, an overgrown and thick-kneed Captain with huge feet, & a voice like Donald Duck attempts to restore order. 2000 British officers reply " Quark, quark, Quark. Quark!" He tries again. Again " Quark, Quark. Quark! " He leaves & a fury, giving orders to the Sentries to keep us on parade & disappears. There is a concerted rush for the exits. The parade disappears. We reach our rooms & sit down. to breakfast. or the cold + daunted square 10 bewildered Sentries are still standing.

Appel 9 am. Bugle has blown. Very few overcoats in evidence. Nearly all have a book or newspaper. The companies fall in, the sentries and inspecting officer arrive for the count. Suddenly someone laughs, loudly, deliberately and offensively. "Ha. Ha. Ha. Oh boys look at that. "Achtung" the Commandant".

"Come on down you old bastard. Don't stand there on the bank with your legs apart. We're waiting." "Wot 'yer Blätters old boy. Papers, evening papers, all the winners and prices. Books, feelthy pictures."—Roars of applause as he majestically approaches the parade. Some of the sentries are tittering. They've been in the fighting. The Oberst-Leutnant never heard a bullet in his life.—"Parade 'Shun!" (British orders, and therefore obeyed)—Stand at ease—"Blätters" takes the salute with a click of his podgy legs and walks threateningly towards the leading ranks.

"Blimey he's inspecting us. Yoo-hoo Blätters, you old sod. How are we looking" An awful roar is heard, necks are craned. "What's up?" "He's cursing someone for not looking at him. The f——r, he's put him under arrest."

"Ercher! You bastard. Nach dem Krieg. Mind your own business" "Look out, here he is" Jerry P. has carefully removed his overcoat and draped it over his shoulders. He takes out a huge volume, stands in front of the rank and reads. Deadly silence. Blätters speechless. Suddenly like a roll of distant thunder it comes. "So was haben wir hier. Ein Britische Offizier, ja." Silence. Louder "Ein Britische offi-Z-I-E-R" all in chorus, "JA."

"Ruhe! Sind Sie Schweine oder Offiziere?" Chorus "Dolmetcher! Interpreter! Speak English you f——r!"

J. P. has his name taken and his book confiscated. The inspection continues. The opposition grows less and less subtle and more vociferous. The sentries are enjoying it hugely. Every now and then there is an ugly rumble of abuse above the banter as Blätters once again rises to the fly, and gives an exhibition of German vocal fury, which is the best that we have ever heard, and we've heard a good deal in our 3 years in Germany. Meantime the parade is in an uproar. I think Blätterbau is beginning to realise we don't like him. He expresses his intention of leaving the parade ground. There is much saluting and heel clicking from junior officers, which is loudly applauded.

Blätters gives up the unequal struggle and leaves amid yells of derision. His junior officer, an overgrown and knock-kneed captain with huge feet and a voice like Donald Duck attempts to restore order. 2,000 British officers reply "Quack, quack, quack, quack!" He tries again. Again "Quack, quack, quack, quack!" He leaves in a fury, giving orders to the sentries to keep us on parade, and disappears. There is a concerted rush for the exits. The parade disappears. We reach our rooms and sit down to breakfast. On the cold and deserted square 10 bewildered sentries are still standing.

26. NIGHTLIFE

One needed an occasional rest from the hectic nightlife of Alexandria, so one or two nights a week we were allotted to raids by sea on enemy coastline with the object of landing small forces (say 10 men) armed with time bombs for the destruction of enemy tanks, m.t. and aircraft and dumps.

The expeditions were usually last minute affairs which meant that prawns for lunch was a gamble. Since the M.T.B.s which we used while the submarine flotillas were all too busy sinking Rommel's convoys to play with us, were very sick-making (acks to Evelyn Waugh). The sea is almost invariably unaccommodating when one intends to do a night landing. Many of our raids were abortive, so that one probably had to paddle about for hours in a canoe looking for a gap in the surf.

Once I was on the bridge of an M.T.B. that was going as close inshore as possible (far closer than was prudent) looking for a landing place. The landing was timed for 11.30 pm. At midnight the Fleet Air Arm were dropping flares for a destroyer shoot on Mersa Matruh about 25 to W. We were behind schedule so thought it might be wiser to go back, as the flares would make us visible. The shore was dimly visible to port. Suddenly I saw what I thought were rocks on the beach, then they seemed much more like tents. I said, "Don't look now, but there's a German encampment about 25 yards to port!"

The N.O. laughed, but not for long. There was a sudden shudder, and ominous grating and the boat stopped. We were aground! We hurriedly went astern which cleared the port screw from the rock it had hit. We then bounded joyously ahead slap into a sandbank. Then two things happened. Car headlights suddenly lit up on land revealing tents and lorries right on the beach only a few yds. away. Then the whole sky lit up like day as numerous flares began to drop slowly earthwards. An aeroplane flew very low over our heads.

We went full speed astern and luckily got clear. By this time Germans were running about on the beach. We disappeared back to Alex. as fast as our remaining screw would carry us, firing a farewell burst on the machine guns as we left.

Prawns for lunch next day were a certainty as we seldom went out two nights in succession.

Michael Alexander

27. AND SO TO GREECE—TILL 15 APRIL '41

That land of scenic grandeur, evergreen mythology and unsurpassed maidenly complexions. But alas, not to dally by seductive hillside taverns—sipping on that mellow nectar, for which she is so renowned. Nay to repel an ominous invader of everything peaceful. While a mere handful of stalwart Australians were accustoming weary limbs to steep mountain gradients after a seemingly endless plain of desert sands, the rumble of enemy armour and artillery confident of its at least numerical superiority came ever nearer. The days of pleasant exercising in surroundings steeped, though strategic, in the lush hues of early Spring were all too soon brought to a close by the dread tidings that the foe had crossed the Jugoslavian frontier. On to more spartan country positions in heights Spring had not yet touched. Tents, diffused with camouflage on a green backdrop, gave way to widely separated positions, deeply

One needed an occasional rest from the hectic night life of Alexandria, so one or two nights a week were allotted to sail by sea on enemy coastline with the object of landing small forces (say 10 men) armed with time bombs for the destruction of enemy tanks, etc. & aircraft & dumps. The expeditions were usually last minute affairs which meant that prawns for lunch was a gamble since the M.T.Bs we used while the submarine flotillas were all too busy sinking Rommel's convoys to play with us, were very sick making (acks to Evelyn Waugh). The sea is almost invariably unaccommodating when one intends to do a night landing and many of our raids were abortive, so that one probably had to paddle about for hours in a canoe looking for a gap in the surf.

Once I was on the bridge of an M.T.B going as close inshore as possible (far closer than was prudent) looking for a landing place. The landing was timed for 11.30 p.m. At midnight the Fleet Air Arm were dropping flares for a destroyer shoot on MERSA MATRUH about 25 to W. We were behind schedule so I thought it might be wiser to go back, as the flares would make us visible. The shore was dimly visible to port. Suddenly I saw what I thought were rocks on the beach, then they seemed much more like tents. I said: "Don't look now, but there's a German encampment about 25 yds to port." The N.O. laughed, but not long. There was a sudden shudder, an ominous grating and the boat stopped. We were aground! We hurriedly went astern & heard the port screw free from the rock it had hit. We then bounded forwards ahead slap onto a sandbank. Then two things happened. Car headlights suddenly lit up on land revealing tents & lorries on the beach only a few yds. away. Then the whole sky lit up as numerous flares began to drop slowly eastwards. An aeroplane flew very low over our heads. We found full speed astern & luckily got clear. Germans were this time running about on the beach. We disappeared back to Alex. as fast as our remaining screw would carry us, giving a farewell burst on the machine guns as we left. Prawns for lunch next day were a certainty as we didn't go out two nights in succession.

Michael Alex

AND SO TO GREECE, that land of scenic grandeur, ever-green mythology, and unsurpassed maidenly complexions. But alas, not to dally by seductive hillside taverns _ sipping of that mellow nectar, for which she is so renowned. Nay to repel an ominous invader of everything free & peaceful. While a mere handful of stalward Australians were accustoming weary limbs to steep mountain gradients after a seemingly endless plain of desert sands, the rumble of enemy armour and artillery, confident of its, at least numerical superiority, came ever nearer. The days of pleasant exercising in surrounding steeped, though strategic, in the lush hues of early Spring, were all too soon brought to a close, by the dread tidings that the foe had crossed the Jugoslavian frontier. On to more spartan country _ positions in heights Spring had as yet not touched. Tents, diffused with camouflage on a green backdrop, gave way to widely separated positions, deeply dug in snow where no camouflage was needed to disguise the grimness of our plaintive shelters. Yet, so well were emplacements sighted in that naturally rugged stronghold, that there was no tremor in the quiet confidence of men who had already vanquished one enemy from a continent where such undreamt of cover had not existed.

Now, just as they were standing to, every man eager to come to grips _ the fates of war decided otherwise. By a sudden swoop on the part of the enemy across the low-lying Macedonian Plains, they were in danger of being cut off; and without a moment's hesitation, everything but essential arms, and what ammunition and rations could be loaded on to unwilling donkeys, had to be abandoned before embarking on a seven days trek across what seemed like every bleak and forbidding mountain range that scarred the country's back, _ only at rare intervals dipping down to a, by now deserted village _ a stream to be crossed, whilst keeping well away from roads that were no longer ours to come.

Each time a stand at some vantage point in the hills _ a deeply defiled pass _ a good tactical fmand. river position, was made, frontages and fire tasks were of necessity extended, as was also the value of each round of steadily dwindling ammunition. Yet the enemy stopped to our bidding, suffering heavy casualties at every attempt to break through _ and particularly from the devastating onslaught of nightly carrier raids. However, numbers must tell in the end, and artillery is scarcely an adequate match for an unmolested Luftwaffe; so on we had to march ever southwards, with a stealth and efficiency that must have caused many a surprise in the morning. Eventually there came a time when we no longer planned to withdraw. We had had a fair innings, and got away from each encounter with scarcely any losses. Now it was another's turn, a battalion of New Zealanders who had stoically held at bay in the deepest of passes, where road, railway, and river _ all rendered completely useless _ converged; a pretty pressing enemy. So pressing was their demand for thoroughfare, that many recce. patrols probing ahead to see what Jerry was up to, failed to return and report, eventually only volunteers being mustered for such unenviable tasks.

The relief each man felt at our arrival needed no expression, and no sooner had we shaken down into positions that were not confined to any one front, than they began to pull out _ lucky blighters. It did not take those deadly Stukkas long to pick out newly brought up field units, though men in the rugged slopes were harder to locate, and on them alone _ with the realisation that there was no turning back _ did all those withdrawing forces depend. A night of standing to _ for our part, bellies sunk in the mud of the river bank, with Brens trained to sweep with considerable effect any attempted crossing _ gave way to day. A day that spelt the end for many times our number of Germans; a day of intermittant L.M.G. fire _ ample opportunity for the snipper; the eventual crossing on a large front of river bend presenting an ideal job for suitably sited Vickers, had we had them; and finally the onslaught _ not from across the water, or out of the narrow pass, but from over the tops of neighbouring ridges _ across such rugged & steep grades, thought to be insurmountable, _ and would have been _ to any but Jerry's crack Gebirgsjaeger, cleanlimbed men with giant, studded, boots, and quite unmolested by all the paraphernalia we were wont to decorate our necks with.

The encounter was short and sharp. We already were one with the many jagged crags and scrubs, and could not readily be seen, whereas even before they appeared, litterally in their hordes, over the skyline. (P.T.

dug in snow where no camouflage was needed to disguise the grimness of our plaintive shelters. Yet so well were emplacements sighted in that naturally rugged stronghold, that there was no tremor in the quiet confidence of men who had already vanquished the enemy from a continent where such undreamt of cover had not existed.

Now, just as they were standing to, every man eager to come to grips,—the fates of war decided otherwise. By a sudden swoop on the part of the enemy across the low-lying Macedonian Plains, they were in danger of being cut off, and without a moment's hesitation, everything but essential arms, and what ammunition and rations could be loaded on to unwilling donkeys, had to be abandoned before embarking on a seven day trek across what seemed like a very bleak and forbidding mountain range that scarred the country's back,— only at rare intervals dipping down to a by now deserted village, a stream to be crossed, whilst keeping away from roads that were no longer ours to command.

Each time a stand at some vantage point in the hills—a deeply defiled pass—a good tactical river position was made, frontages and fire tasks were of necessity extended, as was the value of each round of steadily dwindling ammunition. Yet the enemy stopped to our bidding, suffering heavy casualties at every attempt to break through—and particularly from the devastating onslaught of nightly carrier raids. However, numbers must tell in the end, and artillery is scarcely an adequate match for an unmolested Luftwaffe; so on we had to march ever southwards, with a stealth and efficiency that must have caused many a surprise in the morning. Eventually there came a time when we no longer planned to withdraw. We had a fair innings, and got away from each encounter with scarcely any losses. Now it was another's turn, a battalion of New Zealanders who had stoically held at bay in the deepest of passes, where road, railway and river—all rendered completely useless—converged a pretty pressing enemy. So pressing was their demand for thoroughfare, that many recce patrols probing ahead to see what Jerry was up to, failed to return and report, eventually only volunteers being mustered for such unenviable tasks.

The relief each man felt at our arrival needed no expression, and no sooner had we shaken down into positions that were not confined to any one front, than they began to pull out—lucky blighters. It did not take those really deadly Stukkas long to pick out newly brought up field units, though men in the rugged slopes were harder to locate, and on them alone—with the realisation that there was no turning back—did all those withdrawing forces depend. A night of standing to—for our part, bellies sunk in the mud of the river bank, with Brens trained to sweep with considerable effect any attempted crossing—gave way to day. A day that spelt the end for many times our number of Germans; a day of intermittent L.M.G. fire;—ample opportunity for the sniper; the eventual crossing on a large front of river bend presenting an ideal job for suitably sited Vickers, had we had them; and finally the onslaught—not from across the water, or out of the narrow pass, but from over the tops of neighbouring ridges— across such rugged and steep grades, thought to be unsurmountable,—and would have been—to any but Jerry's crack Gebirgsjaeger, clean-limbed men with giant, studded boots, and quite unmolested by all the paraphernalia we were wont to decorate our necks with.

The encounter was short and sharp. We already were one with the many jugged crags and scrubs, and could not readily be seen, whereas even before they appeared, literally in their hordes, over the skyline (P.T.O.) [*original text continued on page 28 of diary*], could the concise fire orders of their Officers and N.C.O.s be heard. On they came, with only an intermittent shot giving evidence to our presence, till but a couple of hundred yards separated us from a perfect though well-extended target. Then, knowing it to be our last opportunity, every man with a rifle, Bren, even Tommy gun spent his ammunition in one glorious, prolonged burst of rapid fire.

The outcome, when smoke and debris had at length subsided, showed that a heavy toll had been taken among the German ranks: many were dead and dying. Yet, after a scarcely perceptible hesitation, the gaps were again filled—and the advance continued. Needless to say, our relatively few numbers suffered a similar fate, only an odd man here and there managing to break clear, or lying wounded, be picked up by the enemy, and so ultimately in German Gefangenshaft, –– as ––

R. Holroyd, Lt. A.I.F.

28. BELGIUM 1940

The Bn. withdrew from its position on the Charleroi Canal at Hal (S. of Brussels) at 2245 hrs. on May 17. "A" Coy. had orders to hold two of the main roads on our side of the canal until 2330 hrs. to protect the withdrawal.

At 2330 hrs. Capt. C., the Coy. Commander, gave the order to withdraw and remained behind until the last section had moved off. He himself was just on the point of moving off when he heard footsteps coming up the street towards him. Having seen the last of his men off, he thought naturally that they were Germans. He didn't know whether to go away as fast as possible or to remain and try and shoot a few of them. He decided that discretion was the better part of valour and was just on the point of moving after his Coy. when the owners of the footsteps loomed up out of the darkness—four indistinct figures carrying what Capt. C. thought were ammunition boxes.

He stepped quietly into a shop doorway and cocked his revolver. He had aimed and was just about to fire when one of the figures, in a very strong county Fermanagh accent said something about something being "too bloody heavy". They were four "skins" of his own Coy. and were carrying 3 crates of beer between them!

A. R. A. Cocksedge Lt.
2/R Inniskilling Fusiliers

29. LONDON 1940

My house is situated in the centre of a triangle formed by (1) Woolwich Arsenal (2) North Weald Fighter Aerodrome, and (3) Enfield Small Arms Factory; all frequent targets of the German bombers, whose raids on London were at that time taking place day and night.

the Bn. withdrew from its position on the Charleroi Canal at Hal (S. of Brussels) at 2245 hrs. on May 17. "A" Co had orders to hold two of the main roads on our side of the Canal until 2330hrs. to protect the withdrawal

At 2330 hrs., Capt. C, the Coy. Commander, gave the order to withdraw & remained behind until the last section had moved off. He himself was just on the point of moving off when he heard footsteps coming up the street towards him. Having seen the last of his men off he thought, naturally, that they were Germans. He didn't know & whether to go away again as fast as possible or to stay & shoot a few of them. He decided that discretion was the better part of valour & was just on the point of moving after his Coy. when the owners of the footsteps loomed up out of the darkness. — Four indistinct figures carrying what Capt. C. thought were ammunition boxes. He stepped quietly into a shop doorway & cocked his revolver. He had aimed & was just about to fire . . . . when one of the figures, in a very strong County Fermanagh accent said something about something being "too bloody heavy" They were four "skins" of his own Coy. & were carrying 3 crates of beer between them.

a. R. a. Cockredge Lt.
2/R. Inniskilling Fusili

GREECE (Continued)   (Colditz - 29.11.43)

could the concise fire orders of their Officers and N.C.O.s be heard. On they came, with only an inter-mittant shot giving evidence to our presence. till but a couple of hundred yards separated us from a perfect though well-extended target. Then, knowing it to be our last opportunity, every man with rifle, Bren, even Tommy gun spent his ammunition in one glorious, prolonged burst of rapid fire.

The outcome, when smoke and debris had at length subsided, showed that a heavy toll had been taken among the German ranks; many were dead and dying. Yet after a scarcely perceptible hesitation, the gaps were again filled — and the advance continued. Needless to say, our relatively few numbers suffered a similar fate; only an odd man here and there managing to break clear, or lying wounded, be picked up by the enemy, and so ultimately in German Gefangenschaft. — o —

My home is situated in the centre of a triangle formed by (1) Woolwich Arsenal (2) North Weald Fighter Aerodrome, and (3) Enfield Small Arms Factory; all frequent targets of the German bombers, whose raids on London were at that time taking place day and night.

I was fortunate in being at home throughout the entire Battle of London. My ship was commissioning at Tilbury, about 30 miles away, and I was able to get home each evening. I shall always owe a debt of gratitude to Fate that I was able to be at home during this period. The daily and nightly visits of the Nazi youth who fondly believed they were smashing London into subjection left me, as they left most Londoners, singularly undisturbed. One's nerves were undoubtedly a little strained, and in most cases the prospect of a peaceful sleep after the day's work was little more than a fond dream. But London certainly did carry on. My wife, as conductress of a Green Line coach did her job bravely and well - but no better, nor more bravely - than did thousands of other women who were doing men's jobs. I was unworried because I was near my wife. I felt that because of that she would be safe - nothing could possibly happen to us. (What egotistical creatures men are!) Or if it did we would at least be together. The people who in my opinion suffered most were those on active service - or in prison camps far away from their homes - who could do nothing but read the glaring headlines with a feeling of utter impotence. Hoping - hoping - hoping - and yet dreading the news that each day might bring.

Such was the state of affairs in October 1940. My wife and I were sitting by the fire about nine o'clock one evening. The sirens sounded, but apart from a glance at the blackout we took no notice. We talked and listened to the wireless. My dog "Flip" scratched and whined at the kitchen door as he always does when the sirens go - we let him in and he took up his favourite position on the hearthrug. Soon the bombs began to fall in the distance. The regular evening symphony of those days had once more commenced. We hardly interrupted our talking although Flip jumped onto my lap and snuggled up close. The heavy guns in the field opposite my house opened up. Boom! Boom! All the windows & doors shook - Flip trembled and looked at me; wondering perhaps at the murderous folly of men. But he too was well used to this kind of entertainment - He too felt safe while he was near to those he loved.

Suddenly the roar of planes was heard approaching and a terrific crash sounded uncomfortably near. Then another. and another. each louder than the one before. Rena flung herself into my arms and Flip whined and crawled under an armchair. Then CRASH! The house shook violently - the lights went out - there was a noise of glass & wood shattering, and the plaster from the roof fell on to us. We flung ourselves on the floor in the corner. Rena was shaking & crying - She clung to me - I did my best to calm her - but I, too, was far from calm. Anger - a mad-blind pitiful anger seized me. My God. how I hated Hitler - the Nazis - Germans. Had I had the power to destroy every one of them in that moment I would have used that power ruthlessly. War !!! Glory. God and Fatherland. trumpets blowing & flags flying? or thousands of fine young men dying on the battlefields while their women & children are being slaughtered at home. And this is civilisation !! As if the power of all the war lords in the world are worth one hair from my wife's head or one tear from her eyes. My God - how I hated them !

A few seconds - minutes - hours. I don't know how long - we clung together. The planes passed - the din died down - I could hear screams - so we made our way outside. Roofs doors windows were gone from my house, but we were alive & uninjured. The next street was completely destroyed - already nothing remained but a few walls and piles of bricks & mortar which hid mutilated human bodies - The bodies of wives - mothers - children - Sweethearts. Such is Total war, and such. thank God was the spirit of the people of London in those dark months that London still lives - and in the midst of the scars that remain her women can still say with pride that "London could take it."

L. A. Hoovan,
Pay. Lieut. R. N. R.   (16.10.43)
P.O.W. 110599. OFLAG ĪVC

I was fortunate in being at home throughout the entire Battle of London. My ship was commissioning at Tilbury, about 30 miles away, and I was able to get home each evening. I shall always owe a debt of gratitude to Fate that I was able to be at home during this period. The daily and nightly visits of the Nazi youth who falsely believed they were smashing London into subjection left me, as they left most Londoners, singularly undisturbed. One's nerves were undoubtedly a little strained, and in most cases the prospect of a peaceful sleep after the day's work was little more than a fond dream. But London certainly did carry on.

My wife, as conductress of a Green Line coach, did her job bravely and well—but no better, nor more bravely—than did thousands of other women who were filling men's jobs. I was unworried because I was near my wife. I felt that because of that she would be safe. Nothing could possibly happen to <u>us</u>. (What egotistical creatures men are!) Or if it did we would at least be together. The people who in my opinion suffered most were those men on active service—or in prison camps far away from their homes—who could do nothing but read the glaring headlines with a feeling of utter impotence. Hoping—hoping—hoping—and yet dreading the news that each day might bring.

Such was the state of affairs in October 1940. My wife and I were sitting by the fire about nine o'clock one evening. The sirens sounded, but apart from a glance at the blackout we took no notice. We talked and listened to the wireless. My dog "Flip" scratched and whined at the kitchen door as he always does when the sirens go. We let him in and he took up his favourite position on the hearthrug. Soon the bombs began to fall in the distance. The regular evening symphony of those days had once more commenced. We hardly interrupted our talking although Flip jumped onto my lap and snuggled up close. The heavy guns in the field opposite my house opened up. BOOM! BOOM! All the windows and doors shook. Flip trembled and looked at me, wondering perhaps at the murderous folly of men. But he too was well used to this kind of entertainment. He too felt safe while he was near to those he loved.

Suddenly the roar of planes was heard approaching and a terrific crash sounded uncomfortably near. Then another—and another—each louder than the one before. Rena flung herself into my arms and Flip whined and crawled under an armchair. Then CRASH! The house shook violently—the lights went out—there was a noise of glass and wood shattering and the plaster from the roof fell on to us. We flung ourselves on the floor in the corner. Rena was shaking and crying. She clung to me. I did my best to calm her—but I too, was far from calm. Anger—a mad blind hateful anger seized me. My God how I hated Hitler. The Nazis. Germans. Had I had the power to destroy every one of them in that moment I would have used that power ruthlessly. War!!! Glory. God and Fatherland—trumpets blowing and flags flying? Or thousands of fine young men dying on the battlefields while their women and children are being slaughtered at home. And this is civilization!! As if the lives of all the war lords in the world are worth one hair from my wife's head or one tear from her eyes! My God—how I hated them!

After a few seconds—minutes—hours—I don't know how long—we clung together. The planes passed. The din died down. I could hear screams, so we made our way outside. Roof, doors and windows were gone from my house, but we were alive and uninjured. The next street was completely destroyed—already nothing remained but a few walls and piles of bricks and mortar which hid mutilated human bodies. The bodies of wives, mothers, children, sweethearts. Such is total war, and such, thank God was the spirit of the people of London in those dark months that London still lives—and in the midst of the scars that remain her women can still say with pride that "London could take it."

(16.10.43)
J. M. Moran, Pay Lieut. R.N.R.
P.O.W. 110599 Oflag IVC

30. COMMUNICATION PROBLEMS IN A FD. REGT. R.A. IN NORMANDY JUNE 1940

1.   The signals personnel of a Fd. Regiment R.A. were of two kinds (a) gunner signallers who were arty. men formed into a section which was responsible for the communications within a Fd. Bty, and (b) the Royal Signals section whose responsibility was communication within a Fd. Regt, i.e. between the Fd. Btys. and Regt. H.Q.

2.   The signalling equipment throughout the regiment was very good, but untried in war; the only drawback was found to be lack of accumulator charging facilities. The Royal Signals section alone possessed a charging engine (a 550 watt single cylinder petrol engine), and charging boards on the wireless trucks—these latter enabled the accumulators of the wireless set inside the truck to be charged on the move, off the car engine. Thus we were faced with the problem of charging the 56 accumulators belonging to the gunners on our small and quite inadequate 550-watt engine. Naturally the gunners' wireless communication suffered.

3.   Both wireless sets and motorcycles suffered from lack of maintenance. The dust of the hot dry roads of Normandy seemed to get everywhere. The gunner signallers, who had also to assist with the guns, had very little time to clean their sets. The lack of replacements for M/Cs and the large mileage they had to do made their maintenance doubly important.

4.   Operation in battle: (1) Wireless. Two drawbacks: (a) The strict wireless silence regulations in the B.E.F. during the war until the "Blitz" hampered training and operators could not become efficient in the working of their sets; thus the general standard of netting and operating was low. (b) The inadequate accumulator charging facilities mentioned in para 2. Even in the Somme wireless silence was enforced in the calm periods, and sets had to be netted ready to open up instantly on the words "break wireless silence"; consequently the operators had to keep a "listening watch"—a tedious business. On one occasion such an operator had tuned in to a dance music programme from Rugby and was discovered by the C.O.; the explanation given was: "I was making sure my receiver was working, Sir."

1. The signals personnel of a Fd. Regt R.A. were of two kinds: (a) gunner signallers who were arty. men formed into a section which was responsable for the communications within a Fd. Bty, and (b) the Royal Signals section whose responsability was communication within a Fd. Regt, i.e. between the Fd. Btys and Regt. H.Q.

2. The signalling equipment throughout the regiment was very good, but untried in war; the only drawback was found to be lack of accumulator charging facilities. The Royal Signals section alone possessed a charging engine (a 550 watt single cylinder petrol engine), and charging boards on the wireless trucks — these latter enabled the accumulators of the wireless set inside the truck to be charged on the move, off the car engine. Thus we were faced with the problem of charging the 56 accumulators belonging to the gunners on our small & quite inadequate 550-watt engine. Naturally the gunners' wireless communication suffered.

3. Both wireless sets & motorcycles suffered from lack of maintenance. The dust of the hot dry roads of Normandy seemed to get everywhere. The gunner signallers, who had also to assist with the guns, had very little time to clean their sets. The lack of replacements for M/cs and the large mileage they had to do made their maintenance doubly important.

4. Operation in battle: ① Wireless. Two drawbacks: (a) The strict wireless silence regulations in the B.E.F. during the war until the "Blitz" hampered training, + operators could not become efficient in the working of their sets; thus the general standard of netting and operating was low. (b) The inadequate accumulator charging facilities mentioned in para 2. Even on the Somme wireless silence was enforced in the calm periods, and sets had to be netted ready to open up instantly on the words "break Wireless Silence"; consequently the operators had to keep a "listening watch" — a tedious business. On one occasion such an operator had tuned in to a dance music programme from Rugby + was discovered by the C.O.; the explanation given was: "I was making sure my receiver was working, sir."

   ② D.Rs. The Royal Signals section's establishment of D.Rs. was two. To fulfil efficiently our letter service between Regt. H.Q. and Fd. Btys. we needed at least five, and obtained one from R.H.Q. one from each bty; but as these three men had two masters, the position was unsatisfactory.

   ③ Line. Once a line had been laid it needed constant repair due to the damage to it at Bty. H.Q. which was often shelled. We laid always alternate routes from a point on the line near to Bty.H. e.g. R.H.Q. ▭━━━━━━▭ Bty. H.Q. The signal section occasionally had to help out the regt. signallers by laying a line from R.H.Q. to O.P. After a lack of cable at the start of our retreat in Normandy, there was plenty to be had.

5. Recent improvements:
   (a) To accumulator charging equipment. Each wireless truck has now a separate 300 watt petrol charging engine mounted on the truck. This is entirely adequate. This has ceased to be a probl.
   (b) In maintenance discipline. The corps of signals has given the lead to maintenance of sets within the division. Every set is examined regularly by a Royal Signals electrician, and the operator of any set suffering from lack of maintenance is liable to punishment.
   (c) To netting of sets. For this purpose there are improved aids on the sets. Also, wireless operators receive careful training in netting. This has ceased to be a problem.
   (d) Establishment of D.Rs. Until March 1942 the problem still existed. However, Regt. H.Q. has a number of Jeeps which are used by D.Rs. instead of M/cs.

   Modern signals communication depends much on electricity and wireless, which have great possibilities, so that the efficiency of communication is increasing all the time.

J. K. V. Lee.
Lt. Royal Signals.

OFLAG IVC   15 Jan 44.

Looking through the bars of my cell window I saw a gathering of about 50 people - fellow prisoners - Poles. They were of all ages, and dressed very scantily, just as they had been hurriedly hustled out of their cells, although snow lay deep on the ground of the small courtyard, and the temperature was well below zero. Pale and weak they hesitated, standing unsteadily in the unaccustomed freedom of the air and light. The German guards, heavily muffled in their fur coats, plied the metre-long whips they carried, and formed a straggling column of the men before them. Harsh shouts rent the air, and the men began to run round the courtyard, beating a path in the snow with their feet. Those who spluttered, staggered, stumbled, or attempted to walk were savagely beaten with the whips, and forced to continue. Those who, endurance at an end, fell, were beaten till they rose and staggered on. There was no sound except the shouts of the guards and the thud of the whips. This macabre race went on for 15 minutes. Then all were made to lie flat on the snow, and wriggle round the circuit flat on their bellies. Any who attempted to raise themselves on hands or knees were beaten till they lay flat. All were intent on the play, none of the guards spared a glance for my window, where the sight of my face could have caused a shot. Another 10 minutes and the prisoners, exhausted, chilled, plastered with snow were hustled in to their cells and dry themselves as they could. The courtyard emptied. Only the track left remained as evidence that I had not dreamed the scene.

Peter C. Winton Lt

(2) D.Rs. The Royal Signals section's establishment of D.Rs. was two. To fulfil efficiently our letter service between Regt. H.Q. and Fd. Btys. We needed at least five, and obtained one from R.H.Q. and one from each Bty; but as these three men had two masters, the position was unsatisfactory.

(3) Line. Once a line had been laid it needed constant repair due to the damage to it at Bty. H.Q. which was often shelled. We laid always alternate routes from a point on the line near to Bty. H.Q. e.g. R.H.Q. ()--------(--)Bty. H.Q. The Signal section occasionally had to help out the Regt. Signallers by laying a line from R.H.Q. to O.P. After a lack of cable at the start of our retreat in Normandy, there was plenty to be had.

5.   Recent improvements: (a) To accumulator charging equipment. Each wireless truck now has a separate 300 watt petrol charging engine mounted on the truck. This is entirely adequate. This has ceased to be a problem. (b) In maintenance discipline. The Corps of Signals has given the lead to maintenance of sets within the division. Every set is examined regularly by a Royal Signals electrician, and the operator of any set suffering from lack of maintenance is liable to punishment. (c) To netting of sets. For this purpose there are improved aids on the sets. Also, wireless operators receive careful training in netting. This has ceased to be a problem. (d) Establishment of D.R.s. Until March 1942 the problem still existed. However, Regt. H.Q. has a number of Jeeps which are used by D.R.s instead of M/Cs.

Modern signals communication depends much on electricity and wireless, which have great possibilities, so that the efficiency of communication is increasing all the time.

OFLAG IVC 15 Jan 44.

J. K. V. Lee.
Lt. Royal Signals.

31. IN A GESTAPO PRISON IN POLAND—1942

Looking through the bars of my cell window I saw a gathering of about 50 people—fellow prisoners—Poles. They were of all ages, and dressed very scantily, just as they had been hurriedly hustled out of their cells, although snow lay deep on the ground of the small courtyard, and the temperature was well below zero. Pale and weak they hesitated, standing unsteadily in the unaccustomed freedom of the air and light. The German guards, heavily muffled in their fur coats, plied the metre long whips they carried, and formed a straggling column of the men before them. Harsh shouts broke the air and the men began to run round the courtyard, beating a path in the snow with their feet. Those who faltered, struggled, stumbled, or attempted to walk were savagely beaten with the whips, and forced to continue. Those who, endurance at an end, fell, were beaten till they rose and staggered on. There was no sound except the shouts of the guards and the thud of the whips.

This macabre race went on for 15 minutes. Then all were made to lie flat on the snow, and wriggle round the circuit flat on their bellies. Any who attempted to raise themselves on hands or knees were beaten till they lay flat. All were intent on the play. None of the guards spared a glance to my window, where the sight of my face would have caused a shot! Another 10 minutes and the prisoners, exhausted, chilled, plastered with snow were herded in to be in their cells and dry themselves as they could. The courtyard emptied. Only the track left remained as evidence that I had not dreamed the scene.

Peter C. Winton Lt.

Ogflag IVC 16/10/43

32. EFFICIENCY 1940

Nov. '40. A three quarter moon and excellent visibility. The Hun was bombing London and we were intruding against his aerodromes on the Continent, giving him mixed doses off anti-personnel and delay action.

"Aircraft taking off 20 degrees to port" came the observer's voice on the R/T.

A quick turn and there was the perfect target—hangars, runways and flare-path clearly visible in the moonlight and another aircraft taxiing out to take off.

Full throttle and here we go up the flare-path at 400 ft. "Bombs gone" from the Observer and a hit of Flak from the ground to help us on our homeward way. "See any bomb flashes?" "No" from Observer, "Yes!" from Rear Gunner.

Report to I.O. on our return:– "Whole load dropped on aerodrome X. Couldn't miss the bastards. Aerodrome probably U/S 5-6 hours!" "Good work" from the G/C and so to a plate of eggs and bacon and bed.

Next morning out to the satellite aerodrome to fly the a/c back. A quick glance to see if any flares had dropped with the bombs. Yes, some flares had gone—but what the hell are all those yellow things? They're a complete bomb load.

RESULT.—Hefty raspberry from B/C for us for having failed to carry out necessary checks; 56 days for the armourer who forgot to plug in the bomb racks and a damned good laugh for the occupants of the "U/S" aerodrome.

M. L. McColm, S/Ldr. R.A.F.

33. FORT NEUILLY—CALAIS 1940

On May 23rd, 1940, the company I belonged to was in the neighbourhood of Sangatte, about 5 miles to the west of Calais. Shortly after midday we received orders to send one platoon to reinforce the troops already in Fort Neuilly, about a mile and a half to our left

Nov. '40. A three-quarter moon & excellent
visibility. The Hun was bombing London
and we were intruding against his aerodromes
on the Continent; giving him mixed doses
of anti-personnel & delay-action.

"Aircraft taking-off 20° to Port" came
the Observer's voice on the R/T.

A quick turn and there was the perfect
target – hangars, runways and flarepath
clearly visible in the moonlight and another
aircraft taxying out to take off.

Full throttle and here we go up the flare-
path at 400 ft. "Bombs gone" from the
Observer and a bit of Flak from the ground
to help us on our homeward way. "See any
bomb flashes? "No" from Observer. "Yes!" from
Rear-gunner.

Report to I.O. on return:– "Whole load dropped on
aerodrome X. Couldn't miss the bastards. Aerodrome
probably u/s 5–6 hours!" "Good work" from
the G/c & so to a plate of eggs & bacon & bed.

Next morning out to the satellite aerodrome
to fly the a/c back. A quick glance to see if
any flares had dropped with the bombs. Yes,
some flares had gone – but what the hell are
all these yellow things? They're a complete bomb-
load.

RESULT. Hefty raspberry from B/c for me for
having failed to carry out necessary checks;
56 days for the armourers who forgot to plug in
the bomb racks and a damned good laugh
for the occupants of the "U/s" aerodrome.

On May 23rd, 1940, the company I belonged to was in the neighbourhood of Sangatte, about 5 miles to the west of Calais. Shortly after midday we received orders to send one platoon to reinforce the troops already in Fort Neuilly, about a mile & a half to our left rear: this was done. On the following day, having in the meantime found an abandoned French lorry, & having also "acquired" some tinned food & chocolate, we sent the Colour Sergeant — with the M/T. Corporal to drive him & one of the cooks as escort — to Fort Neuilly to see how that platoon was getting along & to take them their share of the bag. The C/Sgt drove up, was challenged, & after some delay was admitted. "How the devil did you get here?" "By road, Sir." "Damn it all, we've been surrounded since 4 o'clock this morning & we had a hell of a time keeping the Bosche out: & now you roll up in your truck as calm as though you were on your ration round." "Well, so I am, Sir: we've managed to make a bit of grub, & there's enough stuff here to last the platoon till to-morrow. And there aren't any Jerries about now, Sir." "Don't you believe it: how on earth you dodged them, I don't know, but now you're here you'll have to stay." "Sorry, Sir: can't do that very well. Company Commander's orders to get back as quick as I can, Sir." "Oh. Very well, then. Take this casualty return with you & tell Captain B— that apart from these we're O.K. Better get out as quick as you can." "Very good, Sir."

Now since Fort Neuilly was about a mile to our rear, we at Company H.Q. were considerably surprised when the truck returned with the whole of the wind-screen smashed & the C/Sgt bleeding from a graze on the cheek & a deep cut over one eye. He reported as follows — "6 Platoon casualty return, Sir: apart from these they're O.K. Mr N— says he's surrounded, Sir." What had actually happened was this: very soon after leaving the Fort, the truck had run into a platoon of German infantry, whereupon the Corporal, who was driving, put his foot down & kept it there. The Germans got in one frontal burst, which damaged the windscreen considerably & the C/Sgt slightly; & Rifleman B—, the cook in the rear of the truck, emptied his magazine over the tail-board, took a fresh charger & managed to get off 3 more rounds before they were clear. As he was something of a marksman, I asked him how he had got on firing over a bouncing tail-board. "Rotten, Sir," he said, disgustedly, "8 bleeding rounds & never a proper sight once: but (more cheerfully) I couldn't let the Corps down in front of the Jerry, Sir, so I declared 'em all 'Correct' at the top of my voice".

Fort Neuilly had not finished with us yet, though. I heard the sequel a day or so later, when we had fallen back to the outskirts of Calais & joined forces with a company of the 60th. I was talking to the Sergeant of the carrier platoon, & since he & our C/Sgt had once been corporals together I told him about the latter's little fracas at Fort Neuilly. "That — place!" he said; "I was out there myself yesterday afternoon — detailed to take carriers there as reinforcement to the garrison. Well, we got there all right, but the only bloomin' garrison in sight was a Bosche one, & they didn't look as though they needed any reinforcements. There we were, 5 bleedin' carriers stuck nose to tail in a narrow sunken cul-de-sac, Jerry looking down at us from all sides, & me looking like Joe-bleedin'-Soap again in the front carrier."

"How did you get out?" I asked.

"Well, Sir, the place had been in Jerry's hands so bleedin' long they didn't think we were real: so we turned each carrier round & drove off quite quiet & sedate like, lobbing out hand-grenades right & left like the bleedin' battle of flowers at Monte Carlo."

J. M. Courtenay
Lt. Q.V.R.

rear; this was done. On the following day, having in the meantime found an abandoned French lorry, and having also "acquired" some tinned food and chocolate, we sent the Colour Sergeant—with the M/T Corporal to drive him and one of the cooks as escort—to Fort Neuilly to see how that platoon was getting along and to take them their share of the bag.

The C/Sgt. drove up, was challenged and after some delay was admitted. "How on earth did you get here?" "By road, Sir". "Damn it all, we've been surrounded since 4 o'clock this morning and have had a hell of a time keeping the Bosche out; and now you roll up in your truck as calm as though you were on your ration round."

"Well, so I am Sir: we've managed to 'make' a bit of grub and there's enough tin stuff here to last the platoon till tomorrow. And there aren't any Jerries about now, Sir."

"Don't you believe it: how on earth you dodged them I don't know, but now you're here you'll have to stay."

"Sorry Sir, can't do that very well. Company Commander's orders to get back as quick as I can, Sir."

"Oh, very well then. Take this casualty return with you and tell Captain B—that apart from these we're O.K. Better get out as quickly as you can." "Very good, Sir."

Now since Fort Neuilly was about a mile to our rear, we at Company H.Q. were considerably surprised when the truck returned with the whole of the windscreen smashed and the C/Sgt bleeding from a graze on his cheek and a deep cut over one eye. He reported as follows: "6 Platoon casualty return, Sir. Apart from these they're O.K. Mr. N— says he's surrounded, Sir."

What actually happened was this. Very soon after leaving the fort, the truck had run into a platoon of German Infantry, whereupon the Corporal, who was driving, put his foot down and kept it there. The Germans got in one frontal burst, which damaged the windscreen considerably and the C/Sgt. slightly. Rifleman B—, the cook in the rear of the truck, emptied his rifle over the tail-board, took a fresh charger and managed to get off 3 more rounds before they were clear. As he was something of a marksman, I asked him how he had got on firing over a bouncing tailboard. "Rotten, Sir." he said disgustedly, "8 bleeding rounds and never a proper sight once: but (more cheerfully) I couldn't let the Corps down in front of the Jerry, Sir, so I declared 'em all 'Correct' at the top of my voice."

Fort Neuilly had not finished with us yet, though. I heard the sequel a day or so later, when we had fallen back to the outskirts of Calais and joined forces with a company of the 60th. I was talking to the Sergeant of the carrier platoon, and since he and our C/Sgt. had once been corporals together I told him about the latter's little fracas at Fort Neuilly. "That —— place!" he said, "I was there myself yesterday afternoon—detailed to take 5 carriers there as reinforcement to the garrison. Well, we got there all right, but the only bloomin' garrison in sight was a Bosche one, and they didn't look as if they needed any reinforcements. There we were, 5 bleedin' carriers stuck nose to tail in a narrow sunken cul-de-sac, Jerry looking down at us from all sides and me looking like Joe-bleedin'–Soap again in the front carrier."

"How did you get out?" I asked.

"Well, Sir, the place had been in Jerry's hands so bleedin' long they didn't think we were real; so we turned each carrier round and drove off quite quiet and sedate like, lobbing out hand-grenades right and left like the bleedin' battle of flowers at Monte Carlo."

J. M. Courtenay
Lt. Q.V.R.

34. LA MORT D'UN LEGIONNAIRE*

You have asked me, my dear Commander, to write an anecdote about the Foreign Legion? The best tale I can think of is the death of Troufimof, one of my legionnaires of whom I was particularly fond because of his bravery in battle. He was of Scandinavian origin, built like Hercules, but as gentle as a lamb. (Thank God, because he could have dispatched a man with one blow). In the Legion he was given the opportunity to quench his thirst for action and adventure.

Although he was very quiet and reserved. One evening in camp he told me the story of his life.

At thirteen he had been a cabin boy on a Norwegian sailing ship and had travelled across the oceans from China to the Chaco, from the Chaco to Abyssinia, during times when arms smuggling was a profitable venture.

One day, by chance, when his ship had put into Le Havre, he and another sailor decided to sign up for five years with the Legion, their intention being to get in some lion hunting. Unfortunately, though there are no lions in Morocco, there are plenty of those famous rebel warriors who give the legionnaires ample scope for roaming about under the scorching sun.

His comrade could not stand up to the rigorous daily life of the Legion, so he deserted, but Troufimof was in his element and signed on again for a period of five years. He distinguished himself in battle and won Corporal's stripes, but once the campaign was over he handed in his stripes and asked to be employed as a stretcher-bearer. He was admirable at his job and seemed the most peace-loving of men. Just at this time the war broke out in Tunisia.

My squadron, which was a Special Assault Group, was ordered to proceed to the front in December 1942. Troufimof woke up at the news and begged me to take him along with me and let him have a machine-gun for himself. I gave into his request and transferred him, much to the disgust of the M.O. I must say I never had to regret it because he was particularly valuable to me once we reached the line and was always extremely active on patrols or guard duty or when engaged in setting traps for enemy patrols. As a matter of fact, I had quite a lot of trouble to prevent him from taking unnecessary risks and getting himself killed to no good purpose.

One morning, in January 1943, my unit was ordered to make a surprise attack on a strongly defended enemy position. The operation was a delicate one and it was essential that it be carried out with dispatch. Fighting started at dawn and at first things went well, but when the enemy had recovered from the initial surprise, they reacted violently with machine-gun fire and immobilized our leading platoon, which was supposed to make an opening in their position. If we had been held up for a few minutes more the whole operation would have

---

* *The Death of a Legionnaire*

Vous me demandez, mon cher camarade, de vous conter une anecdote de Légion Étrangère?... Que puis-je faire de mieux que de vous narrer la mort de TROUFIMOF, un de mes légionnaires que j'aimais beaucoup pour sa bravoure au combat. D'origine Scandinave, bâti en Hercule, mais doux comme un agneau (Dieu merci car il aurait assommé un homme d'une chiquenaude) il trouva chez nous un champ d'action convenant à ses goûts du risque et de l'aventure.

Quoique peu loquace, il me conta, un soir au bivouac, l'histoire de sa vie. Mousse à bord d'un voilier Norvégien, à 13 ans il parcourt les océans. De Chine au Chaco... en Éthiopie pendant les périodes troubles où le trafic d'armes l'intéresse. Un jour, au hasard des voyages, faisant escale au Havre il décide, avec un autre matelot, de prendre un engagement de 5 ans à la Légion, avec l'espoir fantaisiste de chasser le lion. Hélas! si au Maroc les lions n'existent plus, il en est presque de même des fameux guerriers rebelles... procurent aux légionnaires l'occasion de "barouder" sous le soleil brûlant.

Son camarade ne pouvant tenir le pénible régime de la légion, déserte alors que Troufimof se trouve chez nous en plein dans son élément et rengage pour 5 ans; se distingue au combat, gagne le grade de "Brigadier", mais, les combats terminés, remet ses galons et demande de tenir le paisible emploi d'infirmier. Il remplit ces fonctions admirablement et semble le plus pacifique des hommes. Voici que la guerre se rallume en Tunisie. Mon escadron (formation spéciale d'assaut) est désigné pour rejoindre le front en décembre 1942. C'est alors que Troufimof se réveille; me supplie de l'emmener, de lui confier un F.M. pour lui seul. Cédant à ses instances, au désespoir du "Toubib" je le fais remplacer et n'aurai pas à le regretter. Dès notre arrivée en lignes, toujours prêt aux "coups durs" vaillant, fraternel, tendant des pièges aux patrouilles ennemies il m'est d'un concours précieux, j'ai toutes les peines du monde à l'empêcher de commettre des imprudences et de se faire "descendre" inutilement. Un matin de janvier 43 mon unité reçoit ordre de s'emparer par surprise d'une belle position ennemie; c'est une opération délicate et importante que l'affaire tout menée "dardare". L'attaque commence au petit jour. Débute favorablement, mais l'ennemi revenu de sa surprise réagit violemment avec ses mitrailleuses et cloue au sol le premier peloton qui doit ouvrir la brèche sur la position dominante. Quelques minutes d'hésitation et le coup est manqué!! C'est alors que Troufimof s'infiltre en avant, aborde le nid de mitrailleuses ennemi, massacre les servants sur leurs pièces, et, debout, calme, sous le crépitement de la bataille, signale à ses camarades le passage libre; l'assaut est lancé, le peloton pénètre dans les positions, en quelques minutes l'ennemi est assailli, débordé, neutralisé. 130 prisonniers Italiens et Allemands restent entre nos mains, de nombreuses armes dont 4 canons, anti-tanks et 6 mortiers. Hélas! mon brave Troufimof n'eut pas la joie de voir le succès car, son Héroïque action achevée, une balle lui fracassa la tête. Je fus profondément attristé en apprenant la mort de ce beau Suédois, qui ignorait le danger.

Ainsi, mon cher camarade, mourut un légionnaire qui n'avait pour famille que notre régiment, au service duquel, sans soutien être pieusement consenti, comme tant d'autres.

CAPITAINE *Gitte*

1er RÉGT ÉTRANGER DE CAVALERIE

FEZ - MAROC

M— and myself, walking South towards the unoccupied zone, had been arrested, and brought to the district Kommandantur. Escort:— "Sir! These men were told they could not cross the Somme at — as their papers were not in order. They tried to find another place to cross and were arrested." Kommandant:— "Why were you trying to cross the Somme without papers?" Myself:— "My brother here is a Belgian. I too am Flemish, but have French citizenship. I came to France as a refugee. Here is my identity card." — "He has no identity card?" — "No." — "Where have you come from?" — "Péronne." — "Why didn't you cross the Somme at Péronne?" — "Because my brother had no papers." — "I see you are 19 why aren't you in the army?" — "I have a weak heart and was never in the army." — "Oh you have a weak heart, have you?" — "Yes." — "You are a Prisoner of War!" — "Prisoner of war? no no no! Look at my civilian identity card." — "If you are going back to Belgium, how is it you say you come from Péronne? That is north of the Somme. Sentry, they were coming from the south weren't they?" — Escort (walking in) — "Yes Sir!" — Myself:— "I didn't say I was coming from Péronne, I said I was going to Péronne." — "Where were you coming from?" — "Rouen." — "What address did you stop at in Rouen?" — "5 rue Beauvoisine." — "What is that?" — "What do you mean?" — "Was it a house, or a flat or a lodging house?" — "A lodging house." — "What work did you do?" — "As much as I could with my bad heart." — "What work I said!" — "I worked in the ruins." — "You were in the army, you have a numbered shirt!" — "No, it is a hospital shirt." (the truth!) — "Where were you in hospital?" — "In Rouen." — "In a military hospital!" — "No a civilian hospital." — "With your weak heart I suppose" — "Yes" — "How did you get the shirt? You stole it!" — "Yes" — "I say you are a prisoner of war" — "No I am not" — To M— "If you are Flemish you must be able to speak German; can you?" — M— (who spoke neither French or German) "Ein Wenig" — To me, "Why are you of French nationality when your brother is Belgian?" — "I was born in France" — "Were you naturalised French?" — "No I was born in France so I have French nationality as I did nothing to alter it." — "And you were going to Belgium?" "Yes" — "Why?" — "I was going with my brother, who lived there." — "Why were you going to Péronne?" — "We were going to stay with an Aunt at Péronne." — "Well, you are not allowed to cross the Somme without proper papers." — "I know that now." — "You must go back to Rouen and get papers" — "Yes". "You will be shot if you try and get across the Somme" — "Yes" — "Fetch the French gendarme." An orderly fetched him. Kommandant to gendarme:— "These men have been trying to cross the Somme without papers to get back to Belgium." Gendarme:— "Yes they tried to cross here, but I did not allow them to." Kommandant:— "Yes, they probably tried everywhere. They are your business now. Release them on the South bank." Gendarme, pointing to the South bank, — "On this bank?" — "Yes on the South bank. Tell them they are not to try to cross, and will be shot if they do." Gendarme:— "You will be shot if you try to cross again without papers." Kommandant:— "You will be shot if you try to cross the Somme again without papers. Do you understand?" — "I understand very well. I promise I will not try." Kommandant:— "Take them away. Here is your identity card" — "Thank you" — Gendarme "Come along". — "You have been lucky!" he said as he released us on the South bank. We agreed with him.

                                                     John Hamilton Baillie
                                                            Lieut R.E.

been a failure. Here was Troufinof's chance. He crawled ahead of the others, stormed into the enemy machine-gun nest and killed off the gunners. Then he stood up with perfect calm, in the midst of a hail of fire, and signalled his comrades that the road was clear. We put in our attack, the various platoons overran the position, and in a very short time the enemy had been attacked, overrun and completely neutralized. Our total bag consisted of 130 German and italian prisoners, a large number of small arms, four anti-tanks guns and six mortars.

Alas, the courageous Troufimof did not live to rejoice in the victory, as a bullet through the head put an end to his heroic action. I was a very sad man when I learnt of the death of this splendid soldier for whom the word "danger" had no meaning.

Well my dear Commander, that is how one of our legionnaires met his death. He was a man who had no other family but the Legion and you can be sure that we shall keep his memory fresh, as we keep that of so many others.

Capitaine G. Ville,
1st Regt Étranger de Cavalerie,
Fez, Maroc

35. OCCUPIED FRANCE—OCTOBER 1940

M _____ and myself, walking south towards the unoccupied zone, had been arrested and brought to the District Kommandantur.

Escort: "Sir! These men were told they could not cross the Somme at _____ as their papers were not in order. They tried to find another place to cross and were arrested."

Kommandant: "Why were you trying to cross the Somme without papers?"

Myself: "My brother here is a Belgian. I too am Flemish, but have French citizenship. He came to France as a refugee. Here is my identity card."

"He has no identity card?"

"No"

"Where have you come from?"

"Peronne."

"Why didn't you cross the Somme at Peronne?"

"Because my brother had no papers."

"I can see you are 19. Why aren't you in the army?"

"I have a weak heart and was never in the army."

"Oh, you have a weak heart do you?"

"Yes."

"You are a prisoner of war."

"Prisoner of war? No, no, no! Look at my civilian identity card!"

"If you are going back to Belgium, how is it you say you come from Peronne? That is north of the Somme. Sentry, they were coming from the south weren't they?"

Escort (waking up): "Yes, Sir!"

Myself: "I didn't say I was coming from Peronne. I said I was going to Peronne."

"Where were you coming from?"

"Rouen."

"What address did you stop at there?"

"65 Rue Beauvoisine."

"What is that?"

"What do you mean?"

"Was it a house or a flat or a lodging house?"

"A lodging house."

"What work did you do?"

"As much as I could with my bad heart."

"What work I said."

"I worked in the ruins."

"You were in the army, you have a numbered shirt!"

"No, it is a hospital shirt." (the truth).

"Where were you in hospital?"

"In Rouen."

"In a military hospital!"

"No, a civilian hospital."

"With your weak heart I suppose."

"Yes."

"How did you get the shirt? You stole it?"

"Yes."

"I say you are a prisoner of war."

"No, I am not."

To M_____ "If you are Flemish, you must be able to speak German; can you?"

M_____ (who spoke no French or German) "Ein Wenig."

To me, "Why are you of French nationality when your brother is Belgian?"

"I was born in France."

"Were you naturalised French?"

"No, I was born in France so I have French nationality as I did nothing to alter it."

"And you were going to Belgium?"

"Yes."

"Why."

"I was going with my brother, who lived there."

"Why were you going to Peronne?"

"We were going to stay with an Aunt of mine?"

"Well you are not allowed to cross the Somme without proper papers."

"I know that now."

"You must go back to Rouen and get papers."

"Yes."

In May 1940, the Highland Division took over a sector of the Maginot Line. Everyone was excited at the prospect of doing some fighting, for these were the days before the Blitzkrieg. Only a few units in the B.E.F. had hitherto been privileged in this way.

My own Company Commander was not only very efficient but was a great stickler for discipline in all its forms. He was meticulously careful in keeping a check of all Company stores. If one bootlace was unaccounted for, or ¼ gallon of petrol more than necessary was used, he was down on the offender like a ton of bricks.

Before our Battalion actually took over our sector in the "Ligne de Contacte" from the French, all platoon commanders were required to spend one day and night with French platoons to study the conditions and positions which we would take over the next day.

I duly arrived at my future platoon post, which was on the edge of a dark and eerie pinewood, and was politely welcomed by the French platoon commander. He showed me round the position then occupied by his platoon, and which would be occupied by my men the following day.

All was dead quiet. No sign of the Germans although they were only a few hundred yards away. But as soon as night fell it was a very different story. First there would be a distant boom of a Maginot gun, which would be answered by a German gun. This desultory fire would generally intensify until a lively 'counter battery' fire would disturb the night. When this was at its height, one would then hear a few machine guns. The fire would then increase in volume and intensity until about one o'clock, when there would be a perfect crescendo of noise from artillery and machine guns.

It was just about this time when all the firing was at its peak that I heard one of the M.G's belonging to my little Frenchman's platoon, firing. Naturally as I was very excited as this was my first experience of warfare, so I said to him in a breathless whisper, and in my best possible French :—

"Les Allemands sont-ils ici ?"

"Non, non," he replied airily

"Mais pourquoi avez-vous tiré ?" I asked, pointing to the French M.G, which was just visible through the darkness a few yards away.

The French platoon commander shrugged his shoulders and said

"C'est notre dernière nuit ici, et cela les amuse."

I wondered what my Company Commander would think !

J.R.B.

Several days after the fighting commenced on Crete, we were viewing the battle raging in the plains below, from our positions in the hills. Canea which lay just below us had just been subjected to a severe bombardment by enemy aircraft, which constantly flew over us making things fairly uncomfortable.

My section corporal Broderick had just returned from Coy. H.Q. with the news that we were moving at 1300 hrs. for a special job at Retimo. There according to Greek information a force of enemy paratroops had occupied a church and an adjoining block house, from which they commanded the main road communications through which supplies in munitions and food were to pass for Australians fighting on the other side. We were told that some 70 enemy troops were holding out in these buildings. They had been without supplies for four days and only a show of force was necessary to make them surrender. We were conveyed to Retimo in Service Corps Lorries stopping at Kalives to pick up an anti tank gun and crew of the R.H.A. We arrived at Retimo late at night. We had previously picked up two Aussies who had waited to guide us to our exact destination. The attack was timed to start at dawn. The blow was to be struck before the enemy could signal to their air force they were being attacked. In the hills to our right the Greeks kept up a steady fire on the German post, which came dangerously close to us as we advanced. Making use of cover we went forward and got close up to our objective. German snipers who expected an attack, constantly probed the country with fire which made things pretty hot for us and compelled us to crawl forward on our stomachs. Eventually we landed up behind a parapet in a vineyard quite close to the church. A Bren gunner was ordered to open fire on an enemy machine gun nest in the Bell Tower. Immediately followed an extremely heavy barrage of machine gun fire by the enemy. Suddenly our Anti Tank gun opened up, although it hit the target it's shots made no effect. Under cover of their barrage a number of enemy troops advanced. They were met by the accurate fire of one of our platoons, but despite this they managed to reach the parapet behind which we had taken cover. A sharp duel followed. Several hand grenades rolled among us and caused casualties. We were ordered to withdraw. Several men had been fatally hit. I found myself among two or three wounded men and assisted one back to base. I discovered later an enemy bullet had made a large dent in my tin hat and considered myself lucky. Our casualties were approx. 25. Several being dead. The enemy lost 40 dead. We learned later the enemy consisted of more than twice the number we were led to believe. Next day supplies were conveyed to the Aussies by torpedo boats

Pt. D. Halfin KRR

"You will be shot if you try and get across the Somme."

"Yes."

"Fetch the French Gendarme!"

An orderly fetched him. Kommandant to Gendarme: "These men have been trying to cross the Somme without papers, to get back to Belgium."

Gendarme: "Yes, they tried to cross here, but I did not allow them to."

Kommandant: "Yes, they probably tried everywhere. They are your business now. Release them on the South bank."

Gendarme, pointing to the South bank: "On this bank?"

"Yes, on the South bank. Tell them they are not to try to cross, and they will be shot if they do."

Gendarme: "You will be shot if you try to cross the Somme again without papers! Do you understand?"

"I understand very well. I promise I will not try."

Kommandant: "Take them away. Here is your identity card."

"Thank you."

Gendarme: "Come along."

"You have been lucky!" he said as he released us on the South bank. We agreed with him.

John Hamilton Baillie,
Lieut. R.E.

The blanks were in the original, presumably to keep German eyes from seeing the identity of the writer's companion.

36. A NIGHT IN THE MAGINOT LINE

In May 1940, the Highland Division took over a sector of the Maginot Line. Everyone was excited at the prospect of doing some "fighting" for these were the days before the Blitzkrieg. Only a few units in the BEF had hitherto been privileged in this way.

My own Company Commander was not very efficient but was a great stickler for discipline in all its forms. He was meticulously careful in keeping a check of all Company stores. If one bootlace was unaccounted for, or ¼ gallon of petrol more than necessary was used, he was down on the offender like a ton of bricks.

Before our Battalion actually took over our sector on the "Ligne de Contacte" from the French, all platoon commanders were required to spend one day and night with French platoons to study the conditions and positions which we would take over the next day.

I duly arrived at my future platoon post, which was on the edge of a dark and eerie pinewood, and was politely welcomed by the French platoon commander. He showed me round the position then occupied by his platoon, and which would be occupied by my men the following day.

All was dead quiet. No sign of the Germans although they were only a few hundred yards away. But as soon as night fell it was a very different story. First there would be a distant boom of a Maginot gun, which would be answered by a German gun. This desultory fire would gradually intensify until a lively 'counter battery' fire would disturb the night. When this was at its height, one would then hear a few machine guns. The M.G. fire would then increase in volume and intensity until about one o'clock, when there would be a perfect crescendo of noise from artillery and machine guns.

It was just about this time when all the firing was at its peak that I heard one of the M.G.s belonging to my little Frenchman's platoon, firing. Naturally I was very excited as this was my first experience of warfare, so I said to him in a breathless whisper, and in my best possible French:

"Les Allemands, sont-ils ici?" (*Are the Germans here?*)

"Non, non," he replied airily.

"Mais pourquoi avez-vous tiré?" (*But why did you fire?*) I asked, pointing to the French M.G. which was just visible through the darkness a few yards away.

The French platoon commander shrugged his shoulders and said: "C'est notre dernière nuit ici, et cela les amuse." (*It's our last night here, and that amuses them*).

I wondered what my Company Commander would think!

J. R. B.

(John R. Boustead, Lieutenant, Seaforth Highlanders)

37. AN ACTION AT RETIMO, CRETE

Several days after the fighting commenced on Crete, we were viewing the battle raging in the plains below, from our positions in the hills. Canea which lay just below us had just been subjected to a severe bombardment by enemy aircraft which constantly flew over us, making things fairly uncomfortable.

My section Corporal, Broderick had just returned from Coy. H.Q. with the news that we were moving at 1300 hrs. for a special job at Retimo. There, according to Greek information, a force of enemy paratroops had occupied a church and an adjoining block house from which they commanded the main road communications through which supplies in munitions and food were to pass for Australians fighting on the other side. We were told that some 70 enemy troops were holding out in these buildings. They had been without supplies for four days and only a show of force was necessary to make them surrender.

We were conveyed to Retimo in Service Corps lorries, stopping at Kalives to pick up an anti-tank gun and crew of the R.H.A. We arrived at Retimo late at night. We had previously picked up two Aussies who had waited to guide us to our exact destination. The attack was timed to start at dawn. The blow was to be struck before the enemy could signal to their Air Force that they were being attacked. In the hills to our right the Greeks kept up a steady fire on the German fort, which came dangerously close to us as we advanced. Making use of good cover we went forward and got close up to our objective. German snipers who expected an attack, constantly probed the

Le 11.11.42, à 19h00, les officiers des formations de l'Air en Tunisie, repliés à Biskra, afin d'échapper à la protection spéciale allemande, sont réunis à la popote, anxieux de nouvelles = la veille, un armistice, mieux, un accord, a mis fin aux résistances sporadiques au débarquement Anglo-Américain en Algérie et au Maroc.

Silence soudain : le doyen des officiers prend la parole et donne lecture du T.O. suivant = ORDRE A TOUTES LES FORCES FRANÇAISES D'A.F.N. D'ADOPTER ATTITUDE HOSTILE AUX TROUPES DE L'AXE.

Spontanément, des poitrines gonflées d'un espoir nouveau la MARSEILLAISE retentit ; en ce jour anniversaire de défaite germanique – 11.11.1918 – la lutte contre l'ennemi reprend. Quelque humiliant qu'ait pu être l'armistice de Juin 40, grâce à lui, toute l'Afrique française est désormais, intacte, aux côtés des Alliés.

FINIS : notre désolante passivité et les 5 à 10h d'entraînement mensuel insuffisant pour maintenir notre forme et instruire les jeunes ;

la tyrannie du contrôle des commissions d'armistice de l'Axe, qui non seulement limitent toute activité aérienne, mais raflent systématiquement à leur profit les productions françaises et africaines ;

les combats d'honneur qui humilient autant de fois l'honneur militaire français et que tant de camarades ont payé de leur sang, en vain.

Quelques jours plus tard, les bombardiers tunisiens rejoignent la plateforme d'Aïn-Oussera – décembre, au cours de transports (essence, munitions etc.) d'Oran et de Casablanca au front tunisien, les équipages renouent la fraternité d'armes avec nos alliés enfin retrouvés. Ils font connaissance avec les appareils nouveaux, splendides, racés, qui pullulent sur les terrains. Le type d'avions qui nous est destiné est l'objet de leur particulière attention et mille questions de détail assaillent les "renards" qui les utilisent. Avec un tel coursier le bon vieux Léo 45 ne sera guère regretté ! Les chasseurs d'en face savent déjà ce qu'il en coûte de s'y frotter = témoins les nombreuses constellations de croix noires sur les fuselages qui symbolisent leurs victoires et leur souveraineté du ciel.

En Février 43 aubaine inespérée = notre groupe est engagé. Des missions de bombardement de nuit nous sont confiées, en coopération avec une flotte aérienne américaine.

Le groupe Lafayette représente momentanément la Chasse française aux côtés des alliés avec du matériel d'outre-atlantique ; le Buffle de l'Ichkeul et le Hibou représenteront le Bombardement avec du matériel français = nul choix ne saurait être d'ailleurs plus apprécié et plus heureux car la totalité du sol tunisien est familier, de jour comme de nuit, à tous les équipages.

Les autres formations aériennes françaises commencent, dès Mars 43, leur entraînement sur les avions Anglo-Américains.

Si un obus de 88 m/m, le 23.3.43 à 01h00, au dessus de Sfax, a coupé mes ailes et clos ainsi le cycle d'immenses espoirs, la pensée que mes camarades participent à la finale prochaine est sérieux réconfort et un puissant tonique – 1.5.1944

... the wording of the official communiqués "Local patrol & artillery activity" & from having read of the Horrors of War, we, who were digging ... on the Belgian frontier, thought we could form a pretty good ... of what was going on. But it was not until February 1940 that we ... the chance to modify this impression by first hand experience on ... Saar Front.

Keyed up for action & dreamily wondering whether to win the ... straight away & get the others later in the week or whether to work ... to it slowly, we arrived on & about the battlefield. Very impressed ... -ded revolver slung uncomfortably on the thigh or held dangerously ... hand we moved from billet to estaminet & estaminet to ... -tinet, selfconsciously upholding the Empire in its fight for Democracy.

Then we observed & were told the Rules of War, or rather the ... cal rules that applied here. It was Strictly Forbidden for villages ... the area of the front to be shelled — as it was very cold & everyone was ... doors. It was Strictly Forbidden to fire on enemy working parties ... an automatic weapon during the hours of daylight — might ... many people at once & cause Questions to be Asked. To give ... little Zest to the proceedings roads which were in view could be ... -lled but otherwise not, because at All costs the fighting sold... ... have their Hot Meal.

A Regular French officer from the Maginot line finished ... picture for us with his account of an Atrocity & the repri... ... -ther down the line were two villages one in French hands one... ... enemy, electricity, water & telephone still joined them toget... ... -ey were not on speaking terms of course but the electricity in the ... -ench village was by courtesy of the OKW. Everyone was very happ... ... one night the Germans were bad mannered enough to cut off ... current. The French took a very poor view of this breach of ... -quette indeed &, invoking their Deity & heavy guns, proceeded ... -hurl a considerable amount of metal, explosive & abuse at the ... -ds of the Perpetrators of this outrage. So much so in fact ... after about half-an-hour the lights were turned on & stayed ... As a sequel: a week or so later the ligh... ... -e more were extinguished, almost simultaneously the 'phon... ... rang & in bad & very excited French came a voice, ... Don't shoot please, we are mending the fuse as quickly as possi...

J'ffrey W—
5th Regt.

country with fire which made things pretty hot for us and compelled us to crawl forward on our stomachs. Eventually we landed up behind a parapet in a vineyard quite close to the church.

A Bren gunner was ordered to open fire on an enemy machine gun nest in the bell tower. Immediately there followed an extremely heavy barrage of machine gun fire by the enemy. Suddenly our anti-tank gun opened up. Although it hit the target, its shots made no effect.

Under cover of their barrage a number of enemy troops advanced. They were met by accurate fire of one of our platoons, but despite this managed to reach the parapet behind which we had taken cover. A sharp duel followed. Several hand grenades rolled among us and caused casualties. We were ordered to withdraw. Several men had been fatally hit. I found myself among two or three wounded men and assisted one back to base. Later I discovered an enemy bullet had made a large dent in my tin hat and considered myself lucky. Our casualties were approximately 25, several being dead.

The enemy lost 40 dead. We learned the enemy consisted of more than twice the number we were led to believe. Next day supplies were conveyed to the Aussies by torpedo boats.

Rfn. D. Halfin, K.R.R.C.

38. SOUS LES AILES FRANÇAISES EN AFRIQUE DU NORD*

On the 11th of November 1942 at 1900 hours, the Air Force officers in Tunisia, safe in Biskra after escaping the special protection of the Germans, were gathered in the Mess anxiously awaiting news. The day before, an armistice or rather an agreement had put to an end the sporadic resistance of the Anglo-American landings in Algeria and Morocco. Sudden silence. The senior officer brought the news and read out the following message: "Order to all French Air Force personnel to adopt a hostile attitude to Axis troops".

Their hearts filled with new hope, those present burst into a spontaneous chorus of "La Marseillaise". On this day, the anniversary of the German defeat 11.11.1918, the fight against the enemy was to be resumed. However humiliating the Armistice of June 1940 may have been, it was in a sense thanks to it that French Africa remained intact and was able now to join the allies. At last this meant an end to the dull passivity of five to ten hours of training a month, which was quite insufficient to maintain our fitness or train recruits.

The tyranny of the Armistice Control Commissions of the Axis powers not only put a curb on all military activity on our part, but systematically plundered French and African production for their own purposes. There were the duels which humiliated French military honour every time they took place and which besides being fought in vain, cost so many of our comrades their blood.

A few days later the Tunisian bombers rejoined the base at Ain Oussera. From December on the course of their transport flights with petrol, munitions and stores from Oran and Casablanca to the front in Tunisia, our air crews renewed their friendly relations with our

* *Beneath the Wings of the French in North Africa*

allies. They also became familiar with the splendid new types of aircraft which were to be found in great numbers on their airfields. The special type of plane which was set aside for their use was of particular interest to them and thousands of detailed questions about them met the lucky fellows who actually flew them. With such a fine craft to fly, nobody would regret the passing of the old Leo 45!

The fighter pilots on the other side soon learnt to their cost what it meant to be up against them and there was plenty of evidence of this fact in the numerous swastikas that decorated their fuselages and symbolized their victories and re-won mastery of the sky.

In February 1943 our group had an unexpected bit of luck! Our whole group went into action. We were given night bombing missions in co-operation with the American Air Group. The Lafayette Group for the time being represented French Fighter Forces on the Allied side with material from across the Atlantic; the Hawk of Ichkheul and the Owl represented the bombers with French equipment. No other choice would have been appreciated so joyfully because the whole of Tunisia was open to the crews, both by day and night. The other French Air formations began their training with British and American aircraft in March 1943.

Although an 88mm. shell over Sfax on 23.03.43 at 0100 hours clipped my wings, and thus also my cycle of great hopes, the thought that my comrades are participating in the next finale is a great source of comfort and a powerful tonic.

Lasalle-A, 1-5-1944

39. THE GENTLEMAN'S WAR

From the wording of the official communiques "Local patrol and artillery activities" and from having read the Horrors of War, we, who were digging holes on the Belgian frontier, thought we could form a pretty good picture of what was going on. But it was not until February 1940 that we had the chance to modify this impression by first hand experience on the Saar front.

Keyed up for action, and dreamily wondering whether to win the V.C. straight away and get the others later in the week or whether to work up to it slowly, we arrived on or about the battlefield. Very impressive! Loaded revolver slung uncomfortably on the thigh or held dangerously in the hand we moved from billet to estaminet and estaminet to cabinet, self-consciously upholding the Empire in its fight for Democracy.

Then we observed and were told the strict Rules of War, or rather the Local Rules that applied here. It was Strictly Forbidden for villages in the area of the front to be shelled—as it was very cold and everyone was indoors. It was Strictly Forbidden to fire on enemy working parties with an automatic weapon during the hours of daylight—might kill too many people at once and cause Questions to be Asked. To give a little zest to the proceedings roads which were in view could be shelled, but otherwise not, because at All Costs the fighting soldiers must have their Hot Meal.

A Regular French Officer from the Maginot Line finished the picture for us with his account of an Atrocity and the Reprisal. Further down the line were two villages, one in French hands, one in the enemy, electricity, water and telephone still joined them together. They were not

After the capture of Bardia & our Bn was resting prior to the projected attack on Tobruk, I was summoned by the and told to command three Italian anti-tank guns & form an anti-tank platoon. I had previously been i/c a sec on the 2 pounder gun, but as there were no guns available the crime was sent back to an infantry platoon. I had no trouble in locating 3 guns in the Bardia perimeter and there were also tons of ammunition lying about. My personnel were drawn from A & B Companies, whose commanders naturally unloaded all the chaps that they wanted least. After having them for a few days I wanted them even less.

To make sure the guns were in working order we fired a few rounds from each, using a long string attached to the lanyard for fear of possible booby traps. We had three porties in the Bn, which are 3 ton trucks specially designed to carry the 2 pounder, enabling the gun to be fired from the truck. I was given these porties but of course the gun did not fit the channels etc on the body. After a lot of trouble we heaved them on board and tied them on with rope. The Iti gun was a 47mm Breeda with hand operated breech and a hand firing mechanism. There was no shield for the crew and altogether it was a vastly inferior weapon to our own. All the range readings were in metres and the sights were outside the ken of anyone but an Italian. For 10 days I tried to instil the first principles of anti-tank gunnery into my gun crews. This was no easy task and when the time came for the attack on Tobruk we were not much further forward. My orders were to go as right flank protection against tanks. This meant that if the Bn was attacked my crews had to man-handle the guns to the ground, about 5 minutes hard work, and beat off the attack.

We attacked Tobruk at dawn on 21 Jan and our Bn was fortunate enough to gain its objective without firing a shot. One of my porties was blown up by a land-mine but thank the merciful heavens we didn't even see an angry tank.

     Jack. W. K. Champ Lieut
     2½th Bn A.I.F

We were standing on the bridge over the moat which surrounded the under
and fort. After 2 days in a train, & a 3 mile walk from the station, carrying
among all our kit, we weren't feeling our best. Machine guns were trained
us from the roof, & every other vantage point.

We had no idea why we had been moved there from Laufen in Bavaria,
& the commandant presently appeared. A typical bull necked Prussian,
brandishing a horse whip, he was followed by the usual satellites, saluting &
ing their heels. He treated us to a tremendous tirade, which very few
lst understood. The gist of it was that, owing to the 'scandalous' treatme
the German officers in Fort Henry, Canada, we were being subjected to similar
ations, until the British government, on our entreaties, he hinted, had taken
able steps.

I shall never forget our first night there. The room, in which we were to
live, & sleep, was so crowded, that all beds were touching, & quite a few peop
to sleep together, in the same bed. The walls were dripping & the blankets full of flea
ll searched our clothes methodically, & chalked up the 'bag' on the door. It
luded eventually fleas (in hundreds), lice, bed bugs, mice, 'various', & beetles
4. watch 1!

The door was locked by guards armed with truncheons, & we were provided w
ucket. But it was treated as a point of honour, to climb through the ventila
the door, & elude the guards on the way to the abort. There were no locker
e chaos was indescribable. The windows were wired, & the view was block
the moat wall, about 10 yards away. The moat itself stank of stagnant
& overflowing aborts. So much for the 'exercise ground'.

We were there from February until the end of June. The first 6 weeks,
g entirely on German rations were grim, after which conditions were
what relaxed. Parcels arrived, we were allowed up on to the roof, &
numbers were reduced from 260 to 200. But the memory of the
days there, will remain with me, as a typical example of German
dictiveness & 'Kultur', at a time when they were supremely confide
victory.
                    Phil Pardoe Lt. 60th Rifles.

on speaking terms of course but the electricity in the French village was by courtesy of the O.K.W. Everyone was very happy, until one night the Germans were bad mannered enough to cut off the current. The French took a very poor view of this breach of etiquette indeed and, invoking their Deity and heavy guns, proceeded to hurl a considerable amount of metal, explosive and abuse at the heads of the Perpetrators of this outrage. So much so in fact that after about half-an-hour the lights were turned on and stayed on.

As a sequel: A week or so later the lights were once more extinguished, almost simultaneously the 'phone bell rang and in bad and very excited French came a voice "Don't shoot please, we are mending the fuse as quickly as possible."

G. S. Drew, Lt.
58th Regt.

40. LIBYA, JANUARY 1941

After the capture of Bardia and our Bn was resting prior to the projected attack on Tobruk, I was summoned by the C.O. and told to commandeer three Italian anti-tank guns and form an anti-tank platoon. I had previously been to a school on the 2 pounder gun, but as there were no guns available at the time was sent back to an infantry platoon. I had no trouble in locating 3 guns in the Bardia perimeter and there was also tons of ammunition lying about. My personnel were drawn from A and B Companies, whose commanders naturally unloaded all the chaps that they wanted least. After having them for a few days I wanted them even less.

To make sure the guns were in working order we fired a few rounds from each, using a long string attached to the lanyard for fear of possible booby traps. We had three porters in the Bn, which are 3-ton trucks specially designed to carry the 2-pounder, enabling the gun to be fired from the truck. I was given these porters, but of course the Iti guns did not fit the channels etc. on the body. After a lot of trouble we heaved them on board and tied them with rope. The Iti gun was a 47 mm. Breeda with hand operated breech and a hand firing mechanism. There was no shield for the crew and altogether it was a vastly inferior weapon to our own. All the range readings were in metres and the sights were outside the ken of anyone but an Italian. For 10 days I tried to instill the first principles of anti-tank gunnery into my gun crews. This was no easy task and when the time came for the attack on Tobruk we were not much further forward. My orders were to go in as right flank protection against the tanks. This meant that if the Battalion was attacked my crews had to man-handle the guns to the ground, about 5 minutes hard work, and beat off the attack.

We attacked Tobruk at dawn on 21 Jan and our Bn was fortunate enough to gain its objective without firing a single shot. One of my porters was blown up by a land mine but, thank the merciful heavens we didn't even see an angry tank.

Jack W. K. Champ, Lieut.
2nd/6th Bn. A.I.F.

Colditz 6 May '44

41. FORT VIII, POSEN, 1941

We were standing on the bridge over the moat which surrounded the underground fort. After 2 days in a train, and a 3 mile walk from the station, carrying or jettisoning all our kit, we weren't feeling our best. Machine guns were trained on us from the roof and every other vantage point.

We had no idea why we had been moved there from Laufen in Bavaria, until the commandant presently appeared. A typical bull-necked Prussian, brandishing a horse whip, he was followed by the usual satellites, saluting and clicking their heels. He treated us to a tremendous tirade, which very few people understood. The gist of it was that, owing to the "scandalous" treatment of the German Officers in Fort Henry, Canada, we were being subjected to similar conditions, until the British Government, on our entreaties, he hinted, had taken suitable steps.

I shall never forget our first night there. The room, in which we were to feed, live and sleep, was so crowded, that all the beds were touching and quite a few people had to sleep together in the same bed. The walls were dripping and the blankets full of fleas. We all searched out clothes methodically and chalked up the 'bag' on the door. It included eventually fleas (in hundreds), lice, bed bugs, mice, 'various', and beetles death-watch!

The door was locked by guards armed with truncheons, and we were provided with a bucket. But it was treated as a point of honour, to climb though the ventilator over the door and elude the guards on the way to the abort. There were no lockers, so the chaos was indescribable. The windows were wired and the view was blocked by the moat wall, about 10 yards away. The moat itself stank of stagnant water and overflowing aborts. So much for the 'exercise ground'.

We were there from February until the end of June. The first six weeks, living entirely on German rations were grim, after conditions were somewhat relaxed. Parcels arrived, we were allowed up on to the roof, and our numbers were reduced from 260 to 200. But the memory of the first days there, will remain with me, as a typical example of German vindictiveness and 'Kultur' at a time when they were supremely confident of victory.

Phil Pardoe, Lt. 60th Rifles

42. JERRY

As a conclusion to the several discussion we had; remember the words of the brainiest man of our era:

"A persecution is always a man hunt, and man hunting is not only a very horrible sport but socially a dangerous one, as it revives a primitive instinct incompatible with civilization. Indeed civilization rest fundamentally on the compact: that it should be dropped."

> If radiance you desire,
> Sunshine to the eyes;
> Go forth create it out of nothingness.

Gerry;

As a conclusion to the several Discussion
we had; remember the words of the brainiest
man, of our era;

" A persecution is always a man hunt, and man
hunting is not only a very horrible sport but
socially a dangerous one, as it revives a primitive
instinct incompatible with civilization. Indeed
civilization rest fundamentally on the compact, that
it should be Dropped."

If Radiance you desire,
Sunshine to the eyes;
Go forth create it out of nothingness
go carve it even from the very ro
Draw it from the misty depths,
of your own heart.....

Simon Hacohen
(Palestinian R.E.

...o'clock on the first evening of the German attack on Crete I was sent up to the
...ime aerodrome with a bearer party from the MDS. to assist an RMO who had
...any casualties on his hands that he could not deal with them all himse..
...as instructed to proceed with a company of the Maori battalion who were
...ng forward as reinforcements to other front-line battalions, because isolated
...hine-gun posts +snipers were still active on the main East to West coastal
...d. Unfortunately or certainly fortunately for me as it turned out, they had
...sed the meeting point 15 minutes before me + in order to catch them up, th..
...ppers gave me a ride along the road till we met them. We had travelled
...ut one mile when we were suddenly confronted by a road-block of about 200
...on who were perhaps unwisely celebrating their first fruits or rather blood of
...cessful engagement - this gathering reminded me very much of a "tangi" At th..
...d of the column I dismounted +met the Company Commander, Captain Rangi Lo..
..."Rangitira" of the Arawa tribe. His greeting to me was "Well boy (pronounced
...e) you are lucky you did not come along here before us" He related how his
...pany had successfully mopped up two enemy machine-gun nests which
...d been blocking the road - hence the "tangi". To most Europeans, the Maori are
...tle known. They are quiet, robust, handsome +intelligent men, slow to rouse..
...t once roused, keen +hard fighters. They are clean +well-disciplined +their natu..
...e of music makes them easy to instruct in those branches of military
...aining where that natural +regular rhythm for which they are so renown..
...encouraged. 2 days after this incident, I saw the whole battalion make th..
...yonet charge on the Maleme drome; the charge was preceded by a "haka" +was led
...ir Colonel. This short interlude with the Maori, ended at the 23rd RAP which
...as part of a dried-up watercourse about 3 feet deep, 6 feet wide +seve..
...dred feet long. The operating position was only about 25 yards from
...ttalion H.Q. (a most unhealthy spot too!) +the holding area was along the w..
...rse in natural caves. Evacuation of walking cases was done at night +lyi..
...ses were never sent back as we had no available means of doing this. S..
...the confidence of human nature that we reckoned a tent-fly stretc..
...r the operating position was sufficient +adequate protection from all the
...uff flying about overhead +I am glad to say this token had a charmed life +
...least our confidence was not misplaced. Our surgical methods were decide..
...mitive +indeed did not even remotely conform to the accepted standa..
...modern procedure, which makes me think that Ambroise Paré's famous
...ords "I dressed the wounds, God healed them" is a fair summoring-up of th..
...nights + 3 days of front-line surgery.

NOTE   MAORI   Should be spelt MAURI +should be pronounced MAÖÖRI (almost MOWR..
                    MAORI   is plural +collective

      TANGI   is the name of the funeral ceremony which continues for varying
                    periods, throughout which there are songs, dances +feasting.
      RANGITIRA   is a Maori chieftain +a very high person in the Maori Race
      HAKA   is the Maori War-dance   R.Moodie Capt. NZMC.

Go carve it even from the very rocks
Draw it from the misty depths,
of your own heart . . .

Simon Hacohen
(Palestinian R.E.)

43. MOSTLY MAORI AND MEDICAL—CRETE, MAY 1941

At 8 o'clock on the first evening of the German attack on Crete I was sent up to the Maleme aerodrome with a bearer party from the M.D.S. to assist an R.M.O. who had so many casualties on his hands that he could not deal with them all himself. I was instructed to proceed with a company of the Maori battalion who were going forward as reinforcements to other front line battalions, because isolated machine-gun posts and snipers were still active on the main East to West coastal road.

Unfortunately or certainly fortunately for me as it turned out, they had passed the meeting point 15 minutes before me, & in order to catch them up the Sappers gave me a ride along the road till we met them. We had travelled about one mile when we were suddenly confronted by a road-block of about 200 Maori who were perhaps unwisely celebrating their first fruits or rather blood of a successful engagement. This gathering reminded me very much of a "tangi". At the head of the column I dismounted and met the Company Commander, Captain Rangi Royal, a "Rangitira" of the Arawa tribe. His greeting to me was "Well boy (pronounced boi), you are lucky you did not come along here before us." He related how his Company had successfully mopped up two enemy machine-gun nests which had been blocking the road—hence the "tangi". To most Europeans the Maori are but little known. They are quiet, robust, handsome and intelligent men, slow to rouse, but once roused, keen and hard fighters. They are clean and well-disciplined and their natural love of music makes them easy to instruct in those branches of military training where that natural and regular rhythm for which they are so renowned, is encouraged. 2 days after this incident, I saw the whole Battalion make their bayonet charge on the Malene 'drome; the charge was preceded by a "haka" and led by their Colonel.

This short interlude with the Maori ended at the 23rd R.A.P. It was part of a dried-up watercourse about 8 feet deep, 6 feet wide and several hundred feet long. The operating position was only about 25 yards from Battalion H.Q. (a most unhealthy spot too!) and the holding area was along the water course in natural caves. Evacuation of walking cases was done at nights. Lying cases were never sent back as we had no available means of doing this. Such is the confidence of human nature that we reckoned a tent-fly stretched over the operating position was sufficient and adequate protection from all the stuff flying about overhead. I am glad to say this token had a charmed life and at least our confidence was not misplaced.

Our surgical methods were decidedly primitive and indeed did not even remotely conform to the accepted standard of modern procedure, which makes me think that Amboise Pane's

On passing through the door Thom had taken off his coat which was now lying in a puddle of water, and was dropping down the terrace side, arresting his progress by grabbing the iron bars which covered the window as he fell past them. It was too late to stop him, and at that moment the guard following us, shouted and raised his rifle to fire, whether he fired or not I can not say, but Thom was then still hanging from the bars of the last window. & the guard in front of us pushed the side unslinging his rifle, and commenced fire, his first shot missing Thom by no less than six inches, as he picked himself up in the flower beds.

He then started to run along the foot of the terrace, the guard in front of us unslinging cartridges into his gun, I managed to catch him by the shoulders and by shaking upset his aim. Thom turned left behind some trees toward the shooting box whose guard thinking he was not going to cross the wire pushed his rifle out of another window while Thom turning right vaulted the wire, rolled down the bank but this time amid a volley of shots from the sentries on the other side of the castle.

G. P. Dickinson F/lt
R.A.F.

Infinately more thrilling than the escape in the film "The Big House" was the attempt for freedom by F/Lt Thom. R.A.F. although at the time it left us rather shaken.

During the previous afternoon, we three F/Lt Thom, P/o Van Rood and myself had been sitting on the terrace during the afternoon exercise discussing the posibilities of escape from our confine.

We were guarded by two posterns with rifles, one at either end of the terrace, while below us some thirty feet down another patrolled the barbe wire, while his companion overlooked us all from a raised shooting box.

The prospect of escape seemed very remote unless the guards could be diverted, and we returned from exercise thinking no more about it.

The following morning at 9 oclock we were fetched by the guards for exercise, and led through the guardroom onto the terrace, one guard proceeded us then myself, Thom, Van Rood, and finally followed up by another Postern.

The Postern door to the terrace was opened and we marched out behind the first guard, I stopped and was just lighting a cigarette when I heard Van Rood say "My God he's mad".

famous words "I dressed the wounds, God healed them" is a fair summing up of those 4 nights and 3 days of front line surgery.

Note:

Maori: Should be spelt Mauri and should be pronounced Maoori (almost Mowree). Maori is plural and collective.

Tangi: Is the name of the funeral ceremony which continues for varying periods throughout which there are songs, dances and feasting.

Rangitira: Is a Maori chieftain and a very high person in the Maori race.

Haka: Is the Maori war-dance.

R. Moody, Capt. N.Z.M.C.

45. COLDITZ OFLAG IVC GERMANY

Infinitely more thrilling than the escape in the film "The Big House" was the attempt for freedom by F/Lt. Thom, RAF, although at the time it left us rather shaken.

During the previous afternoon, we three, F/Lt. Thom, F/o Van Rood and myself had been sitting on the terrace during the afternoon exercise discussing the possibilities of escape from our confinement.

We were guarded by two posterns with rifles, one at either end of the terrace, while below us some thirty feet down another patrolled the barbed wire, while his companion overlooked us all from a raised shooting box.

The prospect of escape seemed very remote unless the guards could be diverted, and we returned from exercise thinking no more about it.

The following morning at 9 o' clock we were fetched by the guards for exercise and led through the guardroom onto the terrace, one guard preceding us, then myself, Thom, Van Rood, and finally followed up by another postern.

The postern door to the terrace was opened and we marched out behind the first guard, I stopped and was just lighting a cigarette when I heard Van Rood say "My God, he's mad." [*Original text continued on page 28 of diary*].

On passing through the door Thom had taken off his coat which was now lying in a puddle of water, and was dropping down the terrace side, arresting his progress by grabbing the iron bars which covered the windows as he fell past them. It was too late to stop him, and at that moment the guard following us, shouted and raised his rifle to fire Whether he fired or not I can not say, but Thom was then still hanging from the bars of the last window. The guard in front of us rushed to the side, unslinging his rifle and commenced to fire, his first shot missing Thom by no less than six inches, as he picked himself up from the flower beds.

He then started to run along the foot of the terrace, the guard in front of us hammering cartridges into his gun. I managed to catch him by the shoulders, and by shaking upset his aim. Thom turned left behind some trees toward the shooting box whose guard, thinking he

29th May 1940.

I was in the 10th C.C.S, situated in a small village called Krombeck, about 15 mi
from Dunkirk. We had received our sentence, and knew that nothing could
save us being taken P.O.W's. There were about 1000 officers and OR's wounded,
and about 200 of the staff of the C.C.S. I will not attempt to describe the scene;
it was all too terrible, the stench of gangrene, the moans of the dying, the lack of
food, water, and attention. The staff were overwhelmed, those who were badly
wounded were left to die, only those whose lives could be saved with certainty
received attention; time could not be spared for those who were on the brink.
About mid-day the Matron and the four Nursing Sisters were ordered to
evacuate themselves in an ambulance. They protested strongly, but in vain,
and were almost forceably put on an ambulance to start their adventurous
journey to Dunkirk, about which six months later we were to hear that
they had completed safely. All day long transport was creeping through the
village, all going northwards. Those of us who were able to walk, disobey
the orders, to stay where we were, and disappeared one by one to scrounge lifts.
One gunner subaltern left wearing only a shirt! Gradually they left, until
only those of us incapable of moving were left. This with the C.C.S. staff
amounted to about 1000 in all.

As the evening drew on the traffic intensified, taking advantage of the
dark, for what was to be their last journey on the Continent for over four years.
The faces of the men wore signs of extreme fatigue, they were dirty, they had
arms, but none that were of any avail against the German Panzas. They
were the remnants of the once proud B.E.F. defeated, but not disgraced,
fighting against odds, which no one could have withstood. However they were
happy, they were going home, and one day they could come back for their revenge.
As the evening drew on, the shelling grew nearer and nearer, and small arms
fire was incessant, the rearguard was falling back. About 10 p.m we heard the
rattle of the tracks of the light tanks of the 13/18th Hussars, useless against
modern armour. Their C.O. came in to see his 2nd i/c who lay seriously
wounded next to me. He wanted to take him back, but he was too bad
to be moved. The Colonel looked grim and tired, he said a few cheery words

shook hands with us all, and with a cheery "Goodbye" and "Good luck" disappeared into the darkness. He was the last British Officer we were to see who was not a P.O.W. Shortly afterwards a few carriers rattled through the village, their Brens blazing defiance, the bursting of shells grew level with us, and shortly afterwards we heard their whine as they sped overhead. The small arms fire grew fainter and fainter, and by midnight there was silence. We knew now that nothing could save us, we were doomed. After a sleepless night, the Germans arrived, and we commenced our lives as P.O.W's.

For over two and a half years we heard nothing but bad news. The threat of invasion, the bombing of England; Greece; Crete; Singapore; Tobruk; to enumerate but a few of our disasters. The blare of the German Sonder meldungs as they announced another victory in the East, or the West, or another convoy sunk, continued with monotonous regularity. When would it stop. 1942 came and in October of that year the tide turned at El Alamein and Stalingrad. At last the sun had broken through.

8th March 1945

Today after nearly five years, the tables are indeed turned. The Russians stand still along the Oder. The British, Canadians, and Americans are streaming across western Germany, it is impossible to keep track of events, it is all moving too rapidly. At last the Germans are being given a taste of their own medicine. Completely overwhelmed, more so than the B.E.F were in the bog and around Dunkirk of 1940, their country is invaded, and they can do nothing about it. In 1940 we were very nearly in a similar position; but we were not invaded, and somehow we knew that we would pull through, how we did not know; just blind faith. But to-day the Germans stand with no hope, their industry gone, their armies disintegrated, they await hopelessly for the inevitable, hoping that it will come quickly.

We have waited nearly five years for this great day. It has been a long road and at times a hard journey, but our patience & faith are rewarded. The end and victory is in sight. At last we can look forward to that great day when we shall be home again.

G. M. Pemberton. Howe.
Capt. R.A.S.C.

28/3/45

was not going to cross the wire, pushed his rifle out of another window while Thom turning right, vaulted the wire, rolled down the bank over the trip wires amid a volley of shots from the posterns on the other side of the castle.

J. P. Dickinson
F/Lt. R.A.F.

46. "EVERY CLOUD HAS A SILVER LINING"

<u>29th May 1940</u>

I was on the 10th C.C.S. situated in a small village called Krombeck, about 15 miles from Dunkirk. We had received our sentence and knew that nothing could save us being taken P.O.W.s. There were about 1,000 officers and O.R.'s wounded and about 200 of the staff of the C.C.S. I will not attempt to describe the scene, it was all too terrible, the stench of gangrene, the moans of the dying, the lack of food, water, and attention. The staff were overwhelmed, those who were badly wounded were left to die; only those whose lives could be saved with certainty received attention; time could not be spared for those who were on the brink.

About mid-day the Matron and the four Nursing Sisters were ordered to evacuate themselves in an ambulance. They protested strongly but in vain and were almost forcibly put in an ambulance to start their adventurous journey to Dunkirk, about which six months later we were to hear that they had completed safely.

All day long transport was creeping through the village, all going northwards. Those of us who were able to walk disobeyed the orders to stay where we were and disappeared one by one to scrounge lifts. One gunner subaltern left wearing only a shirt! Gradually they left, until only those of us incapable of moving were left. This, with the C.C.S. staff, amounted to about 1,000 in all.

As the evening drew on the traffic intensified, taking advantage of the dark for what was to be their last journey on the Continent for over four years. The faces of the men wore signs of extreme fatigue, they were dirty, they had arms, but none that were of any avail against the German Panzers. They were the remnants of the once proud B.E.F., defeated, but not disgraced, fighting against odds which no one could have withstood.

However, they were happy, they were going home, and one day they would come back for their revenge. As the evening drew on, the shelling grew nearer and nearer, and small arms fire was incessant, the rearguard was falling back. About 10 p.m. we heard the rattle of the tracks of the light tanks of the 13/18th Hussars, useless against modern armour. Their C.O. came in to see his 2nd I/C who lay seriously wounded next to me. He wanted to take him back, but he was too bad to be moved. The Colonel looked grim and tired, he said a few cheery words, shook hands with us all, and with a cheery "Goodbye" and "Good Luck" disappeared into the darkness. He was the last British Officer we were to see who was not a P.O.W. [*Original text continued on page 47 of diary*].

Shortly afterwards a few carriers rattled though the village, their Bren guns blazing defiance, the bursting of shells grew level with us, and shortly afterwards we heard their whine as they sped overhead. The small arms fire grew fainter and fainter, and by midnight there was silence. We knew now that nothing could save us, we were doomed. After a sleepless night the Germans arrived and we commenced our lives as P.O.W.s.

For over two and a half years we heard nothing but bad news. The threat of invasion, the bombing of England, Greece, Crete, Singapore, Tobruk, to enumerate but a few of our disasters. The blare of the German Sondermeldungs as they announced another victory in the East, in the desert, or another convoy sunk, continued with monotonous regularity When would it stop. 1942 came and in October of that year the tide turned with El Alamein and Stalingrad. At last the sun had broken through.

28th March 1945

To-day after nearly five years, the tables are indeed turned. The Russians stand all along the Oder. The British, Canadians and Americans are streaming across Western Germany. It is impossible to keep track of events, it is all moving too rapidly. At last the Germans are being given a taste of their own medicine. Completely overwhelmed, more so than the B.E.F. were in the bow and arrow period of 1940, their country is invaded and they can do nothing about it.

In 1940 we were very nearly in a similar position; but we were not invaded, and somehow we knew that we would pull through, how we did not know, just blind faith. But to-day the Germans stand with no hope, their industry gone, their armies disintegrated, they await hopelessly for the inevitable, hoping that it will come quickly.

We have waited nearly five years for this great day. It has been a long and at times a hard journey, but our patience and faith were rewarded. The end and victory is in sight. At last we can look forward to that great day when we shall be home again!

G. M. Pemberton-How,
Capt. R.A.S.C.
28/3/45

49. "THE CALM BEFORE THE STORM"—'CRETE' SUDA BAY

Our Company had the job of unloading cargo from various boats in mid stream or at the jetty and as we were always a target both day and night, one felt like a shag on a rock when on duty. As I was looking after three Officers and acting as Company runner, my unloading activities were entirely confined to the ship's Food Storage rooms and I have pleasant recollections of cooking and eating a nice West Australian groper (fish) during my sojourn at the Bay.

Now to proceed, I had wangled a trip to Canea, a township 4 miles from Suda, and used to go there every afternoon on a Tommy ration truck, to get food for my Officers and grog for myself. I must digress a moment to pay tribute to the Driver, whom no amount of bombing seemed to worry.

séri.
26.3.45

Our Company had the job of unloading cargo from various boats in mid stream at the jetty and as we were always a target both day & night, one felt like a Shag on a rock when on duty. As I was looking after our Officers and acting as Company runner, my unloading activities were entirely confined to the ships Food Storage rooms and I have pleasant reccolections of cooking & eating a nice West Australian Roper (fish) during my sojourn at the Bay. Now to proceed I had wangled a trip to Canea, a township 4 miles from Suda and used to go there every afternoon on a Tommy ration truck to get Food for my Officers and Grog for myself. I must digress a moment to pay tribute to the Driver, whom no amount of bombing seemed to worry.

Upon arrival in Canea and having pleasantly disposed of the swarm of Boot-Blacks who abound everywhere, I proceeded to my favorite Cafe "The Ritz" to be met with the astounding information that no Drink would be served to Soldiers as there was a parachute attack expected. However rules are made to be broken and meeting a large Australian Postal Orderly who had pleasant memories of an afternoon spent in the right way at Barce, Libia, we enlisted a small Cretian and got quite mellow. I may say the Cherry Brandy on site is the best ever. During our aimless wandering my attention was attracted by bright posters advertising a concert party and upon entering found it was real; the Kiwi Concert Party in the flesh, I certainly enjoyed this unexpected show. The Female impersonator was exceedingly good, also the Piano Accordeon player but was he prophetic when he played his solo "Under the Double Eagle". I wonder what became of them.

Well evening drew nigh and no truck, went to Suda Bay or as it "Bombay" after dark for obvious reasons, so I dashed round to get some fodder for the Officers and heavily laden inside and out flagged a wagon ride to the Bay.
Next Morning:-

The Bombs in fury bursting Forth
They churned the waters into Froth
They burst around the poor old York
While all about the batteries talk.

The Aussies scattered round the Bay
Awake to such a lovely day
The bullets whistle through the Grass
Be careful of your Bloody Arse

or Ladies note Just lay low lads and let them pass

Sapper Lionel B. Archer
2nd and Field Park Co.
R.A. Engineers A.I.F.

...... We fixed the door.

If Buggie had jumped when he wanted to we should have all landed plum in the middle of an it
aduct!

Pitch black, raining like stink; perfect in most ways, except that you couldn't see your hand in
front of your face. And those bloody sentries would keep flashing their spotlights up and down the
side of the carriages!

Luckily the engine gave a great belch of flame, which lit up the whole track;
otherwise as sure as God made little apples we'd have been out on that bridge.

I yawned quite a lot; one does.

Lulu had jumped only about half-an-hour before. 'Crash!' 'Twang!' He took
the signal wires like a ton of bricks; but still the sentries hadn't noticed anything.
I stopped cracking futile little jokes after that and looked thoughtful.

What I mean is this: to hear a noise like that above the rattle and roar of the train doesn't
inspire a hell of a lot of confidence; especially when it's your turn next.

I thought: "Lulu – bant, steel wires – head – embankment – bomp! bomp! bomp! – quite
simple – cold meat!"

We all yawned.
Scorgie and Doug thought the same; I asked them afterwards.
One o'clock A.M.

One man was sleeping upright, propped in a corner, on the corridor side; another chap
ce up on the seat. They weren't coming with us. No, they'd done a daylight job on the way back
from Poland. Oh, there was nothing to it; you just jumped and ... There you were. Still
they weren't coming.......

So I took over at the window.
'Flick! Flick! Flick! Flick!' – telegraph poles; I could just make them out.
–uh!! that was a nasty one; didn't see the bastard coming, must have been a signal
tt sei Dank' the down track is on the other side!

"Come on Bobby, for Christ's sake!"
"All right, all right! I'm watching these telegraph poles and I still reckon it's going
bloody fast!"

"well, for God's sake get a move on, or else we won't get a chance at all" –
and so on. Mind you, all this frightfully heartily, with big 'Ha-ha's stuck in here and there
for the benefit of the sentries. They were only about ten feet away and pretty well on the 'qui vive'.
We had to take a chance on it. If they'd understood english it would have been, well ... just
too bad! But they didn't. We took a peek at them over the top of the seat. They
registered complete blank.

More watching....
Suddenly, a shudder of brakes. Or was it? – Yes! now I'm sure it was.
I opened the door.
I hung for a second to the hand rail with my left hand. In my right I had a
ten pound kitbag full of food, clothing, cheap Turkish cigarettes and 'what have you'.

y spectacles were in my pocket and I had a Balaclava on my head and a scarf
round my neck.

The kit-bag went first and I followed in a graceful swallow dive.

Something hit me very hard on the forehead and I bounced three times and
to rest between two heaps of stone-chips.

'clickity-click, clickity-click, clickity-click' — I didn't think a train could
such a length.

Then the red tail light disappearing into the distance.

'clank!' — a signal, just above me changed to red.

Silence . . . . . .

I raised my head cautiously and looked about.

Tracks, tracks everywhere. New ones, old ones, sleepers, signals, huts, —
the devil was this, a bloody marshalling-yard? And then, ... footsteps and
. . . .

"Where the hell's Bobby?"

Jeez! what a relief! My God it felt good! I wanted to laugh and sing and
. . . . . . Doug was in a frightful state. His sweater was torn and he was bleeding
a stuck pig. He'd landed on his back and hit his head a smart blow on a concrete
And, worst of all, he'd lost his pack with half the food in it! Scorgie was o.k.
from a few scratches.

Well, we stuffed some lint on Doug's head and bound it with my scarf.
so good. But the food . . . . . .

We searched high and low for about ten minutes. It was impossible to strike a
because of the wind and the rain; so we decided to give it up. In fact we were
going away when Scorgie happened to notice a bit of silver-paper glinting in the
. It was a bar of chocolate; and just beside it lay the missing pack.

We were so intent on getting Doggie away and were making such a hell of
noise scrambling over piles of stone chips that we never saw that blasted canal!
. . . .

However, as I say, it was raining like stink and we were pretty wet anyway

---

R.H.S. Colt. Lieut.
1st Bn Tyneside Scottish
(The Black Watch)
15th May 1944.

Upon arrival in Canea and having pleasantly disposed of the swarm of boot-blacks who abound everywhere, I proceeded to my favourite cafe "The Ritz" to be met with the astounding information that no drink would be served to soldiers as there was a parachute attack expected. However rules are made to be broken, and meeting a large Australian Postal Orderly who had pleasant memories of an afternoon spent in the right way in Barce, Libya, we enlisted a small Cretian and got quite mellow. I may say the cherry brandy on Crete is the best ever. During our aimless wandering my attention was distracted by bright posters advertising a concert party, and upon entering found it was real. The Kiwi concert party in the flesh, I certainly enjoyed this unexpected show. The female impersonator was exceedingly good, also the piano accordion player, but was he prophetic when he played his solo "Under the Double Eagle". I wonder what became of them.

Well evening drew nigh and no trucks went to Suda Bay or was it "Bombay" after dark for obvious reasons, so I dashed around to get some fodder for the officers, and heavily laden inside and out flagged a wagon ride to the Bay.

Next morning:–

> The bombs in fury bursting forth
> They churned the waters into froth
> They burst around the poor old York
> While all about the batteries talk.
>
> The Aussies scattered round the Bay
> Awake to such a lovely day
> The bullets whistle though the grass.
> Be careful of your bloody arse

or ladies note: Just lay low lads and let them pass.

Sapper Lionel R. Archer
2nd 2nd Field Park Co.
R.A. Engineers A.I.F.

50.   12.45-1.30 A.M. GERMAN STATE RAILWAYS, JUNE 30TH 1941

...... We fixed the door. If Duggie had jumped when he wanted to we should have all landed plum in the middle of an iron viaduct!

Pitch black, raining like stink, perfect in most ways, except that you couldn't see your hand in front of your face. And those bloody sentries would keep flashing their spotlights up and down the outside of the carriages!

Luckily the engine gave a great belch of flame, which lit up the whole track; otherwise as sure as God made little apples we'd have been out on that bridge. I yawned quite a lot; one does.

Lulu had jumped only about half an hour before. 'Crash!' 'Twang!' He landed on the signal wires like a ton of bricks, but still the sentries hadn't noticed anything. We stopped cracking futile little jokes after that and looked thoughtful. What I mean is this: to hear a noise like that above the rattle and roar of the train doesn't inspire a hell of a lot of confidence; especially when it's your turn next. I thought: "Lulu—taut, steel wires—head—embankment—bomp! bomp! bomp!—quite simple—cold meat!"

We all yawned. Scorgie and Doug thought the same; I asked them afterwards. One o'clock A.M. One man was sleeping upright, propped in a corner, on the corridor side; another sprawled face up on the seat. They weren't coming with us. No, they'd done a daylight job on the way back from Poland. Oh, there was nothing to it; you just jumped and . . . there you were. Still they weren't coming . . . So I look over at the window.

Flick! Flick! Flick! Flick!—telegraph poles; I could just make them out. Uh-uh!! that was a nasty one; didn't see the bastard coming; must have been a signal-box. "Gott sei Dank" the down track is on the other side!

"Come on Bobby, for Christ's sake!"

"All right, all right! I'm watching these telegraph poles and I still reckon it's going too bloody fast!"

"Well, for God's sake get a move on, or else we won't get a chance at all"—and so on. Mind you, all this frightfully heartily, with big "Ha-Ha's" stuck in here and there for the benefit of the sentries. They were only about ten feet away and pretty well on the "qui vive". We had to take a chance on it. If they'd understood English it would have been, well . . . just too too bad! But if they didn't. We took a peek at them over the top of the seat. They registered complete blank.

More watching . . .

Suddenly a shudder of brakes. Or was it?—Yes! Now I'm sure it was. I opened the door. I hung for a second to the handrail with my left hand. In my right I had a fifteen pound kitbag full of food, clothing, cheap Turkish cigarettes and "what have you". [*Original text continued on page 51 of diary*]. My spectacles were in my pocket and I had a balaclava on my head and a scarf around my neck. The kitbag went first and I followed in a graceful swallow dive. Something hit me very hard on the forehead and I bounced three times and came to rest between two heaps of stone-chips.

"Clickety-click, clickety-click, clickety-click"—I didn't think a train could be such a length. Then the red taillight disappearing into the distance. "Clank!" —a signal just above me changed to red.

Silence . . . I raised my head cautiously and looked about. Tracks, tracks everywhere. new ones, old ones, sleepers, signals, huts—what the devil was this, a bloody marshalling yard? And then . . . footsteps and voices . . . "Where the hell's Bobby?"

Jeez! what a relief! My God it felt good! I wanted to laugh and sing and shout . . . Doug was in a frightful state. His sweater was torn and he was bleeding like a stuck pig. He'd landed on his back and hit his head a smart blow on a concrete post. And, worst of all, he'd lost his pack with half the food in it! Scorgie was O.K. apart from a few scratches. Well, we stuffed some lint on Doug's head and bound it with my scarf. So far so good. But the food. . . !

We searched high and low for about ten minutes. It was impossible to strike a light because of the wind and rain; so we decided to give it up. In fact we were just going away when Scorgie happened to notice a bit of silver paper glinting in the dark. It was a bar of chocolate, and just beside it lay the missing pack.

AFTER A WAR
—

Sleepless I hear the city's morning note:

Footsteps, gears grinding, then the gathered heart,

Like a ship's engine, masterful, remote,

Where I am part and yet am not a part.

The dust of evening, settling drop by drop;

The broadcast, eddying through smoky bars;

The top rooms glow; the sounds of business stop;

The ages cross the rope-bridge of the stars,

And statesmen speak, and conferences meet,

And ships come home, and parliaments prepare

Rewards for all, and dancing in the street.....

.....I had my son and he will not be there.

Michael Burn

   Sept 1944

      Colditz

— No change of clothes, no-soap, no water, no blanket, nothing to while away the hungry hours; — just lying, lost in my own thoughts, — interrupted only by the shout of a guard, the smash of a whip, the scream of a tortured prisoner, the shot of a pistol or machine gun, or the faint monotonous hum of some little tune issuing through the wall from the cell next door. — These were the conditions in the underground cells of Pawiak prison, where I had been kept for two weeks in August 1942.

When I had been moved up. to a cell on the ground floor which was in a section of the prison usually reserved for spies and German prisoners, my experiences were very little changed. The cell, however, was cleaner, and, a bucket, a basin and water; all things which had been lacking in the cells down below, — were provided.

My new cell was on a different side of the prison and among the sounds I already knew, I heard another and rather different one. — Almost every night at the same time, a dog began to bark wildly. The barking was coupled with the indescribable screams of a human being in abject terror. I was prompted to climb onto my stool and peep cautiously out of my semi-circular window.

Outside I saw a group of S.S. guards applauding while a man (probably a Jew) was brought in. (These victims of what follows were always old, poorly clothed, thin and often stumbling with fear and weakness) — "LAUFE — and the whip would be used to flog him into action. As soon as he began to run, the dog would be released and barking savagely would dash after him spring at him and pull him to the ground, it would maul him and tear his clothes before being called off. — "AUFSTEHEN," — and the whip would be brought down repeatedly until he rose. — "LAUFEN," and the 'game' would begin once more. In the end the man would become completely exhausted, with his wounds beginning to show through his torn clothes, and would be dragged away out of my sight apparently unconscious.

The cries of the victims of this treatment were indescribable, but the more there were the better pleased seemed the audience who laughed and cheered throughout the performance, and ended by clapping when the bodies lay still and motionless.

We were so intent on getting Duggie away and were making such a hell of a noise scrambling over piles of stone-chips that we never saw that blasted canal! However, as I say, it was raining like stink and we were pretty wet anyway!

R. H. D. Colt, Lieut.
1st Bn. Tyneside Scottish
(The Black Watch)
15th May 1944

52. AFTER A WAR

Sleepless I hear the city's morning note:
Footsteps, gears grinding, then the gathered heart,
Like a ship's engine, masterful, remote,
Where I am part and yet am not a part.

The dust of evening, settling drop by drop;
The broadcast, eddying through smoky bars;
The top rooms glow; the sounds of business stop;
The ages cross the rope-bridge of the stars.

And statesmen speak, and conferences meet,
And ships come home, and parliaments prepare
Rewards for all, and dancing in the street . . .
. . . I had my son and he will not be there.

Michael Brown
Sept 1944 Colditz

53. IN PAWIAK PRISON, WARSAW—J. A. CRAWFORD, LT., QUEENS OWN HIGHLANDERS. 29.10.43

—No change of clothes, no soap, no water, no blanket, nothing to while away the hungry hours;—just lying, lost in my own thoughts,—interrupted only by the shout of a guard, the smack of a whip, the scream of a tortured prisoner, the shot of a pistol or machine gun, or the faint monotonous hum of some little tune issuing through the wall from the cell next door.—These were the conditions in the underground cells of Pawiak Prison, where I had been kept for two weeks in August 1942.

When I had been moved up to a cell on the ground floor which was in a section of the prison usually reserved for spies and German prisoners, my experiences were very little changed. The cell, however, was cleaner, and a bucket, a basin and water,—all things which had been lacking in the cells down below,—were provided.

My new cell was on a different side of the prison and among the sounds I already knew, I heard another and rather different one.—Almost every night at the same time, a dog began to bark wildly. The barking was coupled with the indescribable screams of a human being in abject terror. I was prompted to climb onto my stool and peep cautiously out of my semi-circular window.

Outside I saw a group of S.S. guards applauding while a man, (probably a Jew) was brought in. (These victims of what follows were always old, poorly clothed, thin and often stumbling with fear and weakness.)—"LAUFEN"—and the whip would be used to flog him into action. As soon as he began to run, the dog would be released and barking savagely would dash after him, spring at him and pull him to the ground, it would maul him and tear his clothes off before being called off.—"AUFSTEHEN," and the whip would be brought down repeatedly until he rose.—"LAUFEN," and the 'game' would begin once more. In the end the man would become completely exhausted, with his wounds beginning to show through his torn clothes, and would be dragged away out of my sight apparently unconscious.

The cries of the victims of this treatment were indescribable, but the more there were, the better pleased seemed the audience who laughed and cheered throughout the performance, and ended by clapping when the bodies lay still and motionless.

54. WILLIBALDSBURG, JUNE 1943

The cells in the Eichstätt Kommandanteur were soon filled. Every few hours saw the arrival of yet more escaped prisoners. The stories told were but a variation of the same theme— ambushed by Hitler Jugend, halted by Landwache or rounded up by troops. The countryside was alive with armed personnel—they combed the woods, patrolled the lanes, guarded bridges—so that only a handful of the sixty-five of us got through.

The German staff of the camp were more than usually unpleasant. The magnitude of the escape no doubt meant severe repercussions from O.K.W. and the harassed security officer saw no reason to treat us with consideration, notwithstanding the fact that we had employed 60,000 area guards.

After a few days, when the majority had been recaptured, we were marched through the outskirts of Eichstätt and up the hill leading to Willibaldsburg—an old castle that dominated the valley and in which the Canadians of Dieppe fame had been incarcerated and handcuffed some months previously.

We were escorted with troops in depth for the whole journey until we entered an outer courtyard. [*Original text continued on page 55 of diary*]. Here our names were called and we filed into an inner yard, collected our blankets and passed down into a white-washed dungeon—a long narrow room jammed with beds and hopelessly overcrowded. Guards prevented exit—except for the purpose of relieving nature, four at a time, in a filthy little nook just off the main quarters. Two hours exercise was eventually allowed, when we were

The cells in the Eichstätt Kommandantur
were soon filled. Every few hours saw the
arrival of yet more escaped prisoners. The stories
told were but a variation of the same theme —
ambushed by Hitler Jugend, halted by handwach
& rounded up by troops. The countryside was
alive with armed personnel — they combed the
woods, patrolled the lanes, guarded bridges
so that only a handful of the sixty-five
of us got through.

The German staff of the camp were more
than usually unpleasant. The magnitude of the
escape no doubt meant severe repercussions
from O.K.W. & the harassed Security Office
saw no reason to treat us with consideration
notwithstanding the fact that we had employed
10,000 area guards.

After a few days, when the majority had been
recaptured, we were marched through the
outskirts of Eichstätt & up the hill leading
to Willibaldsburg — an old castle that
dominated the valley & in which the Canadians
of Dieppe fame had been incarcerated &
handcuffed some months previously.
We were escorted with troops in depth
for the whole journey until we entered

...ter courtyard. Here our names were called
– we filed into an inner yard, collected
blankets & passed down into a whitewashed
dungeon — a long narrow room jammed
with beds & hopelessly overcrowded. Guards
prevented exit – except for the purpose of
relieving nature four at a time, in a filthy
little nook just off the main quarters.

Two hours exercise was eventually allowed,
when we were permitted to circle round the
inner yard, a small space overshadowed
by towering walls, & in the mornings we
were taken to the nearby S.S. barracks to
wash.

So great were the precautions & so petty the
restrictions that they obviously sprang from
the personal spitefulness of the security captain.
Our complaints were either refused a hearing
or dismissed. The food was entirely German,
therefore we remained hungry. The lights
were left on all night & guards wandered
back & forth along the room & it was
only after many attempts that we managed
to get the windows open after dark – despite
the adequate bars.

Our refusal to clean out the latrine buckets
resulted in five girl convicts being brought
in to do them. They were clothed in white

canvas slacks of were handled by a wardress
who fed them with crusts of bread in the
approved story book style.

Then, as a concession, the doors of a
genuine 15th Century lavatory, situated off
the yard, were thrown open to us & we had
the novel experience of using a 100. foot drop
& combating a very strong upward draught.

Those of us who had remained ten days
in these conditions were moved to another
room of the castle, and allowed considerable
more freedom. A magnificent view, Red X
food & more comfortable sleeping conditions
made life more tolerable, even though the
same sanitary arrangements prevailed.
After a few more days we were searched
& marched down to Eichstätt railway
station. Our destination was unknown to
us. But what matter anyhow? Sufficient that
Lager VII B. was fast becoming just a memory

Ian Bruce MacErskine

Lieut. R.W.K. R.

like the cracking of artillery. I was still in the search light beam & made slow going to the wire as the search light swept over me several times. I reached the wire & lay very still for the patrolling sentry approached; he stopped, then suddenly screamed & ran towards me he didn't shoot & I was taken to the cells.

What me had not accounted for was the fact I would steam, my warm & wet body was condensing the cool night air.

The guard told me afterwards that he couldn't make out where the "Smoke" was coming from.

F/Lt. Vincent Parker R.A.F.

It was just another idea. The football field which was in another compound to ours, was covered with snow, 2 ft deep in places. The Camp Commandant must have been rather surprised when we asked for permission to play Rugger as it hadn't been used for several weeks.

Permission was granted but the football hour was changed from 16.00 - 17.00 hrs. to 14.00 - 15.00 hrs. quite an obstacle as you will see.

Only players were allowed in the playing compound, 31 for Rugger, 23 for Soccer. Players were lined up, counted, then taken through the gates. The field itself was controlled by 2 towers & 2 guards who controlled the wire. A S/Pilot had been shot & killed here 3 weeks before, having cut the wire from his compound & attempted to crawl across the playing field at night.

Two games were necessary before a furrow was carefully made in the snow about the size of a man's body — then the big game arrived.

I read about sheep buried under snow for 3 weeks or more surviving, so decided that I could last 6 hrs alright; you see it meant a wait from 2.30 until about 8.30, then it was quite dark.

We succeeded in faking the count getting an extra man among the players & the game started. I had 2 pr trousers, 2 jackets, 4 pr socks & numerous layers of underclothing on & hardly moved in the first half.

Immediately after half time we got a scrum over the furrow, I slipped through the scrum, slipped a sort of white periscope gadget over my face & lay full length in the trench to be covered over with snow by the front row forwards, the scrum half following the ball in & adjusted everything perfectly leaving my small periscope just clear of the snow. My only track of time was to count the changes of Guard when they marched by.

Those six hrs were an eternity, my legs grew wet, ached, became numb; I couldn't move.

As I broke to the surface the breaking of snow seemed

permitted to circle round the inner yard, a small space overshadowed by towering walls, and in the mornings we were taken to the nearby S.S. barracks to wash.

So great were the precautions and so petty the restrictions that they obviously sprang from the personal spitefulness of the security captain. Our complaints were either refused a hearing or dismissed. The food was entirely German and therefore we remained hungry. The lights were left on all night and guards wandered back and forth along the room and it was only after many attempts that we managed to get the windows open after dark—despite the adequate bars.

Our refusal to clean out the latrine buckets resulted in five girl convicts being brought in to do them. They were clothed in white canvas slacks and were handled by a wardress who fed them with crusts of bread in the approved story book style. [*Original text continued on page 56 of diary*].

Then, as a concession, the doors of the genuine 15th Century lavatory, situated off the yard, were thrown open to us and we had the novel experience of using a 100 foot drop and combatting a very strong upward draught.

Those of us who had remained ten days in these conditions were moved to another room of the castle, and allowed considerably more freedom. A magnificent view, Red X food and more comfortable sleeping conditions made life more tolerable, even though the same sanitary arrangements prevailed.

After a few more days we were searched and marched down to Eichstätt railway station. Our destination was unknown to us. But what matter anyhow? Sufficient that Lager VII B was fast becoming just a memory.

Ian Bruce MacAskie
Lieut. R.W.K. Regt.

59. "SMOKE"–STALAG LUFT 1, JANUARY 1942

It was just another idea. The football field which was in another compound next to ours, was covered with snow, 2 feet deep in places. The Camp Commandant must have been rather surprised when we asked for permission to play Rugger as it hadn't been used for several weeks.

Permission was granted but the football hour was changed from 1600-1700 hours to 1400-1500 hours; quite an obstacle as you will see.

Only players were allowed in the playing compound, 31 for Rugger and 23 for Soccer. Players were lined up, counted, then taken through three gates. The field itself was controlled by two towers and two guards who patrolled the wire. A S/Pilot had been shot and killed here three weeks before, having cut the wire from his compound and attempted to crawl across the playing field at night.

Two games were necessary before a furrow was carefully made in the snow about the size of a man's body—then the big game arrived.

I read about sheep buried under snow for three weeks or more and surviving, so decided that I could last 6 hrs alright; you see it meant a wait from 2.30 until about 8.30, then it was quite dark.

We succeeded in faking the count, getting an extra man among the players, and the game started. I had 2 prs trousers, 2 jackets, 4 prs socks and numerous layers of underclothing on and hardly moved in the first half.

Immediately after half time we got a scrum over the furrow. I slipped through the scrum, slipped a sort of white periscope gadget over my face and lay full length in the trench to be covered with snow by the front row forwards, the scrum half followed the ball in and adjusted everything perfectly leaving my small periscope just clear of the snow; my only track of time was to count the changes of guard when they marched by.

Those six hours were an eternity, my legs grew wet, ached and became numb; I couldn't move. As I broke to the surface, the breaking of snow seemed [*original text continued on page 58 of diary*] like the cracking of artillery. I was still in the searchlight beam and made slow going to the wire as the searchlights swept over me several times. I reached the wire and lay very still, for the patrolling sentry approached, he paused, stopped, then suddenly screamed and ran towards me. He didn't shoot and I was taken to the cells.

What we had not accounted for was the fact that I would steam, my warm and wet body was condensing in the cool night air.

The guard told me afterwards that he couldn't make out where the "Smoke" was coming from.

F/Lt. Vincent Parker R.A.F.

60. THE ONE THAT GOT AWAY. . .

Those last few days in France and Belgium were not very amusing. Ours were mobile guns and we did not lack opportunity of firing them, for we seldom had a whole day in our position. The ration problem was difficult and but for Regimental reserves some of us would have been very hungry. Nobody seemed to know what was happening and the one thing certain was that we were fighting a retreat—we did not dare call it a rout, even to ourselves. The general trend was westward and towards the end that could only mean one thing—HOME: if ever we got that far.

The German tactics became obvious. We were constantly attacked from the air and intermittently the scream of artillery fire could be heard overhead. Through it all there seemed to be amazingly little damage, either personal or material. Only when we went through a village or crossroad did we see the effect of the bombardment. Every defile was plastered with H.E. but as soon as the way was blocked, the barrage would lift and when we got to the coast the same plan was in evidence. Although the greater part of the B.E.F. was crowding the sands, fire was directed entirely at the shipping offshore. The intention was to block our retreat. If we could be held up in retiring, then we could be rounded up or destroyed at leisure.

Those last few days in France and Belgium were not very amusing. Ours were motor guns and we did not lack opportunity of proving them for we seldom had a whole day in position. The ration problem was difficult and but for Regimental reserves some of us would have been very hungry. Nobody seemed to know what was happening and the one thing certain was that we were fighting a retreat — we did not dare call it a rout, even to ourselves. The general trend was westward and towards the sea, that could mean only one thing — HOME, if ever we got that far.

The German tactics soon became obvious. We were constantly attacked from the air & intermittently the scream of artillery fire could be heard overhead. Through it all there seemed amazingly little damage, either personal or material. Only when we went through a village or crossroad did we see the effect of the bombardment. Every defile was plastered with H.E. but as the way was blocked the barrage would lift and when we got to the coast the same plan was in evidence. Although the greater part of the B.E.F. was crowding the sands, fire was directed entirely at the shipping offshore. The intention was to block our retreat. If we could be kept up in retiring then we could be rounded up or destroyed at leisure.

It seemed a lifetime before we got within range of Dunquerque and when we made our final rendezvous the news that greeted us was that the harbour was out of action. The alternative was the beaches north east of the town, a long flat plage, in peacetime a fashionable holiday resort, now the only strip of coast left in our hands. Then we really saw how desperate the position had become. How we were to get away from there none of us could understand & if the truth be told, very few of us cared. A reconnaissance showed that the roads were blocked by abandoned vehicles, so the order was given to select what could be carried on the person & destroy the rest.

Guns were blown up and essential parts scattered to the four corners. Tractors were destroyed as far as they could be and all M.T. was made unusable. Stores and personal belongings were thrown in ponds and streams or soaked in oil and petrol. The one thing we must not do was to leave our stuff. Then at seven o'clock in the morning of 31st May we set off on our last thirteen miles on foot and we soon found out why Gunners are mounted. To complete our misery it was raining. That statement probably conveys very little and I suppose the rain made not difference to most of us, who were already soaked to the skin. Most of the time we had to leave the roads & the low-lying country was almost completely under water. During our infrequent halts we lay down in wet ground, sometimes in pools.

We did that thirteen miles in just four hours, not from inclination but of necessity. But if we were to be blown after us and even in our state we didn't feel like swimming if we could avoid it. We marched seven miles without a halt but we had to slack off after that. When we arrived at the railway station Bras Dunes we were directed to the beach and bivouacked among the sand-hills to await instructions & embarkation. Officers were given various jobs and I was detailed to the beach to find the Movement Control authorities and arrange with them for the embarkation of the Regiment, now some six hundred strong.

The scene on the beach was amazing, miles of flat sand with seemingly hundreds of thousands of troops of all nationalities, British, French, Belgian, Dutch and even one group of Poles. But to seaward there shipping of all types, naval units, passenger ships, private yachts, fishing boats, everything that could float, and precious little seemed to be floating. Of some, only the topmasts were visible above ... To the ... two steams appeared out of the sea and northwards a cruiser was on fire at the ... and amidships. A huge cloud of black smoke hung over Dunquerque and at night we saw the oil-tanks were ablaze, as was also much of the abandoned M.T. on the roads.

I hadn't been long on the beach, when there was a commotion on the Promenade, which I was curious enough to investigate. One of our subalterns had arrived, with three of his guns. How he ... the fourth and why he had brought the others I didn't inquire. Presumably his orders had ... the same as ours, if he received any, but getting these guns through must have been ... ... to try Hercules. One didn't ask. One helped him put them in action and wished him ... shooting, which incidentally he had.

Leaving Bill I went back to my job, the impossible search for the fabled Movement Control people. Nobody knew anything about them until I found a cheerful Welshman who ... me to try the Casino. Everyone seemed to turn up there sooner or later. On my way along ... Promenade I fairly ran into a R.E. Captain wearing a white armband. I don't know what was on it but I remember wondering at the time about the amazing organisation of British Army which was capable of producing such a thing at such a time. To my question ... he was Movement Control he cheerily answered "Yes old boy, what is it you want?" and ... the greatest difficulty in preventing myself from crying "I want to go home". Instead, I told ... about the Regiment and my job and how disappointed they would be if I got no results, ... here, mercifully he interrupted. "I'm afraid old boy" he said "I have a shock for you. We ... had a signal that the Navy won't play so it looks as if we will just have to sit down and ... for Jerry to make us in. Nice prospect, what?"

It was a shock all right, so we were already virtually prisoners! He went on talking ... he said I don't know, until it appeared that he was offering me a drink, so we went off ... ... to his "kennel", where I was fortified with whisky and bully-beef sandwiches. While we ... eating and drinking, a message came in which he read and handed to me, saying "You see ... boy, the Lord does provide after all." Briefly, it was an instruction to have all troops ... at concentration areas easily available to stated point on the beach, ready to ... when night fell. Each unit, even French and Belgians, was allocated to one or other of ... embarcation points but no order of precedence was given. So long as there was control and no ... , troops would be taken off as they came. I was co-opted on the spot as Unpaid Acting ... Assistant Movement Control Officer so, having conveyed my instructions to the Regiment ... returned to the beach and my new duties.

Throughout the day, even in the worst bombing and shelling there was a complete absence ... panic. Probably most of us had gone beyond that. Men were arriving every minute, in ones, twos ... of dozens, all with the same story: "I've lost my Platoon, Sir. I've lost my Battery, Sir. I've lost my ... adron Sir, What am I to do?" When one knew to which Division or Corps a man's unit belonged ... was sent to the appropriate concentration area. If one did not know he was sent to one's own unit

It seemed a lifetime before we got within range of Dunquerque, and when we made our final rendezvous the news that greeted us was that the harbour was out of action. The alternative was the beaches north-east of the town, a long flat plage, in peace time a fashionable holiday resort, now the only strip of coast left in our hands. Then we finally saw how desperate the position had become. How we were to get away from there none of us could understand and, if the truth be told, very few of us cared. A reconnaissance showed that the roads were blocked by abandoned vehicles, the order was given to select what could be carried on the person and to destroy the rest.

Guns were blown up and essential parts scattered to all four corners. Tractors were destroyed as far as they could be and all M.T. was made unusable. Stores and personal belongings were thrown in ponds and streams or soaked in oil and petrol. The one thing we must not do was to burn our stuff. Then at seven o'clock in the morning of 31st May we set off on our last thirteen miles on foot and we soon found out why Gunners are mounted. To complete our misery it was raining. That statement probably conveys very little and I suppose the rain made not much difference to most of us, who were already soaked to the skin. Most of the time we had to leave the roads and the low-lying country was almost completely under water. During our infrequent halts we lay down, always on wet ground, sometimes in water.

We did that thirteen miles in just four hours, not from inclination but of necessity. Bridges had to be blown after us and even in our state we didn't feel like swimming if we could avoid it. We marched seven miles without a halt but we had to slack off after that. When we arrived at the railway station of Brae Dunes we were directed to the beach and bivouacked among the sand-hills to wait for instructions for embarkation. Officers were given various jobs, and I was detailed to the beach to find the Movement Control authorities and arrange with them for the embarkation of the Regiment, now some six hundred strong.

The scene on the beach was amazing, miles of flat sand with seemingly hundreds of thousands of troops of all nationalities, British, French, Belgian, Dutch and even one group of Poles. Out to sea there [*original text continued on page 61 of diary*] was shipping of all types, naval units, passenger ships, private yachts, fishing boats, everything that would float, and precious little seemed to be floating. Of some, only the topmasts were visible above water. To the west two sterns appeared out of the sea and northwards a cruiser was on fire at the bows and amidships. A huge cloud of black smoke hung over Dunquerque and at night we saw that the oil-tanks were ablaze, as was much of the abandoned M.T. on the roads.

I hadn't been long on the beach when there was a commotion on the promenade which I was curious enough to investigate. One of our subalterns had arrived with three of his guns. How he lost the fourth and why he had brought the others I didn't inquire. Presumably his orders had been the same as ours, if he received any, but getting those guns through mud must have been a labour to try Hercules. One didn't ask. One helped him put them in action and wished him good shooting, which incidentally he had.

Leaving Bill, I went back to my job, the impossible search for the fabled Movement Control people. Nobody knew anything about them until I found a cheerful Welshman who advised me to try the Casino. Everyone seemed to turn up there sooner or later. On my way along the Promenade I fairly ran into a R.E. Captain wearing a white armband. I don't know yet what was on it but I remember wondering at the time about the amazing organization of the British Army which was capable of producing such a thing as such a time. To my question whether he was Movement Control he cheerily answered "Yes old boy, what is it you want?" and I had the greatest difficulty in preventing myself from crying "I want to go home". Instead, I told him about the Regiment and my job and how disappointed they would be if I got no results, and here, mercifully, he interrupted. "I'm afraid old boy" he said, "I have a shock for you. We've just had a signal that the Navy won't play, so it looks as if we will just have to sit down and wait for Jerry to rake us in. Nice prospect, what?"

It was a shock alright. So we were already virtually prisoners! He went on talking, what he said I don't know, until it appeared that he was offering me a drink, so we went off together to his "kennel", where I was fortified with whiskey and bully-beef sandwiches. While we were eating and drinking, a message came in which he read and handed to me, saying "You see old boy, the Lord does provide after all". Briefly, it was an instruction to have all troops marshalled at concentration areas easily available to stated points on the beach, ready to embark when night fell. Each unit, even French and Belgians, was allocated to one or other of the embarkation points but no order of precedence was given. So as long as there was control and no panic, troops would be taken off as they came. I was co-opted on the spot as Unpaid Acting Deputy Assistant Movement Control Officer so, having conveyed my instructions to the Regiment I returned to the beach and my new duties.

Throughout the day, even in the worst bombing and shelling there was a complete absence of panic. Probably most of us had gone beyond that. Men were arriving every minute, in ones, twos, half-dozens, all with the same story—"I've lost my Platoon, Sir. I've lost my Battery, Sir. I've lost my Squadron, Sir. What am I to do?" When one knew which Division or Corps a man's unit belonged he was sent to the approximate concentration area. If one did not know he was sent to one's own unit [*original text continued on page 62 of diary*] so that the Regiment, which started around six hundred, was just under a thousand when night fell.

It couldn't be said that darkness fell for there seemed to be no diminution of the light. Fires were blazing all around, in Dunquerque, out to sea, on the roads, fires which we later learned were visible across the Channel. The only difference was that there were no planes overhead, although the guns kept pumping away. Then we saw that new ships had silently appeared and soon the signal started between sea and shore and our dispersal arrangements began to bear fruit.

The beach at that sector is sandy and very slow shelving for a considerable distance out to sea. The result was that shipping of any draft could come no closer that about a quarter mile offshore. A ferry system had to be run between ship and shore, consisting usually of a power launch towing five or six R.E. pontoons. These, again, could not come beyond a depth of three feet, which meant fifty yards from dry land. Ships as they arrived across Channel went to the various embarkation points and when they were all filled by the ferries sailed off home.

All kinds of craft were employed, from the heaviest literally to the lightest. Several rowing boats even made the journey. The tide was falling with night until about midnight it turned. All night long lines of phosphorescence were visible where the troops walked across the wet sand and the water's edge was aglow for miles. When a "ferry" arrived, parties of fifteen men waded out to each pontoon while the officers stood by on traffic control.

...o that the Regiment, which started around six hundred, was just under a thousand when w...

It couldn't be said that darkness fell for there seemed to be no diminution of the light. ...were blazing all around, in Dunquerque, on the roads, out to sea, fires which we later learned were visible across the Channel. The only difference was that there were no flames overhead, although ...was kept pumping away. Then we saw that new ships had silently appeared and soon the sig... started between sea and shore and our dispersal arrangements began to bear fruit.

The beach at that sector is sandy and very slow shelving for a considerable distance an... sea. The result was that shipping of any draft could come no closer than about a quarter mile offshore. A ferry system had to be run between ship and shore, consisting usually of a power lau... towing five or six R.E. pontoons. These, again could not come beyond a depth of about three feet which meant fifty yards from dry land. Ships as they arrived across Channel went to the war... embarcation points and when they were filled by the ferries sailed off home. All kinds of craft ... employed, from the heaviest literally to the lightest. Several rowing boats even made the journey. ...de was falling with night until about midnight it turned. All night long lines of phosphorescence ...were visible when the troops walked across the wet sand and the water's edge was aglow for miles ...hen a "ferry" arrived, parties of fifteen men waded out to each pontoon while the officers stood by ...in traffic control.

At last the long time came to an end and it was our turn, some of us after, two and a h... ...was in the water, up to the waist. We tumbled into the pontoon and almost had to be hoisted ...aboard our destroyer. We were sent below to the Wardroom where we were given ship's cocoa a... ...while our clothes were taken by a boy to dry in the engine room. Almost at once we started ...move but after a few minutes we have to and there were sounds of more men coming aboard. ...new we must start before daylight or we should be blown out of the water. The clock said ...o thirty and dawn was about four thirty at that time of the year. In my anxiety I could ...ardly take my eyes off the clock - three o'clock, three thirty, four, four thirty, five o'clock - ...ell - what's the difference? I couldn't have moved from my chair for Gabriel's horn.

I must have slept for when I looked again it was nine-fifteen, broad daylight, an... ...boy was laying out our dry clothes. "Dover in half an hour sir. Better get dressed sir." Dover ...that's in England. There's something about a war in France. But of course! We blew our... ...us yesterday. Or was it yesterday? "It might be sir. We only left France at seven this ...orning. The Boss wouldn't move until he couldn't take any more".

So we came home.

Lt. R.A.

36 hours at sea ..... 2300 hrs. Red light to starboard, Good. the much looked
for Navigation light on H.M.S Submarine — dead on our course.
Ahead, the sky is lit by searchlights & flak, as our bombers fly over our objective,
St Nazaire. ..... Now we cross the sandbanks in the mouth of the R. Loire. the shores loom
faintly on either side.   The bombers have gone, all is quiet, just the swish of our
own wave, the padding of rubber shod feet, the occasional chink of metal as we stand
"Action Stations". The decks are cleared for action, scaling ladders lie ready
in the bows. Assault & Protection parties look to their guns Tommy gunners,
bombardiers report all correct, below, the Demolition officer checks his party who
stand tensed, waiting for the word. The suspense of waiting is awful. "Will we
ever land?".... At last we see the silhouette of cranes on the dockside as we swing
past anchored ships. "We might get in without a shot being fired"! But it is
not to be. Searchlights on both sides of the river spring to life, a solitary shore
gun opens up. They aren't quite sure who we are. "6 PEN FIRE", the order rings down
convoy then hell let loose.   The night is filled with noise & streaks of light, as
shore batteries & AA on roofs & towers open up with tracer. we retaliate with 6erlikon
Pom-pom & Bren gun .... One ....two lights go out.   The river is covered with burning
oil as several M.Ls are hit & blow up, but nothing can stop the H.M.S
Campbeltown, which glides in at 18 knots & hits her objective the Dry Dock gates
with a shudder. Hardly has she come to rest than Demolition & Assault parties
are landed & are racing under heavy fire for their objectives .... two
hrs later tasks completed they return to there re-embarkation point. The C.O.
gives his last orders. "Fight your way through the town" first stop Gibraltar
the transport as usual has not arrived.   This last does not apply to me. I'm
in the drink.

Richard F Morgan

LIEUT.

No -. Commando

At last the long line came to an end and it was our turn, some of us after two and a half hours in the water up to our waist. We tumbled into the pontoon and almost had to be hoisted aboard the destroyer. We were sent below to the Wardroom where we were given ship's cocoa and rum while our clothes were taken by a boy to dry in the engine room. Almost at once we started to move but after a few minutes we hove to and there were sounds of more men coming aboard. I knew we must start before daylight or we should be blown out of the water. The clock said two-thirty, and dawn was about four-thirty at that time of the year. In my anxiety I could hardly take my eyes off the clock—three o'clock, three-thirty, four, four-thirty, five o'clock—Oh Hell what's the difference? I couldn't have moved from my chair for Gabriel's Horn.

I must have slept, for when I looked again it was nine-fifteen broad daylight, and the boy was laying out our dry clothes. "Dover in half an hour, Sir. Better get dressed,—Sir" Dover? But that's in England. There's something about a war in France. But of course! We blew our guns yesterday. Or was it yesterday? "It might be, Sir. We only left France at seven this morning. The Boss wouldn't move until he couldn't take any more.

So we came home.

D. K. Hamilton

Lt. R.A.

63. ST. NAZAIRE—NIGHT 28/29TH MARCH 1942

36 hours at sea . . . 2300 hrs. Red light to starboard. Good, the much looked for Navigation light on H.M.S. Submarine—dead on our course.

Ahead, the sky is lit by searchlights and flak, as our bombers fly over our objective, St. Nazaire . . . Now we cross the sandbanks in the mouth of the R. Loire, the shores loom faintly on either side. The bombers have gone, all is quiet, just the swish of our bow wave, the padding of rubber shod feet, the occasional chink of metal as we stand to "Action Stations".

The decks are cleared for action, scaling ladders lie ready in the bows. Assault and Protection parties look to their guns. Tommy Gunners, Bombardiers report all correct. Below the Demolition officer checks his party who stand tensed, waiting for the word. The suspense of waiting is awful.

"Will we ever land?" . . . At last we see the silhouette of cranes on the dockside as we swish past anchored ships.

"We might get in without a shot being fired!" But it is not to be. Searchlights on both sides of the river spring to life, a solitary shore gun opens up. They aren't quite sure who we are.

"Open Fire", the order rings down the convoy, then hell let loose. The night is filled with noise and streaks of light, as shore batteries and A.A. on roofs and towers open up with tracer. We retaliate with Oerlikon machine guns and Bren guns . . . one . . . two lights go out. The river is covered with burning petrol as several M.L.s are hit and blow up, but nothing can stop the H.M.S. Campbeltown, which glides in at 18 knots and hits her objective, the Dry Dock gates with a shudder. Hardly has she come to rest than Demolition and Assault parties have landed and are racing under heavy fire for their objectives . . . Two hours later, tasks completed, they return to the re-embarkation point.

The C.O. gives his last orders: "Fight your way through the town" first stop Gibraltar.

The transport as usual has not arrived. This last does not apply to me. I'm in the drink.

Richard F. Morgan Lieut.
No–. Commando

64. N.W.E.F.—1940*

In the dim and comparatively distant days of April 1940, a brigade of infantry left France for a destination that was known only to a privileged few. After the lapse of five days, during which time the Bde had steamed across the channel, had trained through England, had camped and assembled in Scotland and had cruisered and destroyered across the North Sea, the Bde was fighting a German armoured div. in Norway.

I don't know whether you have ever been to Norway, Jerry, but I am certain that when you do go you will be as greatly impressed as I was by the splendour of the snow-covered mountains, and by the tranquillity and sleepiness of the few villages that exist in the north. Those were just my first impressions formed during the first 24 hours of my service in Norway. Later on when I found myself a hospital patient and a prisoner into the bargain, and was able to converse with the Norwegians, my admiration and sympathy for them exceeded what I had previously felt. It did not take me long to realize how sacrilegious it was to have allowed the Huns to drive their beastly war machine through the heart of a country so sincerely peaceful and peaceloving. (As it transpired, of course, Jerry, even with the best will in the world, we could not have prevented them at that time).

Though they have not had to fight a war for 150 years, they have not allowed this delightful and enviable period of peace to affect them. They have as much "guts" as the next man. Ever hear the story of the lorry drivers who were commandeered by the Hun to transport a party of Bosches up the valley? They drove their lorries into a ravine. The Norwegian C-in-C is still a prisoner as far as I know. He went into captivity as a token to show that, although her King had been chased out of the country and a Queasling set up instead, and although her armed forces had been compelled to surrender, Norway was still at war with Germany.

Yes, Jerry, Andalsnes where we landed; Lesja le Coq where I found myself underneath a train; Dombass, Otta and Kvam where we fought; Dovre, Lillehammer and Oslo where I was in hospital: these are the names of places which I am certain I will remember as long as I live.

Before I stop I must tell you something curious. At Oslo a badly burnt airman was brought in. He told me his story. A year later I arrived here. I told his story to the first Air Force type I saw. He said, "I was the pilot of that kite." You've got his line. Don Donaldson his name.

J. deD. Yule, Lieut. R. Signals.

* *North Western Expeditionary Force*

In the dim and comparatively distant days of April 1940, a [...] of infantry left France for a destination that was known only to a priv[...] few. After the lapse of five days, during which time the bde had steamed [...] the channel, had trained through England, had camped and assembled in [...] and had cruised & destroyed across the North Sea, the bde was fighting [...] German armoured div. in Norway.

     I don't know whether you have ever been to Norway, but I am certain that when you do go you will be as greatly imp[...] as I was by the splendour of the snow-covered mountains, and by the tranquillity and sleepiness of the few villages that exist in the north. [...] were just my first impressions formed during the first 24 hours of my s[...] in Norway. Later on when I found myself a hospital patient and a prisoner into the bargain, and was able to converse with the Norwegians [...] admiration and sympathy for them exceeded what I had previously [...] It did not take me long to realise how sacrilegious it was to h[...] allowed the Huns to drive their beastly war machine through the [...] of a country so sincerely peaceful & peace loving. (As it transpired, [...] course, Jerry, even with the best will in the world, we could not have prevented them at that time). Though they have not had to fight [...] war for 150 years, they have not allowed this delightful and envia[...] period of peace to affect them. They have as much "guts" as the [...] man. Ever hear the story of the lorry drivers who were commandeer[...] the Hun to transport a party of Bosches up the valley? They drove [...] lorries into a ravine. The Norwegian C-in-C. is still a prisoner as far [...] I know. He went into captivity as a token to show that, although t[...] King had been chased out of the country and a Quisling set up in [...] and although her armed forces had been compelled to surrender, Norway [...] was still at war with Germany.

     Yes, Jerry, Andalsnes where we landed; Lesja he Cog where I found myself [...] -neath a train; Dombaas, Otta & Kvam where we fought; Dovre, Lillehammer [...] Oslo where I was in hospital; these are names of places which I am [...] certain I will remember as long as I live.

     Before I stop I must tell you something curious. At Oslo a badly burn[...] airman was brought in. He told me his story. A year later I arrived here [...] told this story to the 1st airforce type I saw. He said "I was the pilot of that [...] You've got his line. I can tell you his name.   J. des. Yule. Lieut. R. Signals.

...ltenant Cazaumayou numéro trente deux soixante quinze". With this sentence and dressed in a rather shabby French uniform I managed to leave ...litz for Lübeck with a party of French officers. With me were two British officers similar disguises. The trip up was uneventful, none of us daring to utter ...re than a few well rehearsed sentences as our French was by no means perfect ...r days after our arrival at the Lübeck camp, Hamilton and Sandbach were discovered ...ed following day my name was was called out on parade. Another French ...cer impersonated me and went out in my place. The German officer said with a ...-satisfied smile — "Meester Barott, say good-bye to all your friends as thees ees the ...t time them you weel see". Didler duly waved good-bye amid the loud laugh ...ll present thus leaving me safe for another few days at least. The following ...nday, after my understudy had left again with the other two for Colditz, I was ...vealed from beneath a pile of sacks on board a truck leaving the camp. I was ...ried off to the German cells where I gave my name as Didler. After struggling ...wer the many questions flung at me as regards my family etc. in my best ...ool boy French, I was asked if I would rather speak English! The game was ...- the puzzle was unsolved for the Germans as to how two British officers of the ...me name and number happened to be at Lübeck at the same time under different ...ises!　　At about ten o'clock that night the sirens went and all the Germans ...ped down to the cellars. After a few minutes there were distant rumbles and the ...increasing thuds of ack ack, then the throbbing roar of a thousand motors. Shell ...ead rising above the now deafening crash of guns just outside my window. Shell ...ments were clattering on the roofs all around. My feelings were mixed — I wanted ...boys to blow the whole place to pieces but on the other hand I didn't want to ...o close to an 8000 pounder! Fortunately for me they put all their eggs in one bas ...that basket was Hamburg, 50 kms away. The following day they came over again ...ated such a fuss in my cell that the guard took me to the lavatory window where ...I get a better view. The shells were bursting all over the sky and the planes ...d be heard but not seen. Suddenly a glint of silver appeared amid the ever ...hening barrage of bursting steel. It grew bigger and bigger as it lost height ...the while twisting and weaving, like a huge bird, to free itself from the now ...less trap. It went into a vertical dive at about 6000 ft and tried to pull out ...out 500. Small arms fire was now in play and the whole earth seemed to open up ...devour the helpless machine in a sheet of flame about 2 km away. Dead silence followed ...a column of smoke rose into the sky. Four white dots... [illegible] ... I returned to my cell with a dull ...sadness pressing hard upon me. For the following six nights, with one excep ...treatment was repeated. The citizens of London, Coventry and many other English ...s had once more been avenged. The city of Hamburg was in ruins an ...he lips of all the Germans was the one sentence — "alles, alles ist weg ...ungen", which when translated into a civilized tongue means — "all, all ...gone".

T M Barott Lieut.
1st Bn THE BLACK WATCH (RHR) OF CANADA.

65. LÜBECK–JULY 1943

"Lieutenant Cazamayou numero trente deux soixante quinze."

With this short sentence and dressed in a rather shabby French uniform I managed to leave Colditz for Lübeck with a party of French officers. With me were two British officers in similar disguises. The trip up was uneventful, none of us daring to utter more than a few well rehearsed sentences as our French was by no means perfect.

Four days after our arrival at the Lübeck camp, Hamilton and Sandbach were discovered and the following day my name was called out on parade. Another French officer impersonated me and went out in my place. The German officer said with a self-satisfied smile—"Meester Barott, say goodbye to all your friends as thees ees the last time them you weel see." Didler duly waved good-bye amid the loud laughter of all present thus leaving me safe for another few days at least.

The following Saturday, after my understudy had left again with the other two for Colditz, I was extricated from beneath a pile of sacks on board a truck leaving the camp. I was marched off to the German cells where I gave my name as Didler. After struggling to answer the many questions flung at me as regards my family, etc., in my best school-boy French, I was asked if I would rather speak English! The game was up but the puzzle was unsolved for the Germans as to how two British officers of the same name and number happened to be at Lübeck at the same time under different aliases!

At about ten o'clock that night the sirens went and all the Germans trooped down to the cellars. After a few minutes there were distant rumbles and the ever increasing thuds of ack ack, then the throbbing roar of a thousand motors overhead rising above the now deafening crash of guns just outside my window. Shell fragments were clattering on the roofs all round. My feelings were mixed—I wanted the boys to blow the whole place to pieces but on the other hand I didn't want to be too close to an 8,000 pounder! Fortunately for me they put all their eggs in one basket and that basket was Hamburg, 50 kms away.

The following day they came over again and I created such a fuss in my cell that the guard took me to the lavatory window where I could get a better view. The shells were bursting all over the sky and the planes could be heard but not seen. Suddenly a glint of silver appeared amid the ever thickening barrage of bursting steel. It grew bigger and bigger as it lost height, all the while twisting and weaving like a huge bird, to free itself from the now hopeless trap. It went into a vertical dive at about 6,000 ft. and tried to pull up at about 500. Small arms fire was now in play and the whole earth seemed to open up and devour the helpless machine in a sheet of flame about two km. away. Dead silence followed and a column of smoke rose into the sky. Four white dots could be seen floating down against a blue background. I returned to my cell with a cloud of sadness pressing hard upon me. For the following six nights, with one exception, this treatment was repeated. The citizens of London, Coventry and many other English towns had once more been avenged. The city of Hamburg was in ruins and on the lips of all the Germans was the one sentence—"Alles, alles ist Weg gegangen," which when translated into a civilized tongue means—"All, all is gone."

T. M. Barott Lieut.

1st Bn. The Black Watch (RHR) of Canada

66. SUSPENSE

After an uncomfortable night spent in an attic room, Hank, Don and I were marched out through the inner courtyard where the night before we had passed a small forlorn looking group of prisoners surrounded by numerous guards with rifles at the ready.

As we passed through the outer courtyard and down a narrow path across a small bridge and though a wood to be halted finally in front of a white stone wall, I remembered that our guards of yesterday had said we had been sent here to be shot.

Strange thoughts passed through my mind and in imagination I heard the N.C.O. giving his final instructions to the guard.

He spoke to us in German but none of us understood the language. He turned to the waiting guards. It seemed a pity that the first three British officers in Colditz were leaving so soon.

The N.C.O. shouted an order at the waiting soldiers who marched off the edge of the clearing and left us free to enjoy our first exercise in the park.

Keith Milne.

Page 67 is blank.

68. PETITE HISTOIRE DE CAPTIVITÉ*

It was in the gloomy light of a room full of captured French officers in Oflag VIII F in Silesia, during one of the first winters in captivity, interminable because even though the hope of allied victory was firmly anchored in the hearts of the prisoners, the realization of our wishes seemed far away.

It was four o'clock in the afternoon.

It was our time of day to, explain, comment and discuss the military operational picture as interpreted from the daily bulletin while we sat around a well-stoked stove; we killed time as best we could while we waited for our supper.

Less patient than the others, one of our comrades was eating a bar of chocolate and some biscuits. The "Verdunklung" (blackout) Orderly made his daily appearance and walked over to the torn black paper curtain in front of the window. When he finished he was just about to leave the room when his attention was caught by the huge chocolate bar our comrade was devouring with such obvious satisfaction.

He stopped completely, stared silently for a moment and then walked out. We were still chuckling over this scene when the door opened again and the same orderly entered the room again and walked over to the window, even though there was nothing for him to do there. This time he took his time. With a comical expression of envy directed towards the happy

* *Short Story of Captivity*

After an uncomfortable night spent in an attic room, Hank, Don and I were marched out through the inner courtyard where the night before we had passed a small forlorn looking group of prisoners surrounded by numerous guards with rifles at the ready.

As we passed through the outer courtyard and down a narrow path across a small bridge and through a wood to be halted finally in front of a white stone wall I remembered that our guards of yesterday had said we had been sent here to be shot.

Strange thoughts passed through my mind and in imagination I heard the N.C.O. giving his final instructions to the guard.

He spoke to us in German but none of us understood the language. He turned to the waiting guards. It seemed as if that the first three British officers in Colditz were leaving so soon.

The N.C.O. shouted an order to the waiting soldiers who marched off to the edge of the clearing and left us free to enjoy our first exercise in the

Keith Milne.

chocolate-eater, he said to him with great conviction,

"Es schmeckt gut?" (Does it taste good?)

Then pointing a finger at the object of his desire, he said in a voice that sounded as if he were drooling in anticipation, "Ah Schokolade! Scho ko la a de!"

The officer, who was a decent chap, gave way to a momentary impulse of pity for his—temporary—conqueror who was obviously in so much distress, broke his chocolate bar into two pieces and gave him one.

We were witnessing a very curious scene.

The chocolate disappeared swiftly down the wide open throat of the Orderly. When he had finished, there were still visible traces around the edges of his mouth of his breach of rules.

He straightened his wedge cap on his shaven head and, when he reached the door, put one finger to his lips and uttered a long "ssshhh" as a request for our discretion and silence regarding the whole matter.

Then he sprang to attention, saluted smartly, shouted "Fife La France!" . . . and with all the dignity he could muster, he marched off.

3/4/45 This short story is dedicated to my friend Jerry as a token of friendship. I hope very much to continue with him in France the strong relationship that began in captivity.

Charles Froger

69. FAMOUS LAST WORDS

The sky which, a second ago was as dark as tar is suddenly set ablaze by the star shells fired ahead and on our port side. The ship in front has found at last the convoy we were seeking, and thanks to the skill of his gunners, the whole hive of enemy ships is now silhouetted against the light of the flares—The Germans must have been caught unawares, and they can't see us now with all that blinding light in their eyes. We're lucky, it is just like an exercise.

Now, as in a well pre-arranged ballet, the Germans carry out their usual dispersal, but we know the trick and they have been too slow reacting and in altering course, we'll be able to catch them easily.

"Charles, we'll take the cargo on our port bow as target, get your sight ready, torpedoes in readiness; Bill, give your order to load to the guns but keep them patient; I don't want any firing as long as they haven't seen us.

"Target turning right! Starboard ten, half ahead both. Midships! Steady! Slow ahead both!

"Can you see him Charles?—Yes, I see him O.K.!

"Right ho! I'll go in now. Half ahead both. Speed of target 10—target moving right . . . . Starboard torpedo stand by . . . . Fire!

"Hard to port! full ahead both! Watch the target . . . Midships, steady . . . steer North ten East . . . Hurrah! Charles it's a splendid hit."

On the side of the tramp, clearly cut against the light of the flares, a huge geyser in black and white rises and blots out the silhouette of her bridge. She "had it"! Our little SGB raises her

Petite histoire de Captivité.

C'est dans la lumière triste d'une chambre d'officiers français prisonniers à l'Oflag VIII F en Silésie, au cours d'un des premiers hivers de captivité, hiver lugubre, interminable, car si l'espoir de la victoire des alliés restait ancrée à nos cœurs de captifs, la réalisation de nos vœux nous paraissait plus lointaine.

Il est 4 heures du soir.

C'est l'heure du communiqué où s'expliquent, se commentent et s'interprètent les événements militaires et politiques, autour d'un calorifère chichement garni ; on tue le temps comme on peut.

MM les Officiers prisonniers attendent leur soupe.

Moins patient que les autres un de nos camarades mange une barre de chocolat avec des biscuits.

Le posten de service aux "Verdunklung" fait son apparition quotidienne, il vient baisser le rideau de papier noir déchiré devant la fenêtre. Il avait fini et allait sortir quand son attention fut attirée par la grosse barre de chocolat que notre camarade croquait à belles dents.

Il s'arrêta net, le regarda un instant en silence et s'en alla.

A peine les sourires provoqués par cette scène avaient-ils cessé que le même posten fit irruption dans la chambre, il alla de nouveau à la fenêtre où — selon toute apparence — il n'avait plus rien à faire ; mais décidé cette fois à prendre son temps il considéra avec une comique expression d'envie l'heureux mangeur de chocolat et lui dit avec une indéniable conviction.

— Es schmeckt gut ?

Puis montrant du doigt l'objet de sa convoitise il ajouta avec cet accent particulier que donne l'eau à la bouche :

Ah ! Schokolade ! Schokola a de !!

Bon garçon, cédant à un sentiment d'humanité, peut-être de pitié pour un vainqueur — provisoire — et combien dépourvu ! notre camarade cassa une barre de chocolat et la tendit généreusement à son geôlier.

Alors nous assistâmes à une scène curieuse:

Le chocolat disparut dans la bouche avide du posten, englouti en un temps record. S'étant ainsi régalé, et les commissures des lèvres portant nettement les traces de cette infraction aux règlements du camp il assujettit son calot sur son crâne rasé, et à la porte, un doigt sur la bouche, nous fit un long: Chut !!.... pour nous recommander la discrétion.

Puis s'étant mis au Garde-à-vous, il salua militairement cria : "Fife la France !".... et très digne, s'en alla.

4/45 Cette petite histoire est dédiée à mon ami Jerry en gage de sympathie. J'espère beaucoup continuer avec lui en France les bonnes relations commencées en captivité. Charly [?]

Famous last words   Summer 1942

The sky which, a second ago was as dark as tar is suddenly set ablaze by the star shells fired ahead and on our port side. The ship in front has found at last the convoy we were seeking, and thanks to the skill of his gunners, the whole line of enemy ships is now silhouetted against the light of the flares - the Germans must have been caught unawares, and they can't see us now with all that blinding light in their eyes. We're lucky, it is just like an exercise.

Now, as in a well pre-arranged ballet, the germans carry out their usual dispersal but we know the trick and they have been too slow reacting & in altering course, we'll be able to catch them easily.

"Charles, we'll take the cargo on our port bow as target, get your sight ready, torpedoes in readiness; Bill, give the order to load to the guns but keep 'em patient; I don't want any firing as long as they haven't seen us

"Target turning right! Starboard ten, half ahead both, Midships! Ready! Slow ahead both!

"Can you see him Charles? — Yes, I see him O.K!

"Right ho! I'll go in now. Half ahead both. Speed of target 10 - Target swing right ——... Starboard torpedo stand by.... Fire!

"Hard to port!, full ahead both! Watch the target ... Midships, steady... Steer North ten East...... Hurrah! Charles it's a splendid hit.

On the side of the tramp, clearly cut against the light of the flares, a huge tower in black & white rises and blots out the silhouette of her bridge, she "had it" our little SGB raises her nose and the foam sweeps across the bridge, we must [be] doing thirty now, and still increasing.

"Ship on starboard bow Sir!

"Port ten, up a hundred. I can see her, she's one of their big schnells open fire as soon as she's in range. Midships! steady!

In a split second a hail of bullets & small shells pierces the darkness & the tracers weave on the glittering surface of the sea a dazzling web [of] bright colours.

"Pom-pom out of action - Starboard turret out of action!"

The fire seem to slow down from opposite too; the ferry seems to take a list and disappears in the darkness. Quite time too!

Suddenly a rush on the ladder and a stoker out of breath appears [on] the bridge: "'Scuse me Sir! The boiler's hit!

"What? bad?

"Yes, pressure is going down fast! in a minute we'll be stopped

"Any hope of repairing it.

"No Sir, it's in the casing. Dockyard job, at least —

"Gosh! Charles, tell the w/T to send a message for one of the boys to take us in tow, if they are still around. That's bad luck! If they're already gone it'll be Gefangenschaft for us. I hope not ----

R. Barrett

Indian Politics. An allegory.

The following is true. I have suppressed names to avoid heart-burnings. In the summer of 1942, two thousand British prisoners were in a camp in Westphalia. Among them were some 40 Indian officers. The Indian army commissions were before the war of two kinds. The King Emperor's entitled the recipient to the same privileges and the same military status as any other British officer. The Viceroy's commission beginning I believe, to give to the Indian army sufficient junior officers under the Indianisation scheme for the Indian army, gave to the recipient a status between that of warrant officer and officer. There is no corresponding rank in the British army unless it be that of P.S.M. (now abolished). The Indian officers in the camp were all viceroy commission officers. There were among them a number of clerks or were not commissioned, but being civilian-turned-soldiers, had warily clung to the officers in order to avoid despatch to troops camps where their position would have been a difficult one. They were however a difficulty because they insisted on discussing highly controversial political subjects, & drawing into the debates the regular soldiers who were under oath to refrain from doing so. I do not propose to go into a discussion of the morality of such an oath. The story arises from facts as they were, not as they should or might be, or should not be. The facts were then. In two small small adjoining rooms was crowded a mixture of old & young Indian army soldiers, from sappers, R.I.A.S.C, & crack cavalry regiments. They had been captured after a heroic defence of an important oasis in Libya, during the first British retreat from Benghazi. At the order to withdraw, the majority had fought their way through the German tanks at night. These prisoners represented the unlucky rear-guard. Great fighters they were, like many soldiers all over the world, ill equipped for political discussion. It was my privilege to be liaison officer between them & the British Brigade office. Having had no experience of the Indian army. I learned much from my 6 month contact with them, of their courage, their country, their enthusiastic loyalty, & their readiness again like soldiers the world over, to put something across if they thought they could get away with it. The political, religious & caste questions I expected to crop up hardly ever appeared, yet here were Hindu, moslem & Sikh, high caste & not so high, regular soldiers & young clerks packed together for 24 hours a day in the closest proximity. I have never ceased to marvel at & be encouraged by their readiness to sink their fundamental differences for the good of the community. Their Senior officer was a man of long service & much wisdom. His most difficult problem was to check the endless & acrimonious debates on the subject of British policy in India. This problem was embarrassed by the reports in the German papers of the Cripps mission to India. This wise soldier kept his head for many weeks, but the subject seemed as alive & inexhaustible as ever. He decided to end it. He called all of them together, & asked the Hindus, the moslems & the Sikhs to get together & get out a plan for the future constitution of India. He gave them 10 days. At the end of that time he asked for a summary of their views. They had devoted much labour to the problem, but confessed a disability to settle the problem as they were unable to agree to a plan satisfactory to all parties. "Well stop talking about it, then" he replied. They did. A bit unfair perhaps, but a masterly stroke of the diplomacy of this old officer. But I often think of the goodwill which, though not apparent on paper, enabled these officers to live for all that time without a single serious dispute.

The Almost Perfect Raid   July 1940.

Target for the night was the Bayer Chemical Factory - area 1 mile by 2 miles - location Leverkus 7 miles north of Cologne. A fine moonlight night. Two hours out from England, we were swinging round over Cologne, the silvered Rhine, acting as signpost. Cologne laid out in semi circles centring on the Hohenzollern bridge wasn't much interested. A few guns were firing, more to make it look like a raid than to hit us. The bombing run in was a dream from Bombing School. A fire already started, showed up the long factory buildings. Height 6000 ft, Running up – Bombs gone. As we swung and flames already were tearing up the sky. Seventy miles away our tail gunner saw the last of the flames. A good landing and one taxied up to the hangar thinking that was worth the extra 2/6 on Income Tax or at least 1/5. Collected all the maps & shit that go to swell the bulky navigators satchel. Went forward to get down the ladder, stepped out – onto nothing The thump on hitting the ground + the resultant sprained ankle and language was good, I reckon for all the subsequent rise in Income Tax.

D Bruce

F/LT   RAF.

nose and the foam sweeps across the bridge, we must be doing thirty now, and still increasing.

"Ship on starboard bow Sir!

"Port ten, up a hundred. I can see her, she's one of their big Schnellboots. Bill, open fire as soon as she's in range. Midships! Steady!"

In a split second a hail of bullets and small shells pierces the darkness and the tracers weave on the glittering surface of the sea a dazzling web of bright colours.

"Pom-pom out of action—Starboard turret out of action!"

The fire seem to slow down from opposite too; the Jerry seems to take a list and disappears in the darkness. Quite time too! Suddenly a rush on the ladder and a stoker out of breath appears on the bridge:

"'Scuse me Sir! The boiler's hit!

"What? Bad?

"Yes, pressure is going down fast! In a minute we'll be stopped!

"Any hope of repairing it.

"No Sir, it's in the casing. Dockyard job, at least—

"Gosh! Charles, tell the W/T to send a message for one of the boys to take us in tow, if they are still around. That's bad luck! If they are already gone it'll be Gefangenschaft for us—I hope not . . .

R. Barnet Lieut. R.N.

70. INDIAN POLITICS—AN ALLEGORY

The following is true. I have suppressed names to avoid heart burnings. In the Summer of 1942, two thousand British prisoners were in a camp in Westphalia. Among them were some 40 Indian officers. The Indian Army Commissions were before the war of two kinds. The King' Commission entitled the recipient to the same privileges and the same military status as any other British officer. The Viceroy's Commission being, I believe, to give to the Indian Army sufficient junior officers under the Indianisation Scheme for the Indian Army, gave to the recipient a status between that of warrant officer and officer. There is no corresponding rank in the British Army unless it be that of P.S.M. (now abolished). The Indian officers in the camp were all Viceroy Commission Officers. There were among them a number of clerks who were not commissioned, but being civilian-turned-soldiers, had wisely clung to the officers in order to avoid despatch to troops camps where their position would have been a difficult one. They were however, a difficulty because they insisted on discussing highly controversial political subjects and drawing into the debates the regular soldiers who were under oath to refrain from doing so.

I do not propose to go into the morality of such an oath. The story arises from parts as they were, not as they should or might be. The parts were there. In two small adjoining rooms were crowded a mixture of old and young Indian army soldiers, from Sapper, R.I.A.S.C. and crack cavalry regiments. They had been captured after a heroic defence of an important oasis in Libya, during the first British retreat from Benghazi. At the order to withdraw, the majority had fought their way through the German tanks at night. These prisoners represented the unlucky rearguard, great fighters. They were, like many soldiers all over the world, ill equipped for political discussion.

It was my privilege to be liaison officer between them and the British Brigade Office. Having had no experience of the Indian army, I learned much from my 6 months contact with them, of their courage, their courtesy, their enthusiastic loyalty, and their readiness again like soldiers the world over, to put something across if they could get away with it.

The political, religious and caste questions I expected to crop up hardly ever appeared, yet here were Hindu, Moslem and Sikh, high caste and not so high, regular soldiers and young clerks packed together for 24 hours a day in the closest proximity. I have never ceased to marvel at and be encouraged by their readiness to sink their fundamental differences for the good of the community.

Their Senior Officer was a man of long service and much wisdom. His most difficult problem was to check the endless and acrimonious debates on the subject of British policy in India. This problem was emphasized by the reports in the German papers of the Cripps Mission to India. This wise soldier kept his peace for many weeks, but the subject seemed as alive and inexhaustible as ever. He decided to end it. He called them all together and asked the Hindus, the Moslems and the Sikhs to get together and get out a plan for the future constitution of India. He gave them 10 days. At the end of that time he asked for a summary of their views. They had devoted much labour to the problem, but confessed a disability to settle the problem as they were unable to agree to a plan satisfactory to all parties.

"Well stop thinking about it, then" he replied. They did. A bit unfair perhaps, but a masterly stroke of the diplomacy of this old officer. But I often think of the goodwill which, though not apparent on paper, enabled these officers to live for all that time without a single serious dispute.

H. [*Capt. The Earl of Hopetoun, Lothian and Borders Yeomanry*].

71.   THE ALMOST PERFECT RAID—JULY 1940

Target for the night was the Bayer Chemical Factory—area 1 mile by 2 miles—location—Leverkusen, 7 miles north of Cologne. A fine moonlight night. Two hours out from England, we were swinging around over Cologne, the silvered Rhine acting as a signpost. Cologne laid out in semi circles centring on the Hohenzollern Bridge, wasn't much interested. A few guns were firing, more to make it look like a raid than to hit us. The bombing run-up was a dream from Bombing School. A fire already started, showed up the long factory buildings.
Height 6,000 ft, running up—Bombs gone. Around we swung and flames already were tearing up the sky. Seventy miles away our tail gunner saw the last of the flames. A good landing and one taxied up to the hangar thinking that was worth the extra 2/6 on Income Tax or at least 2/5.

Collected all the maps and shit that go to swell the bulky navigators satchel. Went forward to get down the ladder, stepped out—onto nothing. The thump on hitting the ground and the resultant sprained ankle and language was good, I reckon for all the subsequent rise in Income Tax.

D. Bruce,
F/Lt. RAF.

Two soldiers left the hospital one afternoon. Next day the Germans assured us they would shoot ten men for every one that escaped; we were fools enough to take the threat seriously. Having been successfully bluffed, we had to wait until we were discharged before escaping. It was in fact September before we were suddenly sent to a very squalid transit camp in an old textile factory at Lokeren. Previously it had been very easy to leave unofficially. We were however a small party, only three British, and nine French officers. And so though the troops could move within the perimeter after dark, the Germans were able to guard us effectually by placing a sentry on the door of our own little room at dusk. This forced us to try and leave by day. After various reconnaissances, we found a door leading to the outside world, a locked door, but after all only half an inch of wood held in place by a steel mechanism was between us and freedom. Too easy we thought particularly when we found a good iron bar excellently suited to breaking through doors. Great consultations took place. A plan was made and in mid-day we started on the door itself. Needless to say when success was in sight, a long procession of Germans appeared, and off we went to an improved cell. Silence and a crowbar had not proved a happy combination. The crowbar was an easy winner.

It was quite different later. We had keys, pick-locks, wires, rope, forges, money, maps, papers, civilian clothes, files, hacksaws, compasses and experts. We also had locked doors, iron bars, horizontal wire, lines of vertical wire, dogs, machine guns, sound detectors and snow.

The problem however remained constant. It was always as easy to escape as it was in a transit camp in Belgium in September 1940. It was always a question of who was that one move ahead.

Colin Mackenzie Lt
Seaforth Highlanders

July 1944.

where lives – dressed up as the four doctor!

It was all Harry & Nick's idea. We'd play the trick successfully once, & I just won't work up enough interest to do it again. The trouble was that most of these new arrivals had seen me before, in Laufen, 1940, & I didn't like to risk being recognised in the middle of a practical joke. The mat lows after all had been complete strangers to me in Sept. 1942, when I'd waded in on them going as the German Stabsarzt, slightly crazy of course, & given them a thorough & shame making examination. But this time we had no German hat to fix the disguise.

Still, Harry persisted, & I agreed to give the boys a laugh. The French dent. me me his white surgery dress. One of the Dutch lent me his green riches of forage cap. This latter, with a red, white & blue blob sewn front rounded off one end, boots & spurs the other. Bosun Chrisp as medical orderly.

We gave them hell! Bo went ahead to get the names of those who'd arrived the camp the night before. They were all in bed naturally. Harry & his & a little quiet propaganda about the awful doctor fellow. At 10.15 went into the British quarters yelling & roaring 'Achtung' – 'Aufstehn' only a goon can, & there we were. They were shaken. They were worse they were bloody frightened. They were, some of them, as jelly in my hands Blitz in factories living up to its reputation in Oflag VII-B & prior to that to War. They were dragged out, in alphabetical order, stripped, sounded & stethoscoped. I prowled in their hair for lice, examined their teeth, tweaked their eye lids about, smeared them with some filthy mixture of decayed barley & mildewed cornflour (for crabs), & as a special treat painted portions of selected victims a dubious blue (to taste). A stream of comment & abuse flowed from me all the time made the German language sound very, very nasty. And they took it abs. All except one, whose back chat earned him a threat of court-mar less he apologised, which he did. None suspected anything. It all made a bit noisy – but quite normal to the Kriegie in goon land. Even when I asked for a cigarette I got it, although when I wouldn't give how his towel sack except for a packet of ten, he had the presence mind to make it an empty one. "Verdammt! Donnerwetter! Schweine!"

It all came to a head after ¾ of an hour when I ran out of adjectives & pinched my stethoscope. I'd examined over 30 people & was wondering how to make a good exit. I called the room to order, threatened to have them locked in for a week (applause), confinement called / loud applause finally promised not to 'report to the Kommandant'.

Harry just saved the stethoscope from destruction. It belonged to Col...

(MR...

72. A CONSTANT PROBLEM

Two soldiers left the hospital one afternoon. Next day the Germans assured us they would shoot ten men for every one that escaped. We were all fools enough to take the threat seriously. Having been successfully bluffed, we had to wait until we were discharged before escaping. It was in fact September before we were suddenly sent to a very squalid transit camp in an old textile factory at Lokeren. Previously it had been very easy to leave unofficially. We were, however, a small party; only three British, and nine French Officers. And so, though the troops could move within the perimeter after dark, the Germans were able to guard us effectively by placing a sentry on the door of our evil little room at dusk. This forced us to try and leave by day. After various reconnaissances, we found a door leading to the outside world—a locked door, but after all only half an inch of wood held in place by a steel mechanism was between us and freedom. Too easy, we thought, particularly when we found a good iron bar excellently suited to breaking through doors. Great consultations took place—a plan was made—and finally we started on the door itself. Needless to say, when success was in sight, a long procession of Germans appeared, and off we went to an improvised cell. Silence and a crowbar had not proved a happy combination—the crowbar was an easy winner.

It was quite different later. We had keys, pick locks, wire, ropes, stooges, money, maps, papers, civilian clothes, files, hacksaws, compasses and experts. We also had locked doors, iron bars, horizontal wire, three lines of vertical wire, dogs, machine guns, sound detectors and snoops.

The problem however remained constant. It was always as easy to escape as it was in a transit camp in Belgium in September 1940. It was always a question of who was that one move ahead.

Colin MacKenzie Lt.
Seaforth Highlanders

July 1944

73. FUN IN COLDITZ—HORRID HOAX BY HOWARD GEE

And there I was—dressed up as the Goon Doctor!

It was all Harry Elliot's idea. We'd played the trick successfully once, and I just couldn't work up enough interest to do it again. The trouble was that most of these new arrivals had seen me before, in Laufen, 1940, and I didn't like to risk being recognised in the middle of a practical joke. The matlows after all had been complete strangers to me in Sept, 1942, when I'd roared in on them, posing as the German Stabsarzt, slightly crazy of course, and given them a thorough and shame-making examination. But this time we hadn't even a German hat to fix the disguise.

Still, Harry persisted and I agreed to give the boys a laugh. The French dentist gave me his white surgery dress. One of the Dutch lent me his green breeches and forage cap. This latter, with a red, white and blue blob sewn on the front, rounded off one end, boots and spurs the other. Bosun Chrisp acted as medical orderly.

We gave them hell. Bo went ahead to get the name of those who'd arrived at the camp the night before. They were all in bed naturally. Harry and friends did a little quiet propaganda about the awful doctor fellow. At 10.15 I burst into the British quarters yelling and roaring "Achtung" "Aufstehen" as only a Goon can, and there we were. They were shaken. They were worried. They were bloody frightened. They were, some of them, as jelly in my hands. Colditz in fact was living up to its reputation in Oflag VIIB and points N., S., E. and West. They were dragged out, in alphabetical order, stripped, probed and stethoscoped. I prowled their hair for lice, examined their teeth, tweaked their eye-lids about, smeared them with some filthy mixture of decayed barley and mildewed cornflour (for crabs) and as a special treat painted portions of selected victims a dubious blue, (for art's sake). A stream of comment and abuse flowed from me all the time. I made the German language sound very, very nasty. And they took it all like lambs. All except one, whose back-chat earned him a threat of court-martial unless he apologised, which he did. No one suspected anything. It all seemed a bit noisy—but quite normal to the Kriegie in Goonland. Even when I asked for a cigarette I got it, although when I wouldn't give a fellow a towel back except for a packet of ten, he had the presence of mind to make it an empty one. "Verdammt! Donnerwetter! Schweinerei!"

It all came to a head after ¾ of an hour when I ran out of adjectives. They pinched my stethoscope. I'd examined over 30 people and was wondering how to make a good exit. I called the room to order, threatened to have them locked up for a week (applause), court-martialled (loud applause) and finally stormed out to "report to the Kommandant"

Harry just saved the stethoscope from destruction. It belonged to the Poles.

Gee (Mr.)

74. "SEA RESCUE" BY FLYING OFFICER CENEK CHALOUPKA, ROYAL AIR FORCE

Four hurricanes flying low on the water, skimmed over the Channel bound for Belgium. It was somewhere near twelve, midday, on 29th August 1941, a lovely warm day with a soft haze cutting down our visibility. We carried assorted armament between us. Two of the "kites" with 12 machine guns each, one with four cannons and one, myself, with two 250 lb bombs.

We crossed the coast with no opposition from hostile flak, and wheeling left soon picked up a canal which we were to follow inland for some twenty miles before reaching our target, a concentration of German Flak Ships in some small canal harbour.

The unexpected always occurs, however! Some miles before reaching our objective we came over a single flak ship in the canal. Immediately the C.O's voice came over the radio: "Attack... Attack... Go!" Down went one after another, myself with the eggs last. I pressed the button and down went a bomb scoring a hit on the flak ship. Contrary to expectations however the bomb burst immediately instead of the usual seven second delay before detonation which enables the aircraft to reach a safe distance before the explosion. My aircraft rocked violently in the explosion and I caught the sound of a false note in the engine. I reported this to the

Four Hurricanes flying low on the water, skimmed over the Channel bound for Belgium. It was somewhere near twelve, midday, on 29th August 1941, a lovely warm day with a soft haze cutting down our visibility. We carried assorted armament between us. Two of the 'kites' with 12 machine guns each, one with four cannons and myself, with two 250 lb bombs.

We crossed the coast with no opposition from hostile flak and whilst left soon picked up a canal which we were to follow inland for some twenty miles before reaching our target, a concentration of German Flak ships in some small canal harbour.

The unexpected always occurs however. Some miles before reaching our objective we came over a single flak ship in the canal and immediately the CO's voice came over the radio "Attack.... Attack.. Go." Down we went one after another, myself with the 'eggs' last. I pressed the button & down went a bomb scoring a hit on the flak ship. Contrary to expectations however the bomb burst immediately instead of the usual seven second delay before detonation which enables the aircraft to reach a safe distance before the explosion. My aircraft rocked violently in the explosion & I caught the sound of a false note in the engine. I reported this to the CO & duly received instructions to join the formation and continue for the target.

Soon the harbour & six flak ships appeared and in we once more to the attack. After a fast and furious engagement we pulled away & headed for the coast. Things were going from bad to worse however with my engine and with my speed down to 140 m.p.h. it was decidedly unpleasant when a heavy barrage opened up at us as we crossed the coast. The old 'hurribus' staggered on however until some thirty miles from the English coast, the inevitable happened and smoke & fire began to come up from the cockpit floor. I did not waste much time by pulling out my back & dropping out of the aircraft. My parachute had hardly opened when I hit the water & down & down went swallowing most of the channel before reaching surface again. O was circling overhead & sending back my position by wireless as it with the inflatable dinghy. A little later two Spitfires were overhead patrolling and two and a half hours later, by means of a smoke flame dropped by the Spitfires, I was picked up by an R.A.F Sea Rescue boat and taken to Ramsgate in nice time for a celebration party that night.

When France capitulated in 1940, why didn't the British march into Syria? We nearly did: in Palestine the 1st Cavalry Division stood by for the ride north, packed saddles lay ranked along the horse lines, trumpeters waited ready to sound ... the frontier was open .... in Syria the French expected us & hoped for us, having no taste for the ignominious armistice signed on their behalf in France. But the trumpeters blew 'Stables' instead, for the word never came. Disappointed, numbers of Poles & Frenchmen crossed into Palestine, & in a week the Axis commission had reached Beyrout, the frontier was closed, & Syria lost. A year later it was blood not flowers along the Damascus road.

The subaltern's conclusion (subalterns are notoriously right) is that for want of a bold decision we handed Syria to the enemy. But the following points show, perhaps, why the bold decision was lacking. The French had about 2½ divisions in Syria (modest estimate): in Palestine, odds & sods excepted, there was only the 1st Cav. Div. & one Australian brigade with another ditto just arriving. And Italy had entered the war & was threatening a very thin line in Egypt from the Western Desert. It should also be remembered that the firepower of mounted troops is small: we had one LMG per troop & one H.M.G. troop per regiment, & in dismounted action every fourth man is a horseholder. The case was an understandable though not an excusable one, & might be equated as – no stuff = no bluff.

Michael Riviere Lt Notts. Yeomanry.

C.O. and duly received instructions to join the formation and continue for the target.

Soon the harbour and six flak ships appeared and in we went once again to the attack. After a fast and furious engagement we pulled away and headed for the coast. Things were going from bad to worse, however, with my engine and with my speed down to 140 mph was decidedly unpleasant when a heavy barrage opened up at us as we crossed the coast. The old "hurribus" staggered on however until some thirty miles from the English coast the inevitable happened. Smoke and fire began to come up from the cockpit floor.

I did not waste much time in pulling onto my back and dropping out of the aircraft. My parachute had hardly opened when I hit the water and down and down I went swallowing most of the channel before reaching surface again. My C.O. was circling overhead and sending back my position by wireless as I got into the collapsible dinghy. A little later two Spitfires were overhead patrolling and two and a half hours later, by means of a smoke flare dropped by the Spitfires, I was picked up by an R.A.F. Sea Rescue boat and taken to Ramsgate in nice time for a celebration party that night.

Cenek.

75. MIDDLE EAST—JUNE 1940

When France capitulated in 1940, why didn't the British march into Syria? We nearly did; in Palestine the 1st Cavalry Division stood by for the ride north, packed saddles lay ranked along the horse lines, trumpeters waited ready to sound . . . the frontier was open . . . in Syria the French expected us and hoped for us, having no taste for the ignominious armistice signed on their behalf in France.

But the trumpeters blew "Stables" instead, for the word never came. Disappointed, numbers of Poles and Frenchmen crossed into Palestine, and in a week the Axis commission had reached Beyrout, the frontier was closed and Syria lost. A year later it was blood not flowers along the Damascus road.

The subaltern's conclusion (subalterns are notoriously right) is that for want of a bold decision we handed Syria to the enemy. But the following points show, perhaps, why the bold decision was lacking. The French had about 2½ divisions in Syria (modest estimate). In Palestine, odds and sods excepted, there was only the 1st Cav. Div. and one Australian Brigade with another ditto just arriving. And Italy had entered the war and was threatening a very thin line in Egypt from the Western Desert. It should also be remembered that the fire power of mounted troops is small. We had one L.M.G. per troop and one H.M.G. troop per regiment, and in dismounted action every fourth man is a horseholder. The case was understandable though not an excusable one, and might be equated as—no stuff = no bluff.

Michael Riviere, Lt. Notts. Yeomanry

Page 76 is blank.

An Episode whilst on working party

POW 19/41 Gogolin Oberschlesia Germany

One Evening after I returned to the Lager where I was Billhetted
Our Room was on potato peeling of coarse at that time
things were very bad as regards food besides which made things
more unpleasant was the Shortage of Red X parcells I was known through
the Camp for getting any Buckshie soup when ever the oppertunity arose-
enough that I was clamied The Buckshie King-now this evening in
perticular all we Boys were busy peeling spuds the Sgt who was i/c said to me
Bucky- if you want some Buckshie soup there is a full pail out in the yard which the Frau-
lein in the German kitchen have Left Becareful she dosent see you take it without hesitation
I went for it full of glee on my way back the Frau had Seen me take it and kept
calling me back but I took no notice of her but hurried into the Billett I got my
mess Bowls besides my own and Set to Lobling the soup I happened to Look
round and Seen that the Sgt was laughing I asked him what was afloat he
then replied that the reason why the frau went off the deep end because what
was in the pail was not soup but pig swill I can assure you I felt a fool
when I realysed my mistake and the disapointment in not having soup.
was all there & then I Lost my name Buckshie King-The following
morning The frau & the pigs absolutly ignored me.

Can you Blame them?.

I always kept my distance
from soup after that.

With Best Wishes.
Buckshie King.
R.E.

24th
"/43

...alk we waited in a wood until it was dark. Soon after w...
...tarted again we passed a few scattered houses, where ...
...og barked & someone opened a window. It was here tha...
...re first aroused suspicion, as we subsequently discove...
...e walked for another 5 or 6 miles & came to a railw...
...ridge over the road, where we realised that we had ...
...issed a turning. While we were discussing what ...
...hould do, we heard footsteps on the road behin...
...o we walked on quickly intending to get well ...
...head & then stop for another discussion of plans ...
...e were going through a small village & had come t...
...ide road, when suddenly men armed with all kind...
...f weapons sprang on to the road all round us ...
...houting at us to halt & to put our hands up. Prot...
...ing our innocence we were hustled into a n...
...by inn where there was a Gestapo man, wh...
...vas apparently in charge of the local frontie...
...guards. He scorned our papers & excuses & s...
...s under escort to Singen police station, f...
...vhere we eventually returned crestfallen t...
...ichstätt.

J. McDonnell
Royal Norfolk Regt.

3/7/44
Coldit...

st 25th 1939. I have just made port after a pleasure cruise to the Atlantic Isles, and war
being imminent I am not surprised when I receive my papers and am
ted to "H.M.S Vandyck". My ship is an A.M.C (Armed Merchant Cruiser), later known under
sobriquet of "Admiralty Made Coffins".

. 2nd 1939. We clear port on our first commission, our destination New York. Our
cargo is of great value, Bullion and American citizens returning ho
y War is declared, but death is close on our heels.

. 3rd 1939. We received wireless notification of the declaration of War. All watertight
s are permanently closed and crew are at action stations. 4 P.M. a loud explosion is
d, and the Anchor liner "Athenia", a few miles astern has been torpedoed, the first
m of the submarines. We are told to proceed on our course, and without further incid
e at our destination.

. 18th 1939 We proceed to Halifax to escort convoy to England. After seven miserable
lying in Bedford Basin without shore leave the convoy is finally assembled, and on
28th we proceed to sea with the cruiser "Berwick" and four Canadian Destroyers
attendance. One old tramp cannot make the convoy speed, and the cruiser orders her to
n to port. After 36 hours the destroyers circle the convoy and then return to Halifax. Before
the cruiser signals "safe voyage and happy return" and then steams away and the
responsibility for the safety of the convoy rests with us. It is a monotonous and
ng job, keeping ships in station, changing speed continually, circling the
voy, ahead, astern, both sides, one escort vessel to protect 14 merchant ships fr
marine attack. It is the second convoy to leave for England with food and war
terial and rather uneventful, with no incidents during the voyage. We are met by
British destroyers off the coast of Ireland, but a storm blows up and they return to po
le we turn into the storm to avoid pooping by the following seas, and ride out the
m. Next morning the weather having abated we again proceed on our original
se once more the destroyers picked us up. The convoy splits up as we approac
channel, two destroyers escorting the ships due in southern ports, whilst the other
e and ourselves proceed north bound for Liverpool. The voyage completed the next
we are once more ready to proceed to sea. After four months of convoy work we ar
ered by the news we are to be relieved, and take over contraband control work
h the Northern Patrol, a much more exciting and interesting occupation. Our
k consists of stopping suspected vessels, sending them into port for searching
ing as mother ship to the armed trawlers attached to the patrol, and ready for
ight with any enemy vessel we chance to meet. We spend three months on th
k and then we are ordered to the Orkneys as base ship to the R.A.F & R.N.F.A
are once more back at a damn monotonous job, but only for a short time
t in May we receive orders to sail for Liverpool for a six weeks refit. Thing
k look good for leave and a good time ashore, to paint the town red, but
fortunately as often happens in war time our orders are cancelled, and we
eive notice to escort the troopships to Narvik for the evacuation of Norway.
sailed from Liverpool on the 29th May 1940 to meet the troopers at Greenoc
e convoy consisted of the following ships, Orient liners "Oronsay" "Ormonde,"
ama, Blue Star liner "Arandora Star", Irish S.P. Ships, Ulster "Monarch" and

77. AN EPISODE WHILST ON WORKING PARTY POW 19/41/ GOGALIA, OBERSELISIA,* GERMANY

One evening after I returned to the Lager where I was billetted, our room was on potato peeling. Of course at that time things were very bad as regards food, besides which made things more unpleasant was the shortage of Red X parcels. I was known though our camp for getting any Buckshie soup whenever the opportunity arose. Through that I was claimed the Buckshie King.

Now this evening in particular all we boys were busy peeling spuds. The Sgt. who was in charge said to me, Taffy, if you want some Buckshie soup there is a full pail out in the yard which the Frau from the German kitchen has left. Be careful she doesn't see you take it.

Without hesitation I went for it, full of glee. On my way back the Frau had seen me take it and kept calling me back, but I took no notice of her but hurried into the Billet. I got my chums' bowls besides my own and set to lobbing the soup. I happened to look around and seen that that the Sgt. was laughing. I asked him what was afloat. He then replied that the reason why the Frau went off the deep end because what I had in the pail was not soup but pig swill. I can assure you I felt a fool.

When I realized my mistake and the disappointment in not having soup, after all there and then I lost my name "Buckshie King". The following morning the Frau and the pigs absolutely ignored me.

Can you blame them?

I always kept my distance from soup after that.

> With best wishes
> Buckshie King
> "R.E."   24th 11/43

(*Sapper Jones, Royal Engineers*)
*Obersilesia

79. CONVOY AND ESCORT DURING 1939-40 NORTHERN PATROL AND WESTERN APPROACHES

August 25th 1939
I have just made port after a pleasure cruise to the Atlantic Isles, and war being imminent I am not surprised when I receive my papers and am posted to "HMS Vandyck." My ship is AMC (Armed Merchant Cruiser), later known under the sobriquet of "Admiralty Made Coffins".

Sept 2nd 1939
We clear port on our first commission, our destination New York. Our cargo is of great value. Bullion and American citizens returning home before war is declared, but death is close on our heels.

<u>Sept 3rd 1939</u>

We receive wireless notification of the declaration of war. All water-tight doors are permanently closed and crew are at action stations. 4 pm a loud explosion is heard, and the Anchor Liner "Athenia" a few miles astern has been torpedoed, the first victim of the submarines. We are told to proceed on our course, and without further incident arrive at our destination.

<u>Sept 18th 1939</u>

We proceed to Halifax to escort convoy to England. After seven miserable days lying in Bedford Basin without shore leave, the convoy is finally assembled, and on Sept 28th we proceed to sea with the Cruiser "Berwick" and four Canadian Destroyers in attendance. One old tramp cannot make the convoy speed and the Cruiser orders her to return to Port. After 36 hours the destroyers circle the convoy and then return to Halifax. 12 hours later the Cruiser signals "safe voyage and happy returns" and then steams away and the full responsibility for the safety of the convoy rests with us. It is a monotonous and boring job keeping ships in station, changing speed, continually circling the convoy, ahead, astern, both sides, one escort vessel to protect 14 merchant ships from submarine attack. It is the second convoy to leave for England with food and war material and rather uneventful, with no incidents during the voyage.

We are met by four British destroyers off the coast of Ireland, but a storm blows up and they return to port while we turn into the storm to avoid pooping by the following seas and ride out the storm. Next morning, the weather having abated, we again proceed on our original course and once again the destroyers pick us up.

The convoy splits up as we approach the Channel, two destroyers escorting the ships due in southern ports, whilst the other two and ourselves proceed north bound for Liverpool.

The voyage completed the next day, we are once more ready to proceed to sea. After four months of convoy work we are cheered by the news we are to be relieved and take over Contraband Control work with the Northern Patrol, a much more exciting and interesting occupation. Our work consists of stopping suspected vessels, sending them into port for searching, acting as mother ship to the armed trawlers attached to the patrol, and ready for a fight with any enemy vessel we chance to meet. We spend three months on this work and then we are ordered to the Orkneys as base ship to the RAF and RNFAA.

We are once more back at a damn monotonous job, but only for a short time, and in May we receive orders to sail for Liverpool for a six weeks refit. The prospects look good for leave and a good time ashore to paint the town red, but unfortunately as often happens in war time our orders are cancelled and we receive notice to escort troopships to Narvick for the evacuation of Norway.

We sailed from Liverpool on the 29th May 1940 to meet the troopers at Greenock. The convoy consisted of the following ships: Orient Liners "Oronsay", "Ormonde", "Orama", Blue Star Liner "Arandora Star"; Irish S.P. Ships, "Ulster Monarch", and [*original text continued on page 80 of diary*] "Ulster Prince"; with escort vessel "HMS Vandyck" and four destroyers. We sailed north up the west coast of Scotland and the Hebrides (pleasant memories of cruise day in peace time) and pick up two ships joining the convoy from Kirkwall in the Orkneys.

"Ulster Prince", with escort vessel "H.M.S. Vandyck", and four destroyers. We sailed north up the west coast of Scotland and the Hebrides, (pleasant numar of cruise days in peace time), and pick up two ships joining the conuoy from Kirkwall in the Orkneys. The following day after dropping depth ch the destroyers left the convoy and we took over full charge. On Tuesday 3 June a ship was sighted astern, rapidly overhauling the convoy. Action station were sounded, but she was identified as the C.P.R. liner Duchess York sent to join the convoy. On the 5th June the Cruiser Squadron p us up and the troopships were escorted into Harstad for the evacua whilst we were ordered to patrol the coast to the "North Cape." Our cou was a sixty mile triangular one due North, then west and then South E to our original position, to rejoin the Cruiser Squadron after the evacua was completed. By Sunday the 8th June our triangular sailing seemed to h become circular and made us dizzy, with no sign of any Cruiser to rel us. About 07.30 hrs a message was picked up from the relieving Cruis asking for "Vandyck" position, but unfortunately we must have been R.D by the enemy shore stations and at 10.00 hrs a plane was sighted a head. Action Stations once more and the plane proved to be an enemy "Focke Wulf Condor" a large four motored bomber. The bomber circled s several times, but observing our formidable armaments, which at that ea stage of the war consisted of 2 Four inch Anti-Submarine guns, and t Lewis Guns for defense against aircraft, he decided to attack. Comin in from astern, his first bombs missed the target and he received a load of lead in his guts. The force of the explosion seemed to lift the shi with all her 21,000 tons displacement right out of the water and th down again with a God almighty smash. Steam pipes and joins burst all over the Engine Room. Circling once more the bomber attacks from the stern and ca s low scores three direct hits with thousand pounders, which cause considerable damage a et the ship on fire. The bomber is also seriously hit and makes off towards the coast without trying to machine gun the decks. The water mains damaged beyond repair the fires becom unmanageable, and we are forced to abandon ship. After 3½ hrs in the boats the longest and coldest spell I have ever experienced, we made a landfall on the Island of Ande in the Lofoten Group off the North West coast of Norway. We landed only to be inform hat Norway was capitulating at midnight, and we would be interned until taken prisoners by the Germans. We watched "Vandyck" from our internment camp for a wee coming in on the tide and out again as the tide receded the fires still raging. It took a the old girl to sink, but eventually she did so the the Jerry's did not have the sat of Making her into port. My Birth day gift from the Germans three one thousand pounders I last words on leaving home, I shall be back in fourteen days, it now seems like four years

COLDITZ 24th NOVEMBER 1943.   Ernest Champion.

                                              Lieut [?] R.N.R.

Lieutenant J. E. R. Wood MC, Royal Canadian
Engineers. 'Jerry' Wood was the leading
organiser behind the *Wartime Log* at Colditz.

Lieutenant A. M. (Mike) Sinclair, (1918-1944).
Sinclair attempted to escape on 25 September
1944. He climbed over the fencing, was hit
over the head by the butt of a gun by the
security, but, continued running. The guards
fired at him, one bullet pierced his shoulder,
bouncing off and penetrating his heart. He
was shot dead. He was the only prisoner to
be killed during an escape attempt at Colditz.
The Germans buried him in Colditz cemetery
with full military honours—his coffin was
draped with a Union Flag made by the
German guards, and he received a seven-gun
salute. Both images are taken from *Detour*.

OFLAG IV C
COLDITZ

Séni
31.3.45

To Those who have Governed Us.

This time they died with a cynical smile
A few twisted thoughts and a muttered word,
"Peace in our Time" was the slogan they'd heard
While hysterical crowds were shouting "Sieg Heil".
They knew you'd bungled and would bungle more
But were too tired for anger, too hopeless
To worry about the grim bloodiness
Of the war that followed "War to end War".
Remember they died strong in conviction
That "Peace Everlasting" is only fiction:
But think no less of them for that blast you,
Remember those men your smugness slew
Died with a shrug and a lop-sided grin
Paying the price of your Party's sin.

May — 1944

Lest we forget!

In November 1941 I was living 'incognito' in a certain town in Poland. My hosts at this particular time had a flat near the outskirts of the town. One bright, cold morning I was having breakfast when seven shattering explosions shook the town. "Friendly planes," exclaimed my host, "Come on." We bundled ourselves into coats and rushed out into the street.

I shall never forget the sight that met our eyes. The streets were crowded with people of every age and hundreds more were pouring from their houses. Many were pointing and gazing at the sky, most were hurrying towards the centre of the town. My host grabbed me and rushed me through the mélée till we reached the tram terminus, where people fought to get on the vehicles. At last we got on and bought tickets "to the bombs."

Everywhere people, thousands of them it seemed, were moving rapidly in the same direction. At last we got out near a small square 100 yards from the station. The crowds were very thick, but I could see several ruined houses, some dead horses, ambulances, stretchers, quite a lot of dead, dying or wounded people and masses of broken glass. As each ambulance drove away the throng burst into delirious cheering. "Why are they cheering?" I asked. "They have come to see Germans who have been hacked up by the bombs," was the reply. "Some are dead, others will have much pain and may be mutilated for life. It is good." "But were they all Germans who got hit?" I asked again. My host shrugged. "The majority, I suppose, were our people, but if twenty Germans were killed today, it is worth while."

"It is worth while." That is what Poland thinks today. The Polish armies have long since disappeared, but the people carry on the war. In the concentration camps and prisons, in the gangs of forced labour, or face to face with the firing squad, they remain true to their ally, England. Will England remain true to them?

Grismond Davies-Scourfield.
Lt. 60ᵗʰ Rifles.

From cake tins to—....?

Early one morning, shortly after the recrudescence of the World War in 1939, & as a result of an urgent telephone message from the W.O., two officers - a major & a capt - set off on a secret mission to Reading.

On arrival at Reading they proceeded to the works of Messrs Huntley & Palmer where one of the principals was awaiting them.

The two officers were escorted round that part of the factory devoted to the manufacture of cake & biscuit tins. In these articles the officers took a great deal of interest and, eventually — after all types had been inspected and after much discussion — a particular cake tin was selected.

The representative of H. & P. seemed to be very puzzled and intrigued by the strange behaviour of the military gentlemen — more so when he was asked if he could supply 250,000 of the cake tins within 3 weeks. He agreed that this could be done but could not conceal his curiosity as to the purpose for which they were required. His curiosity was not satisfied, but the reader of this — if there is one — will be luckier.

First, a little explanation is required. Before the war the military authorities had spent a great deal of time & thought in devising an Anti-Tank mine. Eventually they designed what they considered the perfect mine, & even went to the expense of producing one or two which — rumour had it — were kept under glass cases at Chatham!!

This mine was built like a watch & with as much precision. It was beautifully machined and nothing was spared to make it a high grade article — which it was. Unfortunately, in war time mines do not serve their purpose under glass cases, however beautiful they may be; and they are required in millions — not in one's and two's!

When the blue prints of the mine were sent out the manufacturers held up their hands in horror! It was not a practicable proposition to make them in vast numbers, and that is why a cake tin, filled with explosive, and with a strengthened lid and cheap fuze, is

Bombardement de Milan (août 1943).

Le vendredi 13 août 1943, à minuit 35, la sirène réveilla brusquement les prisonniers de guerre blessés et malades de l'hôpital 207 de Milan. Les alertes précédentes, assez nombreuses, d'ailleurs, n'avaient été que rarement suivies du bombardement de la ville par quelques dizaines d'avions alliés. Cependant, la descente aux abris s'effectua comme d'habitude, dans l'ordre et le calme, les grands éclopés étant transportés sur des brancards par les "orderlies" britanniques. Un peu avant une heure du matin, nous entendîmes les premières bombes et le tir de la D.C.A. italienne. Il nous semblait que le bombardement était, cette fois, très sérieux, et effectué par un nombre d'avions considérable. Vers une heure cinq une violente explosion nous fit sursauter, toutes les vitres des portes et soupiraux de l'abri se brisèrent, blessant légèrement quelques prisonniers. Quelque deux ou trois minutes après une seconde explosion ébranla les murs de la cave servant d'abri et le plafond s'écroula avec un bruit effroyable ensevelissant une vingtaine d'officiers et d'orderlies. Je fus plaqué au sol et je sentis les poutres et les pierres s'abattre sur moi. J'avais, heureusement, la tête et une partie du corps sous un banc ce qui me permit de respirer et de ne pas être broyé par les pierres. Au bout de quelques minutes, les secours s'organisèrent et les prisonniers valides commencèrent à délivrer leurs camarades ensevelis sous les décombres. Les sauveteurs, que les soldats italiens n'aidèrent en aucune façon, se dépensèrent sans compter, au milieu de la fumée opaque, au bruit des bombes qui tombaient de tous côtés, à la lueur rouge des incendies et s'attendant à chaque instant à être écrasés sous les ruines de l'hôpital qui menaçait de s'écrouler. Je fus délivré au bout de trois heures d'efforts et certains de mes camarades ne purent être dégagés qu'à l'aube. Le bilan de la catastrophe se soldait par 10 morts, dont 7 officiers britanniques, français et américains et 3 orderlies néo-zélandais, et quelques blessés. La bombe qui avait causé l'effondrement des quatre étages de l'hôpital sur notre abri était une bombe à souffle de grande puissance tombée à environ une trentaine de mètres du bâtiment. Plusieurs qui se trouvaient à quelques centaines de mètres de l'hôpital avaient détruites et brûlèrent jusqu'au matin. Avec une quinzaine de mes camarades je fus transporté dans la matinée au centre des Mutilés de Milan qui devait être évacué le jour même par les blessés italiens qui s'y trouvaient. La première nuit se passa bien mais la nuit suivante eut lieu un bombardement violent. Notre hôpital fut atteint par une bombe explosive et une bombe incendiaire. La nuit suivante, au cours d'un raid non moins important que le précédent, cinq bombes éclatèrent sur l'hôpital qui fut en grande partie détruit. Grâce à Dieu l'abri où nous étions descendus ne fut pas touché et le lendemain matin nous étions évacués sur l'hôpital de Baggio, dans un des faubourgs de Milan. Quelques jours après, nous rejoignîmes le gros de nos camarades...

My home is situated in the centre of a triangle formed by ① Woolwich Arsenal ② North Weald Fighter Aerodrome, and ③ Enfield Small Arms Factory; all important targets of the German bombers, whose raids on London were at that time taking place day and night.

I was fortunate in being at home throughout the entire Battle of London. My ship was commissioning at Tilbury, about 30 miles away, and I was able to get home each evening. I always owe a debt of gratitude to Fate that I was able to be at home during this period. The daily and nightly visits of the Nazi youth who fondly believed they were smashing London into subjection left me, as they left most Londoners, singularly undisturbed. One's nerves were undoubtedly a little frayed, and in most cases the prospect of a peaceful sleep after the day's work was little more than an idle dream. But London certainly did carry on. My wife, as conductress of a Green Line coach did her job bravely and well - but no better, nor more bravely - than did thousands of other women who were doing men's jobs. I was unworried because I was near my wife. I felt that because of that she would be safe - nothing could possibly happen to us. (what egotistical creatures men are!) Or if it did we would at least be together. The people who in my opinion suffered most were those on active service - or in prison camps far away from their homes - who could do nothing but read the glaring headlines with a feeling of utter impotence. Hoping - hoping - hoping - and yet dreading the news that each day might bring.

Such was the state of affairs in October 1940. My wife and I were sitting by the fire at nine o'clock one evening. The sirens sounded, but apart from a glance at the blackout we took no notice. We talked and listened to the wireless. My dog "Flip" scratched and whined at the kitchen door as he always does when the sirens go - we let him in and he took up his usual position on the hearthrug. Soon the bombs began to fall in the distance. The recurring symphony of those days had once more commenced. We hardly interrupted our talking though Flip jumped onto my lap and snuggled up close. The heavy guns in the field opposite the house opened up. Boom! Boom! All the windows & doors shook - Flip trembled and looked up, wondering perhaps at the murderous folly of men. But he too was well used to this kind of entertainment - He too felt safe while he was near to those he loved.

Suddenly the roar of planes was heard approaching and a terrific crash sounded uncomfortably near. Then another - and another - each louder than the one before. Rena flung herself into my arms and Flip whined and crawled under an armchair. Then CRASH! The house shook violently - the lights went out - there was a noise of glass & wood shattering, and the plaster from the ceiling fell on to us. We flung ourselves on the floor in the corner. Rena was shaking & crying - She clung to me - I did my best to calm her - but I, too, was far from calm. Anger - a mad - blind primeval anger seized me. My God - how I hated Hitler - the Nazis - Germans. Had I had the power to destroy every one of them in that moment I would have used that power ruthlessly. War!!! Glory - God and the Fatherland - trumpets blowing & flags flying? or thousands of fine young men dying on the battlefields while their women & children are being slaughtered at home. And this is civilization!! As if the glory of all the war lords in the world are worth one hair from my wife's head or one tear from her eye. My God - how I hated them!

A few seconds - minutes - hours - I don't know how long - we clung together. The planes passed - the din died down - I could hear screams - so we made our way outside. Roof, doors & windows were gone from my house, but we were alive & uninjured. The next street was completely destroyed - already nothing remained but a few walls and piles of bricks & mortar which hid mutilated human bodies - The bodies of wives - mothers - children - sweethearts. Such is Total War - and such, thank God was the spirit of the people of London in those dark months that London still lives - and in the midst of the scars that remain her women can still say with pride "London could take it."

L. M. Horan.
President P.N.P.   (16.10.43)

Vous me demandez, mon cher camarade de vous conter une anecdote de la Légion Étrangère ?... Que puis-je faire de mieux que de vous narrer la mort de TROUFIMOF, un de mes légionnaires que j'aimais beaucoup pour sa bravoure au combat. D'origine Scandinave, bâti en Hercule, mais doux comme un agneau (Dieu merci car il aurait assommé un homme d'une chiquenaude) il trouva chez nous un champ d'action convenant à ses goûts du risque et de l'aventure.

Éveloppé par la grâce, il nous conta, un soir au bivouac, l'histoire de sa vie : mousse à bord d'un voilier Norvégien, à 13 ans il parcourt les océans, de Chine au Chaco du Chaco en Éthiopie hantant les périodes troubles où le trafic d'armes l'intéresse : Un jour, au hasard de ses voyages, faisant escale au Havre il s'écrie, avec un autre matelot, ... première un engagement de 5 ans à la Légion, avec l'espoir fantaisiste de chasser le lion. Hélas ! si au Maroc les lions n'étaient plus, il n'en est pas de même des fameux guerriers rebelles offrant aux légionnaires l'occasion de "barouder" sous le soleil brûlant.

Son camarade ne pouvant tenir le pénible régime de la Légion, déserta alors que Troufimof se trouve chez nous en plein dans son élément et rengage pour 5 ans ; se distingue au combat, gagne le grade de Brigadier. Ses les combats terminés, remet ses galons et demande à tenir le pénible emploi d'infirmier. Il remplit ces fonctions admirablement et semble le plus pacifique des hommes. Voici que la guerre se rallume en Tunisie. Mon escadron (formation spéciale d'assaut) est désigné pour refaire le front en décembre 1942. C'est alors que Troufimof se réveille ; me supplie de l'emmener, de lui confier un F.M. pour lui seul. Cédant à ses instances, au désespoir du "Toubib", je le fais remplacer et n'aurai pas à le regretter. Dès notre arrivée en lignes, toujours prêt aux "coups durs" veillant, patrouillant, tendant des pièges aux patrouilles ennemies il m'est d'un concours précieux, j'ai toutes les peines du monde à l'empêcher de commettre des imprudences et de faire "l'escarmouche" inutilement. Un matin de janvier 43 mon unité reçoit ordre de s'emparer par surprise d'une saillie position ennemi ; c'est une opération délicate il importe que l'affaire soit menée "sans bavure". L'attaque commencée au petit jour s'élance favorablement, mais l'ennemi remis de sa surprise réagit violemment avec ses mitrailleuses et cloue au sol le premier peloton qui doit ouvrir la brèche sur la position dominante, quelques minutes d'hésitation et le coup est manqué !! C'est alors que Troufimof s'infiltre en avant, aborde le nid de mitrailleuses ennemi, mitraille les servants sur leurs pièces, et là debout, calme, dans le déchaînement de la bataille, signale à ses camarades le passage libre ; l'attaque est lancée, ils pénètrent dans les positions, en quelques minutes, l'ennemi est assailli, débordé, neutralisé 180 prisonniers Italiens et Allemands restent entre nos mains, de nombreuses armes dont 4 canons anti-tanks et 6 mortiers. Hélas ! mon brave Troufimof n'eut pas la joie de voir le succès car, son héroïque action achevée, une balle lui fracassa la tête. Je fus profondément attristé en apprenant la mort de ce beau dévouement, qui ignorait le danger.

Ainsi, mon cher camarade, mourut un légionnaire qui avait pour famille que notre régiment, au besoin un héros, son souvenir sera pieusement conservé, comme tant d'autres.

CAPITAINE Gitte

1er RÉG' ÉTRANGER DE CAVALERIE
FEZ - MAROC

Infinitely more thrilling than the escape in the film "The Big House" was the attempt for freedom by F/Lt Thom. R.A.F. although at the time it left us rather shaken.

During the previous afternoon, we three, F/Lt Thom, P/O Van Rood. and myself had been sitting on the terrace during the afternoon exercise discussing the posibilities of escape from our confinement

We were guarded by two posterns with rifles, one at either end of the terrace, while below us some thirty feet down another patrolled the barbed wire, while his companion overlooked us all from a raised shooting box.

The prospect of escape seemed very remote unless the guards could be diverted, and we returned from exercise thinking no more about it.

The following morning at 9 oclock we were fetched by the guards for exercise, and led through the guardroom onto the terrace, one guard proceeding us then myself, Thom, Van Rood, and finally followed up by another Postern.

The postern door to the terrace was opened and we marched out behind the first guard, I stopped and was just lighting a cigarette when I heard Van Rood say "By God he's mad".

séri.
26.3.45

was aware of a pungent smell and the throbbing pain in my ankle. My cloth
maps and the floor were wet with some dark liquid. For one moment I
ght it was blood, but when I rubbed my fingers together it didn't
ght for that. There was the familiar yet unplaceable smell too. Oil! The
hat it was – oil. I called Webster up and told him about the oil. "Stand by for one
engines to cut," I told him. I sniffed and rubbed my fingers together again.
didn't seem to be engine oil somehow. Then it must be oil from the hydraulic
stem. Must be. I informed Webster of this, and told him not to forget to test
aps and the undercarriage before he went in to land, for their unexpected fa
the last moment had killed many an unwary crew.

Then, lying in the gangway about eight feet behind me i
saw some infernal looking thing which again set my heart pounding
th an unreasonable fear. It looked like an iron drum lying on its s
ther like a small edition of the depth charges they drop over the stern o
stroyers. The only answer was to drop it through the escape hatch – and qui
went for the thing expecting to hear it fizzing or ticking away the second
til it should blow us all to Kingdom Come. I reached it, and with
vous clammy hands grabbed hold of it – and then my eyes fell on the
gend printed on its side. It was –

CHEMICAL
ELSAN
LAVATORIES

I was too relieved and too shaken to laugh at my groundless fears. "Good old Elsan
thought. "Dear little lavatories," and sat back to gather my scattered wits
w I knew what the dark liquid was, and the pungent smell. Disinfectan

Only those who know the interior of a Hampden can realise what
volutions the machine must have gone through for the lavatory to e
where it did. It had come adrift from way down aft, rolled
ong the roof, hit the pilot's sheet of armour plating, then dropped do
well into the navigator's position where it emptied itself over the
ckless me.

When we arrived back at our base and I was helped
obble along to the sick bay, there was much hearty laughter at us a
r machine, the latter somewhat tattered and with disinfectan
ipping from here and there. I too felt in a mood for laughte
nt when I got to bed that morning and thought back – especi
f the moment when I wanted to be sick, I laughed again. H
still do – just like that. Ha, ha.

Z

Sorry it's so long – you asked for it!

un arrivons en bordure des aires de dispersion des aérodromes.

Brusquement, deux fusées apparaissent dans le ciel et, quelques secondes après, les feux, pistes s'allument et un avion atterrit. Nous apprendrons plus tard que la patrouille néo-zélandaise est allée cueillir l'équipage à sa descente d'avion et s'est retirée avec deux prisonniers après avoir placé une bombe à retardement dans l'appareil.

A 1 heure, l'heure H prévue, formés en ligne sur un rang, nous pénétrons sur l'aérodrome, à une vitesse d'environ 15 km à l'heure, faisant feu de toutes nos pièces les premiers avions en vue. Nos balles traceuses font un feu d'artifice éblouissant.

Au signal de trois fusées vertes, tirées par le major Stirling et les voitures des ailes, nous adoptons la formation en U renversé figurée ci-contre, que nous conserverons pendant toute la durée de l'opération. Nous parcourons alors méthodiquement un itinéraire, préparé à l'avance sur photos aériennes, parmi les concentrations d'avions, et

navigateur

mitraillons les avions sur notre passage. Certains prennent feu en quelques secondes, sur une rafale d'une dizaine de cartouches. D'autres encaissent deux trois cents balles sans s'enflammer. La défense, évidemment prise au dépourvu et intimidée notre feu, ne réagit qu'au bout d'une vingtaine de minutes et, d'une manière générale, le tir des mitrailleuses et des deux 20 mm Breda qui se manifestent est peu efficace.

A 1 h 45 l'opération est terminée. Une évaluation prudente des résultats, qui sera remise par le major Stirling au Q.G. de la VIIIᵉ Armée, donne 18 avions incendiés et gravement endommagés. Nos pertes se réduisent à un homme tué, un blessé, et une voiture, mise hors d'action, abandonnée sur le terrain.

L'opération est terminée, mais il nous reste à rejoindre notre base. Nous savons qu'à le lever du jour, nous serons pris en chasse par l'aviation ennemie. Aussi avons nous l'ordre, par groupes de deux ou trois voitures, de prendre le plus de champ possible pendant les heures de nuit qui nous restent, d'être camouflés à l'aube au moment des premières reconnaissances ennemies et de passer la journée sur place sans mouvements d'aucune sorte. Tout se passe bien, dans la journée du 24, pour la plupart des détachements. malheureusement, deux voitures françaises, ralenties pendant la nuit par plusieurs crevaisons, sont repérées et attaquées par trois Stukas à la fin de la matinée, et l'aspirant André ZIRNHELD, croix de guerre, M.C., l'un des meilleurs officiers parachutistes français d'Orient, est tué par une rafale de mitrailleuse.

Dans la nuit du 24 au 25 juillet, tous les détachements rejoignent notre base dans le désert.

Colditz, Juin 1944

Cᵐ A. Jordan

Forces aériennes françaises

Captain	F. W. C	Weldon,	R. H. A
Lieut.	J. R. E.	Hamilton-Baillie,	R. E.
Captain	G. P.	Campbell-Preston	Black Watch
Captain	D. H.	Walker	Black Watch
Lieut.	M. G.	Wittett	Royal Scots
Lieut.	I. B.	Macaskie	Q. O. R. W. K.
Captain	Sir P.	Greenwell	Surrey & Sussex Yeoma
Captain	K. E.	Hermon	D. L. I.
Lieut.	M.	Scott	D. L. I.
Lieut.	L. R. A.	Cocksedge	R. I. Fusiliers
Captain	J. A.	Tweedie	Cameron Highland
Captain	R. R.	Baxter	A. I. F.
Lieut.	J. W. K.	Champ	A. I. F.
Lieut.	M. A.	Howard	A. I. F.
Lieut.	C. E.	Sandbach	Cheshire Yeomanry
Lieut.	E. A.	Hannay	Seaforth Highland
Captain	D. A.	Crawford	A. I. F.
Lieut.	J. L.	Pumphrey	Northumberland Hu
Lieut.	D. N.	Moir	R. T. R
Lieut.	M.	Farr	D. L. I
Lieut.	J. T. P	Mellor	Arg. & Suth.
Major	B. D. S.	Ginn	R. E. M. E.
Captain	C. H.	Keenlyside	Q. O. R. W. K.
Lieut.	F. M.	Edwards	R. W. Fusiliers
Lieut.	P.	McLaren	Arg. & Suth.
Lieut.	S. C. T	Elms-Neale	R. A.
Captain	M. J.	Gilliatt	K. R. R. C.
Lieut.	P.	Pardoe	K. R. R. C.
Lieut.	H. B.	Collett	Yorkshire Hussars
Captain	W. J.	Burton	Yorks & Lancs
Captain	J.	Fawcus	Northumberland F
Lieut.	C. A.	Elson	R. Norfolk R.
Lieut.	H. C. W.	Ironside	R. T. R.
Lieut.	J. P.	Fergusson	R. T. R.
Lieut.	G. S.	Drew	Northumberland R

(Copy)

─── EICHSTÄTT EPIC ───

Once in days of Blätterbauer. Frank and Baillie had a thought,
Decided not to waste an hour; so a plan they straight way sought.
Campbell-Preston, David Walker, helped to make a wondrous scheme,
And at last they had a corker, so began to form a team.
And they formed a team of wonder-specialists of every rank
Names which made the heavens thunder — names which in our nostrils stank
Michael Wittet 'ersatz' Scotsman — worked with Bruce both night and day;
Peter Greenwell, Kenneth Hermon, Michael Scott who could not stay;
Alan Cocksedge and John Tweedie worked together on a shift.
Rex and Jack and young Mark Howard tried so hard great rocks to lift.
Young men, old men, men like Sandy, worked along with men like Ed.
Dougie Crawford Laurie Pumphrey worked 'till they were nearly dead.
Duggie Moir — great man of spirit — Michael Farr to help him on
Worked so hard with Jimmy Mellor — dug the record five feet long.
'Skelly' Ginn, a one-eyed monster, kept the lamp and kept it good.
Keenlyside and Michael Edwards stowed the earth and pinched the wood
Pat McLaren and Elms-Neale — stooging hard from every crack
Martin Gilliatt, and Phil Pardoe pulling hard to bring earth back.
Harry Collett and Bill Burton — silent men, but very strong.
Types like Fawcus, Clem and Hugo — all these men could do no wrong

Worthy men! and none were pupils; men prepared to die or do
Men in fact just lacking scruples — men like Fergusson and Drew.

Then was made a wondrous tunnel — almost perfect, very grand
With an entrance by a lat. seat, room enough inside to stand.
Fitted up with every comfort, cigarettes and pipe to hand.
Efficient air pipe, sucking madly, also used as telephone
(Upstairs just remove the stopper, hear the wretched workers groan.)
Bells and bags and ropes and trolleys. Oh! What chaos down below.
Stacking bags and rocks and rubbish — how we did it, I don't know
Stooging was our greatest bug-bear; stooging here and stooging there,
In the post room, in the attic — we were stooging everywhere.
Tons of earth in little packets, packets slung on canvas bands,
Carried miles to be well hidden — Had to have some extra hands.

(P. T. O.)

Lieut. the Hon. D.		Fellows	Rifle Bde.
Captain the Lord		Arundell of Wardour,	Wiltshire R
Captain the Earl		of Hopetoun	Lothian & Border H
Lieut.	C. R.	Weld-Forester	Rifle Bde.
Lieut.	P. H.	Parker	K. R. R. C.
Lieut.	E. A. J.	Lochrane	Seaforth Highlande
Lieut.	C. I. C.	Dieppe	A. I. F.
Lieut.	J. M.	Courtenay	Q. Y. R.
Lieut.	A. L.	McCall	Cameron Highland
Captain	R. W.	Leah	Cameron Highlan
Lieut.	A. J. R.	Bissett	Seaforth Highlande
Lieut.	S. N.	Martin	R. A. S. C
Lieut.	D. E.	Bartlett	R. T. R
Lieut.	W. H.	Scott	Essex Scottish (Cana
Lieut.	G.	Bolding	A. I. F.
Lieut.	J. W.	Beaumont	D. L. I.
Lieut.	T. M.	Barott	Black Watch (Cana
Sgt. Maj.	S.	Perry	R. T. R
Lt.-Col.	C. C. I.	Merritt, V.C.	Saskatoon Rifles
Lieut.	J. E.	Wood	Royal Can. Engrs.
Major	G. M.	Rolfe	Royal Can. Signals
Lieut.	W. A.	Millar	Royal Can. Engrs
Lieut.	M. Y. B.	Rivière	Notts Yeomanry.
Captain	S. C.	Wright	9th Q. R. Lancers
Lieut.	J. R.	Penman	Arg. & Suth.
Lieut.	J. H.	Roy	Fus. Mont. Royal
Lieut.	A. G.	Vandalac	Fus. Mont. Royal
Lieut.	A. R.	Marchand	Fus. Mont. Royal
Lieut.	J. R.	Millett	A. I. F.
Lieut.	D. K.	Hamilton	R. A.

First of all came David Fellowes, willing stooge in every camp.
Lords appeared, both John and Charlie, working in onto the ramp.
The other Charlie, Peter Parker helped to swell this élite throng
John Lochrane, Dieppe and Courtenay present with his whiskers long,
McCall and Leah (both brawny Scotsmen), Bissett too, the damned old ram.
Paddy Martin, Denis Bartlet – all were sharing in the jam,
Two colonials, Scott and Bolding, came to join in on the fun
All were very willing workers, helping things to smoothly run.

Numbers big, but still undaunted, "Siggy" Jackson called for more.
Combed the camp from top to bottom, begging chaps: "Come in and draw."
In the draw came all the loafers – men with just the faintest hope,
Men like Beaumont men like Barott – tried to bribe their way with soap
Men like Sgt.Maj. Perry (quite a different type, its true
He'd escaped from every Stalag; the loafing game he quite well knew)
Col. Merritt had a partner, but the wretched man got stuck,
So a miner "Craggy Jerry" had the greatest stroke of luck.
Gordon Roffe and "Dopey" Millar came along with Mike Revière.
"Screwy" Stephen and John Penman, neither of them knowing fear.
Frank chose Penman as a guide post, but left Stephen in the rear
In their normal charming manner, French-Canadians sent in three
Jack and Hamish waking early, both got up to go and pee,
Got mixed up with Hector Christie — being sleepy, did agree.
So they passed right up the tunnel : early morning found them free.

But there is no happy ending to this epic which is sad,
For the Goons just combed the country 'till they found us – which was bad.
Back into the cells at Eichstätt, then up to the Schloss were sent.
What its like, I cannot tell you, because up there I never went.
Now we are at happy Colditz — budding men of spirit we,
With the embryonic madmen, some as mad as mad can be.
If with this, you are offended, then dear Reader please be kind
Not your fault, and not the writers, but the rhyme's so hard to find.

Composed and written,
   31. January 1944,
      Oflag. IV C., Colditz.

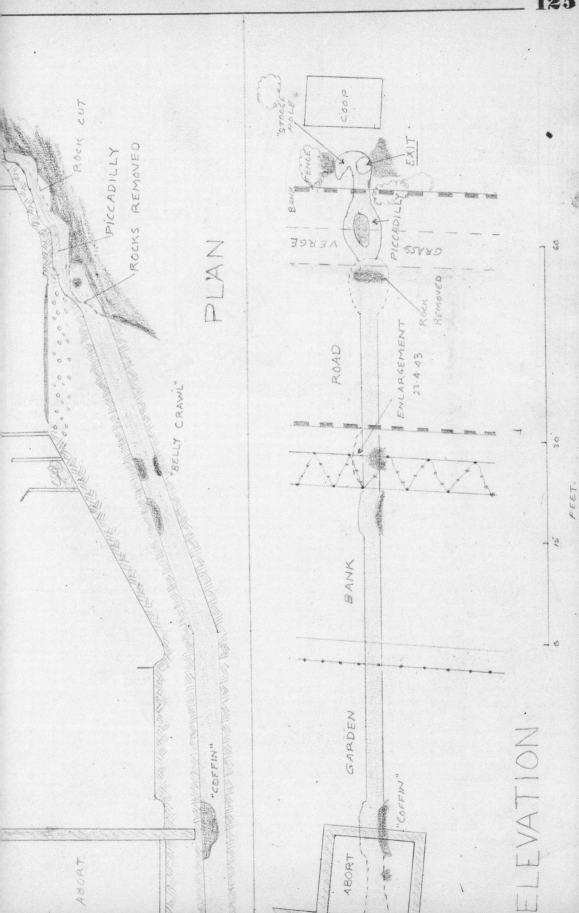

possible. When Bill struck the dummy, the rope broke about 20' from
ground. When Dougie and I went down it was impossible to keep it wound as
fast so we had little control and as a result Dougie sprained his ankle,
wrenched my spine and nearly knocked myself cold from a knee to the jaw —
very pretty show though.

We sorted ourselves out in the best way possible, collected our poor
little dummy and after recovering for a few minutes, moved as quick as
may from the Sellers. The undergrowth was thick and was a great misery to
Dougie and I due to injuries. Also it was very noisy. Eventually we came to
a village below, circled around it after going through a stream which was
to the thighs, and reached the railway track we planned to follow.
Going about 300 yards along the track we were challenged. At the
girl was leading by about 15 yards, Dougie hobbling along at centre
brought up the rear. On being challenged I turned towards our chal-
thinking Bill and Dougie would be able to run for it. Bill ran but
ankle was too troublesome so he turned back towards me. Our captor
S.S. soldier who had been in a "waiting booth" beside the railway
track with a rather attractive girl friend. What a life ..... in the bag.

S. W. Rolfe, Sgt
R.C. Signals

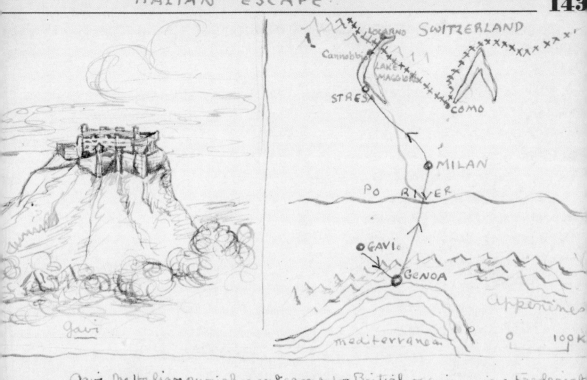

Gavi

Gavi, the Italian punishment camp for British officers, is a Frederick barossa medieval fortress 40 miles north of Genoa, built solidly onto a needle rock which rises from a rolling plain of vineyards and grain, and looks south to the Ligurian mountains. Behind it to the north, and only 10 miles away, Marengo, scene of Napoleon's greatest Italian victory.

Inside the fortress in close seclusion live 180 British officers. Three hundred guards are employed on the task of picketing the battlements; 20 carabinieri (the Italian soldier-police) look after inside security; and a carabinieri Brigadier General is Commandant with a staff of 15 officers under him. Comparing Gavi with its German equivalent at Colditz (where I fetched up a year later) it seemed to me that although the Germans employed the same laws and careful security measures, the Italians were more expert and effective at this kind of work. For one thing, Italian guards were better — more alert, more suspicious — and the Italians interfered more with your private life, if a prisoner can be said to have one, so that work was difficult.

Now it is April, 1943. Eight officers and 2 batmen are watching the weather with anxiety. An escape, 8 months in preparation, is due to break, and success depends on very special weather conditions.

There are 4 South African officers: Palm, Pole, Wuth and Patterson. They discovered the intricate route, and have been responsible with the 2 batmen for most of the hard work. Then there is Cram, in peacetime an Edinburgh lawyer, now the most-escaped officer in Italian hands; Medical officer with his Sapper partner Daly; Stirling, recently captured at Tunis; myself; and finally 2 batmen: Macrae and Headley. The

Above left: Lieutenant Colonel C. C. I. Merritt, VC, South Saskatchewan Regiment.

Above right: General Bór-Komorowski, Polish Army.

Above left: Lieutenant John Roy, Fusiliers, Mont Royal.

Above right: Lieutenant Simon Hacohen, Royal Engineers.

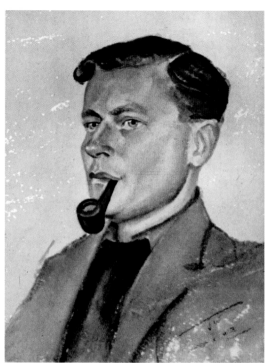

Above left: Light Lieutenant A. Van Rood. 'A Dutchman in the Royal Air Force'.

Above right: Lieutenant-Commander L. W. Harvey, Royal Navy.

Above left: Major G. L. Rolfe DSO, Royal Canadian Signals.

Above right: Captain G. M. Pemberton How, Royal Army Service Corps.

Above left: Flight Lieutenant Cenek Chalupka, Royal Air Force.

Above right: Flight Lieutenant M. W. Donaldson, Royal Air Force.

Above left: Lieutenant T. M. Barott, 1st Battalion the Black Watch (RHR) of Canada.

Above right: Lieutenant J. M. Courtenay, Queen Victoria Rifles.

Above left: Lieutenant W. H. Scott, Essex Scottish Regiment of Canada.

Above right: Lieutenant Alan Campbell, Royal Artillery.

Above left: Flying Officer Keith Milne, Royal Air Force.

Above right: Lieutenant D. E. Bartlett MC, 3 Battalion Royal Tank Regiment.

Above left: Captaine Charles Jordan MC, Free French Force.

Above right: Flight Lieutenant Vincent Parker, Royal Air Force.

Above left: Captain I. Schrire, Royal Army Medical Corps.

Above right: Flying Officer Peter D. Tunstall, Royal Air Force.

Above left: Captain D. J. Rogers, Royal Engineers.

Above right: Howard Gee

Above left: Paymaster-Lieutenant J. N. Moran, Royal Naval Reserve.

Above right: Lieutenant C. W. B. Purdon MC, Commando.

Oflag IVc at night.

A volley ball game in the courtyard.

Collecting Red Cross
Parcels.

An aerial view of Colditz *c.* 1946.

Oflag IVc has been dramatized many times on television and in film. This atmospheric still is from the 1955 Guy Hamilton film, *The Colditz Story*.

Two modern photographs of Colditz Castle. *Wikimedia Commons*

...e had been waiting in a washroom in the camp hospital for ab...
...mins one fine winter morning, when we were told to start. Th...
...e of us, disguised as a Sonderführer, three Frenchmen & a...
...try with rifle, went down the stairs, out on to the road &...
...ned left towards the gate twenty yards away. The ge...
...n sentry opened the gate as he saw us approaching &...
...od to attention as we passed. We turned left on t...
...main road running past the camp & as we pass...
...sentry tower at the corner of the camp George ...
...Sonderführer, turned to Stewart Walker, the sent...
...said in German, "A bit quicker, Meyer," apart from...
...& Stewart's orders to the other three of us no one said...
...thing, the Germans apparently assuming that we were...
...usual French party for the dentist. We walked along...
...road, George occasionally acknowledging a salute,...
...ned left on the outskirts of the village & made our way to a wo...
...the hill south of the village. Here we hid our French clothes...
...German uniforms & tidied the civilian clothes which we...
...re wearing underneath our disguise.   Then, Stew...
...wart Walker, who had chosen a different route from ou...
...other four of us split into two parties of two & started the...
...ble walk to Eichstätt junction. Terence Prittie & I reached...
...station in good time & after a short wait we caught the mid...
...ning train to Munich. We did not see Tom Acton & George agai...
...er we got on the train until we reached Tuttlingen the next da...
...ad to wait fifteen hours in Munich, because we could only be su...
...voiding an inspection of our papers by travelling on slow trains &...
...e were few of these.   We arrived in Munich at about...
...lock in the afternoon, &, as we had already decided to avoid the...
...tion during our wait, we went to the cinema. Until 11 o'clock th...
...ht we spent the time in cinemas & in a bar, after which we...
...lked round & round the town till the train for Ulm left at 4:...
...next morning. I was very tired when we boarded the train &...
...pt all the way to Ulm, where we changed into a train which...
...th us to Tuttlingen, about 20 miles from the Swiss frontier. W...
...no trouble on the trains apart from almost being locked in a lavatory in...
...ema & my asking Terence for some soap in English in the station lavatory...
...e was no crisis in Munich.   At Tuttlingen we met George & Tom...
...ted to walk to the frontier which we hoped to reach early the next...
...ning; it was then 4 o'clock in the afternoon. After an ho...

[cont. p.78

The following day after dropping depth charges, the destroyers left the convoy and we took full charge. On Tuesday 3rd June a ship was sighted astern, rapidly overhauling the convoy. Action stations were sounded, but she was identified as the C.P.R. Liner "Duchess of York" sent to join the convoy.

On the 5th June the Cruiser Squadron picked us up and the troopships were escorted into Harstad for the Evacuation whilst we were ordered to patrol the coast to the "North Cape". Our course was a sixty mile triangular one due north, then west and then south-east to our original position, to rejoin the cruiser squadron after the evacuation was completed. By Sunday the 8th June our triangular sailing seemed to have become circular and made us dizzy, with no sign of any cruisers to relieve us. About 0730 hours a message was picked up from the relieving cruiser asking for "Vandyck's" position, but unfortunately we must have been R.D.F.ed by enemy shore stations as at 10.00 hours a plane was sighted dead ahead. Action stations once more and the plane proved to be an enemy, a "FockeWulf Condor", a large four-motored bomber.

The bomber circled around several times, but observing our formidable armaments, which at that early stage of the war consisted of 2 four-inch anti-submarine guns, and two Lewis guns for defence against aircraft, he decided to attack. Coming in from astern, his first bombs missed the target and he received a load of lead in his guts. The force of the explosion seemed to lift the ship with all her 21,000 tons displacement right out of the water and then down again with a God Almighty smash, stem pipes and joints bursting all over the Engine Room.

Circling once more the bomber attacks from the stern and coming in low scores three direct hits with thousand pounders, which cause considerable damage and set the ship on fire. The bomber is also seriously hit and makes off towards the coast without trying to machine gun the decks.

The water mains damaged beyond repair, the fires become unmanageable, and we are forced to abandon ship. After 36 hours in boats, the longest and coldest spell I have ever experienced, we made a landfall on the Island of Andhoy in the Lefoten Group off the north-west coast of Norway. We landed only to be informed that Norway was capitulating at midnight and we would be interned until taken prisoners by the Germans. We watched "Vandyck" from our internment camp for a week coming in on the tide and out again as the tide receded, the fires still raging. It took a week for the old girl to sink, but eventually she did. The Jerrys did not have the satisfaction of taking her into port. My birthday gift from the Germans, three one thousand pounders. My last words on leaving home, I shall be back in fourteen days, it now seems like fourteen years.

Colditz 27th November 1943

Ernest Champion, Lieut. (E) R.N.R.

81. ESCAPE FROM EICHSTÄTT

We had been waiting in a washroom in the camp hospital for about 10 mins, one fine winter morning, when we were told to start. The five of us, disguised as a Sonderführer, three Frenchmen and a sentry with rifle, went down the stairs, out onto the road and turned left towards the gate twenty yards away. The German sentry opened the gate as he saw us approaching and stood to attention as we passed. We turned left on to the main road running past the camp and as we passed the sentry tower at the corner of the camp George Kane, the Sonderführer, turned to Stewart Walker, the sentry and a." Apart from this and Stewart's orders to the other three of us, no one said anything. The Germans apparently assumed that we were the usual French party for the dentist. We walked along the road, George occasionally acknowledging a salute, turned left on the outskirts of the village and made our way to a wood on the hill south of the village. Here we hid our French clothes and the German uniforms and tidied the civilian clothes which we were wearing underneath our disguise.

Then, leaving Stewart Walker, who had chosen a different route from ours, the other four of us split into two parties of two and started the 2 mile walk to Eichstätt Junction. Terence Prithie and I reached the station in good time and after a short wait we caught the mid-morning train to Munich. We did not see Tom Acton and George again after we got on the train until we reached Tuttlingen the next day. We had to wait fifteen hours in Munich, because we could only be sure of avoiding an inspection of our papers by travelling on slow trains, and there were few of these.

We arrived in Munich at about 1 o'clock in the afternoon, and as we had already decided to avoid the station during our wait, we went to the cinema. Until 11 o'clock that night we spent the time in cinemas and in a bar, after which we walked round and round the town till the train for Ulm left at 4.30 the next morning. I was very tired when we boarded the train and slept all the way to Ulm, where we changed into a train which took us to Tuttlingen, about 20 miles from the Swiss frontier. We had no trouble on the train and apart from almost being locked in a lavatory in a cinema and my asking Terence for some soap in English in the station lavatory, there was no crisis in Munich.

At Tuttlingen we met George and Tom and started to walk to the frontier, which we hoped to reach early the next morning; it was than 4 o'clock in the afternoon. After an hour's [*original text continued on page 78 of diary*] walk we waited in a wood until it was dark. Soon after we started again we passed a few scattered houses, where a dog barked and someone opened a window. It was here that we first aroused suspicion, as we subsequently discovered. We walked for another 5 or 6 miles and came to a railway bridge over the road, where we realised that we had missed a turning. While we were discussing what we should do we heard footsteps on the road behind, so we walked on quickly intending to get well ahead and then stop for another discussion of plans.

We were going through a small village and had come to a side road, when suddenly men armed with all kind of weapons sprang on to the road all round us, shouting at us to halt and to put up our hands. Protesting our innocence we were hustled into a nearby inn where there was a Gestapo man, who was apparently in charge of the local frontier guards. He scorned our papers and excuses and sent us under escort to Singen police station, from where we eventually returned crestfallen to Eichstätt.

J. McDonnell, Royal Norfolk Regt.
3/7/44 Colditz

En Syrie après l'armistice de Juin 1940, et l'appel du Général de Gaulle les sympathisants, au mouvement créé par ce dernier, s'étaient groupés en solides n... dans chaque garnison. Malheureusement les événements ultérieurs devaient, plus q... la propagande de Vichy, dissoudre ces groupes, si sincères et enthousiastes. Je parle en particulier, de ce qui concerne le groupe de R... où je me trouvais. Le premier bomb... effectué sur la Syrie au mois de mai ... alors que les hostilités n'étaient pas encore déclarées, et que rien, tout au moins pour R... ne motivait un pareil acte.

Nous étions malgré les défections qui se produisirent, assez nombre... à R... et comme nous avions depuis janvier 1941 pris contact avec les Français libres de Palestine étions à même d'agir comme par le passé. Notre action se bornait à renforcer le mouvem... par une propagande active en faveur de la résistance, à faciliter, à tout ceux qui désiraient le passage de la frontière à destination de la Palestine. Et enfin à fournir a... moyen d'un poste radio émetteur. tout les renseignements concernant... les commissions d'armistice et leurs agissements.

Après le bombardement dont j'ai parlé plus haut, notre situa... devint critique du fait, que dans les éléments qui nous avaient quittés, plusieurs étaient partiellement au courant de notre activité. Elle fut aggravée par les m... prises par la police et l'armée à la suite de la destruction parfaitement réussie... plusieurs trains d'armes et d'explosifs, dirigés sur l'Irak par les Allemands, pour... rebelles alors en lutte contre les Alliés. La parade à notre activité devait se faire sentir rapidement puisque le 3 juin 1941 quelques jours après le fait précédemment cité, un coup de filet géant était donné sur la région de R... le 3 au matin la Sûreté Générale assistée de la gendarmerie et de sections de Légion Étrangère restées fidèles à Vichy nous encerclaient et arrêtaient tout les suspects gaullistes. La veille que so... ayant eu à passer des messages par radio. J'étais chargé du poste. Je n'y étais pas au mess pour dormir et je dus à cela de n'être pas arrêté dans les premiers. J'étais chez un camarade qui logeait en ville. Remarquant une agitation anorm... en ville, nous comprîmes immédiatement la raison. Je m'habillais avec d... vêtements arabes que nous avions en prévision d'un départ toujours possible. et réussis à passer ainsi les barrages organisés pour interdire toute sortie.

Sorti de la ville je gagnais les montagnes du Liban où... pouvais trouver un abri pour quelques jours relativement sûr. Je réussis à prendre contact avec des amis fidèles qui étaient très inquiets de mon ... car, il avait été annoncé que j'avais été tué en essayant de fuir. Ils m'appr... également qu'un autre camarade le Sergent Chef R... avait aussi réussi s'enfuir, je pris rendez vous avec eux pour plus tard dans le cas où L... viendra... aussi les voir, de manière à ce que nous puissions nous joindre. J'emportais des pro... pour plusieurs jours, pain arabe que se conserve très longtemps, ail, tomates, et je co... sur les jardins se trouvant dans la montagne pour végéter plus longtemps. Le ... juin les hostilités étaient ouvertes et cet acte me coupait irrévocablement le ch... de la frontière. Je vécus pendant dix jours, dehors, changeant continuellement... place transi de froid la nuit, manquant d'eau le jour dans un grand état de faiblesse n'étant pas nourri suffisamment. Après ce temps je m'en fus au rendez vous dont j'ai parlé, où j'eus la joie de retrouver L... nous repartim... tout deux ayant adopté ma manière de vivre comme étant la plus sûre n'exposant pas la sûreté, des personnes qui auraient pu consentir à nous ca...

Nous vécûmes ainsi durant quarante sept jours. constamment en alerte, et à bout de forces, lorsque les premiers élém...

britanniques firent leur apparition.

Notre aventure faillit se terminer tragiquement pour nous car ne tenant compte ni de notre méconnaissance de l'anglais, ni de l'aspect quelque peu bizarre que nous avions dans nos vêtements arabes, avec nos longues barbes sales. L'Officier britannique à qui nous nous présentâmes dit nous prendre pour des fous ou des espions, ce que j'aurais sans doute fait à sa place, et nous fit mettre sous surveillance jusqu'à l'arrivée d'un interprète. nous pûmes obtenir de téléphoner à notre officier le capitaine R.P. qui fit le nécessaire immédiatement et le soir même douchés, rasés et habillés de neuf nous étions assis à la table devant un superbe repas auquel nous ne fîmes pas l'honneur qu'il méritait, notre estomac serré depuis longtemps se refusant à tout travail. Nous l'avions échappé belle mais hélas! ce n'était que partie remise –

Sgt E.C. COLDITZ 10/11/.

Castanet

2 Cie PARATROOP

82. SYRIE—MAI-JUIN 1941*

In Syria after the Armistice of June 1940 and General de Gaulle's appeal, his followers rallied in solid little groups in each garrison. Unfortunately subsequent events, far more than any Vichy propaganda, proved strong enough to dissipate these groups, sincere and enthusiastic though they were. I refer, particularly to the group at R . . . where I was stationed. The first bombs were dropped in Syria in May 41 though hostilities had not yet been declared and, as far as R . . . was concerned, there seemed no motive for such an act.

Though a number of people left us, we still remained fairly numerous at R . . . and as, since June 41, we had established contact with the Free French in Palestine, we were in a position to do something. For the time being our action consisted of strengthening the movement by an active propaganda campaign in favour of the Resistance and in providing facilities for people who wanted to cross the Palestinian frontier. Finally we managed to set up a radio set and send out information regarding the Armistice Commissions and their nefarious doings.

After the bombardment which I mentioned above, our position became rather critical as some of the individuals who left us were in a position to know all about our activities. Matters became worse because of steps taken by the police and the army resulting in the complete destruction of numerous German trains headed for Iraq, loaded with arms and explosives for the rebels, who were then fighting against the Allies. The counter measures against us were not long in making themselves felt for on 3 June 41, a few days after the incident referred to above, a mass raid was carried out in the district of R . . . At three in the morning, the Security Police assisted by the local police and patrols from the Foreign Legion, who had remained loyal to Vichy, surrounded us and arrested all Gaullist suspects. The evening before, as there had been messages to transmit by radio, I had taken a tour of duty. I did not go back to the mess to sleep and it is to that I owe the fact that I was not arrested among the very first. I had gone to stay with a friend of mine who was lodging in town. When we noticed that there seemed to be an abnormal amount of animation in the town, we understood at once what was happening. I dressed myself in Arab clothes, which had been kept ready for just such an emergency, and managed to pass through the controls set up to prevent any exit from town.

After making my escape, I headed for the Lebanese mountains where I knew I could find a safe refuge for a few days. I managed to make contact with some trusted friends of mine whom I found very worried about what might have happened to me, for the news had been given out that I had been killed while attempting to escape. I also learnt from them that another friend of mine, Sergeant Major L . . . had likewise succeeded in escaping. I made an arrangement with them to let me know should L . . . also come to see them and in this way we would be able to get together.

I set off again with enough food for several days. This consisted of Arab bread, which keeps for a long time, as well as garlic and tomatoes, and I counted on living off the gardens which are to be found in the mountain country. On the sixth of June hostilities commenced, and this act cut off irrevocably my route to the frontier. I lived out of doors for the next ten days, moving

---

* *Syria—May-June 1941*

constantly from place to place. I suffered severely from cold at night and lack of sufficient water to drink in the day-time. I was also very weak indeed as I had insufficient to eat. At the end of this time I went to the rendezvous which I had spoken about and to my great joy found L . . . there. We set off together and followed the same tactics that I had previously adopted, as it meant that we did not have to endanger other persons by asking them to hide us.

We lived like this for 47 days, constantly on the alert and pretty well at the end of our tether, when the forward [*original text continued on page 83 of diary*] British troops made their appearance.

Our adventure nearly ended tragically for us because we forgot to take into account our ignorance of English and our bizarre appearance because of our Arab clothes and our long scruffy beards. The British officer we presented ourselves to must have taken us for lunatics or spies and I would certainly have done the same in his place. He kept us under guard until an interpreter could be fetched. We got permission to telephone to our C.O, Capt. R.P., who at once took all the necessary steps and that very evening, after a shower and a shave and dressed in new clothes, we sat down to a sumptuous meal to which, unfortunately, we failed to do adequate honour. We had been starving for so long that our stomachs were unable to cope.

We had had a lucky escape, but unfortunately, it was only a matter of time.

Sgt. C.C.
Castanier, 2Cie Paratroops
Colditz 10/11/43

85. REPORTED KILLED IN ACTION—ST. OMER—12 APRIL 42

Our wing was climbing slowly as we flew along the South Coast on our way to the rendezvous with the Bostons and the other fighter wings. Target: Hasebrouck at noon. We were detailed as Freelance Wing to intercept the German fighters from St. Omer Jägerhorst. Visibility was practically unlimited, the Channel a grey steel plate, Sussex a smoky smudge and the French cliffs sharply outlined. The Wing kept the wide flung, difficult battle formation beautifully as we climbed thru' a layer of cold air at 25 thousand feet, leaving conspicuous and betraying vapour trails, which broke off abruptly as the Wing rose above it. The three squadrons, strung out in line abreast, stepped down a thousand feet at a time to the sun, at half mile intervals; each squadron a miniature replica of the whole Wing, with the three sections in line abreast stepped down with 300 yard intervals. The four planes or each section are "snaking thro'" flying in a very slightly zigzagged line astern, which as a whole "weaves" imperceptibly. The Wing moves fast at this height, it performs majestic sweeping half circles while it climbs to its final operational ceiling round about 35 thousand feet. The accurate coordination of all these individual highly mobile planes, within their gigantic but supple organism forms a huge three-dimensional tactical unit, which manoeuvres as one thinking whole.

Along the South Coast, from the Isle of Wight to Beachy Head, we climbed steadily in a straight line. Over Beachy Head we met and left the bombers behind us, and their escort of nine wings: Bee Hive, Medium Support and Topcover, a flexible unity many times greater

There, at last, a "kette" of six F.W.'s coming down, making for our lowest section. They dive past us and the Wing commander orders the middle section to engage them, and then, as an afterthought, we to join middle section. After them! I pull the nose of my aircraft up and over into a steep dive and curse the middle which has several hundred feet altitude start on me. A voice: "On your tail, Red Three, on your tail." I hardly turned my head when the first tracer appears to enmesh my plane like whipthongs and simult- ly holes the size of my fist appear in my port wing. I remember thinking they were too large for M.G., too sm for 20 mm cannon. But I have instinctively jerked my plane up and round, toward the left, toward the a He makes an astonishing error, turns in behind me — does he think he can out turn me? We make our ti blacking out, juddering, half stalled circle — and there he is, in my sight. I feel the recoil of my cann and he suddenly straightens out, large fragments of fuselage are ripped out of his plane and fly by Again I fire — the Focke Wulf rears up like a live animal, and breaks in two with one big flame from petrol tank between cockpit and engine.

I see the pilot slump out of the wreckage and then my cockpit is filled with tracer smoke, the in ments on my dash board lose their faces, rapid heavy thudding against the back armour of my seat, la holes are torn in the Perspex. As I turn the plane over on its back to dive out of this cone of fire I reali my engine is hit, too. Oil is blown back in greenish waves over the cowling and flows black thru' the up Perspex into my face, over my goggles. I keep on diving, a tight spiral dive, that second Boche w be able to follow me in that. Tearing my goggles off, I see that the airscrew is no longer turning — a airbrake in front of the heavy, useless weight of my wounded engine. Somehow the sight of the airs standing still, a sight which I have never before seen while airborne, brings out all the fear wh I was too busy to feel a minute ago, and a great hopelessness takes the place of the warm confiden which I've always had in my Merlin. At about 18 thou' I pull out and tear the lacerated, oild cockpit cover back. I am roughly 3 miles North of St. Omer, not far from the Channel. Perha I will be able to glide that far — in the Channel I have at least the chance of being picked up by o Air Sea Rescue units. I notice that my right leg is numb and flaccid, blood gushing out of a large on the inside of the thigh, my flying boot on that foot warm and squelching with blood. I try the plane into a proper glide, but with the airscrew not even turning over, and the streamlin cockpit cover destroyed she glides very badly — I am losing too much height. Glancing behi me, an automatic action in a fighter pilot, wherever he is, I see two F.W.'s rapidly overtaking Christ, I will never reach the Channel now. I let them come closer without altering course, and as th one opens fire, I jerk the plane violent bently into a spin. This is a last trick of desperation — ma they'll think I've had it and not follow me down. Pulling out at about three thousand feet — she doe recover properly, the middle must have caught it too — I find I haven't fooled them. They were a back bot at once — and the next thing I know is, that a sheet of flame bursts thru' the dashboard, I tear the pin of the Sutton harness, kick the stick forward, the blinding, unbearable tear of petrol flame enve me, and, as I am thrown violently out of the exploding plane by the centrifugal force of the sudden dow turn, I feel my oxygen mask being torn off my face by the tube, still connected to the plane. The ground rushing up, I jerk the ripcord, nothing seems to happen for ages, and then, as everything inside contracts, anticipating the inevitable collision with the earth, the violent jerk of the opening cano and almost simultaneously I hit some ploughed ground, my legs crumpling under me. —

A. van Rood F/Lt
RAFVR
ROYAL NETHERLANDS AR

COLDITZ,
XMA
4

Wing was climbing slowly, as we flew along the South Coast on our way to the rendez-vous with the Bombers and the fighter-wings. Target: Hazebrouck at noon. We were detailed as freelance Wing to intercept the German fighters St. Omer Jägerhorst. Visibility was practically unlimited — the Channel a grey steel plate, Sussex a smoke dye and the French cliffs sharply outlined. The Wing kept the wide flung, difficult battle formation tidily as we climbed thro' a layer of cold air at 25 thousand feet, leaving conspicuous and betraying vap..., which broke off abruptly as the Wing rose above it. The three squadrons, strung out in line abreast, ste... a thousand feet at a time to the sun, at half mile intervals; each squadron a miniature replica of the whole w... the three sections in line abreast stepped down with 300 yd intervals. The four planes of each section are "on alig... flying in a very slightly zigzagged line astern, which as a whole "weaves" imperceptibly. The Wing moves thro' height, it performs majestic sweeping halfcircles while it climbs to its final operational ceiling ...about 35 thousand feet. The accurate coördination of all these individual, highly mobile planes, within the ...ntire but supple organism forms a huge three-dimensional tactical unit, which manoeuvres as one ...ing whole.

Along the South Coast, from the Isle of Wight to Beachy Head, we climbed steadily, in a straight lin... ...r Beachy Head we met and left the bombers behind us, and their escort of nine wings: beehive, med... ...port and topcover, a flexible unity many times greater than ours. Crossing the Channel the Wing steadil... ...pared for battle: the arrow-straight course becomes a cautious sweeping and turning, gun switches ar... ...t from "Safe" to "Fire", radiators are closed to ensure unfrozen cannons and machineguns, Sutton harness st... pulled tighter, gauntlets removed to leave thumbs free for the gun-button, optical sights and automatic cam... switched on. Soon we would cross the French Coast and break the R.T. silence. Up to that moment the ether ha... ...silent, to escape the German Direction Finding Stations. Up to that moment we have climbed from sea... ...el to an altitude of 7 miles, the temperature has fallen to −40 or −50°C, the air has become thinner a... ...iner and our hearts beat faster and faster.

Our squadron had the most difficult & dangerous place in the Wing, farthest down-sun, high above t... ...e other squadrons. I am sub-section leader, the third plane in my section, which in its turn is the high... ...the three sections. My altimeter reads 38,600 ft. My flight-commander and his number two in front of... ...number two, a sergeant pilot newly arrived from OTU, behind me. But he is not flying well, lagging behind ...ning up too far, sometimes losing height on turns — suddenly he waggles his wings to attract my attention ...thout breaking the R.T. silence. He gestures, points at his oxygen mask and sweeps away in a steep downward ...rn, which takes him back over the Channel. He must have trouble with his oxygen, I think, but Christ, I do... ...he being left without a N° 2 to guard my tail, if we meet those Focke Wulfs we are after.

As we cross the Coast, the ether is suddenly filled with the clicking of R.T. sets being tested, ...nd orders from leaders to their unit. Somebody else has been flying badly and "Whales" Squadron ...ommander leaves little doubt as to what he thinks of the unfortunate pilot. At last there i... ...a gap in the Babel of our resound voices and I report the loss of my number two. By now we ar... ...over St. Omer and beginning the first of a series of great series circle, squadrons ^(crossing over) inside the Wing ...ections inside the squadrons, so that at all times the Wing and the squadrons in it are stepped ...down to the sun. A grand coördinated sweeping, which ensures that at each point in the orbit ...lon' which the Wing turns the higher squadrons guard the lower ones from the most dangerous ...part of the sky, the sun. Voices from the lower units begin to report enemy fighters, appa... ...ly climbing steeply toward us. Should we really have brought it off, and caught them off their ...guard, on the ground? Usually they are waiting for us, with their extra 2 thousand feet altitude ...ince the German R.D.F. is quite effective when given a headstart of 20 minutes. Soon the first ...section of the lowest squadron peels off, and sweeps in a steep dive toward the enemy. The Wing ...commander's voice comes, collected and faintly, than ours as always: "Steady, boys, stick ...your stations, eyes in the sun". He has hardly finished when two-three excited voices report ...Focke Wulfs, above us, many of them, South of us, in the sun. They are difficult to see, necks are ...craned back, eyes squinting into the sun, but they are there, many dark spots, weaving apparently with... ...order, waiting their chance to swoop down on us and get the initial advantage of diving speed and first squ... ...in. We can do no more than wait, circling and sweeping over our comrades in the lower squadrons, most of wh... ...are already joined in a wild dance with the Focke Wulfs which so gamely climbed up to them.

CONT. P. 84

than ours. Crossing the Channel the Wing steadily prepared for battle: the arrow straight course becomes a cautious sweeping and turning, gun switches are put from "Safe" to "Fire", radiators are closed to ensure unfrozen cannons and machine guns, Sutton harness straps are pulled tighter, gauntlets removed to leave thumbs free for the gun-button, optical sights and automatic cameras are switched on. Soon we would cross the French Coast and break the R.T. silence. Up to that moment the ether has been silent, to escape the German Direction Finding Stations. Up to that moment we have climbed from sea-level to an altitude of 7 miles, the temperature has fallen to -40 or -50° C, the air has become thinner and thinner and our hearts beat faster and faster.

Our squadron had the most difficult and dangerous place in the Wing, farthest down sun, high above the two other squadrons. I am Subsection Leader, the third plane in my section, which in its turn is the highest of the three sections. My altimeter reads 38,600 feet. My Flight Commander and his Number Two in front of me, my Number Two, a Sergeant pilot newly arrived from O.T.U. behind me. But he is not flying well, lagging behind, coming up too far, sometimes losing height on turns,—suddenly he waggles his wings to attract my attention without breaking the R.T. silence. He gestures, points at his oxygen mask and sweeps away in a steep downward turn which takes him back over the Channel. He must have trouble with his oxygen, I think, but Christ I don't like being left without a No. 2 to guard my tail, if we meet those Foche Wulfs we are after.

As we cross the coast, the ether is suddenly filled with the clicking of R.T. sets being tested, curt orders from leaders to their units. Somebody else has been flying badly and "Whaler Squadron" Commander leaves little doubt as to what he thinks of the unfortunate pilot. At last there is a gap in the Babel of our refound voices and I report the loss of my Number Two. By now we are over St. Omer and beginning the first of a series of great series circles, squadrons crossing over inside the Wing, sections inside the squadrons, so that at all times the Wing and the squadrons in it are stepped down to the sun. A grand coordinated sweeping, which ensures that at each point in the 'orbit thru' which the Wing turns the higher squadrons guard the lower ones from the most dangerous part of the the sky, the sun.

Voices from the lower units begin to report enemy fighters, apparently climbing steeply towards us. Should we really have brought it off, and caught them off their guard, on the ground? Usually they are waiting for us, with their extra 2 thousand feet altitude, since the German R.D.F. is quite effective when given a head start of 20 minutes. Soon the first section of the lowest squadron peels off, and sweeps in a steep dive toward the enemy. The Wing Commander's voice comes, collected and faintly humorous as always: "Steady boys, stick to your stations, eyes in the sun". He has hardly finished when two, three excited voices report the Foche Wulfs above us, many of them, south of us in the sun. They are difficult to see, necks are craned back, eyes squinting to the sun, but they are there, many dark spots, weaving apparently without order, waiting their chance to swoop down on us and get the initial advantage of diving speed and first squirt in. We can do no more than wait, circling and sweeping over our comrades in the lower squadrons, most of which are already joined in a wild dance with the Foche Wulfs which so gamely climbed up to them. [*Original text continued on page 84 of diary*].

There, at last, a "kettle" of six F.W.s, coming down, making for our lowest section. They dive past us, and the Wing Commander orders the middle section to engage them, and then, as an afterthought, me to join the middle section. After them! I pull the nose of my aircraft up and over into a steep dive and curse the middle section which has several hundred feet altitude start on me. A voice: "On your tail, Red Three, on your tail". I have hardly turned my head when the first tracer appears to enmesh my plane like whip thongs and simultaneously holes the size of my fist appear in my port wing. I remember thinking that they were too large for M.G., too small for 20 mm cannon. But I have instinctively jerked my plane up and round, toward the left, toward the attacker. He makes an astonishing error, turns in behind me—does he think he can out-turn me? We make our tight, blacking out, juddering, half stalled circle—and there he is in my sight. I feel the recoil of my cannons—and he suddenly straightens out, large fragments of fuselage are ripped out of his plane and fly by me. Again I fire—the Foche Wulf rears up like a live animal, and breaks in two with one big flame from its petrol tank between cockpit and engine.

I see the pilot slump out of the wreckage and then my cockpit is filled with tracer smoke, the instruments on my dash-board lose their faces, rapid heavy thudding against the back armour of my seat, large holes are torn in the perspex. As I turn the plane over on its back to dive out of this cone of fire I realise that my engine is hit too. Oil is blown back in greenish waves over the cowling and flows back thru' the shot-up Perspex into my face, over my goggles. I keep on diving, a tight spiral dive, that second Boche won't be able to follow me in that. Tearing my goggles off, I see the airscrew is no longer turning—an airbrake in front of the heavy, useless weight of my wounded engine. Somehow the sight of the airscrew standing still, a sight which I have never before seen while airborne, brings out all the fear which I was too busy to feel a minute ago, and a great hopelessness takes the place of the warm confidence I've always had in my Merlin.

At about 18 thou' I pull out and tear the lacerated, oil-dripping cockpit cover back. I am roughly 3 miles north of St. Omer, not far from the Channel. Perhaps I will be able to glide that far—in the Channel I have at least the chance of being picked up by our Air Sea Rescue Units.

I notice that my right leg is numb and flaccid, blood gushing out of a large hole on the inside of the thigh, my flying boot on that foot warm and squelching with blood. I try to trim the plane into a proper glide, but with the airscrew not even turning over, and the streamlined cockpit cover destroyed, she glides very badly—I am losing too much height.

Glancing behind me, an automatic action of a fighter pilot, wherever he is, I see two F.W.s rapidly overtaking me. Christ, I will never reach the Channel now. I let them come down without altering course, and as the first one opens fire, I jerk the plane violently into a spin. This is a last trick of desperation—maybe they'll think I've had it and not follow me down. Pulling out at about three thousand feet—she doesn't recover properly, the rudder must have caught it too—I find I haven't fooled them. They now attack both at once—and the next thing I know is, that a sheet of flame bursts thru' the dashboard.

I tear the pin out of the Sutton harness, kick the stick forward, the blinding, unbearable sear of petrol flame enveloping me, and, as I am thrown violently out of the exploding plane by the centrifugal force of the sudden downward turn, I feel my oxygen mask being torn off

arrived at Laufen early in July 1940, together with some hundreds of other British officers, mostly [of] the 51st Div. The camp had been previously occupied by Polish officers, but after the collapse of F[rance] [it] became entirely a British OFLAG. At the time of my arrival there were already over 1000 [off]icers there, some of whom had been there about a month. My first impressions on arrival we[re] [th]ose of infinite relief that the Horrors of the "march" from France were over. After a fortnigh[t] [on]ward - on foot, by Train, and by Barge up the Rhine my whole being was longing, above a[ll] [fo]r a bed in which to sleep and for some form of organised life once more. [I] was also delighted, beyond words, to meet again the officers of my own Regiment from whom [I had] been separated for six weeks. Like most new prisoners, I had little idea of what [to] expect in a permanent camp. I certainly did not anticipate any high degree of luxury. [I] had visions of fairly small rooms of from 6 to 12 occupants, of libraries and silen[ce] Rooms, of well-furnished Dining Rooms, of some form of games facilities, and of a [diet] Ration on which I could exist in adequate health. I was quickly disillusioned. [A] few hours after arrival, and before our release into the camp we were "fallen in" for [a] Head shaving". The horror of standing in a long queue and gradually moving neare[r] the machine, which, to my imagination, almost resembled the guillotine, will always live in my memory. Had our morale been higher, or had we been less miserably ti[red] and hungry, the sight of some hundreds of British officers gingerly approaching the chair [and] doom looking fairly normal, sitting for a few seconds under the electric shears, an[d] getting up looking like phantoms from a H.G. Wells futuristic Film, might have appealed to our much vaunted British sense of humour. Under the circumstances the w[hole] affair seemed to me to strike a note of sombre warning of things to come during the [ear]ly part of captivity. After the head-shaving followed a Search of what few miserable possessions we had, then a "De-lousing", and at long last we were dispatched to o[ur] rooms. I was fairly lucky for 2 Reasons: I managed to remain [with] [sever]al particular friends of the line of march, and I was detailed to a room which [co]ntained only 50 officers, all nominally Captains. My good luck was only relative to [the] [c]onditions in which I found myself compared to many others. Most of the rooms for more [than] [50] officers contained 100 or more bodies; bodies which in most cases ate, lived and slep[t] [i]n one portion of the 3 Tier Beds with which the rooms were filled. In my room we ha[d] [2] Tier Beds because the ceiling was too low to permit 3 Tiers, and by dint of packing the Beds tight against each other managed to obtain enough space on the fl[oor] [to] insert a few Tables and stools at which most of us were able to sit when not [l]ying in a state of listless apathy on our beds. In other respects my [d]isillusionment was quickly completed. No sort of library, no Silence Room, no Din[ing] Room, little enough chance to play games, even if one had had the strength to wish [t]o do so, and merely the normal German prison ration. I must digress here for a few lines on the subject of the daily ration. The Qual[ity] of the rations at Laufen was normal except for one appalling exception which w[as] of the greatest importance to us in our semi-starved condition - The Potat[oes] were bad. That bald statement can not begin to describe the degree of badn[ess] [o]r the quantity thereof - Whole cellars of Potatoes were merely rotting, stinking [,] slimy scum, and these at the beginning constituted our only potato rat[ion.] It was a case of "Take them or leave them", and have no potatoes. In our folly [a]nd through our hunger we took them, and one by one - and there were few [e]xceptions, we went down with Dysentry in a mild or severe form.

...plaints went in. Representations were made. The Commandant was approached; all to no avail. Those ...tes must be issued to us, they were too foul for the pigs. To most of us who were at Laufen the stink ...rotting potatoes which permeated the entire camp, will be a memory which we shall never lose.

...a few days we developed some kind of a daily routine — that inevitable stand by of all ...ons — and we existed. The days passed somehow in an apathetic, miserable stream. ...m afraid we were filled with self-pity, and with a few gallant and splendid exceptions, our Moral ...s not good. Life was utterly empty and futile. We had the certainty of no mail ...the "IN" or "OUT"]. There were no books. There were no parcels. We had no clothes except what ...e stood up in and also slept in. And we were in most cases suffering from a form ...Dysentry — and perhaps worst of all — although it was not very vivid, deep down in each ...us we had the ghastly, gnawing fear that "Britain would be the next". The might of germa... ...d struck down Poland, Belgium, Holland and France in a matter of weeks. We all knew the inadequac... ...our Home Defences at that time. Those of us who could read german papers or who had spoken ...germans received only one impression; that Britain must fall, when and as the Führer directed ...God knows this was a miserable, defeatist attitude, but to many of us at that time, although ...e tried never to put it into words, the thought was ever present, that our Hearth and Home ...ould be ravaged, that the Britain which we had all thought was unassailable would be struck down ...Therefore, we just existed in this nightmare. Those of us who had the health and energy ...ced round the court yard, or feverishly hurried from lecture to lecture, usually on subjects ...which we were totally uninterested and totally ignorant. On one day I attended lectures ...n such different subjects as Bee Keeping, Income Tax, Greek History and The Wine Trade. I do ...t think I absorbed much of any lecture, but at least these lectures helped to deaden the ...pangs of hunger and to quicken our troubled spirits. And here I want to pay a tribu... ...to those who, at that time and in those conditions, were brave enough to stand — an ...exhausting process then — and give of their best to distract us, an audience of comatose ...shaven-headed sheep.

...Little by little things improved. The Pianists and amateur actors began to give shows; ...the first tiny Bulk issue of Red X food appeared; a few cigarettes arrived; at last ...a tiny bag of mail came in; the occasional book was produced; and even the ...canteen began to sell fruit and vegetables of various kinds to those who could ...afford to buy them. At the same time our Morale quickly picked up. All ...except a few of the worst pessimists began to feel that somehow — though we could ...not exactly guess how, Britain would repel the invasion which we still felt certain ...must come. The first letters from home of course altered the whole vista ...of life. I do not intend to stress the attitude of the germans towards us. ...I do not feel that it is of any interest for me to describe a number of small ...incidents. Prisoners of war during the first few months of confinement are seldom ...mentally in a good position to judge dispassionately of such things. In some ways, b... ...our bearing and lack of morale in the early days, we deserved the treatme... ...which we received.

...the Darkest days there were very dark, and soon after affairs improved I was ...moved to another camp, but the memories of the early days at Laufen will remain ...vividly in my memory until the end of my life.

M. J. Gilliat.

60th Riflec.

6:11:43.

my face by the tube, still connected to the plane. The ground comes rushing up. I jerk the ripcord.

Nothing seems to happen for ages, and then, as everything inside me contracts, anticipating the inevitable collision with the earth, the violent jerk of the opening canopy and almost simultaneously I hit some ploughed ground, my legs crumpling under me.

A. van Rood F/Lt RAFVR
Royal Netherlands Army
Colditz
Xmas 43

86. EARLY DAYS AT LAUFEN—SUMMER 1940

I arrived at Laufen early in July 1940, together with some hundreds of other British officers, mostly of the 51st Div. The camp had been previously occupied by Polish officers, but after the collapse of France it became entirely a British Oflag.

At the time of my arrival there were already over 1,000 officers there, some of whom had been there about a month. My first impressions on arrival were those of infinite relief that the horrors of the "march" from France were over. After a fortnight of travel—on foot, by train and by barge up the Rhine my whole being was longing above all else, for a bed in which to sleep and for some form of organised life once more.

I was also delighted, beyond words, to meet again the officers of my own Regiment from whom I had been separated for six weeks,

Like most new prisoners I had little idea of what to expect in a permanent camp. I certainly did not anticipate any high degree of luxury, but I had visions of fairly small rooms of from 6 to 12 occupants, of libraries and silence rooms, of well-furnished dining rooms, of some form of games facilities, and of anyhow, a ration on which I could exist in adequate health. I was quickly disillusioned. A few hours after arrival, and before our release into the camp we were "fallen in" for "head shaving". The horror of standing in a long queue and gradually moving closer to the machine, which, to my imagination, almost resembled a guillotine, will always live in my memory. Had our morale been higher, or had we been less miserable, tired and hungry, the sight of some hundreds of British officers gingerly approaching the chair of doom, looking fairly normal, sitting for a few seconds under the electric shears, and getting up looking like phantoms from a H. G. Wells futuristic film, might have appealed to our much vaunted British sense of humour—under the circumstances the whole affair seemed to me to strike a note of sombre warning of things to come during the early part of captivity. After the head-shaving followed a search of what few miserable possessions we had, then a "de-lousing" and at long last we were dispatched to our rooms.

I was fairly lucky for 2 reasons: I managed to remain with my particular friends of the line of march, and I was detailed to a room which contained only 50 officers, all nominally Captains. My good luck was only relative to the conditions in which I found myself compared to many others. Most of the rooms for more Junior officers contained 100 or more bodies; bodies which in most cases ate, lived, and slept in one portion of the 3 tier beds with which the rooms were filled. In my room we had 2 tier beds because the ceiling was too low to permit 3 tiers, and by dint of packing the beds tightly against each other managed to obtain enough space on the floor to insert a few tables and stools at which most of us were able to sit when not lying in a state of listless apathy on our beds.

In other respects my disillusionment was quickly completed. No sort of library, no silence room, no dining room, little enough chance to play games, even if one had the strength and wish to do so, and merely the normal German prison ration.

I must digress here for a few lines on the subject of the daily ration. The quality of the rations at Laufen was normal except for one appalling exception which was of the greatest importance to us in our semi-starved condition. The potatoes were bad. That bald statement can not begin to describe the degree of badness or the quantity thereof—whole cellars of potatoes were merely rotting, stinking, slimy scum, and these at the beginning constituted our only potato ration. It was a case of "take them or leave them", and have no potatoes. In our folly and through our hunger we took them, and one by one—and there were few exceptions, we went down with dysentery in a mild or severe form. [*Original text continued on page 87 of diary*]. Complaints went in—representations were made—the Commandant was approached; all to no avail. Those potatoes must be issued to us. They were too foul for the pigs. To most of us who were at Laufen the stink of rotting potatoes, which permeated the entire camp, will be a memory which we shall never lose.

After a few days we developed some kind of daily routine—that inevitable stand by of all prisoners—and we existed. The days passed somehow in an apathetic, miserable stream. I am afraid we were filled with self pity, and with a few gallant and splendid exceptions, our morale was not good. Life was utterly empty and futile. We had the certainty of no mail (either "IN" or "OUT")—there were no books—there were no parcels—we had no clothes except what we stood up in and also slept in—and we were in most cases suffering from a form of dysentery—and perhaps worst of all—although it was not very vivid, deep down in each of us we had the ghastly, gnawing fear that "Britain would be next". The might of Germany had struck down Poland, Belgium, Holland and France in a matter of weeks—we all knew the inadequacy of our Home Defence at that time—those of us who could read German papers or who had spoken to Germans received only one impression; that Britain must fall, when and as the Führer directed. God knows this was a miserable, defeatist attitude, but to many of us at that time, although we tried never to put it into words, the thought was ever present, that our Hearth and Home would be ravaged, that the Britain which we had all thought was unassailable would be struck down.

Therefore, we just existed in this nightmare—Those of us who had the health and energy paced round the courtyard, or feverishly hurried from lecture to lecture, usually on subjects of which we were totally uninterested and totally ignorant. On one day I attended lectures on such different subjects as Bee-Keeping, Income Tax, Greek History and the Wine Trade. I do not think I absorbed much of any lecture, but at least these lectures helped to deaden the pangs of hunger and to quieten our troubled spirits. And here I want to pay a tribute to

Well, I didn't ask to go, the Germans just told me I was going. It was a mansion situated in South Germany, "freedom from the barbed wire for a period of one month for long-term prisoners. I left my camp Spangenberg (Oflag IX a) in the company of a handful of elderly senior officers. I was all set for an escape once I was at the other end, they had sent me as interpreter. I had maps, civilian clothes, a compass and all the necessities. On arrival we found a comfortable white building situated in its own grounds. There were four sentries to patrol the area which was on parole all day, in fact everything was on parole except by night. 50 officers were gathered here, including many colonels and ten Naval officers. I found two other officers who were interested in escape and we set to work to formulate a plan. The rest of the camp on the whole was anti-escape, they considered they were there for their health and were in need of a change of air, many of them seemed to forget they were British officers and what that entailed. Each day there were long walks into the country in parties of twelve; in a short space of time we were very fit. Eggs, white bread and Schnapps were easy to obtain from the sentries who were only too willing to trade them for cigarettes and soap. There were girls about in the neighbourhood and came very near the camp. Of course after four years of captivity the affect of female proximity on love-starved prisoners was not small. Several Naval boys became infatuated, but had little chance of approaching the objects of their affections. Food was good, the messing on a communal basis. We received extra meat and bread from the Germans by means of bribery. Appetites were large due to the abnormal amount of exercise taken. The Germans were very friendly and organised visits to the local town situated on the Danube where we went to the cinema. A means of escape from the camp by night was found. It consisted of picking the lock of a door on the second floor which led into the verandah, from where by means of sheets tied together you could climb down onto the ground. The guards on sentry duty had to be standing in certain positions before the scheme could be put on. Three of us decided to escape in this way at the end of May, it might be before the invasion started, and that might happen any time. A general tightening-up of movement within Germany would follow the invasion, which spelt danger to us. We made our preparations, dyed clothes, made caps and duplicated maps. Many officers viewed our preparations with disgust, we were going to ruin their holiday. A meeting of senior officers was called to decide whether we should be allowed to put on this scheme, as this was a "holiday" camp and we should not spoil the pleasure of others. Our action was liable to bring about the shutting down of this new type of camp. 11 colonels met and only two of them were definitely in favour of our attempt, whereas more than a few stood out against any such effort on our part. The Naval officers refused to cooperate, saying that they had received orders from their camp Senior to discourage any escaping attempts from this camp. That was what we were up against. Luckily a South African colonel was of our number and permission from the senior British authorities in the camp were grudgingly given, though General Fortune, Senior British Officer in captivity, had stated before our departure from Spangenberg that escapes should be made if the chance arose. It was our duty at all times, to escape or aid others to that end; many of the officers sent to this camp seemed to have forgotten that, many of them had been specially chosen by the Germans to come to this camp, they were enjoying "German Kindness". We had great difficulty in finding six officers to cooperate in the internal organization the night of our escape. It was May 30th 1944, the 4th anniversary of my capture, and it would be my 4th escape, a good augury I felt. The Germans had sent me, they knew I had escaped before, and well I would naturally take any chance I saw.

The night was clear with bright moonlight, not a leaf stirred, as the lock was picked & we crawled out singly onto the verandah above the sentries' beat. We feared that we would be heard, all was dead still. We had obtained the cooperation of a large, strong major who acted as our anchor holding the sheet-rope while we climbed down. I was the first to go over, clasping in my teeth my brief-case full of food and necessities, and my shoes by the laces. The party was on, it was thrilling in the extreme. In a few seconds I was down and away. Freedom at last, and I made my way towards the Danube lying some miles to the South. I was going alone, the other two together, but I did not wait for them. They both followed me over, loaded with heavy packs on their backs, for they were proceeding on foot and not off to catch a train like myself. Unfortunately the last one in his excitement let go of the rope half-way down and fell with a clatter to the ground, thus arousing the Germans and spraining his ankle into the bargain.

I was caught next morning crossing the Danube in the town of Straubing where I was going to catch a train to Innsbruck. The police had been warned of our escape and were patrolling the bridge. I tried to bluff my way out saying I was a workman, but it did not wash at all. I was arrested and put in a Gestapo gaol with a lot of very unsavoury inmates. I had practically nothing to eat, and I could well understand how people went mad after months of solitary confinement in such cells. I was then taken back to the Rest Camp where the other two were also; they did not last long, with only a few minutes start early recapture was to be expected. The authorities were furious at our abuse of their "Kindness and goodwill"!!, even some of the British looked the other way when we returned. – "By Jove, chaps, bad show this, play the game you cads, not bad fellows these Germans"! – here was the attitude we struck among our own kind, not sporting, what, what???!! – no wonder we failed with all the lack of cooperation we received. That camp contained regular senior officers, and also a number of young men, whose attitude cannot be excused. They thought far more of trying to gain contacts with German women. It was pitiful – young officers of the British army. – –

The German authorities quickly sent us back to our camps after we had tried to disturb the peace, we were glad, the camp could continue without us and the inmates could cooperate with the Germans without interference from "tiresome individuals". Yes, I am afraid this is true, a case where the British govt. more trouble than the hated enemy, luckily such incidents are precedential in prison-life.

Stewart Walker Lieut.
9th Batt. Durham Light Infantry.

Going back to Dec 1940 the uncertainties of
that time decided me to to something how
ever small that might enable France to
regain her rights and be once more one of
the leading countries, I hope the near future
shall not prove me wrong, the best way I
might help was to take an active part
in fighting for the Allies, the only way
possible was to join the Free French forces
who were being formed in England by General
de Gaulle, Having applied for enlistment
to the F.F. Delegation in N.Y.C. I was sent
to Montreal to embark for England.

We left Montreal on a two thousand ton
ship of the Court Line, the convoy formed itself
at Sidney (Canada) three days later. We left
Sidney the following morning about fifty
ships all told. The beggining of the trip
was unexciting except for the usual changing
of courses every few hours. The sixth day at
eight thirty five P.M, the forward right and
center of the convoy was attacked, almost
simultaneously four ships (tankers) were in
flames sending great sheets of flame skyward
The rest of the convoy changed course and full
speed ahead for about an hour changing course
every fifteen minutes we went ahead and
seemed to have eluded the submarines when
the ship in front of us just seemed to
blow up (we found out later it carried munitions
it looked like a signal for the other ships
to be torpedoed because in as many minutes
even more were hit (ours excluded)
Afterwards we just kept going straight
and as fast as the machines would
permit there were three other ships
besides ours that kept on the same
course and speed,

those who, at that time and in those conditions, were brave enough to stand—an exhausting process then—and give of their best to distract us, an audience of comatose, shaven-headed sheep.

Little by little, things improved. The pianists and amateur actors began to give shows; the first tiny bulk issue of Red Cross food appeared; a few cigarettes arrived; at last a tiny bag of mail came in; the occasional book was produced; and even the canteen began to sell fruit and vegetables of various kinds to those who could afford to buy them.

At the same time our morale quickly picked up. All except a few of the worst pessimists began to feel that somehow—though we could not exactly guess how, Britain would repel the invasion which we still felt certain must come.

The first letters from home of course altered the whole vista of life. I do not intend to stress the attitude of the Germans towards us. I do not feel that it is of any interest for me to describe a number of small incidents. Prisoners of war during the first few months of confinement are seldom mentally in a good position to judge dispassionately of such things. In some ways by our bearing and lack of morale in the early days, we deserved the treatment which we received.

The darkest days there were very dark, and soon after affairs improved I was moved to another camp, but the memories of the early days at Laufen will remain vividly in my memory until the end of my life.

M. J. Gilliat,
60th Rifles
6:11:43

88. THEY SENT ME TO A "REST CAMP". . . . MAY 1944

Well, I didn't ask to go, the Germans just told me I was going. It was a mansion situated in South Germany. "Freedom from the barbed wire" for a period of one month for long term prisoners. I left my camp Spangenberg (Oflag IXA) in the company of a handful of elderly, senior officers. I was all set for an escape once I was at the other end, they had sent me as interpreter. I had maps, civilian clothes, a compass and all the necessities. On arrival we found a comfortable white building situated in its own grounds. There were four sentries to patrol the area, which was on parole all day, everything, in fact, was on parole except by night. 50 officers were gathered here, including many colonels and ten naval officers who were interested in escape, and we set to work to formulate a plan.

The rest of the camp on the whole was anti-escape, they considered that they were there for their health and were in need of a change of atmosphere. They seemed to forget we were British officers and what that entailed. Each day there were long walks into the country in parties of twelve; in a short space of time we were very fit. Eggs, white bread and schnapps were easy to obtain from the sentries who were only too willing to trade them for cigarettes and soap. There were girls about in the neighbourhood and came very near the camp. Of course, after four years of captivity the effect of female proximity on love-starved prisoners was not small. Several naval boys became infatuated, but had little chance of approaching the object of their affections. Food was good, the messing on a communal basis. We received extra meat and bread from the Germans by means of bribery. Appetites were large due to the abnormal amount of exercise taken. The Germans were very friendly and organized visits to the local town situated on the Danube, where we went to the cinema.

A means of escape from the camp by night was found. It consisted of picking the lock of the door on the second floor which led out onto the verandah from where, by means of sheets tied together you could climb down onto the ground. The guards on sentry duty had to be standing in a certain position before the scheme could be put on. Three of us decided to escape this way at the end of May; it must be done before the invasion started and that might happen any time. A general tightening up of movement within Germany would probably follow the invasion, which spelt danger to us.

We made our preparations, dyed clothes, made caps and duplicated maps. Many officers observed our preparations with disgust; we were going to ruin their holiday. A meeting of senior officers was called to decide whether we should be allowed to put on this scheme, as this was a "holiday" camp and we should not spoil the pleasure of others. Our action was liable to bring about the shutting down of this new type of camp. Eleven colonels met and only two of them were definitely in favour of our attempt, whereas more than a few stood out against any such effort on our part. The naval officers refused to cooperate, saying that they had received orders from their camp senior to discourage any escaping attempts from this camp. That was what we were up against. Luckily, a South African Colonel was of our number and permissions from the senior British authorities in the camp were grudgingly given, though General Fortune, Senior British Officer in captivity, had stated before our departure from Spangenberg that escapes should be made if the chance arose. It was our duty at all times to escape and aid others to that end; many of the officers sent to this camp seemed to have forgotten that many of them had been specially chosen by the Germans to come to this camp, they were enjoying "German Kindness".

We had great difficulty in finding six officers to co-operate in the internal organization the night of our break. It was May 30th, 1944, the fourth anniversary of my capture, and it would be my 4th escape, a good augury I felt. The Goons had sent me here, they knew I had escaped before, and well I would naturally take my chance if I saw it.

The night was clear with bright moonlight, not a leaf stirred, as the lock was picked and we crawled out singly onto the verandah above the sentries' beat. We feared that we would be heard, all was dead still. We had obtained the co-operation of a large strong major who acted as our anchor, holding the sheet-rope while we climbed down. I was the first to go over, clasping in my teeth my briefcase full of food and necessities, and my shoes by the laces. The party was on, it was thrilling in the extreme.

In a few seconds I was down and away. Freedom at last, and I made my way towards the Danube lying some 20 miles to the south. I was going alone, the other two together, but I did not wait for them. They both followed me over loaded with heavy packs on their backs, for they were proceeding on foot and not off to catch a train like myself. Unfortunately, the last one over in his excitement let go of the rope half way down and fell with a clatter to the ground, this arousing the Germans and spraining his ankle into the bargain.

I was caught next morning crossing the Danube in the town of Stauburg where I was going to catch a train to Innsbruk. The police had been warned of our escape and were patrolling the bridge. I tried to bluff my way out saying I was a French workman, but it did not work at all. I was arrested and put in a Gestapo gaol with a lot of very unsavoury inmates. There was practically nothing to eat and I could well understand how people went mad after months of solitary confinement in such cells. I was then taken back to the Rest Camp where the other two were also; they did not last long, with only a few minutes start, early recapture was to be expected. The authorities were furious at our abuse of their "Kindness and Goodwill"! Even some of the British looked the other way when we returned.

"By Jove, chaps, bad show, this, play the game, you cads, not bad fellows these Germans!" — Here was the attitude we struck among our own kind, not sporting, what, what??!!"—no wonder we failed with the lack of cooperation we received. That camp contained regular senior officers, and also a number of young men, where attitude cannot be excused. They thought far more of trying to gain contacts with German women. It was pitiful—young officers of the British Army. . .

The German authorities quickly sent us back to our camps after we had tried to disturb the peace, we were glad to go; the camp could continue without us and the inmates could co-operate with the Germans without interference from "tiresome individuals." Yes I am afraid this is true, a case where the British gave more trouble than the hated enemy. Luckily such incidents are precedential in prison life.

Stewart Walker Lieut.
9th Batt. Durham Light Infantry.

89. PASSING THROUGH

Going back to Dec. 1940, the uncertainties of that time decided me to do something however small that might enable France to reclaim her rights and be once more one of the leading countries. I hope the near future shall not prove me wrong, the best way I might help was to take an active part in fighting for the Allies, the only way possible was to join the Free French Forces who were being formed in England by General de Gaulle.

Having applied for enlistment to the F.F. Delegation in New York City, I was sent to Montreal to embark for England. We left Montreal on a two thousand ton ship of the Court Line. The convoy formed itself in Sidney (Canada), three days later. We left Sidney the following morning about fifty ships all told.

The beginning of the trip was unexciting except for the usual changing courses every few hours. The sixth day at eight thirty five p.m., the forward right and center of the convoy was attacked, almost simultaneously four ships (tankers) were in flames sending great sheets of flame skywards. The rest of the convoy changed course and full speed ahead for about an hour, changing course every fifteen minutes we went ahead and seemed to have eluded the submarines when the ship in front of us just seemed to blow up (we found out later it carried munitions). It looked like a signal for the other ships to be torpedoed, because in as many minutes seven more were hit (ours excluded). Afterwards we just kept going straight and as fast as the machines would permit. There were three other ships besides ours that kept on the same course and speed. [*Original text continued on page 90 of diary*].

Every so often we would hear a distant explosion with light green and red flares telling us that another ship was being abandoned. Early next morning we all slowed down a bit to permit a few stragglers to catch up. By noon all that could reach the rendezvous were present, except twenty ships that undoubtedly were sunk or disabled, and we all proceeded on.

I must admit that it was not exactly the type of action I had anticipated. The feeling of complete hopelessness, fear and rage is so undeniable that it becomes your master. For a layman as myself I could not help but marvel at the coolness and self-assurance of the captain, officers and crew. Others are much more qualified than I to give due praise and to realize the importance of the splendid work that has been accomplished through the single courage of the sailing personnel of the R.M.M.

The rest of the journey was quite quiet. We landed in Loch Ewee, N.W. Scotland. There I was sent to London, then to the F.F. Govt. where I signed my enlistment in the Air Force for the duration and three months afterwards in all the wars the F.F. Government might incur. [*Original text continued on page 91 of diary*].

I was then sent to Camberley (Surrey) to start my training which was interrupted by my being sent to Syria. The trip uneventful but certainly the most uncomfortable journey ever made, passing through Freetown, Capetown, Aden and Port Tawfik, then on to Beyrouth by train and finally Damascus where it was garrison life at its worst. Later on sent to Suez where the training was completed. Various raids were accomplished by the Cie., mostly on enemy airdromes with the intention of destroying as many planes as possible.

The last mission to be undertaken in Africa by the Cie. was in Tunisia in January 43. We set out in the last days of Dec. from Suez and followed the coastal road to Marble Arch where we veered south into the desert to cut up and behind the enemy lines which was permitted by our means of transport that were the American Jeep, equipped and armed with Vickers and Browning .5 and explosives, hand grenades, revolvers and land mines.

On the path of Sfac to Kebili, being separated from the convoy and in the lead with two more following, we were attacked by five German armoured cars all firing at us. I immediately let go a burst of the Browning at the nearest car which ceased firing. I let another burst go into a body of men which were standing to one side. [*Original text continued on page 92 of diary*]. The car being hit, had stopped and we had to make a run for the nearest bushes about sixty yards distant. The cars still firing at us, much too accurately for comfort, we finally managed to get to the hills and started for Gafsa, eighty miles away, and no food nor water. Two days later we met an Arab who offered us the hospitality of his tent. Knowing that when an Arab invites you to share bread and lodgings he considers you his brother, evidently he had no knowledge of the teachings of the Koran, for the next morning we were greeted by about thirty Italians looking very pleased behind their Tommy Guns. We surrendered ourselves to the Italians who took us to Gabes and then to Tunis where we were shipped to Germany by air and finally after interrogations and innumerable threats they sent us to Oflag IV C.

Every so often we would hear
a distant explosion with light
green and red flares telling us that
another ship was being abandoned.
Early next morning we all slowed
down, a bit to permit a few stragglers
to catch up by noon all that could
reach the rendezvous were present,
except twenty ships that undoubtedly
were sunk or disabled, and we all
proceeded on. I must admit that this
was not exactly the type of action
I had anticipated. The feeling of complete
helplessness, fear and rage is so unbearable
that it becomes your master.
For a layman as myself I could not
help but marvel at the coolness and
self assurance of the captain, officers,
and crew. Others are much more qualified
than I to give due praise and to realize
the importance of the splendid work that
has been accomplished through the simple
courage of the sailing personel of the
R.M.M.. The rest of the journey was
quite quiet. We landed in Loch Ewe
N.W. Scotland. There I was sent to
London, then to the F.F. Govt. where
I signed my enlistment in the Air Force
for the duration and three months
afterwards in all the wars that
the F.F. Govt. might incur.

I was then sent to Camberley (Surrey) to start my training which was interrupted by my being sent to Syria. The trip was uneventful but certainly the most uncomfortable journey ever made passing through, Freetown, Capetown, Aden and Port Taufik then on to Beyrouth by train and finally Damascus where it was garrison life, at its worst. Later on sent to Suez where the training was completed. Various raids were accomplished by the C⁴ᵈ mostly on enemy airdromes with the intention of destroying as many planes as possible. The last mission to be undertaken in Africa by the C⁴ᵈ was in Tunisia in January 43. We set out in the last days of Dec. from Suez and followed the coastal road to Marble Arch, where we veered south into the desert to cut up and behind the enemy lines which was permitted by means of transport that were the American jeeps equipped and armed with Vickers and Brownings & explosives, hand grenades revolvers and land mines. On the 10th of Jan. close to Kebili, being seperated from the convoy and in the lead with two more following we were attacked by five German armoured cars all firing at us. I immediately let go a burst of the Browning at the nearest car which ceased firing, & let another burst go into a body of men which were standing to one side

The car having been hit, had stopped
and we had to make a run for the
nearest bushes about sixty yards dista
The cars still firing at us much too
accurate for comfort, we finally
managed to get to the hills and
started for Gafsa eighty miles away
and no food nor water, Two days later
we met an Arab who offered us the
hospitality of his tent, knowing that when
an Arab invites you to share bread
and lodgings he considers you his
brother, evidently he had no knowledge of
the teachings of the Koran for the next
morning we were greeted by about thirty
Italians looking very pleased behind
their Tommy Guns, We surrendered ourself
to the Itollers who took us to Gabes
and then to Tunis where we were
shipped to Germany by air and finally
after interrogations and innumerable
threats they sent us to Oflag IIC,
and now we wait, hope, work, fight
with a certain feeling that you
know you've done your best, and
are only anxious to do it all over
again.

With my sincerest good wishes
Sgt. Vuillont   P.O.W N° 1638

...cornered me at last & won't accept any more excuses. This incident happened in the bar & arrow
..., about 30 m. S of Kassel. A group of railway workers, my captors, were standing me beer &
...so in a pub & we were all gossiping quite amiably. After half an hour the Feld Gendarm...
...in. They were typical German petty officials, & their behaviour to me was not popular with
...y people in the bar. The police marched me out, a disreputable looking tramp in torn
...o still damp from crossing a river. Shortly an army lorry pulled up. Out of it leapt...
...tmann, a Feldwebel & about a dozen men. They were in a vile temper — it was about
...ight on an October Saturday. The usual screaming & shouting followed and I was
...lled into the back with the O.R.s. The lorry went off at ~~great~~ speed, rocking &
...ing. I can't remember how the next part started: all I do know is that quite suddenly I
...d myself the target of the fists, boots & rifle butts of my fellow passengers. For a
...on of a second I nearly lost my temper & wanted to have a real scrap — thank God
...t or I shouldn't be sitting back waiting for Patten now. A bayonet went through my
...e & I was well smashed about. I was almost unconscious & exaggerated my condition
...ere a little frightened now, allowed me to sit down & tried to stop the bleeding. The only amusing thing was
...a rifle butt in missing my head split wide open the nose of another Hun standing
...one side. Even when the lorry stopped about 10 mins. later I was still feeling dazed
...ing like hell. The Hauptmann pushed me into a well lit bar & I felt that this...
...officers' mess at Spangenburg & that my troubles were relatively speaking over. A f...
...ds later found me being marched through a dance hall — quite obviously having
...at all
...ssion with any officers' mess. At the far end the band was on a stage and at a shou...
...my escort stopped playing. I was shoved onto the stage. The Hauptmann mad...
...ort speech — the ~~loud~~ crowd, women, Party members & troops replied by booing
...ing & yelling. As I was being led out the dancers all went for me. During the next few
...tes it was brought home to me forcibly why they are called Huns. ~~They~~ The origin...
...p were now ~~called~~ ordered in to rescue me, & whip off the people. They got me out in
...piece though it didn't feel like it.

I haven't forgotten the Hauptmann's name.

Peter Stone Hugh.
Lieut
April 8th 1945

Now we wait, hope, work, fight with a certain feeling that you know you've done your best, and are only anxious to do it all over again.

With my sincerest good wishes.

Sgt. Vuillant
P.O.W. No. 1638

93. RECAPTURE—FRANCE 1940

You've cornered me at last and won't accept any more excuses. This incident happened in the bow and arrow days of 1940, about 30 m. S. of Kassel. A group of railway workers, my captors, were standing me beer and schnapps in a pub and were all gossiping quite amiably. After half an hour the Feld Gendarmerie came in.

They were typical German petty officials, and their behaviour to me was not popular with the country people in the bar. The police marched me out, a disreputable looking tramp in torn clothes still damp from crossing a river. Shortly an army lorry pulled up. Out of it leaped a Hauptmann, a Feldwebel and about a dozen men.

They were in a vile temper—it was about midnight on an October Saturday. The usual screaming and shouting followed and I was bundled into the back with the O.R.s. The lorry went off at speed, rocking and bouncing. I can't remember how the next part started; all I do know is that quite suddenly I found myself the target of fists, boots and rifle butts of my fellow passengers. For a fraction of a second I nearly lost my temper and wanted to have a real scrap—thank God I didn't or I shouldn't be sitting back waiting for Patten now. A bayonet went through my face and I was well smashed about. I was almost unconscious, and exaggerated my condition.

They were a little frightened now, allowed me to sit down and tried to stop the bleeding. The only amusing thing was that a rifle butt in missing my head split wide open the nose of another Hun standing at one side.

Even when the lorry stopped about 10 minutes later I was still feeling dazed and aching like hell. The Hauptmann pushed me into a well-lit bar and I felt that this must be the Officers' Mess at Spangenburg and that my troubles were relatively speaking, over.

A few seconds later found me being marched through a dance hall—quite obviously having no connection at all with any Officers' Mess. At the far end the band was on a stage. At a shout from my escort it stopped playing. I was shoved onto the stage. The Hauptmann made a short speech. The crowd, women, party members and troops, replied by booing, hissing and yelling.

As I was being led out the dancers all went for me. During the next few minutes it was brought home to me forcibly why they are called Huns. The original thugs were now ordered in to rescue me, and whip off the people. They got me out in one piece though it didn't feel like it.

I haven't forgotten the Hauptmann's name.

Peter Storie Pugh, Lieut.
April 8th 1945

94. FUNNY STORY—PETER TUNSTALL F/LT. RAF—COLDITZ 9.2.44

The crews who had been detailed to fly that night were gathered in the Operations Room to be "briefed". It was 5.30, and as usual our target had not yet been divulged to us. All we knew was that we had a bombing job before us because they loaded the aircraft just before lunch and we could always get a rough idea of what was coming by what was stowed in a our bomb racks. It might be S.A.P.[1] which meant a crack at warships—usually pretty sticky, G.P.s[2] which, with incendiaries, meant almost anything, or it might be a mine. It was nice to see mines being loaded up, because nine times out of ten a mine dropping trip was fairly quiet. On the tenth it was worse than anything else could be. Most of the Squadron's "death or glory" jobs had been dropping these mines from a height of fifty feet into highly defended waters. Casualties on such raids were usually in the region of 70%. Well, we had G.P.s for tonight so only God and the Operations Officer knew what the task in hand was.

The hubbub of conversation faded away as the Ops. Officer came into the room with a file of papers under his arm. He sat at a desk which had a huge wall map of Europe behind it, and opened the file. "The Germans," he said, "have advanced towards Rheims and by now are in occupation of the city. Your target tonight is Rheims, and the object of the raid is to block the main roads through the town and hamper the enemy's movement. It is left to individual crews to decide at which height to bomb. You can expect very little opposition as they haven't had time to install Ack Ack Defences. Times of take off are on board, Target Maps on that table, and the Met. Officer will give you Route Forecasts in a few minutes".

That was that. These 'Penguins', as we called the non-flying people certainly seemed to crackle with crisp efficiency. I liked the bit about 'little opposition', and turned with the other navigators to my maps, and worked out the details of the trip.

I never really enjoyed my supper on the nights I was due for a show, for I always had that 'going to the dentist' feeling. Sitting opposite me was Webster. He was my pilot, and it was a little disconcerting to think that one would be in the hands of a chap with less experience than oneself, especially as he had quite a reputation for doing—to put it mildly—the unexpected in the air. Still, it would be a change to navigate again.

While we were sipping our coffee, a jovial face appeared round the ante-room door. It belonged to Charles Kidd who had been my house captain at school and was now my Flight Commander, a Sqdn. Ldr. with a D.S.O. and 2 D.F.C.s. Charles was killed the next night. He gave us all an expansive grin, and said, "If any of you lucky men are dicing with death tonight, I'll give you a lift down to "Flights" in the van. Going NOW!"

He disappeared followed pell mell by half the contents of the Mess. The first dozen of us to reach his van stuck two fingers up at the rest who would have to walk down to the hangars. (Why it was so important not to walk a few hundred yards in those days if one could possibly ride, I don't know. Now, in prison, we curse our luck because there is nowhere to walk).

The hangars were the usual scene of order in chaos before a raid. Only the flying crews preserved a studied calm as they drew on their bulky clothing and made final preparation for flight. Then we all piled into a lorry waiting on the tarmac and were driven out to the dispersal positions of the aircraft. It was dark now, and every few minutes the lorry would arrest its jolting passage, a voice would call out the last two figures of an aircraft's number, and four men would bid the remainder 'Cheerio' as they jumped over the tail board. Then the "Tumbrill" would rattle on again. Next time it stopped a voice called 'Seven Four.' 'That's us', said Web, and we dropped out of the lorry to stumble under our load of parachutes and other paraphernalia over the rough ground to the huge shadowy form of our machine. Soon we were aboard, and the kite was shaken to life as her engines fired, and with a throaty bellow hurled a challenge to the night skies. There was an infernal shaking and straining as Web tested his engines, then we taxied out to the flare path. Our code letter was flashed to us, and we were roaring and bounding down the lane of lights, each one leaping past us faster than the last, and were away.

Most of our flight was over territory still held by the B.E.F. and the remnants of the French army, so it was uneventful. Then we saw flares dropping from the sky ahead, and our E.T.A.[3] being up, we knew they were our chaps looking for Rheims. There was a certain amount of mist and we had to do a little searching before we found our objective. In view of the Penguins' assurances about flac we had decided to go in at 2,000 feet which is fairly lowish.

Over Rheims a few searchlights were probing the darkness. Dead ahead of us there was one which was systematically combing the sky. Its beam swung down, then along a bit, then up, along a bit more, then down again and so on. [*Original text continued on page 95 of diary*]. As we got near it, I reckoned it would go down in front of us and come up again behind us. "Veree nice!" I thought, but too soon, however, and reckoning without the efficiency of the Luftwaffe. As the beam was dropping down in front of us, it suddenly faltered, then spread itself so that we were picked up in the fringes of its deconcentrated light. Then it concentrated again, smack on us, and five others which until then had been pretty aimless, swung over to dazzle us in their intensity. This was the signal for all hell to let loose around us, and the tracer poured up like illuminated rain going the wrong way. While the kite bucked at the heavies exploding, and there were vicious plonks as stuff hit us. How I wished the damned Penguin was with us—and when we got back and told him—if we ever got back—he would likely as not say, "Nonsense. Impossible".

We were in a very nasty position, and Webster, running true to form, did the unexpected. He blandly told me afterwards, "I thought I'd do a stall turn". Well, you <u>can</u> do a stall turn with a Hampden, but it's not a good thing to do as low as 2,000 feet. As for doing it at night—hardly advisable. As for doing it at 2,000 feet, at night, with a full bomb load, and blinded by searchlights—crazy! Webster was crazy anyhow. The next time he tried this trick a week or two later, the same Sgt. Air Observer was with him, and managed to bail out. His body was washed ashore three weeks after. Perhaps Web tried to do it again for the third time on the night he didn't come back.

Sitting in my navigator's position on the nose, I had a most unpleasant time. My impressions were first of the engines dying down, and the noise of the air stream rising to a tearing crescendo. Then the glass nose started to rise and go up and up until it seemed to be reaching for Eternity. I stopped breathing and grabbed anything that felt solid, certain that Webster had been hit or gone mad. Then I left my seat and brought up on the roof with a

...ews who had been detailed to fly that night were gathered in the Operations Room to be "briefed". It ... and as usual our target had not yet been divulged to us. All we knew was that we had ...mbing job before us because they loaded the aircraft just before lunch, and we could ...ys get a rough idea of what was coming by what was stowed in our bomb racks. ...ight be S.A.P.s [1] which meant a attack at warships – usually pretty sticky, G.P.s [2] which, ...incendiaries, meant almost anything, or it might be a mine. It was nice to see min... ...loaded up, because nine times out of ten a mine dropping trip was fairly quiet. On the ... it was worse than anything else could be. Most of the Squadron's "death or glory" jobs ha... ... dropping these mines from a height of fifty feet into highly defended waters. Casualtie... ...uch raids were usually in the region of 70%. Well, we had G.P.s for tonight, so only Go... the Operations Officer knew what the task in hand was.

The hubbub of conversation faded away as the Ops. officer came into the room with a file of pa... ... his arm. He sat at his desk which had a huge wall map of Europe behind it, and open... ...le. "The Germans," he said, "have advanced towards Rheims, and by now are in occupati... ... city. Your target tonight is Rheims, and the object of the raid is to block the main roads... ...gh the town, and hamper the enemy's movement. It is left to individual crews to deci... ...which height to bomb. You can expect very little opposition as they haven't had time t... ...ll Ack Ack defences. Times of take off are on the board, Target Maps on that table, and t... ...officer will give you your Route forecasts in a few minutes." That was that. These 'Pengui... ...called the non flying people, certainly seemed to crackle with crisp efficiency. I liked... ...t about 'little opposition', and turned with the other navigators to my maps, and work... the details of the trip.

I never really enjoyed my supper on the nights I was due for a show, for I always had that 'going ... ...dentist' feeling. Sitting opposite me was Webster. He was my pilot, and it was a little disconcer... ...ink that one would be in the hands of a chap with less experience than oneself, especially ... ...ad quite a reputation for doing – to put it mildly – the unexpected in the air. Still, ...ld be a change to navigate again.

While we were sipping our coffee, a jovial face appeared round the ante room door. It ... ...ged to Charles Kidd who had been my house captain at school, and was now my flight ... ...mander, a Sqdn. Ldr. with a DSO and 2 D.F.C.s Charles was killed the next night. He gave ... ... an expansive grin, and said "If any of you lucky men are dicing with death tonight ... ...ve you a lift down to "Flights" in the van. Going NOW!" He disappeared followed pa... ...by half the contents of the mess. The first dozen of us to reach his van stuck two ... ...rs up at the rest who would have to walk down to the hangars. (Why it was so importan... ...to walk a few hundred yards in those days if one could possibly ride I don't know. N... ...ison, we curse our luck because there is nowhere to walk.)

The hangars were the usual scene of order in chaos before a raid. Only the flying crews preserved ...odied calm as they drew on their bulky clothing, and made final preparation for flight. ... ... piled into a lorry waiting on the tarmac and were driven out to the dispersal positio... ...aircraft. It was dark now, and every few minutes the lorry would arrest its jolting ...sage, a voice would call out the last two figures of an aircraft's number, and four men ...ld bid the remainder 'Cheerio' as they jumped over the tail board. Then the 'lumbe... ...ed rattle on again. Next time it stopped a voice called 'Seven four.' 'That's us... ... Web, and we dropped out of the lorry to stumble under our load of parachutes a... ...paraphenalia over the rough ground to the huge shadowy form of our machine. S... ...were aboard, and the kite was shaken to life as her engines fired, and with a ...ty bellow hurled a challenge to the night skies. There was an infernal shaking ...a straining as Web tested his engines, then we taxied out to the flare path. ...code letter was flashed to us, and we were roaring and bounding down the the la... ...ghts, each one leaping past us faster than the last, and were away.

Most of our flight was over territory still held by the B.E.F. and the remnants o... ...rench Army, so was uneventful. Then we saw flares dropping from the sky ahead ...d our E.T.A. [3] being up, we knew they were our chaps looking for Rheims. There was a ...ain amount of mist, and we had to do a little searching before we found our ...ctive. In view of the Penguin's assurances about flac, we had decided to go in at ...ject which is fairly lowish. Over Rheims a few searchlights were probing the ...ness. Head ahead of us there was one which was systematically combing the sk... ...eam swung down, then along a <u>bit</u>, then up, along a bit more, then down again, and so o...

to we got near it, I reckoned it would go down in front of us and come up again behind us — nice!" I thought, but too soon, however, and reckoning without the efficiency of the Lufty — the beam was dropping down in front of us, it suddenly faltered, then spread itself so that we were picked up in the fringes of its deconcentrated light. Then it concen— again, smack on us, and five others which until then had been pretty aimless, swu— over to dazzle us in their intensity. This was the signal for all hell to let loose arou— us, and the tracer poured up like illuminated rain going the wrong way, whi— the kite bucked at the heavies exploding, and there were vicious plonks as stuff ho— How I wished that damned Penguin was with us — and when we got back and tol— him — if we ever got back — he would likely as not say, "Nonsense. Impossible."

We were in a very nasty position, and Webster, running true to form, did the unexpected. He blandly told me afterwards, "I thought I'd do a stall turn." Well, — can do a stall turn with a Hampden, but it's not a good thing to do as low a— 2000 ft. As for doing it at night — hardly advisable. As for doing it at 2,000 ft, at n— with a full bomb load, and blinded by six searchlights — crazy! Webster was crazy anyhow. The next time he tried this trick a week or two later, the same Sgt. Air Observer was w— him, and managed to bail out. His body was washed ashore three weeks after. Perhaps Web— tried to do it again for the third time on the night he didn't come back.

Sitting in the navigators position in the nose, I had a most unpleasant time. My impres— are first of the engines dying down, and the noise of the air stream rising to a tearing crescen— then the glass nose started to rise and go up and up until it seemed to be reaching for t— I stopped breathing and grabbed anything that felt solid, certain that Webster had be— hit or gone mad! Then I left my seat and brought up on the roof with a crump th— knocked the wind out of me. I remember struggling with a tangle of tubes and — wires like a demented Laocoön, meanwhile lying on my side looking through — roof at the searchlights which appeared to be pointing down on us from the — Then I sailed off into space again and was sprawled back on the floor with a shoo— pain in my ankle. Web's voice came through the intercom. "Abandon Aircraft. Bail Out! Quick!" Then silence. I could see my parachute in — rack not two feet away. I tried to stretch my arms out to it, but centrifugal — was pulling me back. I exerted myself to the full, but it was as if I were paralys— I tried to move my feet, but they slipped on a litter of apples, bananas, chocolate, round— ammunition, and God knows what spilled everywhere. I gave up the trouble & lay ba— what was the use! All this started at 2000 feet — the big smash and blinding ob— would come any second. I waited for it and wanted to be sick. I remember th— what a rotten way it was to go out. I felt hard done by because there had been n— flashes, no fire, nothing to show for it — all so dark & unimportant it seemed — lying there doing nothing except wanting to be sick —

Suddenly I felt I could move again. The machine was right way up and the b— paralysing force had gone, and with it my helplessness. I felt around me and — my intercom line which had pulled out of its plug. I shoved it back in again, and — heard Web telling the Air Observer to come down and take over the navigation. W— had managed to get half out of his cockpit and then had jammed. When the mac— righted itself over the roofs of Rheims he had dropped back into his seat an— regained control. When he got no answer from me he thought I had manage— to bail out. I told him I was still there, and to level up so that I coul— bomb. The searchlights found us again and the flac opened up once more — dropped the bombs and gave Web a course for home.

Once settled on our course, and with all the immediate navigational — done, I had time to relax. The floor was littered with maps, pans of ammuni— ations, and everything was loose and lying around that could conceivably come loose (—

crump that knocked the wind out of me. I remember struggling with a tangle of tubes and wires like a demented Laocoön, meanwhile lying on my side, looking through the roof at the searchlights which appeared to be pointing down on us from the sky. Then I sailed off into space again and was sprawled off on the floor with a shooting pain in my ankle. Web's voice came through the 'intercom'. "Abandon Aircraft! Abandon Aircraft. Bail Out! Quick!" Then silence. I could see my parachute in its rack not two feet away. I tried to stretch my arms out to it, but centrifugal force was pulling me back. I exerted myself to the full but it was as if I were paralysed. I tried to move my feet, but they slipped on the litter of apples, bananas, chocolate, rounds of ammunition, and God knows what spilled everywhere.

I gave up the trouble and lay back. What was the use! All this started at 2,000 feet—big smash and blinding oblivion would come any second. I waited for it and wanted to be sick. I remember thinking what a rotten way it was to go out. I felt hard done by because there had been no flashes, no fire, nothing to show for it—all so dark and unimportant it seemed—just lying there doing nothing except wanting to be sick. —

Suddenly I felt I could move again. The machine was right way up and the horrible paralysing force had gone, and with it my helplessness. I felt around me and found my intercom line which had pulled out of its plug. I shoved it back in again and heard Web telling the Air Observer to come down and take over the navigation. Web had managed to get half out of his cockpit and then had jammed. When the machine righted itself over the roofs of Rheims, he had dropped back into his seat and regained control. When he got no answer from me he thought I had managed to bail out. I told him I was still there, and to level up so that I could bomb. The searchlights found us again and the flack opened up once more. I dropped the bomb and gave Web a course for home.

Once settled on our course, and with all the immediate navigational jobs done, I had time to relax. The floor was littered with maps, pans of ammunition, rations, and everything was loose and lying around that could conceivably come loose. [*Original text continued on page 96 of diary*]. I was aware of a pungent smell and a throbbing pain in my ankle. My clothing, the maps and the floor were wet with some dark liquid. For one moment I thought it was blood, but when I rubbed my fingers together it didn't feel right for that. There was the familiar yet unplaceable smell too. Oil! That's what it was—oil. I called Webster up and told him about the oil. "Stand by for one of the engines to cut", I told him. I sniffed and rubbed my fingers together again. No, it didn't seem to be engine oil somehow. Then it must be oil from the hydraulics system. Must be. I informed Webster of this, and told him not to forget to test his flaps and the undercarriage before we went in to land, for their unexpected failure at the last moment had killed many an unwary crew.

Then, lying in the gangway about eight feet behind me I saw some infernal looking thing which again set my heart pounding with an unreasonable fear. It looked like an iron drum lying on its side—rather like a small edition of the depth charges they drop over the stern of destroyers.

The only answer was to drop it through the escape hatch—and quickly. I went for the thing expecting to hear it fizzing or ticking away the seconds until it should blow us all to Kingdom Come. I reached it, and with nervous clammy hands grabbed hold of it—and then my eyes fell on the legend printed on its side. It was—

was aware of a pungent smell and the throbbing pain in my ankle. My cloth maps and the floor were wet with some dark liquid. For one moment I ought it was blood, but when I rubbed my fingers together it didn't ight for that. There was the familiar yet unplaceable smell too. Oil! Th hat it was — oil. I called Webster up and told him about the oil. "Stand by for one engines to cut," I told him. I sniffed and rubbed my fingers together again didn't seem to be engine oil somehow. Then it must be oil from the hydraulic stem. Must be. I informed Webster of this, and told him not to forget to test aps and the undercarriage before he went in to land, for their unexpected fa the last moment had killed many an unwary crew.

Then, lying in the gangway about eight feet behind me i saw some infernal looking thing which again set my heart poundin th an unreasonable fear. It looked like an iron drum lying on its ather like a small edition of the depth charges they drop over the stern estroyers. The only answer was to drop it through the escape hatch — and qui went for the thing expecting to hear it fizzing or ticking away the second ntil it should blow us all to Kingdom Come. I reached it, and with rvous clammy hands grabbed hold of it — and then my eyes fell on th gend printed on its side. It was —

CHEMICAL
ELSAN
LAVATORIES

I was too relieved and too shaken to laugh at my groundless fears. 'Good old Elsa thought. 'Dear little lavatories,' and sat back to gather my scattered wite ow I knew what the dark liquid was, and the pungent smell. Disinfecta

Only those who know the interior of a Hampden can realise what volutions the machine must have gone through for the lavatory to e o where it did. It had come adrift from way down aft, rolled long the roof, hit the pilot's sheet of armour plating, then dropped d e well into the navigator's position where it emptied itself over the uckless me.

When we arrived back at our base and I was helped l obble along to the sick bay, there was much hearty laughter at us ur machine, the latter somewhat tattered and with disinfecta ripping from here and there. I too felt in a mood for laught ut when I got to bed that morning and thought back — espe f the moment when I wanted to be sick, I laughed again. still do — just like that. Ha, ha.

Z

Sorry it's so long — you asked for it!

8 octobre 1942, pour la 2ᵉ fois depuis le jour où nous avions été réunis dans l'église
d'Envermeu, près de Dieppe, les Allemands avaient entassé tous les officiers canadiens
dans une vaste salle; mais cette fois-ci, nous sommes solidement enchaî-
nés. — Dans l'église au sol couvert de paille nos préoccupations d'ordre matériel ne nous avaient guère effleurés. Nous étions encore sous l'ahurissement
des premières heures de captivité. Seul importait de savoir quel serait notre
sort. — Puis en Allemagne nous nous étions tant bien que mal installés
dans notre nouvelle vie. Que signifiait donc cette comédie subite ? Pourquoi
encore une fois nous réunir dans une pièce aussi froide et dénudée ? Aucun
évènement durant notre captivité ne semblait justifier cette nouvelle incarcéra-
tion et surtout cet enchaînement. Notre dégoût des Boches était encore plus profond
qu'à Envermeu. — Nous réalisions combien vis à vis de nos ennemis nous ressem-
blions à ces troupeaux que un gardien et ses chiens dirigent à leur guise. —

À l'appel du midi l'on avait fait sortir des rangs les officiers capturés à Dieppe
et sans explication, nous avions été embarqués dans des camions qui nous
conduisirent à la lugubre forteresse qui domine les environs d'Eichstätt. Nous
mîmes pied à terre dans une moyennageuse cour intérieure. Toujours igno-
rants de notre avenir, les pronostics allaient leur plein. "Fusillade !" disaient
les uns en riant. Les fanfaronnades n'empêchaient pas la majorité d'entre
nous d'être assez inquiets. La cour sévère, l'attitude énigmatique des Allᵈˢ,
l'étalage des M.G., rien de cela n'était fait pour nous rassurer. — Nous étions
une centaine environ, y compris quelques blessés portant des bandages. Par
groupes de quatre nous devions quitter les rangs. Je faisais partie du 1ᵉʳ détachement.
Nous sortîmes de cette cour mémorable et sous solide escorte nous fûmes con-
duits vers une aile de ce lugubre château. Je fus introduit seul dans une
chambre basse où 5 ou 6 gaillards m'attendaient avec des câbles prêts. Lecture me
fut faite en guise de cuisine par le Sonderführer d'un ordre de l'O.K.W. J'en devine le sens
plutôt que ne le comprends. Puis mes poignets furent solidement liés. —
Nous fûmes réunis au fur et à mesure dans une grande pièce glaciale — deux
jours sans sortir, dans des conditions hygiéniques abominables, sans tabac et
seulement une soupe et une croûte de pain par jour. — Puis nous retournâmes
au camp, isolés des autres prisonniers. Pour moi, ce calvaire dura jusqu'au 3 juin
date à laquelle je m'évadais. Repris avec soixante de mes camarades, le lecteur
s'étonnera que dans la voûte où nous fûmes entassés, mes bonnes vieilles
menottes me suivirent. Nous étions six dans ce cas. — Avez-vous déjà lavé une
chemise avec menottes aux poings ? En arrivant à l'Oflag IV C, je fus surpris
d'apprendre qu'elles restaient en arrière.

John H. Roy - Lieut.
Les Fus. Mont-Royal.

I was too relieved and too shaken to laugh at my groundless fears. 'Good old Elsan' I thought, 'Dear little lavatories,' and sat back to gather my scattered wits. Now I knew what the dark liquid was, and the pungent smell. Disinfectant!

Only those who know the interior of a Hampden can realize what evolutions the machine must have gone through for the lavatory to end up where it did. It had come adrift from way down aft, rolled along the roof, hit the pilot's sheet of armour plating, then dropped down the well into the navigator's position where it emptied itself over the luckless me.

When we arrived back at our base and I was helped to hobble along to the sick bay, there was much hearty laughter at us and out machine, the latter somewhat tattered and with disinfectant dripping from here and there. I too, felt in a mood for laughter, but when I got to bed that morning and thought back—especially of the moment when I wanted to be sick, I laughed again. Ha, ha. I still do—just like that. Ha, ha.

Sorry it's so long—you asked for it!

(1) Semi Armour Piercing; (2) General Purpose; (3) Estimated Time of Arrival.

97. ENCHAINÉS*

On the 8th October 1942 for the second time since that day we had all been gathered together in the church of Envermeux near Dieppe, the Germans assembled all the Canadian officers in a vast hall. But this time we were tightly shackled. Back in the church with its straw strewn floor, our material worries had seemed of little consequence. We were then still numbed by the first hours of our captivity. The only thing that mattered was to find out what was going to happen to us. Then later on in Germany, we had settled down more or less easily to our new way of life.

What was the reason for this latest piece of nonsense? Why had they brought us all together again in such a cold bare hall? Nothing that had happened during our captivity seemed to excuse this new form of imprisonment and particularly this use of handcuffs. We felt even more contempt for the Goons than we had at Envermeux. We realized how much in our relation to our enemies we resembled a herd of sheep that can be sent this way and that at the whim of some shepherd and his dogs.

At the noon role call all Canadian officers captured at Dieppe were called out of the ranks. Then, with no word of explanation, we were loaded into trucks and taken to the grim fortress that commands the heights near Eichstätt. We disembarked in a medieval looking inner courtyard . We had no idea what was going to happen to us so everybody had some suggestion to make. "They are going to shoot us" said some with a laugh. This devil-may-care attitude didn't prevent most of us from feeling pretty uneasy. The grim court yard, the

* *Shackled*

sphinx-like attitude of the Germans, the unusual number of machine guns; none of those things were exactly reassuring.

There were about a hundred of us there including a few wounded still wearing their bandages. We were called out in groups of four, and I found myself in the first group. We left the never-to-be-forgotten courtyard under a very strong guard and were taken to a wing of the forbidding looking castle. I was led alone into a low-ceilinged room where five or six tough looking characters were standing readily with ropes. The Sonderführer read out an order of the O.K.W. in a kind of pidgin English. I did not really understand what he said but more or less managed to gather the general drift. Then my wrists were bound tightly. We were assembled again one by one in a huge chilly room and were kept there for two days on end. We had no tobacco, only a bowl of soup and a crust of bread per day for food,—and the hygiene conditions were abominable. Then we were sent back to the camp, but were kept separate from the other prisoners. As far as I was concerned this martyrdom went on until 3rd June 1943 at which time I managed to escape. When I was caught again with sixty of my comrades my good old handcuffs caught up with me again. There were six of us in the same situation. Have you ever tried to wash a shirt with handcuffs on? But when I arrived at Oflag IVC I was quite surprised to find that I had managed to shake them off at last.

John H. Roy—Lieut.
Les Fus. Mont-Royal

Colditz 5 April –44

98. TRACKS IN GREECE

It is March 9th, 1941—Pyreas Harbour bathed in brilliant sunshine presents a scene of unusual activity. Units of the Royal Navy and Merchant Fleet are disembarking the Armoured Brigade. The black berets of the R.T.R. bob in and out of the admiring Greeks. These courageous people have a charming custom. They wave you away, when they mean "Hullo—Welcome—Come here", a matter of some slight confusion to the troops at first. The sight of tanks being swung over the sides of the Freighters seems to complete their cup of happiness. "English—good." cry the children and the men and women folk smilingly shake their heads in approval. The British have come to fight for them.

Did they, like us, believe that this was only a small advance guard of troops that would soon pour across the seas to their shores? Or unlike us, were they failing to appreciate the true menace of the German War machine massing in Bulgaria.

Others are at the Quayside too—others who have no smile of welcome for us. Officials from the German Embassy. Greece is at war with Italy, but not with Germany. Watchful eyes note the A10's with their two pounder gun and B.S.H. L.M.G.—the light tanks with their thin armour and .5 and .303 M.G.'s. When they count the tanks on the quayside, they find 52 fifteen tonners and 52 light tanks have come to oppose the German menace. The A10 Cruisers were veterans of long marches in England and the Desert, whose engines were well beyond

It is March 9th 1941 – Pyreeus harbour bathed in brilliant sunshine pre
a scene of unusual activity. Units of the Royal Navy and Merchant
are disembarking the Armoured Brigade. The black berets of the A
bob in and out of the admiring Greeks. These courageous people
a charming custom – They wave you away, when they mean – "Hi
Welcome – come here" – a matter of some slight confusion to the troop
first. The sight of the Tanks being swung over the sides of the Freig
seems to complete their cup of happiness. "English – good" – cry th
children and the men and women folk smilingly shake their heads
approval. The British have come to fight for them. Did they – like
believe that this was only a small advance guard of troops tha
would soon pour across the seas to their shores. Or unlike us
were they failing to appreciate the true menace of the Germa
war machine massing in Bulgaria. Others are at the Quayside
too – others who have no smile of welcome for us. Officials from
German Embassy. Greece is at War with Italy, but not with Germa
Watchful eyes note the A 10's with their 2 pounder gun and B.S.
L.M.G – the light Tanks with their thin armour and ·5 and ·303
When they count the Tanks on the quayside they find that 52
15 Tonners and 52 Light Tanks have come to oppose the German Hea
The A 10 Cruisers were veterans of long marches in England an
Desert. whose engines were well beyond their prime and whose
were the despair of all Tank crews. A never-ending source of wo
to us and no doubt one of some satisfaction to the Germans; w
recognise the Tanks that had proved to be of little avail against
P.4 By the 15th March units of the Armoured Brigade are dotte
over a broad front of some 150 miles watching the Bulgarian and
Slavien frontiers. The main body of fighting Troops on the Salonika
Olympus front consist of New Zealand and Australian Troops – abou
1½ Divisions in all. During this period – as tension grows day by
a Mr. Watt in a fast car tours the Mountains and valleys of Greece
never far behind roars one, sometimes two other powerful cars. Ge
Sir Henry Maitland Wilson – C in C. B.E.F Greece – alias Mr Watt is follo
closely by the watchful eyes of the German Embassy as he makes his
positions. Intelligence reports 2 Armoured and 3 Parashute Divisions
be among the German forces assembling in Bulgaria. Ultimatums t
the Greek Government are growing stronger every day. The British mu
be off Greek soil by the 26th March – otherwise Germany will decl
war on Greece and Athens will be considered a Military Target.
Daily reconnaissance along the Greek – Jugo-Slavien border tests

eling of the old Bulgar villages. This strip of territory was ceded to Greece after the Great War. A Nazi salute is not uncommon in some of them. We visit Florina - the gateway to Albania - streams of young Greeks pour through to continue their heroic struggle against the Italians. To-wards the end of March Antony Eden and the C.I.G.S. Sir John Dill fly to Athens from Turkey. Rumours of Turkey's imminent participation off the side of the Allies strengthen. Tension is growing as the Germans move up to the Greek-Bulgarian frontier. On their way to Florina for talks with the Serbs - Eden and Sir John Dill talk tracks with us. They express concern at our reports - promise immediate help - somewhere the slow machinery of advance goes into action to get new tracks to the Tanks in Greece. Out it streams we feel happier. A wave of optimism greets the rising in Jugo-Slavia, but it fails to unit the country against Germany. The Croats side with Germany and loyal Serbs withdraw South into Greece. April 6th 941. The German Forces march and 3 columns strike into Greece.

The scattered units of the Armoured Brigade rush to the Veve Pass over looking Florina Plain. As night falls a lost column of pathetic Italian prisoners from Albania limp through the pass and the Brigade moves in position. The night is quiet - broken only by the roar of the Tanks engines reverberating round the snow and ice capped peaks. With dawn comes the knowledge that the Germans are at the foot of the pass, with their armour moving across the Florina plain. A greek Division with antique equipment is holding our right flank. The German drive checks as they meet the opposing British Forces from Salonika to Veve. For a week the battle rages at Veve - and we have been flown out of the skies. Greece becomes the "Stukas" playground. Our gunners take deadly toll of the attacking Germans - but now 2 Divisions are facing us on the Florina plain. The B.E.F is falling back and on Easter Saturday April 12th the withdrawal from Veve begins. The Tanks as rear-guard. Easter Sunday 13 April. 16 A10's and a weakened armoured Brigade take up positions to receive the first real blow from the German armour. A division of German Tanks moves up - the 2nd R.H.A. are not permitted to shell the village in which they are concentrating - owing to danger to Greek civilians. All day long the German Tanks are thrown back - the Northumberland Hussars doing brilliant work with their 2pdr A.T. guns. By night fall we are nearly surrounded. As we pull out Tank fights Tank - the German Panzers blaze on the hillside and the A10's lumber off on a 70 mile night march to the next point. All night long the Tanks withdraw over night-mare roads; climbing 3000ft - then twisting and turning to the rock strewn valleys below. Dawn finds the last Tanks swaying across a flimsy wooden

their prime and whose tracks were the despair of all tank crews. This was a never ending source of worry to us and no doubt one of some satisfaction to the Germans, who recognized the tank that had proved to be of little avail against the P.4.

By the 18th March units of the Armoured Brigade are dotted over a broad front of some 150 miles watching the Bulgarian and Jugo-Slavian frontiers. The main body of fighting troops on the Salonika-Olympus front consists of New Zealand and Australian troops, about 1½ divisions in all.

During this period—as tension grows day by day, a Mr. Watt in a fast car tours the mountains and valleys of Greece—never far behind roars one, sometimes two other powerful cars. General Sir Henry Maitland Wilson, C. in C. B.E.F. Greece—alias Mr. Watt. is followed closely by watchful eyes of the German Embassy as he makes his dispositions. Intelligence reports 2 Armoured and 3 Parachute Divisions to be among the German forces assembling in Bulgaria. Ultimatums to the Greek Government are growing stronger every day. The British must be off Greek soil by the 26th March—otherwise Germany will declare war on Greece and Athens will be considered a Military Target. Daily reconnaissance along the Greek-Jugo-Slavian border tests the [*original text continued on page 99 of diary*] feeling of the old Bulgar villages. This strip of territory was ceded to Greece after the Great War. A Nazi salute is not uncommon in some of them. We visit Florina—the gateway to Albania—streams of young Greeks pour through to continue their heroic struggle against the Italians.

Towards the end of March Antony Eden and the C.I.G.S. Sir John Dill fly to Athens from Turkey. Rumours of Turkey's imminent participation on the side of the allies strengthen. Tension is growing as the Germans move up to the Greek-Bulgarian frontier. On their way to Florina for talks with the Serbs—Eden and Sir John Dill talk tracks with us. They express concern at our reports—promise immediate help—somewhere the slow machinery of Ordnance goes into action to get new tracks to the tanks in Greece. Clutching at straws we feel happier. A wave of optimism greets the rising in Jugo-Slavia but it fails to unite the country against Germany. The Croats side with Germany and the loyal Serbs withdraw south into Greece. April 6th 1941, the German Forces march and 3 columns strike into Greece.

The scattered units of the Armoured Brigade rush into the Veve Pass overlooking Florina Plain. As night falls a lost column of pathetic Italian prisoners from Albania limp through the pass and the Brigade moves into position. The night is quiet—broken only by the roar of the tank engines reverberating round the snow and ice capped peaks. With dawn comes the knowledge that the Germans are at the foot of the pass; with their armour moving across the Florina plain. A Greek Division with antiquated equipment is holding our right flank. The German drive checks as they meet the opposing British forces from Salonika to Veve. For a week the battle rages at Veve—and we have been flown out of the skies. Greece becomes the "Stukas" playground. Our gunners take deadly toll of the attacking Germans, but now 2 Divisions are facing us on the Florina plain. The B.E.F. is falling back and on Easter Saturday April 12th the withdrawal from Veve begins. The tanks as rear guard. Easter Sunday 13th April. 16 A10's and a weakened Armoured Brigade take up positions to receive the first real blow from the German Armour. A Division of German tanks moves up—the 2nd R.H.A. are not permitted to shell the village in which they are concentrating, owing to danger to Greek civilians. All day long the German tanks are thrown back, the Northumberland Hussars doing brilliant work with their 2 pounder A.T. guns. By nightfall we are nearly surrounded. As we pull out, tank fights tank. The German Panzers blaze on the hillside as the A10's lumber off on a 70 mile night march to the next position.

All night long the tanks withdraw over night-mare roads climbing 3,000 ft —then twisting and turning to the rock strewn valleys below. Dawn finds the last tanks swaying across a flimsy wooden [*original text continued on page 100 of diary*] bridge 300 feet above the swift flowing Ventricos. It is here that we are to join with the 6th Greek Mountain Division. No signs of them as the remaining tanks move into position. The remnants of the Brigade withdraw to Gravena.

The day passes in comparative peace, maintaining and preparing the remaining 13 A10's for the final effort. The next dawn finds us alone. The Brigade is moving slowly back to the Aliakamon. The bridge over the Ventricos is to be blown. Later in the day we see the Mountain Division on foot, winding like a long black snake along the valley and scrub covered slopes, moving south. I ask a Greek where he is going— "Home", he replies, "The Greek Army is on leave".

Stillness descends over the plain. 13 tanks wait and watch in the shimmering heat. The Brigade is reforming 50 miles behind us. The German planes have the sky to themselves. Stukas gambol in the sunshine and drop death and destruction on anything that moves. Towards evening we withdraw: tank by tank on the long trek. 5 reach the Aliakamon. The rest, blown up by their crews lie charred and deserted by the roadside, their tracks a twisted heap.

The whole B.E.F. line is falling back. Conditions are hopeless. Remnants of the Brigade make for the coast. In Larissa, 300 miles from the original front line, we find our new tracks have just arrived. One A10 tank reaches Larissa. South to Athens move the close columns of withdrawing troops. Planes drone overhead all day. No opposition is offered. There are no planes left to fight. The evacuation begins. Co-ordination no longer exists. Personnel and equipment of an Australian base hospital land as base troops embark on the waiting ships. Days drag on—the British Forces are hunted from harbour to harbour, till on the 29th April 1941, the last intact force surrenders to the Germans. Greece is finished. A few hours before capture, I speak to a Greek. He is smiling, "The British will come back", he says and with that funny little beckoning movement of the hand he walked away to the hills saying his 'Good-bye'.

2 British Divisions had opposed 10 German Divisions and the Luftwaffe. 12,000 officers and men were captured in Greece out of a total force of 40,000.

Dennis E. Bartlett, M.C.
Lieut, 3rd Batt, R.T.R.

bridge 300ft above the swift flowing Ventricos. It is here that we are to join with the 6ᵗᴴ Greek Mountain Division. No sign of them as the rolling Tanks move into position. The remnants of the Brigade withdraw to Grevena. the day passes in comparative peace - maintaining and prepar the remaining 13 A10's for the final effort. The next dawn finds us a The Brigade is moving slowly back to the Aliakomon. The bridge over the Ventricos is to be blown. it is never blown. later in the day we see the Mountain Division on foot - winding like a long black snake along the valley and scrub-covered slopes - moving South. I ask a Greek where he is going - "Home" he replies - "The Greek army is on leave". Stillness descends over the plain; 13 Tanks wait and watch in the shimmering hea the Brigade conforming 50 miles behind us. The German planes have the sky to themselves; Stukas gambol in the sunshine and drop death and destruction on anything that moves. To-wards evening we withdraw again by Tank on the long Trek. 5 reach the Aliakomon. the rest, blown up by their crews lie charred and deserted by the road-side - their tracks twisted heap. The whole B.E.F line is falling back. conditions are hopeless. remnants of the Brigade make for the coast. In Larissa, miles from the original front line we find our new Tracks have arrived - 1 A10 Tank reaches Larissa. South to Athens move the columns of withdrawing troops: Planes drone over-head all day - n opposition is offered. there are no planes left to fight. The evacuat begins. - co-ordination no longer exists. Personel and equipment o Australian base hospital land & base troops embark in the waiting Days drag on - the British Force are hunted from harbour to harb till on the 29ᵗᴴ of April 1941 the last intact force surrenders to Germans. Greece is finished. A few hours before capture I speak a Greek. He is smiling - "The British will come back" he says with that funny little beckoning movement of the hand he walks to the hills saying his 'Good-bye'.

2 British Divisions had opposed 10 German Divisions + the Luftw 12,000 Officers and Men were captured in Greece out of a total f of 40,000.

Dennis. E Bartlett. M.C.

a nice spring evening in 1941, ten Wellington bombers took off
~ one of the eastern aerodromes in England. Their crews were all
…, flying with RAF. I happened to be in one of those aircraft as a navi-
…. Everything was ok, we knew eachother very well and it was not one of
first trips we were going on. Our target was the railway station in
…nover. We crossed the english coast just after nine o'clock, climbing
had a full hour before we reach the dutch coast, where we had to
…eet the first signes of the german defence – night fighters, search lights
… flak. We were fully loaded and the climbing went slowly. We had
…0 feet when we came in contact with the first search lights. Now it
… up to the gunners to do their best and be alert, because we came
to the area defended by night fighters. We had still about couple of
…rs of flight before we get near the target. In those two hours we hoped
… reach the hight of 15.000 feet, from which we used to bomb. On our
…ght side the german flak was busy – Amsterdam. The air was clear
… visibility good. Having the dutch coast behind, the search lights were
…s frequent and one felt better about it. We were coming out of the
…ght fighters area into AA, which showed itself only from time to
…me and very feebly. The main show was still waiting for us, till we
…me to Hannover. In front of us, slightly to the right, Osnabrück
…med to realize, what's going on and showed off, while in Essen and
…ther in Ruhr, the Germans seemed to be quite busy. We went on, leaving
…nabrück on our right and were heading for our target. Reached 15.000 feet,
… felt pretty happy. The time shows, that we should be near. Yes, the
…w starts to show its activity. The search lights grow in number and the AA
… It's after midnight. I leave my cabin and go to the bomb-sight. The
…ts are keeping course and are waiting for me to lead them to the target.
…now question only of a minute or two and we shall be in the middle of it.
… down in the front part of the aircraft and am giving the last touch to the

101. FLYING WITH R.A.F.

On a nice evening in 1941, ten Wellington bombers took off from one of the eastern aerodromes in England. Their crews were all Czechs, flying with R.A.F. I happened to be in one of those aircraft as a navigator. Everything was OK, we knew each other very well and it was not one of the first trips we were going on. Our target was the railway station in Hannover. We crossed the English coast just after nine o'clock, climbing. We had a full hour before we reached the dutch coast, where we had to expect the first signs of the german defence—night fighters, searchlights and flak. We were fully loaded and the climbing went slowly.

We had 10,000 feet when we came in contact with the first search lights. Now it was up to the gunners to do their best and be alert, because we came into the area defended by night fighters. We had still about couple of hours of flight before we could get near the target. In those two hours we hoped to reach the height of 15,000 feet from which we used to bomb.

On our right side the German flak was busy—Amsterdam. The air was clear and visibility good. Having the dutch coast behind, the search lights were less frequent and one felt better about it. We were coming out of the night fighters area into A.A., which showed itself only from time to time and very feebly. The main show was still waiting for us, till we came to Hannover. In front of us, slightly to the right, Osnabrück seemed to realize what's going on and showed off while in Essen and farther in the Ruhr, the Germans seemed to be quite busy. We went on, leaving Osnabrück on our right and were heading for our target. Reached 15,000 feet, we felt pretty happy. The time shows, that we should be near. Yes, the town starts to show its activity. The searchlights grow in number and the A.A. too. It's after midnight. I leave my cabin and go to the bomb-sight. The pilots are keeping course and are waiting for me to lead them to the target. It's now question only of a minute or two and we shall be in the middle of it. I lie down in the front part of the aircraft and am giving the last touch to the bombsight. Through the glass I can see the town underneath, the search lights [*original text continued on page 102 of diary*] sweeping the sky and occasionally lighting up the aircraft. The pilot is doing well. Keeping steady course to the target I gave him and simultaneously playing with the engines, in order to mislead the sound detectors. One can see the bursts of the shells all around. From time to time the plane jumps up. That has only one meaning to us—they are exploding much nearer than one would desire. But still, everything goes well. We are over the target. I release the bombs. I can see them coming out of the belly of the aircraft and the plane is jumping up again. This time we know it's not A.A., but each bomb coming out makes the aircraft lighter. Someone has lit the fire in the target before us and we are putting on a bit more in order to keep it going. Our task is accomplished, we are leaving target. Wireless operator sending message home, that target was bombed and we are on our way back. The A.A. is weaker and weaker, we are leaving Hannover behind. Everything goes nicely. It's not one o'clock in the morning yet. We shall be home by four o'clock. That's what we thought but the fate had something else in store for us. The pilots kept the course which we steered happily for about ten minutes when a big flame bursts out of the port engine. We are on fire! The aircraft is turning and we are flying on one side. The pilot employs immediately the fire extinguisher and closes down the petrol for that engine. The fire slowly dies out, but for us, the engine is dead. This event lasted only for about a minute. We had about 15,000 feet height, our speed came immediately down to 100 mph and we were flying with the left wing high above pointing to the sky. That was our situation round about one o'clock in the morning in the middle of Germany. Not very hopeful. The pilot tries to bring the engine to its life again but in vain. We had to go without it and hope that the starboard engine will make miracles—which it really did looking at it now. In order to steer approximately on the home course, we had to fly with the left wing above us, because if we flew with wings on the level [*original text continued on page 103 of diary*], we would be flying round and round, which would not bring us anywhere. I mean anywhere near home. Another our worry was petrol—how long will it last? The starboard engine needed plenty because it was going on full throttle. And the engine working so intensively, for how long can it keep going? We had 15,000 feet but in order to maintain the height, the speed went down. When the speed reached critical point—about 70 mph, we had to lose the height to keep up the speed. And so it went on. Minutes seemed hours, hours eternity. All the time watching: height, speed, petrol, time, distance. Going down to ten, eight, five thousand feet, down and down, still in Germany, not far from the dawn. Every cloud we came across, we had to go around it, because we could not risk to go through with the plane hanging on one engine. Absolutely helpless against searchlights and A.A. Fortunately enough nobody paid us any heed, till about five o'clock in the morning. The day was coming now rapidly and we were over Holland near the coast. We were down at 2,000 feet, recognizing every single farmhouse, the streams running across the fields and every single detail of the country. Not much chance for us, still over the continent and in daylight too. Perfect target for anybody. A single search light shot out, its beam, due to the dawn already progressed, faint, started to circle round us. Nothing happens and after a little while it disappears. We can see the sea now, in front of us. What to do next? There is 120 miles of sea between us and the english coast. We have enough petrol for not quite an hour of flight. Our top speed is about 90 m.p.h. The starboard engine goes well, but for how much longer? We are bound to land somewhere on the sea. Or should we turn south and follow the coast in a safe distance and so go for the narrowest part of the Channel between Dover and Calais, in case we got it to land on sea, not to be too far from the land? But how much longer could we hope not to be spot by the Germans? We decided to go straight across. The rear gunner came out of his turret and stood by the handle for pulling out the dinghy in case of landing. Everything went well, much better [*original text continued on page 104 of diary*] than one would have expected. We had the dutch coast now far behind us and the engine did miracles. It started to climb! We gained 1,000 feet. After an hour everybody started to look for the coast. The petrol was not far from zero. Finally a hazy narrow stripe showed itself and started to grow. We were near the land and home! The hand of the petrol meter was showing zero now. The engine still goes but we shall have to land on the sea any minute, any second. Get ready, boys! Nothing happened. The engine still going but to us it seems singing because with every second we are nearer to the coast and who knows we might even land dry and if the petrol meter is wrong, we might land on the nearest aerodrome. We reached the coast. I left my cabin and went into the pilots' to have chat with them. After a little while we have

sweeping the sky and occasionally lighting up the aircraft. The pilot is a well. Keeping steady course to the target I gave him and simultaneously playing with the engines, in order to mislead the sound-detectors. One can see the bursts of the shells all round. From time to time the plane jumps up. That has only one meaning to us — they are exploding much nearer, to one would desire. But still, everything goes well. We are over the target, release the bombs. I can see them coming out of the belly of the aircraft and the plane is jumping up again. This time we know, it's not A.A., because each bomb coming out makes the aircraft lighter. Someone has lit the fire in the target before us and we are putting on a bit more, in order to keep it going. Our task accomplished, we are leaving target. Wireless-operator sends message home, that target was bombed and we on our way back. The A.A. is weaker and weaker, we are leaving Hannover behind. Everything goes nicely. It's not one o'clock in the morning yet. We shall be home by four o'clock. That's what we thought, but the fate had something else in store for us. The pilots kept the course, which we steered happily for about ten minutes when a big flame bursts out of the port-engine. We are on fire! The aircraft is turning, and we are flying on one side. The pilot employes immediately the fire-extinguisher and closes down the petrol for that engine. The fire slowly dies out, but for us, the engine is dead. This event lasted only for about a minute. We had about 15.000 feet hight, speed came immediately down to 100 m.p.h. and we were flying with the left wing high above us, pointing to the sky. That was our situation round about one o'clock in the morning in the middle of Germany. Not very hopeful. The pilot tries to bring the engine to its life again, but in vain. We had to go without it and hope that the starboard engine will make miracles — which it really did, looking at it now. In order to steer approximately the home course, we had to fly with the left wing above us, because if we flew with wings on the level

would be flying round and round, which would not bring us anywhere,
..eam, anywhere near home. Another our worry was petrol – how long will
..last? The starboard engine needed plenty, because it was going on full
..ottle. And then, the engine working so intensively, for how long can it
..ep going? We had 15.000 feet, but in order to maintain the hight, the
..ed went down. When the speed reached the critical point, – about 70 m.p.h
..e had to lose the hight to keep up the speed. And so it went. Minutes seemed
..urs, hours eternity. All the time watching: hight, speed, petrol, time, distan..
..ing down to ten, eight, five thousend feet, down and down, still in Germany
..t far from the dawn. Every cloud we came across, we had to go round it, be –
..use we could not risk to go through with the plane, hanging on one engine
..solutly helpless against search-lights & A.A. Fortunately enough nobody pai..
..s any heed, till about five o'clock in the morning. The day was coming now ra..
..dely and we were over Holland near the coast. We were down at 2000 feet,
..cognizing every single farm-house, the streams running across the fields and
..ery single detail of the country. Not much chance for us, still over the con –
..ent and in the daylight too. Perfect target for anybody. A single search ligh..
..t out, its beam, due to the dawn already progressed, faint, started to circle round..
.. Nothing happenes and after little while it disappears. We can see the sea
..w, in front of us. What to do next? There is 120 miles of sea between us
..d the english coast. We have enough petrol for not quite an hour of flight.
..r top speed is about 90 m.p.h, the starboard engine goes well, but for how
..uch longer? We are bound to land somewhere on the sea. Or should we
..rn to the south and follow the coast in a safe distance and so go for the
..rrowest part of the Channel between Dover and Calais, in case we got to
..nd on sea, not to be too far from the land? But for how much longer
..n we hope not to be spot by the Germans? We decided to go straight across
..e rear gunner came out of his turret and stood by the handle for pulling
..t the dinghy in case of landing. Everything went well, much better

then one would have expected. We had the dutch coast now far behind us and the engine did miracles. It started to climb! We gained 10 feet. After half an hour everybody started to look for the coast. The petrol was not far from zero. Finely a hazy narrow stripe showed itself and started to grow. We were near the land and home! The hand of the petrol meter was showing zero now. The engine still goes, but we shall have to land on the sea any minute, any second. Get ready! Nothing happened. The engine still going but to us it seems singing because with every second we are nearer to the coast and who knows, we might even land dry and if the petrol-meter is wrong, we might land on the nearest aerodrome. We reached the coast. I left my cabin and went into the pilot's to have a chat with them. After a little while we have heard a crack coming from the inside of the aircraft. I rushed back in my cabin and there it was. The portengine propeller, revolving for so many hours against its will wrenched itself off and thrust into the fuselage, into my cabin. Few seconds after that, the starboard engine ceased to work, because of the lack of petrol. We were about five miles inland. The pilot counterbalanced the aircraft and without taking out the undercarriage, we went for landing. There was not much time to chose the ground and a small field just in front of us seemed to be the right spot. The only hinder were some trees, running alongside the road, behind which the field was and above which we could not lift ourselves. Anyhow the luck was with us till to the end. There was a gap in between two trees, but not wide enough. We run with our right wing into one, which we succeeded to cut in half and happily landed. Better said crushed because there was not much left from the aircraft, what one could call serviceable.

Colditz 17ᵗʰ March 1944.   Capt. J. Zafouk

We were completely dazed and bewildered throughout the two weeks of the march. Reaction forced it on one. For a short month, which had seemed a hell of a lot longer, we had had the all embracing aim of destroying the enemy, of stopping him breaking through. At any rate that was the original idea. Later on most of us, I'm afraid, thought only of holding him off until we could get out of the ever narrowing circle.

The clear notes of a bugle sounded in St. Valery's smouldering pit. "Cease fire!" It couldn't be! Only two hours before, I had heard the General threaten to shoot a Frenchman if he didn't take his white flag down from the Church.

Then I saw the B.M. "Does this apply to us, Sir?" I saluted smartly. One doesn't salute in the field, but things were breaking up. One had to keep discipline going in oneself. "I'm afraid it does." Tears, floods of tears. Rage & bloody fury.

The enemy appeared. Schemes of escape were ended by a polite German officer who said cheerfully. "For you the war is over!" God! what a damn silly remark.

They separated us from our men. We were herded into a field & left to lie there, unbelievably tired but with no wish to sleep. Sleep prepares one for another day's work — we didn't need rest, there was no "other day."

More officers arrived. No men. We were just rubbish, no use to anyone but our own futile selves. Organisation was broken. Half an hour earlier the 51st Division had held St. Valery. Now there was just a lot of poor fools masquerading in khaki.

After two nights' sleep one began to think. But to think was disastrous. Five years in Germany. Possibly more. Even that might be optimistic. What was there to stop them getting to England? — the navy — one had terrific faith in the navy. — At least one tried to make oneself think one had. The enemy were so bloody cocky. "London on August 15th, war over in two months." "No!" you said, "Five years. You'll never beat us." They looked crestfallen. Odd. Lack of confidence somewhere. Your own confidence increased. You believed what you said — you had to — disbelief meant death.

That was the start of a marvellous self-deception. Always the next camp was going to be better. We would get plenty of food. We would get rid of the lice. We would be rescued. British forces had landed in Holland. Grim humour. Funny now.

Airaines, St. Pol, Doullens, Tournai, Alost, the & other towns passed us by on a painted back-cloth. In one place all the inhabitants turned out to receive us. They fed us magnificently & they cheered us. It was more like victory than utter defeat. Poor devils. But it helped them as well as us. The will was still there, even in a beaten nation. Britain would never give up — God give her courage.

We left France. The will wasn't in Belgium. The French had fed us well. The Belgians charged us exorbitant prices for everything. No money? Then you can starve! — They have starved for four years.

Holland breathed courage. The Dutch helped. Sympathy, terrific courage. No sign of defeat there, only proud disdain.

The last stage. A barge up the Rhine. Two thousand officers of all nationalities huddled together on her decks & in her holds. If you turned over at night you hit your neighbour in the face. We passed pleasure craft on the river in canoes. In the hot weather the Dutch girls were lying back in bathing dresses. Men, idly paddling their precious cargoes, looked up at us & winked. We didn't reply. They weren't real, those people being a

heard a crack coming from the inside of the aircraft. I rushed back to my cabin and there it was. The port engine propeller, revolving for so many hours against its will wrenched itself off and thrust itself into the fuselage, right into my cabin. Few seconds after that, the starboard engine ceased to work, because of lack of petrol. We were about five miles inland. The pilot counterbalanced the aircraft and without taking out the undercarriage we went down for a landing. There was not much time to choose the ground and a small field just in front of us seemed to be the right spot. The only hinder were some trees running alongside the road, behind which the field was, and above which we could not lift ourselves. Anyhow, the luck was with us till the end. There was a gap in between two trees, but not wide enough. We ran our right wing into one, which we succeeded to cut in half and happily landed. Better said crashed, because there was not much left of the aircraft, what one could call serviceable.

Colditz 17th March 1944

Capt. J. Zafouk.

105. THE MARCH—FRANCE, JUNE 1940

We were completely dazed, and bewilderment lasted throughout the two weeks of the march. Reaction forced it on one. For a short month, which had seemed like hell of a lot longer, we had had the all embracing aim of destroying the enemy, of stopping him breaking through. At any rate that was the original idea. Later on most of us, I'm afraid, thought only of holding him off until we could get out of the ever narrowing circle.

The clear notes of a bugle sounded in St. Valery's smouldering pit "Cease Fire". It couldn't be! Only two hours before I had heard the General threaten to shoot a Frenchman if he didn't take his white flag down from the church.

Then I saw the B.M. "Does this apply to us, Sir"? I saluted smartly. One doesn't salute in the field but things were breaking up. One had to keep discipline going in oneself. "I'm afraid it does". Tears, floods of tears. Rage and bloody fury.

The enemy appeared. Schemes of escape were ended by a polite German officer who said cheerfully "For you the war is over"! God! What a damn silly remark.

They separated us from our men. We were herded into a field and left to lie there, unbelievably tired but with no wish to sleep. Sleep prepares one for another day's work and we didn't need rest, there was no "other day".

More officers arrived. No men. We were just rubbish, no use to anyone but our own futile selves. Organisation was broken. Half an hour earlier the 51st Division had held St. Valery. Now there was just a lot of poor fools, masquerading in khaki.

After two nights' sleep one began to think. But to think was disastrous. Five years in Germany. Possibly more. Even that might be optimistic. What was there to stop them getting to England?—The Navy—one had terrific faith in the Navy.—At least one tried to make oneself think one had. The enemy was so bloody cocky. "London on August 15th, War over in two months". "No!" you said "Six years. You'll never beat us". . . . . They looked crestfallen.

Odd. Lack of confidence somewhere. Your own confidence increased. You believed what you said—you had to—disbelief meant death.

That was the start of a marvellous self deception. Always the next camp was going to be better. We would get plenty of food. We would get rid of the lice. We would be rescued. British forces had landed in Holland. Grim humour. Funny now.

Airaines, St. Pol, Doulens, Tournai, Alost.* These and other towns passed us by on a painted black cloth. In one place all the inhabitants turned out to receive us. They fed us magnificently and they cheered us. It was more like victory that utter defeat. Poor devils. But is helped them as well as us. The will was still there, even in a beaten nation. Britain would never give up—God give her courage.

We left France. The will wasn't in Belgium. The French had fed us well. The Belgians charged us exorbitant prices for everything. No money? Then you can starve!—They have starved for four years.

The Dutch helped. Sympathy, terrific courage—Holland breathed courage. No sign of defeat here, only proud disdain.

The last stage. A barge up the Rhine. Two thousand officers of all nationalities huddled together on her deck and in her holds. If you turned over at night you hit your neighbour in the face. We passed people on the river in canoes. In the hot weather the Dutch girls were lying back in bathing dresses. Men, idly paddling their precious cargoes, looked up at us and winked. We didn't reply. They weren't real, those people living an [*original text continued on page 106 of diary*] ordinary life. This was reality, field grey uniform, over crowding, stink and hunger.

Germany at last. Nazis and Police. All the ogres we'd heard of when we were alive. Now one hated—with the hatred of anger and of humiliation.

F. A. Lochrane Lt.
The Seaforth Hldrs.

* *Probably Doullens, Tournai and Aalst.*

107. SALONIKA—JUNE 1941

Salonika . . . the name brings a numbness to the mind; just a space in time from which nothing stands out. A barrack square; blazing sun; derelict barracks; rear-seats in a cloud of flies; urinals choking with ammonia fumes . . .

.   .   .   .   .

"Michael, I believe we could make it over the wire behind the de-louser . . ." Then days of surreptitious planning from the barber's window which over-looked the wire, the wall and the road beyond.

ordinary life. This was reality, field grey uniform, overcrowding, stink & hunger

Germany at last. Nazis & police. All the ogres we'd

heard of when we were alive. Now one hated — with the hatred of any

& of humiliation.

Salonika...... the name brings a numbness to the mind; just a space in time from which nothing stands out. A barrack-square; blazing sun; derelict barracks; rear-seats in a cloud of flies; urinals choking with ammonia fumes.....

—   —   —   —   —

"Michael, I believe we could make it over the wire behind the de-louser......" Then days of surreptitious planning from the barber's window which over-looked the wire, the wall and the road beyond.   —   —   —   —   —   —

"Let's try tonight!" A black bag hurriedly crammed with the savings of several days' biscuits and a loaf smuggled in by a Cypriot against his sweaty stomach. Time passing only through an endless day, and preparation for bed as usual as twilight fell. Lying with a crowd of men in a gutter. Last night a rat had run into my foot and squeaked as it hurried on past my face. An Australian tried sleeping inside the building; he came out half an hour later and counted seventy-three bed-bug bites on him. He was swollen up almost beyond recognition.

Light almost gone. "Come on, Michael". A few Serbs were still moving about the camp. An old Greek oven in what had been the cook-house building was to provide a hide-up near the wire until midnight. It was circular and about 5 feet in diameter, so we lay on each side of the little door which was just large enough to squeeze through. Bodies curved against the walls, our feet were some way apart at the back. Michael put out a hand to close the door: "No leave it open, we'll get more air and there will be less chance of anyone looking in."

Horses were stamping and rattling their pickets in the German transport lines close by; otherwise silence. 11.30 p.m - another half hour to go. Twenty minutes, fifteen, ten - sounds of stealthy feet somewhere behind the building. "What's that, Michael?" "Dunno, better wait a bit longer and see". Minutes pass; someone moving in a room to the right of our oven. More noise; people running, quietly, then a snatch of Arabic. "Christ! those bloody Cypriots are trying our place, I believe....."

"Halt! HALT!!" Suddenly we become the centre of a maelstrom of noise. German guards doubling in nailed boots; guttural commands, and a fusillade of shots. A scream cut short by the sound of a body falling. [Two more did not fall. They were still hanging in the wire two days later.] No noise in the oven except a thumping of heart. A flash of a torch passing a few yards away. "God! Michael, they're searching the building...."

We could hear the guards stamping through the out-houses at the back. Then nearer - entering a room just on our right. A shout and a scream - so close it seemed as if we were in the same room - then a rush of German words and a shot.... scream upon scream..... and more shots.... Christ this is cold-blooded German murder.... Oh God

An intense desire to break wind, and no power on earth to stop it.
"Look-out, Michael, they're coming....." Shrinking back into the dark
ness behind the oven-door; burying my head in my arms to stop
spectacles glinting..... the oven-door is still open..... still, KEEP STILL....
Christ! is this the end?.... good-bye, Michael.... torch-beam against
the back of the oven..... didn't he see us?..... are they moving on?....
The next oven-door is opened. They move further away. A flicker
of hope somewhere inside me. "Michael, have we made it? I
reckon the door being open saved us!"

Gradually silence returns, to be broken by the stamp of a boot
a few yards away. Then a shot, quite close, and an answering
one from further away. "Damn! they have left sentries round
the place".

A long night - hardly daring to move - and every half hour the
sentry outside firing a shot to cheer himself up.

Grey dawn and an occasional German passing between us and
the wire, and staring into the building where we lie. 6 o'clock
7 o'clock; one hour to parade. Half an hour now and a Feld-Webel
passing with two sentries. "I believe they're going, Michael...."
"All right, give them five minutes and we'll try and get back".
put my head slowly out of the oven-door and look both ways.
Noone in sight. "Come on, Michael, leave the bag, we'll pick it
up later".

I have not gone two yards when I stop dead. At my feet
lies a Cypriot. Six powder-blackened holes in his tunic and
a trickle of blood drying up to his mouth. "Poor devil ......
My God, what swine ....."

J. S. Shannon. Captain.
Durham Light Infantry.

...ave recently read a book by Ian Hay, in which he describes the ideal of a certain class of British society as being a lifetime of painful solvency followed [by] an elaborate funeral. My experience tends to confirm this view.

Until a few months ago, I was Dental Officer in a troops working camp & witness that funerals were popular & as elaborate as circumstances permitted. For example: One day the Camp Sgt. Maj. came to me and said "There [are] a couple of blokes from Such & Such a camp killed at work & Soon we're sending a party from this camp. Will you go IK the jart pleas" I agreed & next morning found my best uniform laid out with gleaming buttons & my belt beautifully polished, and a few minutes later was ladie of the most beautifully turned out N.C.O. & men out of camp carrying wreathes & accompanied by a German interpreter N.C.O. We marched to the camp from which the deceased came & met the funeral party from there (30 men) & we all set off together with a German Administration Officer & a Stabsfeldwebel with 30 men (firing party) [cross]roads where we met another 30 men from another camp together with the camp Military [guar]d! Well there was the usual German ballgup & the Senior Brit. W.O. came along & [said] "How will we arrange the parade sir?" The officer from the camp of the dead men replied "You carry on Sgt. Maj. You're the expert at this sort of thing!" At this [the] S.M. got busy. He grabbed the Stabsfeldwebel (who was supposed to be I/c) & said "put your men there (behind the barg) & don't move til I tell you." The Stabsfeldwebel replied "Jawhol Herr Stabsfeldwebel." Eventually the C.S.M. had things to his [l]iking & reported Vaiok. So he roared "Carry on Sgt. Maj." He saluted tremendously & [gave] an earsplitting bellow "PARADE TSHUN!!" "BY THE LEFT QUEEEECK MARCH.!!" [The] Germans although ignorant of English caught on & did their best not to ruin what [was] probably the smartest military parade that part of the World had seen since a [certain] Austrian went to Holland for his health. After marching through the [to]wn to the mortuary we halted & a bearer party went in to bring out the coffins. [The] drill was perfect & after the coffins were lodged in the hearse & covered with [wr]eaths the order "PARADE SLOOOOOW MARCH." was given & the band played [Men]delssohn's Dead March. The British troops keeping perfect step & the Germans [try]ing hard not to look too silly. All this mind you was going on in a town [in Ge]rmany with the Hun populace admiring our smart turn out & drill of the [Brit]ish troops. After a few minutes of slow marching, we quick march[ed] [to the] cemetery on the outskirts of the town & at the gates once more slow [marched] in. The Padre conducted the service after which the firing party fired a [vo]lley & the parade broke up to have its photos taken, as if by magic [c]ups of beer, sandwiches, & chocolate appeared. Don't ask me to explain how they ha[d] carried without making bulges in the outline of "properly dressed" soldiers [o]r where. After this al fresco substitute for the funeral baked meats the three [par]ties fell in & marched back to their respective camps with the air of men [wel]l satisfied with their morning's work, the connoisseurs comparing [?] [favourably with previous efforts.

My object in recording the above is not merely to describe a P.O.W. funeral — this funeral was not at[ypica]l, but to try to illustrate the morale of Thomas Atkins after over 3 years of captivity. The 1st year (whe[n] [?] it began to soak in that Germany had lost the war) slight[ly] improved. The next two years [an elabo]rate funeral is Tommy's way of expressing his sympathy & trying to soften the blow for be[reav]ed relatives by sending photographs of the funeral & the gravestone (the latter [?] [sli]ghtly camp subscription) thus showing them that although their dead died in enemy [?] [Jack] was buried with military honours by comrades who obviously thought [a great deal] of him & that a permanent memorial marks his resting place which they [?] [wi]ll be able to identify after the war.

† to be amended when circumstances permit.

                                    J. M. Green Captain
                                    A. D. Corps.

. . . . .

"Let's try tonight!" A black bag hurriedly crammed with the savings of several days' biscuits and a loaf smuggled in by a Cypriot against his sweaty stomach. Time passing slowly through an endless day, and preparation for bed as usual as twilight fell. Lying with a crowd of men in a gutter. Last night a rat had run into my foot and squeaked as it hurried on past my face. An Australian tried sleeping inside the building; he came out half an hour later and counted seventy-three bed-bug bites on him. He was swollen up almost beyond recognition.

Light almost gone. "Come on, Michael." A few Serbs were still moving about the camp. An old Greek oven in what had been the cook-house building was to provide a hide-up near the wire until midnight. It was circular and about six feet in diameter, so we lay on each side of the little door which was just large enough to squeeze through. Bodies curved against the walls, our feet were some way apart at the back. Michael put out a hand to close the door; "No, leave it open, we'll get more air and there will be less chance of anyone looking in."

Horses were stamping and rattling their pickets in the German transport lines close by; otherwise silence. 11.30 p.m.—another half hour to go. Twenty minutes, fifteen, ten—sound of stealthy feet somewhere behind the building. "What's that, Michael?" "Dunno, better wait a bit longer and see." Minutes pass; someone snoring in a room to the right of our oven. More noise; people running, quietly, then a snatch of Arabic. "Christ! Those bloody Cypriots are trying our place, I believe..."

"Halt! HALT!!" Suddenly we become the centre of a maelstrom of noise. German guards doubling in nailed boots; guttural commands and a fusillade of shots. A scream cut short by the sound of a body falling. (Two more did not fall. They were still hanging in the wire two days later.) No noise in the oven except a thumping of heart. A flash of a torch passing a few yards away. "God! Michael, they're searching the building . . ."

We could hear the guards stamping through the out-houses at the back. Then nearer—entering a room just on our right. A shout and a scream—so close it seemed as if we were in the same room—then a rush of German words and a shot . . . scream upon scream . . . and more shots . . . Christ this is cold-blooded German murder . . . Oh God let him die quickly . . . Fear, gripping fear, creeping up from my stomach . . . [*Original text continued on page 108 of diary*]. An intense desire to break wind, and no power on earth to stop it . . . "Look out Michael, they're coming . . ." Shrinking back into the darkness behind the oven-door; burying my head in my arms to stop my spectacles glinting . . . the oven door still open . . . still . . . KEEP STILL . . . Christ, is this the end? . . . Good-bye Michael . . . torch beam against the back of the oven . . . didn't he see us? . . . are they moving on? . . . The oven door is opened. They move further away. A flicker of hope somewhere inside me. "Michael, have we made it? I reckon the door being open saved us!"

Gradually silence returns, to be broken by the stomp of a boot a few yards away. Then a shot, quite close, and an answering one from further away. "Damn! They have left sentries round the place."

A long night—hardly daring to move—and every half hour the sentry outside firing a shot to cheer himself up.

Grey dawn and an occasional German passing between us and the wire, and staring into the building where we lie. 6 o'clock; 7 o'clock; one hour to parade. Half an hour now and a

Feld-Webel passing with two sentries. "I believe they're going Michael . . ."

"All right, give them five minutes and we'll try and get back." I put my head slowly out of the oven door and look both ways. Noone in sight. "Come on Michael, leave the bag, we'll pick it up later."

I have not gone two yards when I stop dead. At my feet lies a Cypriot. Six powder-blackened holes in his tunic and a trickle of blood drying up to his mouth. "Poor devil . . . My God, what swine . . ."

K. E. Herman, Captain
Durham Light Infantry

109. OBERSCHLESISCHE OBSEQUIES 1943

I have recently read a book by Ian Hay, in which he describes the ideal of a certain class of British Society as being a lifetime of painful solvency followed by an elaborate funeral. My experience tends to confirm this view.

Until a few months ago, I was Dental Officer in a troop working camp and can witness that funerals were popular and as elaborate as circumstances permitted. For example . . . One day the camp Sergeant Major came to me and said "There's been a couple of blokes from such and such a camp killed in Wurnick, Saar, and we're sending a party from this camp. Will you go i/c the party, please?" I agreed and next morning found my best uniform laid out with gleaming buttons and my belt beautifully polished, and a few minutes later was leading 20 of the most beautifully turned out N.C.O.s and men out of camp, carrying wreaths and accompanied by a German interpreter N.C.O. We marched to the camp from which the 2 deceased came and met the funeral party from there (30 men) and we all set off together with a German Administrative Officer and a Stabsfeldwebel with 30 men (firing party) to the roads where we met another 20 men from another camp, together with the Camp Military Band! Well there was the usual German balls-up and the Senior British W.O. came along and said, "How will we arrange the parade Sir?" The officer from the camp of the dead men replied, "You carry on, Sgt. Maj. You're the expert at this sort of thing!"

At this the C.S.M. got busy. He grabbed the Stabsfeldwebel (who was supposed to be i/c) and said, "You put your men there (behind the band, and don't move till I tell you!" The Stabsfeldwebel replied "Jawohl, Herr Stabsfeldwebel!"

Eventually the C.S.M. had things to his liking and reported back. On being told "Carry on Sgt. Maj.", he saluted tremendously and let out an earsplitting bellow "PARADE 'TSHUN!! BY THE LEFT QUEEECK MARCH!!" The Germans, although ignorant of English caught on and did their best not to ruin what was probably the smartest military parade that part of the world had seen since Kaiser Bill went to Holland for his health. After marching through the town to the mortuary we halted and a bearer party went in to bring out the coffins. The drill was perfect and after the coffins were lodged in the hearse and covered with wreaths, the order "PARADE SLOOOOW MARCH!" was given and the band played Mendelssohn's Dead March, the British troops keeping perfect step and the Germans trying hard not to look too silly. All this, mind you, was going on in a town in Germany with the Hun populace admiring the smart turn out and drill of the British troops. After a few minutes of slow marching we quick marched to the cemetery on the outskirts or the town and at the gates once more slow marched in. The Padre conducted the service after which the firing party fired a volley and the parade broke up to have its photos taken. As if by magic, bottles of beer, sandwiches and chocolate appeared. Don't ask me to explain how they had been carried without making bulges in the outline of "properly dressed" soldiers—they were.

After this alfresco substitute for the funeral baked meats, the three parties fell in and marched back to their respective camps with the air of men well satisfied with their morning's work, the connoisseurs comparing events favourably with previous efforts.

My object in recording the above is not merely to describe a P.O.W. funeral—this funeral was not typical, but to try to illustrate the morale of Thomas Atkins after over 3 years of captivity. The first year of which was under appalling conditions enforced very often by <u>kind hearted gentlemen</u>* The next two years (after it began to soak in the Germany had lost the war) slightly improved. Another point: this elaborate funeral is Tommy's way of expressing his sympathy and trying to soften the blow for the bereaved relatives by sending photographs of the funeral and the gravestone (the latter bought by camp subscription), thus showing them that although their dead died in enemy hands he was buried with military honours by comrades who obviously thought well of him and that a permanent memorial marks his resting place which they will be able to identify after a war.

*to be amended when circumstances permit.

J. M. Green, Captain

A. D. Corps

110. CALAIS, 23RD MAY 1940

This will always remain one of the most eventful days of my life. On this day I arrived at the port of Calais, and there began a four days action against the Germans.

My unit, the 60th Rifles, had barely managed to unload a few vehicles before the enemies' guns opened up on us. Fortunately they weren't very accurate and our first moments of anxiety and incidentally our initial baptism of fire, was soon overcome. Our object was to stem the forward drive of Hitler's armies, whose main object was that on the port of Dunkirk from which the British Army was evacuating.

How great was my anxiety that I should come through this action safely may well be imagined when I say that my wife was expecting her first born in July. However, fate was kind to me and so I patiently wait to see this son of ours.

My job of work in the engagement was that of a Dispatch Rider and one that proved fatal for a lot of my fellow comrades. It was pretty obvious that our small force could not last very long over the superior numbers of the enemy. However, we had a job to do and it was done to the best of our ability.

The first day saw my company being severely knocked about overlooking a ridge on the south side of Calais, and many messages were transmitted by wireless and myself to Batt' H.Q. requesting help and also orders as to what to do.

Our Bren Carriers had the unenviable task of making contact with the enemy and we watched them go with what might be termed regret, on a dangerous and daring job, from which not much hope of returning could be expected. I only saw one return out of four and the driver of this was terribly injured and his anti-tank gunner died next to him. He performed a very gallant task in getting back to his position. I eventually put him in a hospital but have not since heard from him or about him.

We held this position well into the second day, when after suffering considerable losses, it was found necessary to withdraw into the town itself.

Then began some bitter street fighting and every inch of ground was fought for. The Germans had already got snipers safely installed in the town and they caused us lots of casualties; these received no mercy when we did get them.

On the beginning of the third day we were much surprised to see a solitary figure approaching our lines with a flag of truce raised. This transpired to be a German officer, who when he reached me requested to be taken to our C.O. His object it was found later, was to ask us to surrender. He said if we didn't we should be bombed out by their air force. Our Commanding Officer would not hear of such a thing and so the useless carnage went on.

Already I had some narrow escapes, being on one occasion blown off my motor bike by a trench mortar and narrowly missed by snipers.

How we did curse them!

Then came the most terrorising bombardment by German "Stuka" dive bombers, who let us have it for roughly eight hours. What a chaotic state we were in by the time they had finished. Houses were ablaze for whole blocks, crashing of masonry, terrific explosions, and all of us,—if the truth be told—pretty well scared out of our wits. It was obvious to all that the end couldn't be prolonged much longer. We had already suffered heavy losses.

The fatal 26th of May was now on us. We hadn't slept, eaten or even drunk properly, and slowly and remorselessly we were being driven back towards the beaches.

At about mid-day of the 26th, our C.O. issued the order. "Every man for himself, and the best of luck."

I can't speak too highly of my C.O. and all the other officers. They never failed to inspire us with their courageous actions, and were to be seen at all dangerous positions. This inspiring leadership undoubtedly encouraged us to prolong our desperate fight. [*Original text continued on page 111 of diary*]. Towards five o'clock most of what was left of us had been taken prisoner, and about an hour later the Germans had taken Calais.

So ended a gallant action, fought against terrific odds. It had taken two German divisions four days to subdue three battalions of us, and I think we can claim the honour of having helped make Dunkirk the success it was.

D. M. Nugent
Cpt. 60th Rifles

23rd May 1940

This will always remain one of the most eventful days of my life. On this day I arrived at the front of Calais, and there began a four days action against the Germans.

My Unit the 60th Rifles had barely managed to unload a few vehicles before the enemy's guns opened up on us continually. They weren't very accurate and our first moments of anxiety, and incidental our initial baptism of fire, was soon overcome. Our object was to stem the forward drive of Hitler's armies whose main object was that of the front of Dunkirk, from which the British Army was evacuating.

How great was my anxiety that I should come through this action safely may well be imagined when I say that my wife was expecting her first born in July. However fate was kind to me, and now I patiently wait to see this son of ours.

My type of work in the engagement was that of a Despatch Rider, and one that proved fatal to a lot of my fellow comrades. It was pretty obvious that our small force could not last very long over the superior machine of the enemy. However we had a job to do, and it was done to the best of our ability.

The first day saw my company being severely knocked about overlooking a ridge on the south side of Calais, and many messages were transmitted by wireless and myself to Batt. H.Q. requesting help and also orders as to what to do.

Our Bren Carriers had the unenviable task of making contact with the enemy and we watched them go with what might be termed respect; on a dangerous and daring job, from which not much hope of returning would be expected. I only saw one return out of four and the driver of this was terribly injured and his anti-tank gunner died next to him. He performed a very gallant task in getting to his position and I eventually put him on an hospital ship, but have not since heard from him or about.

We held this position well into the second day, when, after suffering considerable losses, it found necessary to withdraw into the town itself.

Then began some very bitter street fighting and every inch of ground was fought for. The Germans had already got snipers safely installed in the town, and they caused us lots of casualties. These received no mercy when we did get them.

On the beginning of the third day we were much surprised to see a solitary figure approach our lines with a flag of truce raised. This transpired to be a German officer, who, when he reached requested to be taken to our C.O. His object it was found later, was to ask us to surrender, he said didn't we should be bombed out by their air-force. Our commanding officer would not hear of such thing and so the useless carnage went on.

Already I had had some very narrow escapes, being on one occasion blown off my motor-bike by a trench-mortar, and narrowly missed by snipers.

How we did curse them!

Then came the most terrorising bombardment by German "Stuka" dive bombers, who let us have it roughly eight hours. What a chaotic state we were in by the time they had finished. Houses were for whole blocks, masking of masonry, terrific explosions, and all of us, - if the truth were told - very well scared out of our wits. It was obvious to all that the end couldn't be prolonged much longer. We had already suffered very heavy losses.

The fatal 26th of May was now on us. We hadn't slept; eaten or even drunk properly, and so and remorselessly we were being driven back towards the beaches.

At about mid-day of the 26th, our C.O. issued the order, "Every man for himself, and the best of luck".

I can't speak too highly of my C.O. and all other officers. They never failed to inspire with their courageous actions, and were to be seen at all dangerous positions. Their inspiring leadership undoubtedly encouraged us to prolong a desperate fight.

He told me the story of how hope was restored to him......

In the dank foul-smelling cell he had indeed hours to consider his [sen]tence, as he watched the loathsome insects crowding over floor & walls. Never again [wou]ld he smoke, read or speak his own tongue. "Quos vult deus perdere prius [de]mentat". In the torment of mad despair he struck wildly at the insects. In a [mo]ment they returned in myriads through the tiny vent by the ceiling that served as [win]dow, as he collapsed done in, helpless, sobbing, on the metal bars he called his [bed]. Fear consumed, unhinged him, fear of a death so simple and without [ce]remony. None of a spy's honour, a soldier's glory. Just simply a row of [in]nocents facing a machine-gun. "In a few days a hundred hostages will be sh[ot] [You] will be amongst this number." As he had heard this, he had laughed with [the] abandon that now he sobbed. Suddenly he was composed. He knelt before [the] little cross he had scratched on the chink of wall where the evening sun [sett]led a moment.

Three hours later he was in ecstasy. No news had ever elated him so [mu]ch. He had doubled to the Abort at the familiar cries of Los!. Los! [A] man was there, a terrifying spectre with the visionless sunken eyes of a [cl]ock. They spoke together, in French, My friend asked what were his chances of living. [In] a moment's reflection, the other dramatically held up two fingers. Was he [doome]d as the rest? "That means" he said "I too am Deuxième Bureau. They [hav]e been threatening to shoot me for ten months. Have no fear. Your case will be [no] quicker than mine. Be happy to think you may live on here for months, even [year]s." Life was too dear for my friend to be despondent at such a ghastly [pros]pect stretching into a black, pitiless future. He was jubilant and hobbled [bac]k to his cell whistling stridently.

There was a bit of melodramatic journalese about him, but I believe [I] felt every word of his story was sincere....

Ch. Silverwood Cope
Lieut. RA.

[...a]nds five o'clock most of what was left of us had been taken prisoner, and about an hour late[r] [Ger]mans had taken Calais.
So ended a gallant action, fought against terrific odds.
[...]nd taken two German divisions four days to subdue three battalions of us, and I think [we c]an claim the honour of having helped to make Dunkirk the success it was.

[signature] Dugast
Cpl. 6ᵗʰ Rifles

111. PAWIAK PRISON, WARSAW—19TH AUGUST 1942

He told me the story of how hope was restored to him . . .

In the dank foul-smelling cell, he had indeed hours to consider his sentence, as he watched the loathsome insects crowding over floor and walls. Never again would he smoke, read or speak his own tongue. "Quod vult deus perdere primo dementat".

In the torment of mad despair he struck wildly at the insects. In a moment they returned in myriads through the tiny vent by the ceiling that served as window, as he collapsed done in, helpless, sobbing, on the metal bars he called his bed. Fear consumed, unhinged him, fear of a death so simple and without ceremony. None of the spy's honour, a soldier's glory. Just simply a row of innocents facing a machine gun.

"In a few days a hundred hostages will be shot. You will be amongst this number." As he had heard this, he had laughed with the abandon that he now sobbed. Suddenly he was composed. He knelt before the little cross he had scratched on the chink of wall where the evening sun settled a moment.

Three hours later he was in ecstasy. No news had ever elated him so much. He had doubled to the Abort at the familiar cries of Los! Los! A man was there, a terrifying spectre with the visionless sunken eyes of a Morlock. They spoke together in French. My friend asked what were his chances of living. After a moment's reflection, the other dramatically held up two fingers. Was he as mad as the rest? "That means", he said "I too am Deuxième Bureau. They have been threatening to shoot me for ten months. Have no fear. Your case will be no quicker than mine. Be happy to think you may live on here for months, even years." Life was too dear for my friend to be despondent at such a ghastly prospect stretching into a black, pitiless future. He was jubilant and hobbled back to his cell whistling stridently.

There was a bit of melodramatic journalese about him, but I believe he felt every word of his story was sincere . . .

C. L. Silverwood-Cope,
Lieut. R.A.

112. PRISONERS' JOURNEY

After spending ten days of comparative peace living under the bushes and trees and being escorted by Austrian guards to forage the countryside for hens, pigs and potatoes, the officers captured in Crete were flown to Athens.

On arrival at the station there we were met by a German officer—gaunt, thin-lipped, and pale—who barked and spat at us the consequences of an attempt to escape or speak to the Greek civilians. From then on the shouts and screams of the guards increased as we approached Germany.

After a short pause at the station we were roused by the guards, almost one per officer and crammed into 3rd class carriages. Rations of 3 hard biscuits, a lump of salt fish and some cheese had been issued but this was reinforced by the Greeks, who on every opportunity, showered little packages to us in spite of German threats and shots. The Greek generosity stands out as the most memorable feature of one's early captivity. The rest of daylight was punctuated by the wild shouts and shots of the guards at the Greeks.

Mid-night brought the train to a halt and the prisoners were hustled out into the dark. The line had been blown up during the British withdrawal, was not yet repaired and we were to march over the Thermopylae Pass and pick up another train 25 miles away.

We staggered over the pass in the dark, hugging our worthless but highly-prized possessions, descended into the Plain by which time it was scorching day. Those with dysentery were prodded on when they tried to halt, but somehow everyone made it to the station by midday. Another night on the train, this time cattle trucks—our first introduction to them—a halt of 5 minutes in the morning producing a squatting, crouching mass of British officers mixed with Arabs and Cypriots, the whole surrounded by German sentries with rifles threatening, back into the train all too soon and the now familiar "Raus" emptied us into Salonika, raining.

A bedraggled, singing procession through wet streets, German cameras making the most of it and we entered the transit camp, already overflowing with prisoners from Greece. Here we spent 9 weeks, burning bed bugs from our beds, eating ¼ of a loaf of bread, a biscuit and a watery soup per day and trying to pass the long day. The Germans were winning the war, at least so they thought, their Tommy guns and revolvers trying to convince them and interrupting an already disturbed sleep by countless miniature battles. A night visit to the latrine meant running the gauntlet of T.G.s and even hand grenades. German officers seldom appeared and then only to shout insults and to answer to any complaints that his was only a transit camp.

One morning, after a night of shots, shouts and terrified screams, five bullet-riddled Arabs littered the compound and were left for twelve hours as an example to anyone who contemplated escape.

Towards the end of the 9 weeks, health had deteriorated, collapses were frequent and jaundice, malaria and dysentery were common and there were cases of beri-beri.

The final stage to Germany was done in cattle trucks in August, 40 to a wagon, all doors shut and in some cases the small windows boarded up. Stops were twice a day, a matter of minutes whilst everyone hurried to their business. Once the doors were not open for 24 hours and those who suffered from dysentery and their companions had to make the most of it. The guards became more vociferous, drinking water was practically nil and lice were a matter of course. The stench of forty bodies in midsummer may be imagined.

After a week the "organised" camp at Lubeck was reached, there to have most of our highly prized possessions confiscated and to get rid of the small companions who had become so intimate on the journey.

W. J. Burton, Y&L Regt.

Having spent 10 days of comparative peace living under bushes & trees & being sent by Austrian guards to forage the countryside for hens, pigs & potatoes, the officers captured in Crete were flown to Athens.

On arrival at the station there we were met by a German officer - gaunt, tight-lipped & pale - who looked & spat at us in the consequences of an attempt to escape & spoke to the Greek civilians. From then on the shouts & screams of the guard men as we approached Germany.

After a short pause at the station we were passed by the guards, almost past officers, & crammed into 3rd class carriages. Rations of 3 hard biscuits, a bit of salt fish & some cheese had been issued but this was reinforced by the Greeks who on every opportunity, shoved little packages to us in spite of German threats and shots. The Greek generosity stands out as the most memorable feature of one's captivity. The rest of daylight was punctuated by the wild shouts & shots of the guards at the Greeks.

Mid-night brought the train to a halt & the prisoners were hustled out into the dark. The line had been blown up during the British withdrawal & was not yet repaired & we were to march over the Thermopylae Pass & pick up another train 25 miles away.

We staggered over the pass in the dark, lugging our worthless but highly prized possessions, descended into the Plain by which time it was scorching day. Those with dysentery were prodded on when they tried to halt, but somehow every one made the station by mid-day; Another night in a train, this time cattle trucks - our first introduction to them - a halt of 5 minutes in morning producing a squatting crouched mass of British officers mixed with Arabs & Cypriots, the whole surrounded by German sentries with rifles threatening, back into the train all too soon & the now familiar "Raus" & us into Salonika, raining.

A bedraggled, singing procession through wet streets, German cameras making most of it & we entered the Transit camp, already overflowing with prisoners from Greece. Here were spent 9 weeks, burning bed-bugs from our beds, eating 1/5 of a loaf & a bit of watery soup per day & trying to pass the long day. The Germans were amusing themselves, at least so they thought, their tommy guns & revolvers trying to convince them, interrupting an already disturbed sleep by countless miniature battles. A night to the latrine meant running the gauntlet of T.Gs & even hand grenades. German officers seldom appeared & then only to shout insults & to answer to any complaints that this was a transit Camp.

One morning after a night of shots, shouts & terrified screams, 6 bullet-riddled arabs filled the compound & were left for 12 hours as an example to any one who contemplated escape.

Towards the end of the 9 weeks, health had deteriorated, collapses were common, jaundice, malaria & dysentery were common & there were cases of beri-beri.

The final stage to Germany was done in cattle trucks in August, 40 to a van, all doors shut & in some cases the small windows boarded up. Stops were twice a day & a matter of minutes whilst every one hurried to their business. Once the door were open for 24 hours & those who suffered from dysentery & their companions had to make the most of it. The guards became more vociferous, drinking water was practically nil & air was a matter of course. The stench of 40 bodies in mid-summer may be imagined. After a week the organised camp at Lubeck was reached, there we had most of our

A Mk VI B Light Tank troop is travelling across country in extended order, looking a little battered and part-worn perhaps, but going remarkably well considering their almost pre-historic age.

A staff car, travelling at great speed, as staff cars always do, and looking singularly imposing with its HQ penant flying from the radiator cap, approaches the troop commanders tank signalling to him to halt.

"Switch up operator" orders the troop commander, and when the wireless has warmed up "Hullo Bulldog 3, Bulldog calling — halt to cover my present position — Bulldog 3 to Bulldog 3 over" to which order he receives the acknowledgement "Bulldog 3 a — OK — off" and so on from his other tanks.

Thrusting the microphone behind his respirator, the troop commander gropes for the internal communication voice tube of his tank. For the purposes of this exercise it is not lying in a dejected coil on the floor with neither end connected, as is almost invariably the case, but merely needs a series of desperate wriggles to disentangle it from the commanders legs and probably the gunners neck, and wonder of wonders there it is to hand.

"Driver halt — Vickers traverse left 12 o'clock" he orders, and the series of burps and gurgles which issue from the other end of the voice tube seem to get the necessary results, bringing the tank to a halt.

The staff car draws up in rear and out steps the Brigadier who has just recently taken over command.

A digression here over the peculiarities of staff cars in general. Why is it that they must always travel at fantastic speeds, always trail behind them a semi-permanent cloud of dust, and always give the impression that they are carrying, at the very least, the complete army council, when in point of fact they are in all probability taking the sanitary corporal to the local RASC depot to

113. THE FIRST (AND ONLY) ARMOURED DIVISION 1939-1940

A Mk.VIB Light Tank troop is travelling across country in extended order, looking a little battered and part worn perhaps but going remarkably well considering their almost pre-historic age.

A staff car, travelling as great speed, as staff cars always do, and looking singularly imposing with its HQ pennant flying from the radiator cap, approaches the Troop Commander's tank signalling him to halt.

"Switch up operator", orders the Troop Commander, and when the wireless has warmed up, "Hello, Bulldog 3, Bulldog 3 calling—halt to cover my present position—Bulldog 3 to Bulldog 3 over" to which order he receives the acknowledgement "Bulldog 3 A-O.K.—off." and so on from his other tanks.

Thrusting the microphone behind the respirator, the Troop Commander gropes for the internal communication voice tube of his tank. For the purposes of this exercise it is not lying in a dejected coil in the floor with neither end connected, as is almost invariably the case, but merely needs a series of desperate wriggles to disentangle it from the Commander's legs and probably the gunner's neck and wonder of wonders, there it is to hand.

"Driver halt"—"Vickers traverse left 12 o'clock", he orders, and then the series of burps and gurgles which issue from the other end of the voice tube seem to get the necessary results, bringing the tank to a halt.

The staff car draws up in rear and out steps the Brigadier who has just recently taken over command.

A digression here over the peculiarities of staff cars in general. Why is it that they must always travel at fantastic speeds, always trail behind them a seemingly permanent cloud of dust, and always give the impression that they are carrying at the very best the complete army council, when in point of fact they are in all probability taking the sanitary corporal to the local RASC Depot to [*original text continued on page 114 of diary*] collect a supply of Army Form O?

To continue. The Brigadier speaks a few words to the troop commander then drives off, and the tanks continue their advance.

Some time later the following dialogue between the gunner and the driver is faintly heard shouted above the rattle of the tracks, the roar of the engine and the general din of loose paraphernalia in the form of ammunition bins, compartment doors which have an annoying habit of falling off, and so on.

Driver—"I say Bill, who was that b—— that halted us just now?"

Gunner—"The new Brigadier Jock".

Driver—"Was it by G——. What does he look like?"

Gunner—"He looks pretty fierce to me Jock, but he only has one arm."

Driver, after a pause to digest this startling piece of information—"I say Bill, what a f—— awful army this is, no b—— tanks, no b—— guns, b—— civvy lorries, and now they give us a Brigadier with only one f—— arm."

The moral of this story is contained, I think, in that "ye olde Englishe" toast "Floreat Excreta Tauronum".

Douglas N. Moir,
Lt., Royal Tank Regt.

115. SIDI HANEISH (EGYPTE)—23-24 JUILLET 1942

We had been in the desert for nearly three months, close to the Matruh-Siwa trail, approximately 200 kilometres behind stabilized enemy lines at El Alamein, and had carried out many raids on the enemy's advance aerodromes during the week of the 7th to 15th of July.

The unit engaged in these operations was commanded by Major David Stirling, D.S.O., and had a total complement of about 80 officers and men, from which my detachment under my orders of the First Company Parachutists of the Free French Forces in the Middle East.

After having taken part in the operations at the beginning of the month, Major Stirling returned to Cairo and came to rejoin us on the 22nd, by the Qattara depression, with a substantial revitalization of petrol, munitions, explosives, rations, water and whisky! By the same convoy arrived a certain number of the first Jeeps to appear in the desert.

On his arrival, Major Stirling communicated with us his intention to launch an attack the next night on the concentration of enemy aircraft that had been identified by the R.A.F. on the Sidi Haneish aerodrome, 30 kilometres east of Matruh. Our methods of attacking the aircraft on the ground with bombs, known by the enemy, were out of date. Also to achieve the effect of surprise, we were going to attack in force with all the means of fire at our disposal; all the available Jeeps, which were fifteen, carrying a crew of three men armed with twin Vickers machine guns were engaged in the operation. In this way we could concentrate 60 barrels of rapid fire at the same time against the aircraft on the ground and silence the enemy defences.

After a day of intense work on equipment and vehicles, we set out on the 23rd at 2000 hours accompanied by a patrol of the New Zealand Long Range Desert Group who were charged with creating a diversion in a sector adjoining our objective, a quarter of an hour before our main attack.

The distance we were to cover was approximately 100 kilometres. It was a clear night with a full moon. There were no incidents during the journey except that the Long Range Desert Group, which detached itself from us on the route, lost a vehicle on a mine. Our navigation was remarkably precise, and at 0045 hours [*original text continued on page 116 of diary*] we arrived at the edge of the group of aerodromes.

Suddenly two flares appeared in the sky and a few seconds later, the lights along a runway illuminated and an aircraft landed. We discovered later that the New Zealand patrol captured the crew as they got out of the plane and left with two prisoners after placing a time bomb in the aircraft.

At 0100 hours, the chosen time, formed into a single line, we penetrated the aerodrome perimeter at a speed of 15 kilometres an hour, firing all our guns on the leading planes. Our tracer bullets created a splendid display of pyrotechnics.

At the signal of three green Very lights, fired by Major Stirling and the flanking vehicles, we adopted

collect a supply of Army Form O ?

To continue. The Brigadier speaks a few words to the troop commander then drives off, and the tanks continue their advance.

Some time later the following dialogue, between the gunner and driver is faintly heard shouted above the rattle of the tracks, the roar of the engine, and the general din of loose paraphernalia in the form of ammunition bins, compartment doors which have an annoying habit of falling off, and so on.

Driver — " I say Bill, who was that b— that halted us just now?"

Gunner — " The new Brigadier Jock "

Driver — " Was it by G— what does he look like ?

Gunner — " He looks pretty fierce to me Jock, but he has only one arm."

Driver, after a pause to digest this startling piece of information — " I say Bill, what a f— awful army this is, no b— tanks, no b— guns, b— curvy lorries, and now they give us a Brigadier with only one f— arm."

The moral of this story is contained, I think, in that "ye olde englishe" toast " Floreat Excreta Taurorum"

Douglas N. Muir

Lt. Royal Tank Reg

Nous sommes depuis près de trois semaines dans le désert, à proximité de la piste MATRUH - SIWA, soit à 200 km. environ en arrière des lignes ennemies stabilisées à EL ALAMEIN, et avons effectué, dans la semaine du 7 au 15 juillet, plusieurs raids sur les aérodromes avancés de l'ennemi.

La formation engagée dans ces opérations est commandée par le major David Stirling S.O., et a un effectif total d'environ 80 officiers et hommes, dont un détachement sous mes ordres de la 1ère Cie parachutiste des Forces Françaises Libres Moyen-Orient.

Après avoir pris part aux opérations du début du mois, le major Stirling retourné au Caire et vient de nous rejoindre, le 22, par la dépression de QATTARA, avec un ravitaillement substantiel en essence, munitions, explosifs, vivres, eau et whisky ! Par le même convoi nous arrivent également un certain nombre des premières Jeeps à paraître dans le désert.

Le major Stirling nous communique en arrivant son intention d'attaquer, dans la nuit du lendemain, les concentrations d'avions ennemis, signalées par la R.A.F., sur les aérodromes de SIDI HANEISH, à 30 km. à l'est de MATRUH. Nos méthodes d'attaque des avions au sol, à la bombe, connues de l'ennemi, sont désormais périmées. Aussi, pour obtenir l'effet de surprise, attaquerons nous en force, avec tous les moyens de feu dont nous disposons ; toutes les Jeeps disponibles, soit quinze, portant un équipage de trois hommes et munies chacune de deux jumelages de mitrailleuses Vickers K., seront engagées dans l'opération. C'est donc 60 mitrailleuses à tir rapide qui interviendront en même temps pour détruire les avions au sol et réduire au silence les défenses ennemies qui se révéleraient.

Après une journée de travail intense pour l'équipement des véhicules, nous partons le 23 à 20 heures, accompagnés par une patrouille néo-zélandaise du Long Range Desert Group chargée d'opérer une diversion, dans un secteur voisin de notre terrain de chasse, un quart d'heure avant notre attaque principale.

La distance à parcourir est d'environ 100 km. Il fait une claire nuit de pleine lune. Aucun incident pendant le trajet sinon que la patrouille du L.R.D.G, qui s'est détachée de nous en cours de route, perd une voiture sur une mine. Notre navigation est remarquablement précise et, à minuit,

a reverse U formation which we maintained for the rest of the operation. We then set out to follow methodically the itinerary prepared in advance from aerial photographs, among the concentration of aircraft, and machine-gunned the planes as we passed. Some caught fire after a few seconds of receiving a dozen or so rounds. Others took two or three hundred rounds without catching fire. Their defences, taken by surprise and intimidated by our attack, took about twenty minutes to respond, and their machine guns and two 20 mm Bredas were employed with little effect.

At 0145 hours the operation was over. A conservative evaluation of the results, transmitted by Major Stirling to H.Q. Eighth Army, showed 18 aircraft destroyed and 12 badly damaged. Our own losses were one man killed, one wounded and one vehicle out of action and abandoned.

The operation was completed, but now we had to rejoin our base. We knew that as soon as day broke, we would be hunted by enemy aircraft. We were ordered to travel in groups of two and three vehicles and make as much ground as possible during the hours of darkness, and to employ tree camouflage as soon as the first enemy reconnaissance started in the morning, remaining completely still with no movement of any sort. Everything went well during the day of the 24th for most of the detachment.

Unfortunately two French vehicles, slowing down during the night for many reasons, were spotted and attacked by three Stukas at the end of the morning, and Cadet André Zirnheld, Croix De Guerre, M.C., one of the best French parachute officers of the Middle Eastern force, was killed by a machine-gun bullet.

During the night of the 24th to 25th of July, all the detachments rejoined our base in the desert.

Colditz, June 1944

Cne A. Jordan
Forces Aériennes Françaises

117. ST. NAZAIRE—28 MARCH 1942 NIGHT

The Tirpitz was in Kiel Harbour. Apart from the dry dock there, the only other dry dock on the European coast that would enable her to refit was St. Nazaire. To attack our shipping in the Atlantic she must have that port in which to refit.

It was therefore decided to destroy the dry dock and its installations and, as the port was also a large U-boat base, to destroy the vital lock gates into the inner basin, making the harbour tidal and thereby limiting the movements of these craft. The final plan arrived at was that H.M.S. "Campbelltown"*—ex U.S.N. destroyer—specially strengthened for boom charging and loaded with explosive, should ram the south dock gate, be sunk there, and blow up after the attacking force had left. She would also carry troops to destroy the lock installations, and assault and protection parties. This was the primary object. In addition, protection and demolition parties were carried in M.L.'s for the secondary task of destruction, the U-boat basin installations. An M.T.B. fitted with special torpedoes was to destroy a lock gate into this basin and an M.G.B. to deal with enemy gun positions, searchlights and craft. R.A.F. to keep the guns up by bombing certain targets, and the sea-borne force was to pretend

...avions en bordure des aires de dispersion des aérodromes.

Brusquement, deux fusées apparaissent dans le ciel et, quelques secondes après, les feux de piste s'allument et un avion atterrit. Nous apprendrons plus tard que la patrouille néo-zélandaise est allée cueillir l'équipage à sa descente d'avion et s'est retirée avec deux prisonniers après avoir placé une bombe à retardement dans l'appareil.

À 1 heure, l'heure H prévue, formés en ligne sur un rang, nous pénétrons sur l'aérodrome, à une vitesse d'environ 15 km à l'heure, faisant feu de toutes nos pièces sur les premiers avions en vue. Nos balles traceuses font un feu d'artifice éblouissant.

Au signal de trois fusées vertes, tiré par le major Stirling et les voitures des ailes, nous adoptons la formation en U renversé figuré ci-contre, que nous conserverons pendant toute la durée de l'opération. Nous parcourons alors méthodiquement un itinéraire, préparé à l'avance sur photos aériennes, parmi les concentrations d'avions, et mitraillons les avions sur notre passage. Certains prennent feu en quelques secondes, sous une rafale d'une dizaine de cartouches. D'autres encaissent deux trois cents balles sans s'enflammer. La défense, évidemment prise au dépourvu et intimidée par notre feu, ne réagit qu'au bout d'une vingtaine de minutes et, d'une manière générale, le tir des mitrailleuses et des deux 20 mm Breda qui se manifestent est peu efficace.

À 1 h 45 l'opération est terminée. Une évaluation prudente des résultats, qui sera transmise par le major Stirling au Q.G. de la VIII ième Armée, donne 18 avions incendiés et sérieusement endommagés. Nos pertes se réduisent à un homme tué, un blessé, et une voiture mise hors d'action, abandonnée sur le terrain.

L'opération est terminée, mais il nous reste à rejoindre notre base. Nous savons que, dès le lever du jour, nous serons pris en chasse par l'aviation ennemie. Aussi avons-nous l'ordre, par groupes de deux ou trois voitures, de prendre le plus de champ possible pendant les heures de nuit qui nous restent, d'être camouflés à l'aube au moment des premières reconnaissances ennemies et de passer la journée sur place sans mouvements d'aucune sorte. Tout se passe bien, dans la journée du 24, pour la plupart des détachements. Malheureusement, deux voitures françaises, ralenties pendant la nuit par plusieurs crevaisons, sont repérées et attaquées par trois Stukas à la fin de la matinée, et l'aspirant André ZIRNHELD, croix de guerre, M.C., l'un des meilleurs officiers parachutistes français d'Orient, est tué par une rafale de mitrailleuse.

Dans la nuit du 24 au 25 juillet, tous les détachements rejoignent notre base dans le désert.

Colditz, Juin 1944

C⁺⁺ A. Jordan
Forces aériennes françaises

The Tirpitz was in Kiel harbour. Apart from the dry dock there, the only oT dry dock on the European coast that would enable her to refit was at St. Nazai— to attack our shipping in the Atlantic, she must have that port in which to refit. It was therefore decided to destroy the dry dock and its installation and, as the port was also a large U-boat base, to destroy the vital lock gas into the inner basin, making the harbour tidal, and thereby limiting the movem of these craft. The final plan arrived at was that H.M.S. "Campbelltown" — e U.S.N. destroyer — specially strengthened for boom charging, and loaded with explosive, should ram the south dock gate, be sunk there, and blow up af the attacking force had left. She would also carry troops to destroy the doc installations, and assault and protection parties. This was the primary obje In addition, assault, protection and demolition parties were carried in M for the secondary task of destruction, the U-boat basin installations. An M fitted with special torpedoes was to destroy a lock gate into this basin, & an to deal with enemy gun positions, searchlights & craft. R.A.F. to keep the gu up by bombing certain targets, & the sea-borne force was to pretend it was a s bound A/Sub sweep, en route and on arrival. On completion of the task, tr to re-embark & proceed to a pre-arranged R.V. & thence home. After s training & practice, Commando demolition & assault troops, assembled & sailed outside t range of enemy R.D.F. & fighters on a 36-hr voyage. A submarine acting as navigation beacon was contacted at the mouth of the Loire. Having passe heavy coastal guns, the convoy almost passed the guardship, but was fire Fire was returned by all units, when heavy firing broke out on both side H.M.S. "Campbelltown" rammed the dock gate, her troops destroyed the install & returned to the land R.V. She blew up with Germans aboard later, shattering the end of the dock; the primary object was thus achieved. Ow to many M.L.'s being sunk, and those still afloat receiving heavy casualtie the secondary task was not achieved with success, although the M.T.B. wa successful, & certain gun positions were eliminated by assault parties. Tasks completed, those ashore assembled at the R.V., and being unable t re-embark, attempted to fight their way out of the dock area into the to and thence to Spain. Three men were successful, the remainder, after fig in the streets, were rounded up in various houses.

Conan Purdon.

Lieut.

No. 12 Commando.

it was a storm bound A/Sub Sweep, en route and on arrival. On completion of the task, troops to re-embark and proceed to a pre-arranged R.V. and thence home.

After special training and practice, Commando demolition and assault troops assembled and sailed outside the range of enemy R.D.F. and fighters on a 36-hour voyage. A submarine acting as navigation beacon was contacted at the mouth of the Loire. Having passed the heavy coastal guns, the convoy almost passed the guardship, but was fired on. Fire was returned by all units, when heavy firing broke out on both sides.

H.M.S. "Campbelltown" rammed the dock gate. Her troops destroyed the installations and returned to the land R.V. She blew up with the Germans aboard later, shattering the end of the dock. The primary object was thus achieved.

Owing to many M.L.'s being sunk and those still afloat receiving heavy casualties, the secondary task was not achieved with success, although the M.T.B. was successful and certain gun positions were eliminated by assault parties.

Tasks completed, those ashore assembled at the R.V. and being unable to re-embark attempted to fight their way out of the dock area into the town, and thence to Spain. Three men were successful. The remainder, after fighting in the streets, were rounded up in various houses.

Corran Purdon, Lieut.
No. 12 Commando

*   *HMS Campbeltown.*

118. MES NUMEROS MATRICULES*—NOV 1942—FEV 1944

2142—In the "Froggie" army acting as liaison officer with an american armoured division at Mende-el-Bab, (Tunisia). On 9th December 1942 the Goons attacked Mendez-el-Bab from their advance base at Tebourba, 12 kilometres to the east. I obtained authorization to join a patrol of four "General Lee" tanks which had been ordered to make contact. At around 1030 hours we came upon a tank column of five "Mark IV's" equipped with 75mm and one 88mm gun, escorted by two companies of Panzer Grenadiers. Contact was made at 250 metres.

Several hours later I found myself as patient No. 17, Pavillion K, in a Tunis hospital on Christmas Eve. Still, I managed to escape along with a British parachute officer who had had both legs amputated. You see— "It was a push over".

Identity Card No. 039740—Mr. Aymar Musny, farmer, was my civilian description for the next four weeks in Tunis. Life was very exciting, so much so that the Gestapo, who had always lacked a sense of humour, interrupted my lunch one day in a cafe in the centre of Tunis, and instead of enjoying a Chateaubriand steak with fried potatoes, I was soon put in front of a bowl of watery soup in Cell 67, La Kasba Prison. The openings were cemented over and I was in complete blackness—from this moment and and for the next year I was known only by my

*   *My Registered Numbers*

2142 - danoe armée "Froggie". officier de liaison auprès d'une
division blindée USA. Medjez el Bab (Tunisie) - le 9.12
les Goons attaquent M. el Bab en partant de leur
point d'appui de Tebourba situé à 12 km à l'Est. J'obtiens
l'autorisation de prendre place dans une patrouille de
chars "General Lee" chargée de prendre le contact - nous t
sous subitement vers 10h30 sur une colonne (Rendée de 5
Mark IV (75 m/m) et 1 auto comm (88 m/m) escortée de 2
de panzer-grenadier. le contact à 250 m) a été certainement
mis car je me retrouve quelques heures après au
pavillon p° n° 17 à l'Hôpital de Tunis à la veille de Noël
e m'en évade en même temps qu'un officier parachutiste
Britannique au pied des 2 jambes - vous voyez "it was a
push-over".

te d'identité 4°039.740 - Mr Aymar Musny . cultivateur - c
mon état civil d'emprunt pendant 4 semaines dans
Tunis. vie très excitante, à tel point que la Gestapo qui a
toujours manqué d'humour fait irruption à midi dans
un café du centre de Tunis. Mitraillette ... et au lieu de
déguster un chateaubriand aux pommes comme prévu, je
suis mis en présence d'une soupe à base d'eau dans la
cellule 67. Prison de la Kasbah - les ouvertures sont bouchée
au ciment et je suis dans le noir complet - à partir
de ce moment et pendant 1 an je ne serai plus con
nu que par des numeros. Je suis "le 67". 1° avant
départ en avion pour Naples puis "Nach Berlin" - de deli
rieuses jeunes Italiennes qui ne manquent pas d'humo
distribuent des "Tracts" dans notre train intitulés
"Visiter l'Italie" ... nous avons exprimé en termes po
notre regret de ne pouvoir accepter leur aimable in
vitation, ayant un rendez-vous urgent avec Monsie
Himmler -

°63211. Block 16 - Konzentration lager Oranienburg Bei Be
e d'auto, moto, 3 mois de travaux forcés - Mr A. Musny
e même délicieux costume à raies bleues et blanches ç
rendit célèbre son presque homonyme Paul Musy.
67 . cellule dans la "Gestapo Gefängnis" à Berlin de

...alag III A. Block 8 — jusqu'au 14 février 44 avec
3 officiers russes — envoie alors 1re lettre en Afrique du N
1670 — OFLAG IV C que certains appellent "HELL CAMP"
et que personnellement je considère comme
"HEIL CAMP" — y reendosse l'uniforme —

En résumé : 8 numéros —
              11 mois de cellule
              2 mois et ½ de Bagne.
malgré tout des moments bien drôles et bien réconf-
ortants ... par exemple lorsque j'ai appris en Nov. 43
que je bénéficierai du doute et serai considéré comme un normal prisonnier de guerre — Malheureusement
comme disait Goethe, je crains que " Für mich, der
Krieg ist fertig".

              Lt. J.C. TINÉ —
              1er regt de spahis Algériens
                   Mai 44

number. I was "No. 67". On the 1st April 1943 I was taken by plane to Naples, and then on "to Berlin". Some delightful young Italian girls who did not lack a sense of humour walked up and down in our train distributing brochures encouraging us to "Visit Italy". . . Politely we expressed our regret that we would be unable to accept their friendly invitation, because we had to attend an urgent meeting with Mr. Himmler.

No. 63211. Block 15. Concentration Camp in Oranienburg near Berlin; in other words, three months of hard labour. Mr. A. Musny wore the same charming costume of blue and white stripes that brought fame to his virtual homonym, Paul Murin.

No. 37. Cell in the Gestapo Prison in Berlin from July to December 1943, always dressed as a civilian and treated as a civilian prisoner. [*Original text continued on page 119 of diary*]. Stalag IIIA, Block G—until the 14th of February 1944, with three Russian officers, where I wrote my first letters to North Africa.

No. 1670. Oflag IVC, which some referred to as "Hell Camp" and I personally referred to as "Heil Camp", where I wore a uniform once again.

To sum up, 8 numbers, 11 months in a cell, 2½ months of hard labour. In spite of everything, there were amusing and comforting moments, for example when I learned in November 1940 that I was going to be given the benefit of the doubt and treated as a normal prisoner of war. Unfortunately as Goethe said, I believe that "For me, the war is over."

Lt. J. C. Tinè
1st Regt de Spahis Algeriens,
Mai 44

121. EICHSTÄTT EPIC (LIEUT. G. S. DREW)

Once in days of Blätterbauer, Frank and Baillie had a thought,
Decided not to waste an hour, so a plan they straight way sought.
Campbell-Preston, David Walker, helped to make a wondrous scheme,
And at last they had a corker, so began to form a team.
And they formed a team of wonder-specialists of every rank.
Names which made the heavens thunder—names which in our nostrils stank.
Michael Wittet 'ersatz' Scotsman—worked with Bruce both night and day,
Peter Greenwell, Kenneth Hermon, Michael Scott who could not stay;
Alan Cocksedge and John Tweedie worked together on a shift.
Rex and Jack and young Mark Howard tried so hard great rocks to lift.
Young men, old men, men like Sandy, worked along with men like Ed.
Dougie Crawford, Laurie Pumphrey worked 'till they were nearly dead.
Duggie Moir—great man of spirit—Michael Farr to help him on
Worked so hard with Jimmy Mellor—dug the record five feet long.
'Skelly' Ginn, a one-eyed monster, kept the lamp and kept it good.
Keenlyside and Michael Edwards stowed the earth and pinched the wood.

Pat McLaren and Elins-Neale—stooging hard from every crack.
Martin Gilliatt and Phil Pardoe pulling hard to bring earth back.
 Harry Collett and Bill Burton—silent men, but very strong.
 Types like Fawcett, Clein and Hugo—all these men could do no wrong.

Worthy men! And none were pupils; men prepared to die or do.
Men in fact just lacking scruples—men like Fergusson and Drew.

Then was made a wondrous tunnel—almost perfect, very grand,
With an entrance by a lat. seat, room enough inside to stand.
Fitted up with every comfort, cigarettes and pipe to hand.
Efficient air pipe, sucking madly, also used as telephone
(Upstairs just remove the stopper, hear the wretched workers groan).
Bells and bags and ropes and trolleys. Oh! What chaos down below.
Stacking bags and rocks and rubbish—how we did it. I don't know.
Stooging was our greatest bug-bear, stooging here and stooging there.
In the post room, in the attic—we were stooging everywhere.
Tons of earth in little pockets, pockets slung on canvas bands.
Carried miles to be well hidden—Had to have some extra hands.
[Original text continued on page 28 of diary]
First of all came David Fellowes, willing stooge in every camp.
Lords appeared, both John and Charlie, working in onto the ramp.
The other Charlie, Peter Barker helped to swell this elite throng
John Lochrane, Dieppe and Courtenay present with his whiskers long.
McCall and Leah (both brawny Scotsmen). Bisset too, the damned old ram.
Paddy Martin, Denis Bartlett—all were sharing in the jam.
Two colonials, Scott and Bolding, came to join in on the fun
All were very willing workers, helping things to smoothly run.

Numbers big, but still undaunted, "Siggy" Jackson called for more.
Combed the camp from top to bottom, begging chaps "Come in and draw."
In the draw came all the loafers—men with just the faintest hope
Men like Beaumont, men like Barott—tried to bribe their way with soap
Men like Sgt. Maj. Perry (quite a different type, it's true
He'd escaped from every Stalag; the toasting game he quite well knew).
Col. Merritt had a partner, but the wretched man got stuck,
So a miner "Craggy Jerry" had the greatest stroke of luck.
Gordon Rolfe and "Dopey" Millar came along with Mike Riviere.
"Screwy" Stephen and John Penman, neither of them knowing fear.
Frank chose Penman as a guide post, but left Stephen in the rear
In their normal charming manner, French-Canadians sent in three
Jack and Hamish waking early, both got up to go and pee,

Captain	F. W. C	Weldon,	R. H. A
Lieut.	J. R. E	Hamilton-Baillie,	R. E.
Captain	G. P.	Campbell-Preston	Black Watch
Captain	D. H.	Walker	Black Watch
Lieut.	M. G.	Willett	Royal Scots
Lieut.	I. B.	Macaskie	Q. O. R. W. K.
Captain	Sir P.	Greenwell	Surrey & Sussex Yeom
Captain	K. E.	Hermon	D. L. I.
Lieut.	M.	Scott	D. L. I.
Lieut.	L. R. L.	Cocksedge	R. I. Fusiliers
Captain	J. A.	Tweedie	Cameron Highland
Captain	R. R.	Baxter	A. I. F.
Lieut.	J. W. K.	Champ	A. I. F.
Lieut.	M. A.	Howard	A. I. F.
Lieut.	C. E.	Sandbach	Cheshire Yeomanry
Lieut.	E. A.	Hannay	Seaforth Highlan
Captain	D. A.	Crawford	A. I. F.
Lieut.	J. L.	Pumphrey	Northumberland H
Lieut.	D. N.	Moir	R. T. R
Lieut.	M	Larr	D. L. I
Lieut.	J. T. P	Mellor	Arg. & Suth.
Major	B. D. S.	Ginn	R. E. M. E.
Captain	C. H.	Keenlyside	Q. O. R. W. K.
Lieut.	F. M.	Edwards	R. W. Fusiliers
Lieut.	P.	McLaren	Arg. & Suth.
Lieut.	S. C. T	Elms-Neale	R. A.
Captain	M. J.	Gilliatt	K. R. R. C.
Lieut.	P.	Pardoe	K. R. R. C.
Lieut.	H. B.	Collett	Yorkshire Hussars
Captain	W. J.	Burton	Yorks & Lancs
Captain	J.	Fawcus	Northumberland F
Lieut.	C. A.	Elson	R. Norfolk R.
Lieut.	H. C. W.	Ironside	R. T. R.
Lieut.	J. P.	Fergusson	R. T. R.
Lieut.	G. S.	Drew	Northumberland R

(Copy)

—— EICHSTÄTT EPIC ——

Once in days of Blätterbauer, Frank and Baillie had a thought,
Decided not to waste an hour, so a plan they straight way sought.
Campbell-Preston, David Walker, helped to make a wondrous scheme,
And at last they had a corker, so began to form a team.
And they formed a team of wonder-specialists of every rank
Names which made the heavens thunder — names which in our nostrils stank
Michael Wittet 'ersatz' Scotsman — worked with Bruce both night and day;
Peter Greenwell, Kenneth Hermon, Michael Scott who could not stay;
Alan Cockridge and John Tweedie worked together on a shift.
Rex and Jack and young Mark Howard tried so hard great rocks to lift.
Young men, old men, men like Sandy, worked along with men like Ed.
Dougie Crawford, Laurie Pumphrey worked 'till they were nearly dead.
Duggie Moir — great man of spirit — Michael Farr to help him on
Worked so hard with Jimmy Mellor — dug the record five feet long.
'Skelly' Ginn, a one-eyed monster, kept the lamp and kept it good,
Keenlyside and Michael Edwards stowed the earth and pinched the wood
Pat McLaren and Elms-Neale — stooging hard from every crack
Martin Gilliatt, and Phil Pardoe pulling hard to bring earth back.
Harry Collett and Bill Burton — silent men, but very strong,
Types like Fawcus, Uem and Hugo — all these men could do no wrong

Worthy men! and none were pupils; men prepared to die or do
Men in fact just lacking scruples — men like Fergusson and Drew.

Then was made a wondrous tunnel — almost perfect, very grand
With an entrance by a lat. seat, room enough inside to stand.
Fitted up with every comfort, cigarettes and pipe to hand.
Efficient air pipe, sucking madly, also used as telephone
(Upstairs just remove the stopper, hear the wretched workers groan.)
Bells and bags and ropes and trolleys. Oh! What chaos down below.
Stacking bags and rocks and rubbish — how we did it, I don't know
Stooging was our greatest bug-bear; stooging here and stooging there.
In the post room, in the attic — we were stooging everywhere.
Tons of earth in little packets; packets slung on canvas bands.
Carried miles to be well hidden — Had to have some extra hands.

(P.T.O.)

Got mixed up with Hector Christie—being sleepy, did agree,
So they passed right up the tunnel; early morning found them free.

But there is no happy ending to this epic which is sad,
For the goons just combed the country 'till they found us—which was bad.
Back into the cells at Eichstätt, then up to the Schloss were sent.
What's it like, I cannot tell you, because up there I never went.
Now we are at happy Colditz—budding men of spirit we,
With the embryonic madmen, some as mad as mad can be.
If with this, you are offended, then dear Reader please be kind
Not your fault, and not the writer's, but the rhyme's so hard to find.

Composed and written 31 January 1944
Oflag IVC. Colditz

(*These names are listed on the opposite pages to the poem:*)
Capt F. W. C. Weldon, R.H.A.
Lieut. J. R. E. Hamilton-Baillie, R.E.
Captain G. D. Campbell-Preston, Black Watch
Captain D. H. Walker, Black Watch
Lieut. M. G. Wittett, Royal Scots
Lieut. I. B. Macaskie, Q.O.R.W.K.
Captain Sir P. Greenwell, Surrey and Sussex Yeomanry
Captain K. E. Hermon, D.L.I.
Lieut M. Scott, D.L.I.
Lieut. A. R. A. Cocksedge, R.I. Fusiliers
Captain J. A. Tweedie, Cameron Highlanders
Captain R. R. Baxter, A.I.F.
Lieut. J. W. K. Champ, A.I.F.
Lieut. M. A. Howard, A.I.F.
Lieut. C. E. Sandbach, Cheshire Yeomanry
Lieut. E. A. Hannay, Seaforth Highlanders
Captain D. A. Crawford A.I.F.
Lieut. Pumphrey, Northumberland Hussars
Lieut. D. N. Moir, R.T.R.
Lieut. M. Farr, D.L.I.
Lieut. J. T. P. Mellor, Arg. E. Suth.
Major B. D. S. Ginn, R.E.M.E.
Captain, C. H. Keenlyside, Q.O.R.W.K.
Lieut. E. M. Edwards. R.W. Fusiliers
Lieut. P. McLaren Arg. E. Suth.
Lieut. S. C. T. Elm-Neale, R.A.

Captain M. J. Gilliat K.R.R.C.

Lieut. P. Pardoe, K.R.R.C.

Lieut. H. B. Collett, Yorkshire Hussars

Captain W. J. Burton, Yorks & Lancs

Captain J. Fawcus Northumberland Fus.

Lieut. C. A. Elson, R. Norfolk R.

Lieut. H. C. W. Ironside, R.T.R.

Lieut. J. P. Ferguson, R.T.R.

Lieut. G. S. Drew, Northumberland R.

Lieut. The Hon. D. Fellows, Rifle Bde.

Captain the Lord Arundell of Wardour, Wiltshire Reg.

Captain the Earl of Hopetoun, Lothian and Border Horse

Lieut. C. R.Weld-Forester, Rifle Bde.

Lieut. P. H. Parker, K.R.R.C.

Lieut. F. A. J. Lochrane, Seaforth Highlanders

Lieut. C. I. C. Dieppe, A.I.F.

Lieut. J. M. Courtenay, Q.Y.R.

Lieut. A. L. McCall, Cameron Highlanders

Captain R. W. Leah, Cameron Highlanders

Lieut. A. J. R. Bissett, Seaforth Highlanders

Lieut. S. N. Martin, R.A.S.C.

Lieut. D. E. Bartlett, R.T.R.

Lieut. W. H. Scott, Essex Scottish (Canada)

Lieut. G. Bolding, A.I.F.

Lieut. J. W. Beaumont, D.L.I.

Lieut. T. M. Barott, Black Watch (Canada)

Sgt. Maj. S. Perry, R.T.R.

Lt. Col. C. C. I. Merritt, V.C., Saskatoon Rifles

Lieut. J. E. Wood, Royal Can. Engrs.

Major G. M. Rolfe, Royal Can. Signals

Lieut. W. A. Millar, Royal Can. Engrs.

Lieut. M. V. B. Riviere, Notts Yeomany

Captain S. C. Wright, 9th Q.R. Lancers

Lieut. J. R. Penman, Arg. & Suth.

Lieut. J. H. Roy, Fus. Mont Royal

Lieut. A. G. Vandalac, Fus. Mont Royal

Lieut. A. R. Marchand, Fus. Mont Royal

Lieut. J. R. Millet, A.I.F..

Lieut. D. K. Hamilton, R.A.

For pages 124–125 see the colour plate section.

Lieut. the Hon. D.		Fellowes	Rifle Bde.
Captain the Lord		Arundell of Wardour.	Wiltshire
Captain the Earl		of Hopetoun	Lothian & Border H
Lieut.	C. R.	Weld-Forester	Rifle Bde.
Lieut.	P. H.	Parker	K. R. R. C.
Lieut.	E. A. J.	Lochrane	Seaforth Highland
Lieut.	C. I. C	Dieppe	A. I. F.
Lieut.	J. M.	Courtenay	Q. Y. R
Lieut.	A. L.	McCall	Cameron Highlan
Captain	R. W.	Leah	Cameron Highlan
Lieut	A. J. R.	Bissett	Seaforth Highland
Lieut.	S. N.	Martin	R. A. S. C
Lieut.	D. E.	Bartlett	R. T. R
Lieut.	W. H.	Scott	Essex Scottish (Can
Lieut.	G.	Bolding	A. I. F.
Lieut.	J. W.	Beaumont	D. L. I.
Lieut.	T. M.	Barott	Black Watch (Can
Sgt. Maj.	S.	Perry	R. T. R
Lt. Col.	C. C. I.	Merritt, V.C.	Saskatoon Rifles
Lieut.	J. E.	Wood	Royal Can. Engrs.
Major	G. M.	Rolfe	Royal Can. Signals
Lieut.	W. A.	Millar	Royal Can. Engrs
Lieut	M. Y. B.	Rivière	Notts Yeomanry.
Captain	S. C.	Wright	9th. Q. R. Lancers
Lieut	J. R.	Penman	Arg. & Suth.
Lieut.	J. H.	Roy	Fus. Mont. Royal
Lieut.	A. G.	Vandalac	Fus. Mont. Royal
Lieut.	A. R.	Marchand	Fus. Mont Royal
Lieut.	J. R.	Millett	A. I. F.
Lieut.	D. K.	Hamilton	R. A.

First of all came David Fellowes, willing stooge in every camp.
Lords appeared, both John and Charlie, working in onto the ramp.
The other Charlie, Peter Parker helped to swell this élite throng
John Lochrane, Dieppe and Courtenay present with his whiskers long.
McCall and Leah (both brawny Scotsmen), Bissett too, the damned old ram.
Paddy Martin, Denis Bartlet — all were sharing in the jam,
Two colonials, Scott and Bolding, came to join in on the fun
All were very willing workers, helping things to smoothly run.

Numbers big, but still undaunted, "Siggy" Jackson called for more.
Combed the camp from top to bottom, begging chaps: "Come in and draw."
In the draw came all the loafers — men with just the faintest hope,
Men like Beaumont men like Barott — tried to bribe their way with soap
Men like Sgt. Maj. Perry (quite a different type, it's true
He'd escaped from every Stalag; the toasting game he quite well knew)
Col. Merritt had a partner, but the wretched man got stuck,
So a miner "Craggy Jerry" had the greatest stroke of luck.
Gordon Rolfe and "Dopey" Millar came along with Mike Revière.
"Screwy" Stephen and John Penman, neither of them knowing fear.
Frank chose Penman as a guide post, but left Stephen in the rear
In their normal charming manner, French-Canadians sent in three
Jack and Hamish waking early, both got up to go and pee,
Got mixed up with Hector Christie — being sleepy, did agree.
So they passed right up the tunnel: early morning found them free.

But there is no happy ending to this epic which is sad,
For the Goons just combed the country 'till they found us — which was bad.
Back into the cells at Eichstätt, then up to the Schloss were sent.
What it's like, I cannot tell you, because up there I never went.
Now we are at happy Colditz — budding men of spirit we,
With the embryonic madmen, some as mad as mad can be.
If with this, you are offended, then dear Reader please be kind
Not your fault, and not the writers', but the rhyme's so hard to find.

Composed and written,
    31. January 1944,
        Oflag. IV C., Colditz.

127. ESCAPE FROM WILLIBALDSBURG SCHLOSS, EICHSTÄTT, 20 JUNE 1943

Sixty three officers were confined in Willibaldsburg Schloss, Eichstätt upon being recaptured after the tunnel break from Oflag VIIB, Eichstätt on the night 3-4 June, 1943. By 19th June, all officers except twelve had served their sentence of 10 days detention and had either been sent to a new camp or moved to the canteen which adjoined the Schloss. The remaining twelve were held in prolonged confinement pending a decision of the security staff on a charge of wearing civilian clothes and leaving VIIB without permission or an escort.

On the afternoon of 20 June, we were advised by the Under Officer in charge of our guard that we would probably be moved from our cell in the Schloss to join our companions in the canteen. We decided, therefore, that if our plan to escape was to be executed we must carry it out on the evening of the 20th, providing we were not moved before then. Our plan of escape had been formulated and polished during previous days of confinement.

During the late afternoon our friends, English and Canadian, removed the bars from the windows and covered the hole with boxes. This work was carefully stooged by other friends and Mike Scott agreed to act as manager for our actual departure. Dummies were prepared for our beds so that our absence would not be discovered until the following morning.

By 2100 hours we had heard nothing further of the move to the canteen so we got underway on the escape plan. The rope we used for the 50 foot drop was made up from cord smuggled into the Schloss. We made up a dummy of a man, used our food packs as stuffing and about 2130 lowered this from the window. It was a very bright night and since the lowering of the dummy aroused no alarm, we assumed that there were no guards posted in the undergrowth and woods below. We retired to bed at 2200 hours fully dressed.

Our guard, consisting of an under officer and three men occupied the adjoining room. By 2300 hours three were sleeping and one standing watch at our door. Arrangements were made for Guy to go to the lavatory which was located above our cell, and the guard dutifully accompanied him. This left our path clear for an estimated five minutes or so. Bill Millar left the window and slid down the rope. We heard loud crashing sounds in the branches below and soon after a signal that he was O.K. Dougie Moir went out next and loud crashing ensued. It was now my turn and I slid my feet out of the window, sat on the window ledge, grasped the rope with both hands and attempted to wind the rope around one leg. I started to slide down the rope and suddenly found myself sitting on a ledge of the building about 12 feet below the window. We had given Mike instructions to cut the rope as soon as he felt the rope slacken so there we no time to lose . . . "Hold your hats, kids, here we go again" . . . partial blackout.

The rope was very light and served Bill because it had the dummy weight on the end which allowed him to keep it wound around his foot and some control was [*original text continued on page 126 of diary*] possible. When Bill struck the dummy, the rope broke about 20 feet from the ground. When Dougie and I went down it was impossible to keep it wound around a foot so we had little control and as a result Dougie sprained his ankle and I wrenched my spine and nearly knocked myself cold from a knee to the face . . . very pretty stars though.

We sorted ourselves out in the best way possible, collected our pack from the dummy and after recovering for a few minutes, moved as quickly as possible away from the Schloss. The undergrowth was thick and was a great nuisance to Dougie and me due to injuries. Also it was very noisy. Eventually we reached the village below, circled around it after going through a stream which soaked us to the thighs, and reached the railway tracks we planned to follow. After going about three hundred yards along the track we were challenged. At this time Bill was leading by about 75 yards, Dougie hobbling along at centre and I brought up the rear. On being challenged I turned towards our challenger thinking Bill and Dougie would be able to run for it. Bill ran but Dougie's ankle was too troublesome so he turned back towards me. Our captor was an S.S. soldier who had been in a "waiting booth" beside the railway track with a rather attractive girl friend. What a life . . . in the bag again.

G. L. Rolfe, Capt.,
R.C. Signals

128. AU REVOIR PARIS—JUNE 11TH-26TH 1940

After a night of air-raid warnings and sounds of distant bombing, I awoke on the morning of Tuesday, June 11th 1940 in my home in the suburbs of Paris to a weird world.

Though the weather had been particularly fine for some time, though the previous evening the glass had been on "set fine" and though my alarm clock told me it was 5.30 a.m., it was almost dark, and there was no sun.

A black pall seemed to be hanging over the world, which did not tend to brighten one's outlook on life, which in view of current events, was not at all rosy.

Going out into the garden I found that the sky was completely black, as though covered with an immense thunder-cloud, but at one point there was a very pale yellow disc—the sun.

That was the morning I left home. After a frugal breakfast which I did not really want, I packed my suit-case, and set off for the office. We had been advised the previous evening to come prepared for a move, as the office would probably be evacuated on the morrow.

The streets on the way to the station were indicative of the nervous strain everyone was feeling. There were fewer people than usual on their way to business and almost all of them carried a suitcase or two—evidence of their place of business moving out of Paris.

Shopkeepers were on their doorsteps watching the departing city workers. Here and there the family car was loaded to its fullest capacity. There was a gloomy expression on everyone's face, which was in keeping with the gloom in the sky, but whenever words were exchanged there was an expression of hope:—"We shall soon be back again."

On arriving at the station, I found that my face and hands were covered with a film of some black, sooty substance, and my fellow passengers in the carriage on the way back up to Paris were in a similar condition.

A general discussion on the subject ensued, and it was generally presumed that the pall hanging over-head was a smoke-screen thrown over the Paris area by the military authorities

possible. When Bill struck the dummy, the rope broke about 20' from the ground. When Dougie and I went down it was impossible to keep it wound around but so we had little control and as a result Dougie sprained his ankle wrenched my spine and nearly knocked myself cold from a knee to the face — saw pretty stars though.

We sorted ourselves out in the best way possible, collected our packs the dummy and after recovering for a few minutes, moved as quickly as pos way from the Sollers. The undergrowth was thick and was a great nuisance Dougie and I due to injuries. Also it was very rainy. Eventually we reach a village below, circled around it after going through a stream which soa to the thighs, and reached the railway track we planned to follow. Af ing about 300 yards along the track we were challenged. At this ill was leading by about 75 yards, Dougie hobbling along at centre a brought up the rear. On being challenged I turned towards our challe inking Bill and Dougie would be able to run for it. Bill ran but Dou kle was too troublesome so he turned back towards me. Our captor — S.S. soldier who had been in a "waiting booth" beside the railway rack with a rather attractive girl friend. What a life ..... in the bag ag

A. W. Rolfe. Sgt.
R.C. Signals.

Sixty three officers were confined in Willibaldsburg Schloss, Eichstätt upon being captured after the tunnel break from Oflag VII B, Eichstätt on the night 3-4 June 19th June, all officers except twelve had served their sentence of 10 days detention and either been sent to a new camp or moved to the canteen which adjoined the Schloss. The remaining twelve were held in prolonged confinement pending a decision the security staff on a charge of wearing civilian clothes and leaving VII B without permission or an escort.

On the afternoon of 20 June, we were advised by the under officer in charge our guard, that we would probably be moved from our cell in the Schloss to in our companions in the canteen. We decided therefore that if our plan to escape was to be executed we must carry it out on the evening of the 20th, provided we were not moved before then. Our plan of escape had been formulated and polished during previous days of confinement.

During the late afternoon our friends, English and Canadian, removed the bars the window and covered the hole with boxes. This work was carefully aged by other friends and Jake Scott agreed to act as manager for our actual venture. Dummies were prepared for our beds so that our absence would not discovered until the following morning.

By 2100 hrs. we had heard nothing further of the move to the canteen so we underway on the escape plan. The rope we used for the 50' drop was made from cord smuggled into the Schloss. We made up a dummy of a man, using food packs as stuffing and about 2130 lowered this from the window. It was very bright night and since the lowering of the dummy aroused no alarm, we assumed that there were no guards posted in the undergrowth and woods below retired to bed at 2200 hrs. fully dressed.

Our guard, consisting of an under officer and three men occupied the adjoining By 2330 hrs. three were sleeping and one standing watch at our door. arrangements were made for Guy to go to the lavatory which was located along cell, and the guard dutifully accompanied him. This left our path for an estimated five minutes or so. Bill Miller left the window and slid down the rope. We heard loud crashing sounds in the branches below and soon after a signal that he was OK. Douglas Howe went out next loud crashing ensued. It was now my turn and I slid my feet out of the window, sat on the window ledge, grasped the rope with both hands and attempted wind the rope around one leg. I started to slide down the rope and suddenly found myself sitting on a ledge of the building about 12 feet below the window. We had given Jake instructions to cut the rope as soon as he felt the rope slacken there was no time to lose..... "Hold your hats kids, here we go again" without blackout.

The rope was very light and served Bill because it had the dummy weight on and which allowed him to keep it wound around his foot and some control was

After a night of air-raid warnings and sounds of distant bombing, I awoke on morning of Tuesday, June 11th 1940 in my home in the suburbs of Paris to a weird World.

Though the weather had been particularly fine for some time, though the previous evening the glass had been on "set fine" and though my alarum-clock told me that it w 5.30 a.m., it was almost dark, and there was no sun.

A black pall seemed to be hanging over the world, which did not tend to brighten one's outlook on life, which in view of current events, was not at all rosy.

Going out into the garden, I found that the sky was completely black, as though covered with an immense thunder-cloud, but at one point there was a very pale yellow disc — the sun

That was the morning I left home. After a frugal breakfast which I did not really want, I packed my suit-case and set off for the office. We had been advised the previous evening to come prepared for a move, as the office would probably be evacuated on the morrow.

The streets on the way to the station were indicative of the nervous strain everyone was feeling. There were fewer people than usual on their way to business and almost all of them carried a suitcase or two — evidence of their place of business moving out of Paris.

Shop-keepers were on their door-steps watching the departing city workers. Here and there the family car was loaded to its fullest capacity.

There was a gloomy expression on every-one's face, which was in keeping with the gloom of the sky, but whenever words were exchanged there was an expression of hope:- "We shall soon be back again."

On arriving at the station, I found that my face and hands were covered with a film of some black, sooty substance, and my fellow-passengers in the carriage on the way up to Paris were in a similar condition.

A general discussion on the subject ensued, and it was generally presumed that the pall hanging over-head was a smoke-screen thrown over the Paris area by the military authorities to screen the evacuation of the population from enemy air-craft.

I subsequently learnt, whilst on the boat on the way to England, that the smoke came from the oil reservoirs of the Standard Oil Co. at Port-Jérome, near Le Havre, some ninety kilometres away, which they had set fire to in view of the german advance.

A curious picture was presented by the town of Orléans. Sappers were mining the bridge over the river Loire preparatory to destroying it, for it was said that a stand would be made along the banks of the river.

On the Paris side of the bridge, all was noise and confusion. Shops were clos and everyone was packing what belongings could conveniently be taken, and a general s of tension prevailed. The military were erecting pill-boxes on the pavements of the main s leading to the bridge and preparing barriers to place across the street.

But, having crossed the bridge, there was a totally different atmosphere. The people w calm, practically all the shops were open, as was a sub-post-office, and food was plentiful.

A somewhat incongruous sight was that of hutments that had been erected at the beginning of the war to accommodate evacuees from the eastern frontier regions. These were now empty and deserted, their occupants having all joined the general flight southwards.

Bordeaux was reached the day that it was declared an "open town," having been bombed the previous night. Accommodation was unobtainable and food practically so. The British Consulate was closed and a notice was affixed to the door instructing british to proceed to Bayonne for embarcation.

This was eventually accomplished at St. Jean de Luz where evacuees were embarked on small motor-fishing boats holding about fifteen or twenty people. The boat I was in, spent about an hour cruising around in a choppy sea in the rain, at midnight, trying to locate the ship that was to take us to England. When she was finally found, we were faced with the trick job of jumping from the rail of the fishing-boat on to the gangway that had been let down the side the big ship.

This was however accomplished without more than a few bags falling into the sea which were eventually fished out, and we sailed for England, reaching Plymouth after an uneventful passage, on June 26th.

Harold Robshaw Lt. R.A.
OFLAG IVC
COLDITZ
28.9.44

May 1941 was a bad month at Fort Rauch in Posen! Two main roads led East & North-East in sight of the fort, & one secondary road ran past the camp gates. The railway lines, running due East, could be seen in the far distance. All May the transports were passing — going towards Russia. Everyone knew that the conflict between Germany & Russia was about to begin — it was apparent to the dullest of minds. So we all stood day after day & watched. On the railways masses of tanks, guns, armoured vehicles; on the roads long, endless convoys of trucks & cars — empty. We timed the convoys, & made suitable comments. Every now & then a few trucks, Morris trucks & Austins could be recognised much to our annoyance. One evening, at 6.0 p.m. or thereabouts, on the road at our gates a convoy was rolling by. We had counted about 2500 vehicles before the last of the trucks could be seen, & then we saw it was a truck of our own camp bringing back a small work party. They brought up the end of the huge convoy, & as they surged alongside the others a voice from the truck, a rich Scottish voice, called "We're pursuing them!"

The British O.R. may be all his critics say he is, but he has got guts.

J Schrire
Capt. R.A.M.C.

to screen the evacuation of the population from enemy air-craft.

I subsequently learnt whilst on the boat on the way to England, that the smoke came from the oil reservoirs of the Standard Oil Co. at Port-Jérôme, near Le Havre, some ninety kilometres away, which they had set fire to in view of the German advance.

A curious picture was presented by the town of Orléans. Sappers were mining the bridge over the River Loire, preparatory to destroying it, for it was said that a stand would be made along the banks of the river.

On the Paris side of the bridge, all was noise and confusion. Shops were closed and everyone was packing what belongings could conveniently be taken, and a general state of tension prevailed. The military were erecting pillboxes on the pavements on the main street leading to the bridge and preparing barriers to place across the street.

But, having crossed the bridge, there was a totally different atmosphere. The people were calm, practically all the shops were open, as was a sub-post-office, and food was plentiful.

A somewhat incongruous sight was that of hutments that had been erected at the beginning of the war to accommodate evacuees from the eastern frontier regions. These were now empty and deserted, their occupants having all joined the general flight southwards.

Bordeaux was reached the day that it was declared an "open town", having been bombed the previous night. Accommodation was unobtainable and food practically so. The British Consulate was closed and a notice was affixed to the door instructing Britishers to proceed to Bayonne for embarcation.

This was eventually accomplished at St. Jean de Luz where evacuees were embarked on small motor-fishing boats holding about fifteen or twenty people. The boat I was in spent about an hour cruising around in a choppy sea in the rain, at midnight, trying to locate the ship that was to take us to England. When she was finally found, we were faced with the tricky job of jumping from the rail of the fishing boat on to the gangway that had been let down the side of the big ship.

This was however, accomplished without more than a few bags falling into the sea, which were eventually fished out, and we sailed for England, reaching Plymouth after an uneventful passage, on June 26th.

> When shall we three meet again?
> In thunder, lightning or in rain?
> When the hurly burly's done,
> When the battle's lost and won.
> (Macbeth)

Claude Redding, Lt, G. L.
Oflag IVC Colditz 28.9.44

129. WAG MAAR, ALLES SAL REG KOM!*

May 1941 was a bad month at Fort Ranch in Posen! Two main roads led East and North-East in sight of the fort, and one secondary road ran past the camp gates. The railway lines, running due East, could be seen in the far distance. All May the transports were passing—going towards Russia. Everyone knew that the conflict between Germany and Russia was about to begin—it was apparent to the dullest of minds. So we all stood day after day and watched. On the railway, masses of tanks, guns, armoured vehicles; on the roads long, endless convoys of trucks and cars—empty. We lined the wires and made suitable comments. Every now and then Bedford trucks, Morris trucks and Austins could be recognised, much to our annoyance. One evening, at 6.00 p.m. or thereabouts, on the road at our gates a convoy was rolling by. We had counted about 2,500 vehicles before the last of the trucks could be seen, and then we saw it was a truck of our own camp bringing back a small work party. They brought up the end of a huge convoy, and as they surged alongside the wires a voice from the truck, a rich Scottish voice, yelled: "We're pursuing them!"

The British O.R. may be all his critics say he is, but he has got guts.

T. Schrire,
Capt. R.A.M.C.

*Wait though, everything will turn out alright!—Afrikaans

130. "ONCE A GUARDSMAN ALWAYS A GUARDSMAN!" (1929— FOR EVER)

The Brigade of Guards is a part of the British Army. The men are recruited in the same way as for other branches of the service, except that they are required to be of a certain height. The height limit changes from time to time according to the demand and supply of recruits. In 1929 this limit was 5ft 10½ inches. While carrying out its normal duties the Brigade has the special duty of guarding the person of the King! Regiments are usually to be found in and around London, maintaining however one Battalion in Cairo.

The Grenadier Guards, who rejoice in the name of "The First or Grenadier Regiment of Foot Guards" is officially the oldest regiment in the Brigade. Actually the Coldstream Guards are the oldest as they were originally raised in the North of England at a village of that name by Monck for Oliver Cromwell. However their official date is the day on which they laid down their arms on Tower Hill, taking them up again in the name of the King.

The Regiment of the Grenadiers consists of No. 13 and No. 14 Training Companies at the Guards depot at Caterham; the 1st, 2nd and 3rd Battalions each permanently at full strength. The numbers of Companies is consecutive throughout. The 1st Battalion having King's Company, No. 2, 3 and No. 4. The 3rd Bn. No. 6, 7 and No. 8 and so on. The King's Company

The Brigade of Guards is a part of the British Army. The men are recruited in the same way as for other branches of the service, except that they are required to be of a certain height. The height limit changes from time to time according to the demand and supply of recruits. In 1929 the limit was 5 ft 10½ inches. While carrying out its normal duties the Brigade has the special duty of guarding the person of the King. Regiments are usually to be found in and around London, maintaining however one Battalion in Cairo. The Grenadier Guards who rejoice in the name of "The First or Grenadier Regiment of Foot Guards" is officially the oldest Regiment in the Brigade. Actually, the Coldstream Guards are older as they were originally raised in the North of England at a village of that name by Monk for Oliver Cromwell. However their official date is the day on which they laid down their arms on Tower Hill, taking them up again in the name of the King. The Regiment of Grenadiers consists of No 13 & No 14 Training Companies at the Guards Depôt at Caterham. The 1st, 2nd and 3rd Battalions each permanently at full strength. The number of Companies is consecutive throughout. The 1st Bn having King's Company, No 2, 3 & No 4. The 2nd Bn No 5, 6, 7 & No 8 and so on. The King's Company contains only men of 6 ft 2½ in and over and it is used when available as the Guard of Honour at official functions. Each Battalion has the equivalent of three R.S.M's (one R.S.M & 2 Drill Sergeants, the latter is a rank peculiar to the Guards the "Gentlemen" concerned are above C.S.M & below R.S.M). I joined the Grenadiers in September 1929 as a recruit in No 14 Company where I was informed that there was only one Army in the world worthy of the name of Army, and that was the British Army. In the British Army there was really only one Brigade worth anything – that was the Guards Brigade. In this Brigade there was one Regiment much better than all the others. This Regiment was the 1st or Grenadier Regiment of Foot Guards commanded by Major General the Viscount Gort V.C. and whose Colonel-in-chief was none other than the King himself. Also one was informed that "once a Guardsman one is always a Guardsman". Having finally been convinced that I really was a member of the finest Regiment in the world & having been promoted Guardsman I was posted to No 4 Company in the 1st Battalion. Shortly after I became a L/Cpl in No 14 Platoon. There are certain things permitted to ordinary soldiers which in the Guards are either just not done, or frankly forbidden. One of these is to fall out on the line of march. To fall out in this manner is not allowed, it is forbidden & therefore cannot happen!

The incident described below happened in No 14 Platoon sometime in September 1930 when the Battalion was stationed at Pirbright Camp near Aldershot. The 1st Battalion was ordered to march to Ascot (about 15 miles) to march past the Colonel of the Regiment (Major Gen Viscount Gort V.C.) and then march home again (another 15 miles). The day was very hot, but guardsmen are never, never permitted to undo their collar hooks – no matter what the temperature. Having arrived at Ascot safely – marched past "The Colonel", the Battalion started its homeward march. About ⅔ of the way back to Pirbright one member of No 14 Pl began to appear a bit distressed. Firstly he was helped along by his comrades – then they relieved him of his Rifle & Pack (in such a manner that none in authority could see). A mile or two later he became quite unconscious. We all became worried, not for the man but because it really did look as if a Guardsman – a Grenadier at that – was about to fall out! However by holding up, by pushing or by pulling he was eventually brought into camp where he collapsed in a heap on the Parade Ground and was taken to Hospital. Two hours later he was dead – but a Guardsman had not fallen out. "Once a Guardsman always a Guardsman" was very true in his case – the poor devil wasn't given a chance to be anything else. A few days later in Part I orders the following appeared – "The Commanding Officer regrets to announce the death of No 2611xxx Gdsn ——— died of heatstroke."

R.H.T. Bampfort Martin
52nd Light Infantry

It was in August '43 on the KAPORNIK range of mountains, sat on a log talking to DJURIĆ, a subordinate commander of MIKHAJLOVIĆ the Royalist leader, that I first heard of the existence of a "bataillon élite" of the JUGO-SLAV Army. The discussion was one of "ways and means" for organizing to the best advantage, and arming most effectively, the forces actual and potential under DJURIĆ command.

Whilst the discussion was taking place I noticed, seated on his haunches arab fashion, a rather striking figure of a man who was outstanding even amongst such an array of colourful personalities as comprised the JUGO-SLAV ARMY OF THE HOMELAND. He had long black straight hair reaching to his shoulders, a face that somehow gave one the impression that there was a predominant Turkish strain in his ancestry, out of which shone a pair of piercing black eyes that seemed to be ever on the alert; a hooked nose and beautifully white sound teeth completed a head that was topped by the SHUBARA, a hat or cap made from lambskin favoured by many CHETNIK. Broad shoulders on a lean athletic figure completed the man.

I asked that he be introduced knowing that custom on introduction would give me his rank, name, regiment and any outstanding qualification he possessed. I was not disappointed - he was named as PORUCNIK (Lieut) ... the last survivor of the famous (in Jugo-slavia) CRNI GUSURI - The Black Hussars. So much pride was evident at a mention of the name that I asked for further enlightenment re the history etc of this Regiment and learned the following — Every officer and man was a volunteer in the Regiment. Other ranks under 25 yrs of age officers under 30. All ranks unmarried. Their dress both clothing and equipment was all Black (Arms, — pistol, S.M.G., hand grenades, fighting knife and knuckle dusters and last _fatal dose of poison_ !! I was not unnaturally intrigued with the news of the latter and asked for an explanation. Here the officer raised his proud head and said, "GOSPODIN KOMMANDANT we take no prisoners and do not allow ourselves to be taken !!"

Small wonder there was an only survivor.

To cut a long story short such a formation was the ideal for the work to be done when ones country is occupied by an unwelcome military force.

Further talks on later days saw the re-birth of his unit with an Englishman commander with the honorary (unconfirmed) rank of POD-PUKOVNIK-Lieut Col, — in the Royalist army, and PORUCNIK ... , as a very able, keen, efficient and extremely daring second in command. All under his immediate influence he was a fine example in all operations, and, if he lives through the war I can't help but believe he will be covered with well-deserved glory, and be more to go down in his country's history with the much sought title of — —

        — NATIONAL HERO!

16am ... th.
Capt
Royal Engineers.

Royal Engineers

contains only men of 6ft 2½ in and over and it is used when available as the Guard of Honour at official functions. Each Battalion has the equivalent of three RSM's (one RSM and 2 Drill Sergeants, the latter is a rank peculiar to the Guards. The "Gentlemen" concerned are above CSM and below RSM).

I joined the Grenadiers in September 1929 as a recruit in No. 14 Company where I was informed that there was only one army in the world worthy of the name Army, and that was the British Army. In the British Army there was really only one Brigade worth anything—that was the Guards Brigade. In this Brigade there was one Regiment much better than all the others—this Regiment was the "1st or Grenadier Regiment of Fort Guards commanded by the Major General The Viscount Gort V.C. and whose Colonel-in-Chief was none other than the King himself. Also one was informed that "Once a Guardsman, one was always a Guardsman"!

Having finally been convinced that I really was a member of the finest Regiment in the world, and having been promoted "Guardsman" I was posted to No. 4 Company in the 1st Battalion! Shortly afterwards I became a L/Cpl in No. 14 Platoon.

There are certain things permitted to ordinary soldiers which in the Guards are either just not done, or frankly forbidden. One of these is to fall out on the line of march. To fall out in this manner is not allowed, it is forbidden and therefore cannot happen!

The incident described below happened in No. 14 Platoon sometime in August or September 1930 when the Battalion was stationed at Purbright Camp near Aldershot. The 1st Battalion was ordered to march to Ascot (about 15 miles) to march past the Colonel of the Regiment (Major General Viscount Gort V.C.) and then of course march home again (another 15 miles). The day was very hot, but Guardsmen are never never permitted to undo their colour hooks—no matter what the temperature. Having arrived at Ascot safely—marched past "The Colonel" the Battalion started its homeward march. About ⅔ of the way back to Purbright one member of No. 14 Platoon began to appear a bit distressed. Firstly he was helped along by his comrades—then they relieved him of his rifle—then his pack (in a manner that none in authority could see). A mile or two later he became quite unconscious. We all became worried, not for the man, but because it really did look as if a Guardsman—a Grenadier at that, was about to fall out! However by holding up, by pushing and by pulling, he was eventually brought into camp where he collapsed in a heap on the Parade Ground and was taken to Hospital.

Two hours later he was dead, but a Guardsman had not fallen out. "Once a Guardsman always a Guardsman" was very true in his case. The poor devil wasn't given a chance to be anything else.

A few days later in Part 1 orders the following appeared: The commanding Officer regrets to announce the death of No. 2611XXX Gdsn _____ died of heatstroke.

R. P. E. T. Barry, Capt
52nd Light Infantry

131. Црни Хусари (BLACK HUSSARS)

It was in August '43 on the KAPOANIK range of mountains, sat on a log chatting to Djurič, a subordinate commander of MIKHAJLOVIČ the Royalist leader, that I first heard of the existence of a "bataillon élite" of the JUGO-SLAV army. The discussion was one of "ways and means" for organizing to the best advantage, and arming most effectively, the forces actual and potential under DJURIČ command.

Whilst the discussion was taking place I noticed, seated on his haunches Arab fashion, a rather striking figure of a man who was outstanding even among such an array of colourful personalities as comprised by the JUGO-SLAV ARMY OF THE HOMELAND. He had long black straight hair reaching to his shoulders, a face that somehow gave one the impression that there was a predominant Turkish strain in his ancestry, out of which shone a pair of piercing eyes that seemed to be forever on the alert; a hooked nose and beautifully white sound teeth completed the head that was topped by the SHUBARA, a hat or cap made from lambskin favoured by many CHETNIK. Broad shoulders on a lean athletic figure completed the man.

I asked that he be introduced, knowing that custom on introductions would give me his rank, name, regiment and any outstanding qualifications he possessed. I was not disappointed—he was named as PORUCNIK (Lieut.) . . . the last survivor of the famous (in Jugo-Slavia) CRNI GUSARI—The Black Hussars. So much pride was existent at the mention of the name that I asked for further enlightenment re the history of his Regiment and learned the following—Every officer and man was a volunteer in the Regiment. Other ranks under 25 years of age officers under 30. All ranks unmarried. Their dress, both clothing and equipment was all black. Arms,—pistol, S.M.G., hand grenades, fighting knife and knuckle dusters and last <u>a fatal dose of poison</u>!! I was not unnaturally intrigued with the news of the latter and asked for an explanation. Here the officer raised his proud head and said "GOSPODIN KOMMANDANT, we take no prisoners and do not allow ourselves to be taken!!"

Small wonder there was only one survivor.

To cut a long story short such a formation was the ideal for the work to be done when one's country is occupied by an unwelcome military force.

Further talks on later days saw the re-birth of his unit with an Englishman as commander with the honorary (unconfirmed) rank of POD-PUKOVNÌK— Lieut. Col.—in the Royalist Army, and PORUČNIK . . . as a very able, keen, efficient and extremely daring second in command. To all under his immediate influence he was a fine example in all operations, and if he lives through the war I can't help but believe he will be covered with well-deserved glory, and one name to go down in his country's history with the much deserved title of———NATIONAL HERO!

A. H. (Alan Hawkesworth, Capt.)
Royal Engineers

20th Century.

Here I lie
In a great cold castle
And wonder why,
And wonder why we are
What we are
And whither we are going.
From whence we have come
Thence shall we return?
Abraham not knowing whence
He went, went out
Nor could he wonder why;
He had faith
In his Friend
Who knew why.

Mardellamel
Feb 1945

(Kierdegaard "Fear and Trembling"
The Bible story in Genesis and
Hebrews 11 about Abraham)

(This poem may not be published, nor copied for circulation without
the permission of the author in writing, Mardell.)

L'aubade d'un Drapeau

[A]u petit jour, quelques instants avant l'heure prévue [n]ous aperçûmes Castel Forte qui dressait ses murs [a]ntiques, à deux ou trois lieues de vous, masquant [la] plaine verdoyante de la vallée de Liri — notre [ob]jectif —. Le ciel printannier, d'une première [l]impidité, était parsemé d'étoiles scintillantes. [L]a lune, déjà à moitié rognée par l'horizon, jetait [ses] rayons d'argent sur nos casques rouillés; la [fra]îcheur de la nuit promenait encore son exhalation [d]ans ce secteur presque calme cette nuit. De temps [e]n temps un duel d'artillerie se faisait entendre. [Le] murmure d'une conversation voltigeait tel un [lé]ger brouillard autour de nos têtes, interrompu [de] temps à autre par le cri perçant d'une chouette [ou] d'un hibou chassé par la peur vers nous et [qui] faisait dire à nos tirailleurs : chess El abitha [le] cri des revenants.

[Qu]elques agents de liaison, coururent çà et là. L'attente [la plus] espérante commença alors. On n'entendait que [q]uelques mots échangés à voix basse et le cliquetis des [a]rmes. Tout à coup la formidable artillerie [fra]nçaise commença à cracher impitoyablement [u]n déluge de fer sur le Castel Forte —

[A] l'heure "H" les Tirailleurs Tunisiens, sous le [co]mmandement de leurs incomparables chefs [f]rançais, bondirent comme des lions,

132. 20TH CENTURY

Here I lie
In a great cold castle
And wonder why
And wonder why we are
What we are
And whither we are going.
From whence we had come
Thence shall we return?
Abraham no knowing whence
He went, went out
Nor could he wonder why;
He had faith
In His Friend
Who knows why

(Kirdegaard "Fear and Trembling" The Bible story in Genesis and Hebrews 11 about Abraham)

Max de Hamel
Feb 1945

(This poem may not be published, nor copied for circulation without the permission of the author in writing, Max de H.)
A separate note on Intelligence Corps stationery, pasted into the Wartime Log gives permission for publication.

77305 Lt de Hamel
No1 DCS
BOAR

Dear Jerry
Many thanks for your note and circular of Oct 24 which reached me to day. You may certainly publish my poem Here I lie in a great cold castle. I had not agreed to it in case I had wanted to publish some others with it. In that case I wanted them all to appear together. The others are lost!

I look forward to seeing your book in print!

Yours ever

Max de Hamel

133. FRONT D'ITALIE LE 11 MAI 1944—L'AUBADE D'UN DRAPAU*

At dawn, a few minutes before zero hour, we made out Castel Forte whose ancient walls towered two or three leagues from us, concealing the verdant plains of the Liri Valley—our objective—. The spring sky, totally clear, was studded with shining stars. The moon, already half hidden over the horizon, shone rays of silver on our rusty helmets; the coolness of the night gave exhilaration to this otherwise calm sector in the night. From time to time an artillery duel was heard. The murmur of a conversation was heard as a light fog floated around our heads, interrupted from time to time by the piercing cry of a startled owl or night hawk, causing our infantrymen to exclaim: "Hess El Abithax"—the cry of ghosts.

Some liaison officers were running here and there. The exasperating waiting period had begun. Now we heard only the quiet exchange of low conversation and the occasional crash from our weapons. All of a sudden the powerful French artillery began to throw a pitiless deluge of fire towards Castel Forte.

At zero hour the Tunisian riflemen under the command of their incomparable French officers, sprang forth like lions [*original text continued on page 134 of diary*], scaled the rocks, climbed the steep slopes under a rain of fire coming from the concrete emplacements which were deeply embedded in the area facing us.

Under this indescribable avalanche of projectiles, our infantrymens' determination became even more ferocious, firing their rifles, throwing their grenades, fighting hand to hand, and continuing their advance in a savage cheer of "Allah" and "Mohamed", shouted with fanatical exaltation.

Gradually our riflemen infiltrated this insurmountable "chain mail" which constituted the Gustave Line. After several hours of this dreadful combat the resistance of the enemy diminished under the force and fierce persistence of the valiant soldiers of the African Army. Then, all that was left confronting us were the "Minen" six-barelled devices that the Boche had manufactured in large numbers for the destruction of the human race. The panorama presenting itself before our eyes was like the bottom of an abyss; here a man with his head shattered, there another, his chest wide open, a little further a man who seemed to be looking, but had no sight, and how many others, fixed in death or writhing in their last agonies.

Then slowly, like every other day the sun rose. Then the tricolour flag was raised over Castel Forte, although happy shouts of our comrades, fallen as heroes in their last endeavours [*original text continued on page 135 of diary*], were never heard, as the last disappearing stars in the heavens above took with them their departed souls.

The banner unfurled its proud colours and flapped in the clean morning air above the ruin, desolation and death; heedless of the spiteful clatter of the "Minen" watched fervently by our leader, the courageous Commander Jarrot, standing immobile, leaning on his cane, and who uttered the words which are engraved in my heart; " To the Tunisian Riflemen goes the honour."

S/Lieutenant El Khemiri Khelil
4e R.F.F. Capturé le 19 Juin
1944 a Sienne (Mont Amiata, Italie)

* *Salute to a Flag*

escaladant les rochers, grimpant les pentes so
la pluie de fer qui venait des casemattes blindées,
échelonnées en profondeur, là bas, en face.
Sous cette indescriptible avalanche de projectiles, nos
tirailleurs devinrent plus féroces encore, tirant de
leur fusil, lançant leurs grenades, luttant à l'arme
blanche, et ainsi continuaient leur avance dans
un hourra sauvage coupé d'"Allah" et de "Moha
criés avec toute l'exaltation de leur fanatisme.
Peu à peu nos tirailleurs s'infiltrèrent dans cette
infranchissable "maille de fer" que constituait la
ligne "Gustave". Au bout de quelques heures de cet
affreux combat la résistance de l'ennemi faiblit
sous l'impétuosité et la continuité du terrible assau
les vaillants soldats de l'armée d'Afrique. Pu
vous n'eûmes plus à craindre que le "minen", em
à six tube que le Boche fabrique en grand nombe
vour la destruction du genre humain. Ce tablea
s'imposait à nos yeux comme le cauchemar d'un
ond d'abîme; ici un homme, la tête éclatée,
à un autre, la poitrine ouverte, plus loin celui-
qui semble vous regarder mais qui ne voit plus,
t combien d'autres, figés par la mort dans les
contorsions de l'agonie. Puis lentement, comme
haque jour, le soleil se leva. Alors le Drapea
ricolore fut hissé sur Castel Forte sous le vire
joyeux de nos camarades tombés en héros tand

que les dernières étoiles disparaissaient dans le lointain infini du ciel emportant avec elles rs âmes saintes. Le pavois déroula ses fières uleurs qui claquent maintenant dans l'air vis du matin au dessus des ruines, de la solation, de la mort ; indifférentes aux latements rageurs des "Nunens", enveloppées u regard fervent de notre chef, le courageu ommandant Jarrot, immobile, appuyé su a cane et qui nous dira tout à l'heure les nots gravés dans ma mémoire et dans mon ur : « Les tirailleurs tunisiens à l'honneur »

S/Lieutenant El Khemiri Khélil
4e R.T.T. Capturé le 19 Juin
1944 à Sienne (Mont Amiata
Italie —

Gdy w latach młodzieńczych czytałem powieści J. J. Kraszen
osnute na tle życia i obyczajów Augusta Mocnego
w jego pałacach i zamkach saskich nie przyszło
mi nigdy przez myśl, że kiedyś znajdę się tu
w zamku Colditz jako jeniec, żołnierz broniący
wolności swej Ojczyzny i że spotkam tu żołnierz
różnych narodów zachodnich, którzy tak samo jak
naród walczą w imię ideałów Demokracji i wolno
człowieka.

Zamek Colditz 9/III 945

Tadeusz Bór Komorowski
gen.

Translation:

In the days of my youth when I read novels
by J. J. Kraszewski about the life and customs
in the palaces and castles of August the Strong
in Saxony, it never occured to me, that at some
time I would find myself in the castle at Colditz
as a P.O.W., a soldier who had fought for the liberty
of his country, and that I would meet in this castle
the soldiers of different Western nations who had
fought for the same ideals of Democracy and
freedom of mankind, as my nation had fought for

The Castle at Colditz 9th March 1945

136. THE CASTLE AT COLDITZ—9 MARCH 1945

In the days of my youth when I read novels by J. T. Kranewski about the life and customs in the palaces and castles of August the Strong in Saxony, it never occurred to me, that at some time I might find myself in the castle at Colditz as a P.O.W., a soldier who had fought for the liberty of his country, and that I would meet in this castle the soldiers of different Western nations who had fought for the same ideals of Democracy and freedom of mankind as my nation had fought for.

Tadeusz Bór-Komorowski
General

Page 137 is blank.

138. CRETE: 31ST MAY 1941

The rear-guard action on Crete was drawing to an end; stubble-bearded men collected small arms ammunition from those detailed for evacuation from Spharkia. The ammunition was thrown into blankets and carried by jaded fatigue parties to the front line positions. Sometimes a water bottle changed hands, sometimes a tin of bully beef, for both food and water had been short on the rearguard. The passage of thousands of men, thirsty from a pitiless sun and the dusty mountain tracks, had drained the Cretan wells and to a man facing the prospect of another day on the bare rocks, the 2nd water bottle was valuable. Behind this was the entrance to a deep waddi, with vertical sides that shut out the direct sunlight but wide enough for men to pass in single file towards the evacuation point. Australians, Maoris and troops from the United Kingdom passed through the traffic control and disappeared into the obscurity of the waddi. Their khaki shirts were torn and marked by sweat stains, their faces parched and cracked from the heat and lined with furrows of dust. They all looked weary and exhausted.

Out of a tranquil blue sky came the drone of engines and the steady activity ceased; whistles shrilled their warning and the ground once more thick with men and heaving with movement became bare as troops sought cover. A quiet came over the sun-drenched earth as a flight of Stukas dropped low and circled to seek their targets. The quiet that had been oppressive broke in an avalanche of sound. The roar of planes was deafening and there was the spatter of machine gun fire and whine of falling bombs. Explosive bullets kicked up puffs of earth and pillars of dust hung in the still air where the bombs had fallen. In insolent security the planes dived, turned and dived again and then swung out of sight over the encircling hills. Whistles sounded again and activity was resumed on the ground. Men moved briskly into the gloom of the waddi. A company of Commandos with Tommy guns slung, moved towards the right flank and Marines passed obliquely to a defensive position beside a Btn. of the Welsh. Within the thin line of rearguard troops, the stream of evacuees made for the beach.

The rear-guard action on Crete was drawing to an end: stubble-bearded men collected small-arms' ammunition from those detailed for evacuation from Sphak The ammunition was thrown into blankets & carried by jaded fatigue parties to the front line positions. Sometimes a water bottle changed hands, sometimes a tin of bully beef, for both food & water had been short on the rearguard. The passage of thousands of men, thirsty from a pitiless sun & the dusty mountain tracks, had drained the Cretan wells and to a man facing the prospect of another day on the bare rocks, the 2nd water bottle was valued Behind them was the entrance to a deep waddi, with vertical sides that shut out the direct sunlight but wide enough for men to pass in single file toward the evacuation point.   Australians, Maoris & troops from the United Kingdom passed through the traffic control & disappeared into the obscurity of the wad Their khaki shirts were torn & marked by sweat stains; their faces parched & cracked from the heat & lined with furrows of dust. They all looked weary, exhausted.

Out of a tranquil blue sky came the drone of engines & the stead activity ceased: whistles shrilled their warning & the ground once thick with men & heaving with movement became bare so the troops sought cover. A quiet came over the sun-drenched earth as a flight of Stukkas dropped low & circle to seek their targets. The quiet that had been oppressive broke in an avalanc of sound. The roar of planes was deafening & there was the spatter of machine gu fire & the whine of falling bombs. Explosive bullets kicked up puffs of earth & pillars of dust hung in the still air where the bombs had fallen. In insolent security the planes dived, turned & dived again & then swung out of sight over the encircling hills.   Whistles sounded again & activity was resumed on the ground.   Men moved briskly into the gloom of the waddi: A company commander with Tommy guns slung, moved towards the right flank & man passed obliquely to a defensive position beside a Btn. of the Welsh. With the thin line of rearguard troops, the stream of evacuees made for the bea

On the night 31st May - 1st June, the Navy made its last trip to beach at Spharkia. Evacuating Commonwealth troops lined the rocky tra leading to the beach by thousands — some distance away on the hill perime the rearguard troops faced the slowly advancing enemy. The word to retire the beach reached them shortly after mid-night & parts withdrew to the main column.   Shortly before dawn the last ship sailed for Egypt & the Senior Office called for all available officers & read the text of a letter ordering the capitula

Dawn broke swiftly in a flawless sky on the morning of June 1st. No ripple disturbed the blue of the sea & the hills were quiet in the fresh morning air. The day was perfect but there was confusion & weariness amongst the men who thronged the narrow Spharkia valley. The news that Navy could not return had come as a physical shock to them: their act became mechanical. Many settled down to destroy their weapons & equipm some started to forage for food & water while others started the pitiful busin of displaying white flags.   Soon the length of the valley where the rema of Crforce had collected was dappled with white tokens of surrender. From the perimeter came the sound of the crisp crackle of rifle fire which ceased abruptly. Shortly afterwards, a section of Germans came cautiously over the crest.

In a damaged house, some troops had started to boil a

Gavi

Gavi, the Italian punishment camp for British officers, is a Frederick Barbarossa medieval fortress 40 miles north of Genoa, built solidly onto a needle rock which rises from a rolling plain of vineyards and grain, and looking south to the Ligurian mountains. Behind it to the north, and only 10 miles away is Marengo, scene of Napoleon's greatest Italian victory.

Inside the fortress in close seclusion live 180 British officers. Three hundred guards are employed on the task of picketing the battlements; 20 carabinieri (the Italian soldier-police) look after inside security; and a carabinieri brigadier General is commandant with a staff of 15 officers under him. Comparing Gavi with its German equivalent at Colditz (where I fetched up a year later) it seemed to me that although the Germans employed the same lavish and careful security measures, the Italians were more expert and effective at this kind of work. For one thing, Italian guards were better — more alert, more suspicious — and the Italians interfered more with your private life, if a prisoner can be said to have one, so that work was difficult.

Now it is April, 1943. Eight officers and 2 batmen are watching the weather with anxiety. An escape, 8 months in preparation, is due to break, and success depends on very special weather conditions.

There are 4 South African officers: Palm, Pole, Wuth and Patterson. They discovered the intricate route, and have been responsible with the 2 batmen for most of the hard work. Then there is Cram, in peacetime an Edinburgh lawyer, now the most escaped officer in Italian hands; Medd, a naval officer with his sapper partner Daly; Stirling, recently captured in Tunis; myself; and finally 2 batmen: Macrae and Headley. The gap is in the ceiling moulding over their bed.

On the night 31st May–1st June, the Navy made its last trip to the beach at Spharkia. Evacuating Commonwealth troops lined the rocky track leading to the beach by thousands—some distance away on the hill perimeter the rearguard troops faced the slowly advancing enemy. The word to retire on the beach reached them shortly after midnight and parts withdrew to the main column. Shortly before dawn the last ship sailed for Egypt and the Senior Officer called for all available officers and read the text of a letter ordering the capitulation.

Dawn broke swiftly in a flawless sky on the morning of June 1st. No ripple disturbed the blue of the sea and the hills were quiet in the fresh morning air. The day was perfect but there was confusion and weariness amongst the men who thronged the narrow Spharkia valley. The news that the Navy could not return had come as a physical shock to them. Their actions became mechanical. Many settled down to destroy their weapons and equipment; some started to forage for food and water while others started the pitiable task of displaying white flags. Soon the length of the valley where the remnants of Creforce had collected was draped with white tokens of surrender. From the perimeter came the sound of the crisp crackle of rifle fire which ceased abruptly. Shortly afterwards a section of Germans came cautiously over the crest.

In a damaged house, some troops had started to boil a [*original text continued on page 139 of the diary, which is missing. The following two paragraphs are taken from* Detour] handful of dried peas. One glanced up briefly as a German poked his head round the door and then returned to his task. A few yards away, the German Section Leader had taken a large Nazi flag and pinned it to the ground with rocks. Its purpose became clear when the dawn flight of Stukas came into sight over the hills. The squadron dipped white flags. At the lower end they circled and came back, this time bombing and firing into the packed masses below. A small bomb dropped by the damaged house and sent a cloud of dust into the dried peas. The trooper cooking them scooped the dust away and started to eat them hurriedly. Another bomb dropped closer and he wriggled under and adjacent sofa and continued eating ravenously. On the hillside a German soldier sprang to his feet gesticulating wildly at the aircraft. A bullet hit him and he dropped abruptly. Close at hand the wounded were being dragged into a Greek chapel. The capitulation had started.

In the warmth of the late afternoon, a buzzard poised motionless in the still air. His beady eyes watched a ragged column of men struggling up the steep mountain side, pausing wearily on the crest and then trudging on. There were 8,000 men in the column. They were nearing the end of their first day in "Kriegsgefangenschaft".

Lieutenant Sandbach

Pages 139 to 142 (two complete leaves) are missing from the Wartime Log.

143. ITALIAN ESCAPE

Gavi, the Italian punishment camp for British officers, is a Frederick Barbarossa medieval fortress 40 miles north of Genoa, built solidly onto a needle of rock which rises from a rolling plain of vineyards and grain, and looking south to the Lipurian mountains. Behind it to the north, and only 10 miles away, is Marengo, scene of Napoleon's greatest Italian victory.

Inside the fortress in close seclusion live 180 British officers. Three hundred guards are employed on the task of picketing the battlements; 20 Carabinieris (the Italian soldier-police) look after inside security; and a Carabinieri brigadier general is Commandant with a staff of 15 officers under him. In comparing Gavi with its German equivalent (where I fetched up a year later) it seemed to me that although the Germans employed the lavish and careful security measures, the Italians were more expert and effective at this kind of work. For one thing, Italian guards were better—more alert, more suspicious—and the Italians interfered more with your private life, if a prisoner can be said to have one, so that work was difficult.

Now it is April 1943. Eight officers and 2 batmen are watching the weather with anxiety. An escape, 8 months in preparation, is due to break, and success depends on very special weather conditions.

There are 4 South African officers: Palm, Pole, Wuth and Patterson. They discovered the intricate route, and have been responsible with the 2 batmen for most of the hard work. Then there is Cram, in peacetime an Edinburgh lawyer, now the most-escaped officer in Italian hands; Medd, a naval officer with his sapper partner Daly; Stirling, recently captured in Tunis; myself; and finally 2 batmen: Macrae and Headley. The trap is in the ceiling moulding over their bed. [*Original text continued on page 144 of diary*].

At about 4 in the afternoon we decide that the weather is all right—heavy rain and bad visibility. Stirling, Cram and I are carrying 20 days emergency rations. We intend moving only by night, across the Po valley up into the Val d'Aosta, and across into Switzerland by Breuil-Zermatt. Cram knows this crossing well. By one in the morning we are under the dungeons, have swum the 30 yards across the underground pool, climbed the loose rope to the rock ledge where the tunnel starts from. Palm is in the lead, we start. He moves out onto the roof of the fortress below, cuts through the electrified barbed wire, frees a passage. Sentries on the battlements 30 yards above us to the left and right look down onto the illuminated roof where the tunnel comes out.

We move fast; now we are on the lowest edge of the roof. A jump brings us into the courtyard where the guards live. I cannot see Cram and the South Africans ahead of me. They must be all right. Stirling and I cross the lighted yard, passing close by 3 Italian soldiers who don't notice us, their eyes averted because of wind and rain. I climb through some wire on the outside buttress. Behind me a door opens and 2 Italians appear.

Stirling, caught on the wrong side of the wire is picked out by a bright shaft of light. They have spotted him. He makes fast for the keep gate to get through there instead, the other 4 men are behind him. I can't wait any longer. I grab the rope fixed by Palm to take us 30 feet down the outside buttress, it breaks, and I fall headlong. Not hurt.

At about 4 in the afternoon we decide that the weather is all right—heavy rain and bad visibility. Stirling, Cram and I are carrying 20 da[ys]' emergency rations. We intend moving only by night, across the Po val[ley] up into the Val d'Aosta, and across into Switzerland by Breuil-Zerma[tt.] Cram knows this crossing well. By one in the morning we are under [the] dungeons, have swum the 30 yards across the underground pool, clim[bed] the loose rope to the rock ledge where the tunnel starts from. Palm in the lead, we start. ~~moving.~~ He moves out onto the roof of the fortress below[,] cuts through the electrified barbed wire, frees a passage. Sentries on the battlements 30 yards above us to the left and right look down onto 'illuminated roof where the tunnel comes out.

We move fast; now we are on the lowest edge of the roof. A jump b[rings] us into the courtyard where the guards live. I cannot see Cram and the South Africans ahead of me. They must be all right. Stirling and I cro[ss] the lighted yard, passing close by 3 Italian soldiers who don't notice [us,] their eyes averted because of wind and rain. I climb through some wire o[n] the outside buttress. Behind me a door opens and 2 Italians appear. Stirling, caught on the wrong side of the wire is picked out by a bright shaf[t] of light— they have spotted him. He makes fast for the keep gate to get thro[ugh] there instead, the other 4 are behind him. I can't wait any longer. I gra[b] the rope fixed by Palm to take us the 30 feet down the outside buttress[,] it breaks, and I fall headlong. Not hurt.

Now everything starts up. Sentries are firing, the guard company is turning out shouting as only Italians can, sirens are whining, and the spotlights are moving about the hillside trying to pick us up. I slip, ru[n,] fall down the slopes, my heart pounding. No good trying to connect up wi[th] Cram, wherever he may be, or Stirling either if he has made it.

Skirting the village, and wading a river, I arrive in a wood whe[re] I sit down to figure things out. Mist, rain and wind make it pretty saf[e] for me as long as dark lasts. But in my fall I have lost food, maps, compas[s] —everything except 500 lire and some chocolate. Best go south into the Ligurian mountains while the search is on, and then move south to Genoa inside the widening search ring. From there we should see .

For the next 4 days while it rained, I lay by day in dripping bus[hes] on the side of the hills. Alpini troops searching, aimless shepherd[s] and little girls looking after geese, kept me in a constant state of alarm. By night I huddled up in a lean-to, too cold and wet to sleep.

Finally I decided I could risk movement. The day before Good Friday I set out to cross the mountains and reach the coast. I walked 10 hours a day along small mountain tracks. The peasants I encountered were few and far between— most of them had never bee[n] out of their own little valleys — and, believing my story of being a fugitive

. from a group of Italians bound on working party to Germany, fed me well. The accent in my Italian they attributed to my coming from a different province.

Two days later I arrived at the top of a deep gorge; down below I could see the Turin–Genoa railway. Next morning, early, I am at the station, ticket in my pocket.

The difference between travelling in those mountains and in civilized surroundings was considerable. As there were no foreign workers in Italy and very strict document control (more so than I later found in Austria), the odd stranger excited much curiosity. My clothes worried me. Dressed for night marching I had on corduroy trousers, a khaki converted Greek jacket, grey shirt and red tie. By great good fortune, however, the jacket had a black armband on the sleeve which I had left on, as if bereaved. It proved to be the best of all possible disguises. I adopted a sulky, depressed look, with a set frown, and this with the black armband had the effect of discouraging hence conversations – the escaped prisoner's worse danger in friendly, curious Italy.

In the station, after 6 days alone in the hills, the atmosphere was exciting. Every eye seemed to be on me. Fortunately, this was all imagination, and I arrived safely in Genoa which I knew from before the war. Two German newspapers were my first purchase, and these I carried conspicuously at all times as a tacit explanation of my foreign appearance, and also to explain any accent in my Italian. They allowed me to pose as an Italian to Germans, and as a German to Italians.

I spent 2 pleasant days in Genoa, walking about the rich city, old city, looking at the bombing damage, reading the papers in small cafés. Nights were the problem – it was still too cold to sleep without covers and the bombed out ruins were very drafty.

One day I was sitting in a bar drinking beer when 2 Luftwaffe Feldwebels came in; As they spoke no Italian I interpreted for them and got them what they wanted. One of them asked me if I was Italian. I replied that I was a Croat (my 3rd string nationality!). "Well," he said, "you are lucky – the Italians are a despicable race." After finishing their drinks, he & 2 went out. The moment they were gone the barman asked me if I were a German. A Croat, I replied. "A good thing," he said, "the Germans are" – he mentioned a highly objectionable epithet in Italian. Again I heartily agreed, and thought to myself as I finished my beer and called for another that the Italo–German brotherhood could scarcely have had a better commentary.

On Easter Monday, I decided to start for the frontier. After a good deal of wavering, I had decided on a train run: Genoa – Milan–Stresa; and then to foot it 65 k along Lake Maggiore to Switzerland at Locarno.

Now everything starts up. Sentries are firing, the guard company is turning out shouting as only Italians can, sirens are whining, and the spotlights are moving about the hillside trying to pick us up. I slip, run, fall down the slopes, my heart pounding. No good trying to connect up with Cram, wherever he may be, or Stirling either if he has made it.

Skirting the village, and wading a river, I arrive in a wood where I sit down to figure things out. Mist, rain and wind make it pretty safe for me as long as dark lasts. But in my fall I have lost food, maps, compasses, everything except 500 lire and come chocolate. Best go South into the Lipurian mountains while the search is on, and then move south to Genoa inside the widening search ring. From there we should see.

For the next 4 days while it rained, I lay by day in dripping bushes on the side of the hills. Alpini troops searching, aimless shepherds, and little girls looking after geese, kept me in a constant state of alarm. By night I huddled up in a lean-to, too cold and wet to sleep.

Finally I decided I could risk movement. The day before Good Friday I set out to cross the mountains and reach the coast. I walked 10 hours a day along small mountain tracks. The peasants I encountered were few and far between—most of them had never been out of their own little valley—and believing my story of being a fugitive [*original text continued on page 145 of diary*] from a group of Italians bound on a working party to Germany, fed me well. The accent in my Italian they attributed to my coming from a different province.

Two days later I arrived at the top of a deep gorge; down below I could see the Turin-Genoa railway. Next morning, early I am at the station, ticket in my pocket.

The difference between travelling in those mountains and in civilized surroundings was considerable. As there were no foreign workers in Italy and very strict document control (more so than I later found in Austria), the odd stranger excited much curiosity. My clothes worried me. Dressed for night marching I had on corduroy trousers, a khaki converted Greek jacket, grey shirt and red tie. By great good fortune however, the jacket had a black armband on the sleeve which I had left on, as if bereaved. It proved to be the best of all possible disguises. I adopted a sulky, depressed look, with a set frown, and this with my black arm band had the effect of discouraging chance conversations—the escaped prisoner's worst danger in friendly, curious Italy.

In the station, after 6 days alone in the hills, the atmosphere was exciting. Every eye seemed to be on me. Fortunately, this was all imagination, and I arrived safely in Genoa which I knew from before the war. Two German newspapers were my first purchase, and these I carried conspicuously at all times as a tacit explanation of my foreign appearance, and also to explain any accent in my Italian. They allowed me to pose as an Italian to Germans, and as a German to Italians.

I spent 2 pleasant days in Genoa, walking about the rickety old city, looking at the bombing damage, reading the newspapers in small cafés. Nights were the problem—it was still too cold to sleep without covers and the bombed out ruins were very drafty.

One day I was sitting in a bar drinking beer when 2 Luftwaffe Feldwebels came in. As they spoke no Italian I interpreted for them and got them what they wanted. One of them asked me if I was Italian. I replied that I was a Croat (my 3rd string nationality!) "Well," he said, "You are lucky—the Italians are a despicable race!" After finishing their drinks, the 2 went out. The moment they were gone the barman asked me if I were a German. A Croat, I replied. "A good thing." He said, "the Germans are –" he mentioned a highly objectionable epithet in Italian. Again I heartily agreed, and thought to myself as I finished my beer and called for another that the Italo-German brotherhood could scarcely have had a better commentary.

On Easter Monday, I decided to start for the frontier. After a good deal of waivering, I had decided on a train run: Genoa-Milan-Stresa; and then to foot it 65 km along Lake Maggiore to Switzerland at Locarno. [*Original text continued on page 146 of diary*].

I was handicapped by having no maps, compass or documents, and reckoned it was wisest to go quick and far.

Before leaving on Easter Monday afternoon, I went into Genoa Cathedral, sunk on my knees in a dark corner, and tried to get a few hours sleep as I was dead tired. My dreams were of escape—chased by Carabinieri, chased by Germans—. I woke up with a start to find a German officer beside me! Half sleep I sprung to my feet wildly, made the most appalling noise with my boots in the silent gloom of the church, and only when I saw the look of surprise on the German's face did I realize the dream had nothing to do with reality. I knelt again, my head in my hands, but now sleep would not come. I rose wearily and went to the station for the train.

Genoa station and Milan station were like nightmares. To my sensitive nerves every other man seemed to be a Carabinieri or plain clothes policeman, and certainly the ticket queues were most closely observed. In Genoa I had to have 2 quick brandies after 5 minutes in the ticket queue, at Milan I had another 2 to brace me and at Stresa I had a final one with a milliner's assistant whom I had met on the train. I remember this girl because, besides being rather pretty, she asked me if it were true that Paris was entirely underground, or was it like Milan, built on top?

From Stresa I set off on foot along the edge of Lake Maggiore for the frontier. Warmed by the brandy, with a bright mood overhead and Switzerland only 65 kilometres away, who wouldn't be happy? Things went well for me all night, I was able to avoid the police patrols, the way was easy to find with the lake on my right and the villas of Munich, Budapest and Milan millionaires on my left—by dawn I had done 45 kilometres. I lay down in some laurel bushes by the shore just short of Cannobbio, watched the sun rise from behind the mountains across the lake, and saw the Intra-Locarno packet steaming north about half a mile out. I felt very tired but exhilarated by the thought of freedom so close.

Two more hours brought me to the point where I had decided to leave the road and cross the frontier by the mountains. As I sat behind a wall tightening my bootlaces and getting ready for the final effort, I became aware that I was being [*original text continued on page 147 of diary*] watched. Looking over the wall were 2 Carabinieri with revolvers. I was caught.

The sad thing was that my captors had taken me for an escaped convict from Piacenza jail (serving a sentence for rape), and were hoping for a handsome reward. How dull for them to learn the truth. But duller even for me to find myself behind bars again that night. Looking out my cell window to the lights of Locarno, twinkling in the gin clear night air just across the lake.

Jack Pringle Major
8th Hussars

Oflag IVC–Colditz—April 1945

I was handicapped by having no maps, compass or documents, and reckoned it was wisest to go quick and far.

Before leaving on Easter Monday afternoon, I went into Genoa cathedral, sunk on my knees in a dark corner, and tried to get a few hours sleep as I was dead tired. My dreams were of escape – chased by carabinieri, chased by Germans –: I woke with a start to find a German officer beside me! Half asleep I sprung to my feet wildly, made the most appalling noise with my boots in the silent gloom of the churchyard, and only when I saw the look of surprise on the German face did I realize that the dream had nothing to do with reality. I knelt again, my head in my hands, but now sleep would not come rose wearily and went to the station for the train

Genoa station and Milan station were like nightmares. To my sensitive nerves every other man seemed to be a carabinieri or plain clothes policeman, and certainly the ticket queues were most closely observed. In Genoa I had to have 2 quick brandies after 5 minutes in the ticket queue, at Milan I had another 2 to brace me, and at Stresa I had a final one with a milliner's assistant whom I had met on the train. I remember this girl because, besides being rather pretty, she asked me if it were true that Paris was entirely underground, or was it like Milan – built on top?

From Stresa I set off on foot along the edge of Lake Maggiore for the frontier. Warmed by the brandy, with a bright moon overhead and Switzerland only 65 kilometers away, who wouldn't be happy? Things went well for me all night, I was able to avoid the police patrols, the way was easy to find with the lake on my right and the villas of Munich, Budapest and Milan millionaires on my left — by dawn I had done 45 kilometres, and I lay down in some laurel bushes by the shore just short of Cannobbio, and watched the sun rise from behind the mountains across the lake, and saw the Intra-Locarno packet steaming north about half a mile out. I felt very tired but exhilarated by the thought of freedom so close.

Two more hours brought me to the point where I had decided to leave the road and cross the frontier by the mountain as I sat behind a wall tightening my bootlaces and getting ready for the final effort, I became aware that I was being

watched. Looking over the wall were 2 carabinieri with
revolvers. I was caught.

The sad thing was that my captors had taken me for an
escaped convict from Piacenza jail (serving a sentence for rape
and were hoping for a handsome reward. How dull for them to
learn the truth. But duller even for me to find myself behind
bars again that night, looking out my cell window to the lights of
Locarno, twinkling in the gin clear ~~spring~~ night air just across the la
of IV C - Colditz - April 1945.   twinkle

                                                   Maj
                                                   8ª Hussars

If Terry says "go" we must "get-going". He demanded that I should enter the following, to close the book

St. Mt. 17²⁶. "If any man will come after me let him deny himself + take up his cross."

Most people are wondering what the state of things is likely to be in post-war Britain, America, Canada, Australia or whatever place they call home. Until the success of the invasion put such matters out of mind, the future of our own country of the world was the most constant subject of speculation. Men whose interests were industrial + commercial discuss reconverting of the war-potential into a peace-potential. Agriculturist + dairy farmers wondered + are still wondering at extent the Govt. to control their industry. The building trade with all its concomitant trades + professions is well to the fore with its plans for planning. For most people there is a general interest in post-war economics + money — in the unknowable future money-markets in war-despoiled Europe; what stabilization of currency may be expected between the Empire + the Americas; at the true function + utility of the new World Bank created by the Three Powers. People in the Services are naturally anxious about the changes which in four years have put them out of date in their own profession. They are concerned also as to the probable otherwise of the country spending more money than it wishes to on the armed services, or whether it will revert to its former practice of spending as much as possible on immediate pleasure. Judging from the intentions one hears expressed in this camp the latter is probable — + from what one knows of the British taxpayer too who wants his tax as low as low as may be, that his pleasures may be as frequent as can be.

As a christian minister my own thought turns to the place of religion in the post-war world. I fear - wrongly I hope - that in the religion also pleasure may be expected to receive first consideration. Even some of you who are christian people may decide to go on Sunday morning instead of to Church, + most other people will claim a right to do the same kind of thing with the time money that is their own. In religion, I do not visualize the post-war period as being vastly different in essential nature from the period 1918 forward. Half-empty churches may be expected - and I am not one of those who believes that attendance at public worship is the only gauge of religion, but I do believe public worship to be indispensible to christian living! As we have empty churches there will be people of a particular type who will say as has been said before "Christianity has served its day", it is effete + outmoded. Others, like bishop Gore, will beg the question by replying "Christianity has not failed it has never been tried." There will be newspaper articles of a topical variety on the state of the Church: its divisions: its obscurantism and the slavery of some sections of the universal Church to the frozen past. Many earnest folk will be anxious for the future of the Church. Usually they will mean their own particular church + their own practice of Christianity. Personally I have no fears for the future of the Religion of Jesus, but I think it may well be that the Church will receive a violent shaking-up. And I think a Church that claims to have access to the illimitable Power of God + to be the medium of that power on earth - but witnesses two world wars at a time when non-Christians are agreed that war is evil - a Church that is part of an economic order, for the denunciation of which non-Christian theories thrive - such a Church deserves to be shaken up - indeed in the interest of its own survival it must be shaken up. That is not to say that Christianity is to go. The Church in its present form may pass away - I believe it will - but the Religion of Jesus will remain! It will remain because wherever men are interested in the art of good living, the Son of man has no peer; He is incomparable; His conduct wholly good. There is no weak spot in His armour against evil - there is no richer beauty than the family idea on which He bases His world Kingdom- the Realm of God. Though not fearful for the future of the Religion of Jesus:—

I am concerned about the general approach to life which I believe will prevail in the post-war world. My reason for saying this is the fact of my having lived through two world wars. I knew the fathers of the men who are fighting the present war. I knew the girls they married who became your mothers. I heard their conversation, and if you are not their natural sons, then they themselves are here again, doing + saying the same things in the same way as yesteryear. The only way which you men of this generation can make a better job of your post-war than we made of ours, is by being better men than we were. And quite frankly I do not think you are - nor are you more intelligent - nor have you more nor higher ideals - or fewer or worse vices. You know things your fathers did not know, but only about theories, sciences, formulas + the like: not about heroism or cowardice, honour, pain, hatred, love, success, failure, happiness, satisfaction, discontent, hope determined any of those primal things that constitute immediate reality. At the close of the first world war which your fathers fought in, one of the politicians coined the phrase "A world fit for Heroes." It sounded fine + appeared to mean something - and many people it became the focal point of all hope & faith. I wondered then, & am still wondering, what precisely it did mean. If it meant a country from which all perplexity & difficulty were removed by act of Parliament — if it meant a country which called its sons to do roism & sacrifice once in a lifetime and afterwards each hero had an assured income, perhaps a pension, & was superannuated all danger & enterprise, & wrapped for the rest of his life in social cotton wool: if it meant these things, then such a country would never sire another hero having plucked from the nation's womb the very seed of heroism. Yet, I fear, that was the Kind we visualised by many; and there were some who unashamedly asked for a life of that Kind. And is it not true that you have had much the same wish expressed in this camp? and is there not something in all of us that plans a future on golden shores a sunlit sea? But it is a level of life such which no healthy minded man could long be satisfied, and which would revolt — alist, and which a Christian could only regard as vice. Nowhere in the teaching of the N.T. could such living be justified — "If any man would follow after me, let him deny himself & take up his cross". And when one of the scribes, usually of the ruling class alestine, offered himself for discipleship, Jesus pointed out that it would involve a change from physical comfort to discomfort, and added — "The foxes have holes, the birds of the air have nests, but the Son of man hath not where to lay his head". Other occasion speaking much to the same purpose He said "If any man come unto me & hate not his father & mother & children & brethren & sisters — yea and hate not his own life also, he cannot be my disciple". The worlds Jesus as they are noted in the Gospels are not infrequently difficult to understand, but His deeds are infant plain. Of himself & His work He saw a deeds that I do, these bear witness of me". If Jesus had written a book instead of lived a life, there would have been good ground wanting Christianity toned down a little; some of its hardships eliminated & the sacrifices it requires softened down. But Jesus ed a life! And if we take the Gospels as our guide, His words appear to be few indeed while His deeds were many and were characterized by that firm resolve which led Him finally to embrace the cross. He went about doing good, and the substance teaching is little more than a series of comments passed on the deeds done.   After the post war world has had its conflict about Christianity having failed & the Churches inability to keep pace with modern thought about war, economic systems & religions actual life of Jesus on earth will still be the world's highest illustration of noble living while men of noble character, though they reject much that the centuries in an access of overzeal have incorporated in their doctrines about Him, will still see in Jesus & human supremacy that everywhere else is sought in vain. Pardon a very trite phrase from moral philosophy, which in spite triteness is worthy of notice. It is — "The true norm of living is where the best that is in man confronts the highest that is required of him". That aphorism is not higher than Xtian teaching, it is just a philosopher's way of saying in words what Jesus taught de.   It is impossible in a brief sentence to round off all the ragged points left in a sermon of this kind, but the chief thing I have in mind, is clear, I hope viz: that your post war world cannot be better than ours was unless your age dissociates itself from the idea implicit in the phrase "a world fit for heroes" and embraces the idea of a world needing heroes. In this connection the message of the text is thoroughly explicit — "If any man would follow me let him deny himself & take up his cross". A call to be builders of the Realm of God is not a call to a limitative, effortless life in which a man cannot be a man — a life of rich listlessness. It is the hardest life I know: and the phrases "to deny oneself" and to "take up one's cross" are not airy figures speech. They are alive with the tumult of battle — against evil in one's own life first. And if you wish to know how bitter a struggle against evil outside yourself can be, then declare a little war of your own against the vested interests of evil in the area in which you move and see how old friends dismiss you, & how the person who closes his eyes & smiles on everything is honoured & feted — and then tell me if the phrases "to deny oneself" and to "take up one's cross" are airy figures of speech with out invitation. The call to be builders of the Realm of God has none of the specious comfort of self-deception about it. Instead it has the hardness of self-discipline and the stern effort of self-denial. Western civilisation may shortly have to choose between Karl Marx the Jew; and the Jew Jesus of Nazareth." I think the choice finally will be of Jesus of Nazareth: and I think it may be in the process of establishment of that choice that the present aspect of the church may find itself passed by, by a movement less national & less racial in character, and nearer to the ideal of a world unity in the Realm of God.

148. IF JERRY SAYS "GO" WE MUST "GET-GOING"....

. . . He demanded that I should enter the following to close the book. St. Matt 17–24 "If any man will come after me let him deny himself and take up the cross."

Most people are wondering what the state of things is likely to be in post-war Britain, America, Canada, Australia or whatever place they call home. Until the success of the invasion put such matters out of mind, the future of our own country and of the world was the most constant subject of speculation. Men whose interests were industrial and commercial discussed the reconverting of the war potential into a peace potential. Agriculturists and dairy farmers wondered and are still wondering to whatever extent the Govt. to control their industry. The building trade with all its concomitant trades and professions is well to the fore with its plans for planning. For most people there is a general interest in post-war economies and money— in the unknowable future of money markets in a war-despoiled Europe; what stabilisation of currency may be expected between the empire and the Americas; and what the true function and utility of the new World bank created by the Three Powers.

People in the Services are naturally anxious about the changes which in four years have put them out of date in their own profession. They are concerned also as to the probability or otherwise of the country spending more money than hitherto on the armed services, or whether it will revert to its former practice of spending as much as possible on immediate pleasure. Judging from the intentions one hears expressed in the camp the latter is probable— and from what one knows of the British taxpayer too who wants his tax as low as maybe, that his pleasures may be as frequent as can be.

As a Christian minister my own thoughts turn to the place of religion in the post-war world. I fear—wrongly I hope—that in the case of religion also, pleasure may be expected to receive first consideration. Even some of you who are Christian people may decide to go to golf on Sunday morning instead of to Church, and most other people will claim a right to do the same kind of thing with the time and money that is their own. In religion, I do not visualise the post-war period as being vastly different in essential nature from the period 1918 forward. Half-empty churches may be expected—and I am not one of those who believe that attendance as church worship is the only gauge of religion, but I do believe public worship to be indispensable to Christian living! As well as empty churches there will be people of a particular type who will say as has been said before "Christianity has served its day", it is effete and outmoded. Others, like Bishop Gore, will beg the question by replying "Christianity has not failed, it has never been tried".

There will be newspaper articles of a topical variety on: the state of the Church, its divisions: its obscurantism, and the slavery of some sections of the universal Church to the frozen past. Many earnest folk will be anxiously fearful for the future of the Church. Usually they will mean their own particular Church and their own practice of Christianity. Personally I have no fears for the future of the Religion of Jesus, but I think it may well be that the

Church will receive a violent shaking up. And I think a Church that claims to have access to the illimitable Power of God and to be the medium of that power on Earth—but witness two world wars at a time when non-Christians are agreed that war is evil—a Church that is part of the economic order, for the denunciation of which non-Christian theories thrive—such a Church deserves to be shaken up—indeed in the interest of its own survival it must be shaken up. That is not to say that Christianity is wrong. The Church in its present form may pass away—I believe it will—but the Religion of Jesus will remain! It will remain because wherever men are interested in the art of good living, the Son of Man has no peer: He is incomparable; His conduct is wholly good. There is no weak spot in His armour against evil—there is no richer beauty than the family idea on which he bases His World Kingdom—the Realm of God. Though not fearful for the Religion of Jesus:

I am concerned about the general approach to life which I believe will prevail in the post-war world. My reason for saying this is the fact of my having lived through two World Wars. I knew the fathers of the men who are fighting the present war. I knew the girls they married who became your mothers. I heard their conversation, and if you are not their natural born sons, then they themselves are here again, doing and saying the same things in the same way as yesteryear. The only way in which you men of this generation can make a better job of your post-war than we made of ours, is by being better men than we were. And quite frankly I do not think you are—nor are you more intelligent—nor have you more nor higher ideals—or fewer or worse vices. You know things your fathers did not know, but only about theories, sciences, formulae and the like: not about heroism or cowardice, honour, pain, hatred, love, success, failure, happiness, satisfaction, discontent, hope, determination or any of those primal things that constitute immediate reality. At the close of the first world war which your fathers fought and won, one of the politicians coined the phrase "A World fit for Heroes". It sounded fine and appeared to mean something—indeed [*original text continued on page 149 of diary*] for many people it became the focal point of all hope and faith. I wondered then and am still wondering what precisely it did mean. If it meant a country from which all perplexity and difficulty were removed by act of Parliament—if it meant a country which called its sons to deeds of heroism and sacrifice once in a lifetime and afterwards each hero had an assured income, perhaps a pension, and was superannuated from all danger and enterprise, and wrapped for the rest of his life in social cotton wool: if it meant those things, then such a country would never sire another hero having plucked from the nation's womb the very seed of heroism. Yet, I fear, that was the kind of future visualized by many; and there were some who unashamedly asked for a life of that kind. And is it not time that you have heard much the same wish expressed in this camp? And is there not something in all of us that plans a future on golden shores by a sunlit sea?

But it is a level of life with which no healthy man could long be satisfied, and which would revolt an idealist, and which a Christian could only regard as vice. No where in the teaching of the N.T. could such a living be justified—"If any man would follow after me, let him deny himself and take up his Cross."

And when one of the scribes, usually one of the ruling classes of Palestine, offered himself up for disciple-ship, Jesus pointed out that it would involve a change from physical comfort to discomfort and added: "The foxes have holes, the birds of the air have nests, but the Son of Man hath nowhere to lay His head."

On another occasion, speaking much to the same purpose He said: "If any man come with me and leave not his father and mother and wife and children and brethren and sisters—yea and hate not his own life also, he cannot be my disciple." The words of Jesus as they are reported in the Gospels are not infrequently difficult to understand, but His deeds are infant plain. Of Himself and His work He said, "The deeds that I do, these bear witness of me." If Jesus had written a book instead of lived a life, there would have been good ground for wanting Christianity toned down a little; some of its hardships eliminated and sacrifices it requires softened down. But Jesus lived a life! And if we take the Gospels as our guide, His words appear to be few indeed while His deeds were many and were characterized by that firm resolve which led Him finally to embrace the Cross. He went about doing good, and the substance of His teaching is little more than a series of comments passed on the deeds done.

After the post-war world had its confused say about Christianity having failed and the Churches' inability to keep pace with modern thought about war, economic systems etc., etc.—the actual life of Jesus on earth will still be the world's highest illustration of noble living which men of noble character, though they may reject much that the centuries in an excess of overzeal have incorporated in their doctrine about Him, will still see in Jesus that human supremacy that everywhere else is sought in vain.

Pardon a very trite phrase from moral philosophy, which in spite of its triteness is worthy of notice. It is: "The true norm of living is where the best that is in man confronts the highest that is required form him." That aphorism is not higher than Christian teaching, it is just a philosopher's way of saying in words what Jesus taught in deeds.

It is impossible in a brief sentence to round off all the ragged points left in a sermon of this kind, but the chief thing I have in mind is clear, I hope, viz: that your post-war world cannot be better than ours was unless your age dissociates itself from the idea implicit in the phrase "A World fit for Heroes" and embraces the idea of a world needing heroes. In this connection the message of the text is thoroughly explicit—"If any man would follow Me let him deny himself and take up his Cross!" The call to be builders of the realm of God is not a call to a limitative, effete life in which a man cannot be a man—a life of sterile listlessness. It is the hardest life I know: and the phrases "to deny oneself" and to "take up one's Cross" are not airy figures of speech. They are alive with the tumult of battle—against evil in one's own life first. And if you wish to know how bitter the struggle against evil outside yourself can be, then declare a little war or your own against the vested interests of evil in the circles in which you move and see how old friends dismiss you, and how the person who closes his eyes and smiles on everything is welcomed and feted—and then tell me if the phrases "to deny oneself" and to "take up one's Cross" are airy figures of speech with no special investiture. The call to be builders of the Realm of God has none of the spurious comfort and self-deception about it. Instead it has the hardness of self-discipline and the stern effort of self denial. Western civilization may shortly have to choose between Karl Marx the Jew and the Jew Jesus of Nazareth. I think the choice finally will be Jesus of Nazareth: and I think it may be in the process of establishment of that choice that the present aspect of the Church may find itself passed by, by a movement less national and less racial in character, and nearer to the ideal of a world unity in the Realm of God.

J. E. P.

(Captain the Reverend Ellison Platt)

Page 150 is blank.

BRIEF BIOGRAPHIES
OF CONTRIBUTORS

The following is an alphabetical list of the officers and men who wrote articles in the original YMCA Colditz Wartime Log. Although information has been added on some of the contributors, this is limited to snippets of pertinent information, because the intent of this book is not to provide detailed histories of each man, but to allow the reader to experience the stories themselves. Other books have been written by and about the lives of these 'kriegies'.

There are some about whom little is known, while others gained fame during the war because of their daring exploits, and some went on after the war to distinguished peacetime careers in the service of their country.

Alexander, Michael, (1920–2004): Captain, Duke of Cornwall's Light Infantry, Special Boat Service. Captured in North Africa as an SBS Commando, Alexander could have been executed as a saboteur, but with quick thinking, Corporal Gurney who was captured with him, falsely told their captors that Alexander was related to General Alexander and was thus one of the 'Prominente'. He was actually only a distant cousin but enjoyed 'Prominente' status from then on.

Allan, Anthony Murray 'Peter', (1917-2002): Second Lieutenant, Queen's Own Cameron Highlanders. One of the 'Laufen Six', Allan managed to escape by being sewn into an old mattress that was being dumped, the diminutive Scotsman was driven out of Colditz on the back of a lorry. After the mattress was off-loaded, Allan travelled by train and foot to Vienna. As he spoke fluent German, he even hitched a ride with some Gestapo officers. Finally, after being refused help by the American Consulate, tired and hungry, he gave up and turned himself in to a police station.

Archer, G. M., Sapper, 2nd Field Park Company. Royal Australian Engineers, Australian Imperial Force. Captured in 1941 and transferred to Colditz 1943.

Barnet, R., Lieutenant, Royal Navy. Captured 1940, arrived in Colditz 1941.

Barott, Peter T. Murray, Lieutenant, 1ˢᵗ Battalion The Black Watch (R.H.R.) of Canada. Originally from Montreal, Barott was captured 1942 at Dieppe and arrived in Colditz in 1943. He took part in a number of escape attempts including the Eichstätt Job,

Barry, Rupert, Captain, 2ⁿᵈ Light Infantry. Captured and arrived in Colditz 1940. Barry was one of the 'Laufen Six' among the first British prisoners in Colditz, arriving on the 7th November 1940. He made an unsuccessful escape attempt through the well in the Kommandantur in 1942. He corresponded from Colditz with the War Office in London by sending letters to his wife Dodo written in a crossword code. She passed them on to MI9.

Bartlett, Dennis E. A., Lieutenant, 3ʳᵈ Battalion, Royal Tank Regiment. Captured 1941, arrived in Colditz 1943. Bartlett acted as ghost for Mike Harvey's escape, which confused the guards when Bartlett made his own escape via the air raid shelter. He was later awarded the Military Cross.

Best, John 'Jack' W., (1912–2000): Flight Lieutenant, Royal Air Force. Captured after his aircraft ran out of fuel off the coast of Greece, Best was sent to Stalag Luft III from where he escaped by tunnelling, While at Colditz he made a number of escape attempts. For a time he was a "ghost" prisoner, hiding for long periods so the guards would think he had escaped. Best was one of the leaders in building the famous glider that was constructed in the attic of Colditz. He was with Mike Sinclair during his escape using a rope down a wall in 1944.

Bór-Komorowski, Tadeusz, (1895-1966): General, Polish Army. General Count Bór-Komorowski, who took part in the initial fighting in Poland in 1939, became renowned for leading the Warsaw uprising in 1944 as the Soviet forces advanced into Poland from the east. His army surrendered to the Germans in 1944 on condition that all Polish fighters be treated as prisoners of war. He refused however to order all Home Army units to surrender to the Germans. Bór-Komorowski was awarded many distinctive medals.

Boustead, John, Lieutenant, Seaforth Highlanders. Escaped from Colditz in 1941 dressed as a member of Hitler Youth, but was caught. Attempted again in January 1942 using a British snow tunnel over the canteen roof but was detected.

Broomhall, W. M. 'Tubby', (1897-1995): Lieutenant Colonel, Royal Engineers. Captured 1940, arrived in Colditz 1943. Broomhall, who was senior British Officer during much of 1943, was at first suspected of being too compliant with the German captors, but soon gained the respect of his fellow prisoners for taking a tough stand against the Germans on behalf of the 'Prominente'.

Brown, Michael, Captain, No. Commando, AEF. Arrived in Colditz in June 1943.

Bruce, Dominic, (1919–2003): Flight Lieutenant, Royal Air Force. After being ordered to carry boxes up to a third storey store room, Bruce escaped by climbing down a rope from the window to temporary freedom. The next day the guards found a note which read: 'I don't like the air in Colditz. Auf Wiedersehen. Ex-PW Flying Officer Bruce.'

Burton, W. J., Captain, Yorkshire and Lancaster Regiment. Captured in 1941, arrived in Colditz 1943.

Campbell, Alan 'Black', Lieutenant, Royal Artillery. Born in 1917 and a lawyer before the war, Campbell was captured in 1941 in France. He arrived in Colditz 1941, was sent to Spangenberg and returned in 1943. While in Spangenberg, he and Yule attempted to escape across the castle moat, so he was returned to Colditz. During his time there he defended prisoners in German courts martial. Later he became Lord Campbell of Alloway.

Castagnier, C. C., Sergeant, 2ieme Cle Paratroops.

Chaloupka, Cenek, 'Checko', Flight Lieutenant, Royal Air Force. Captured in 1941, arrived in Colditz 1943. Chaloupka, a tall Czech, was in charge of bribery and corruption as part of the escape team in Colditz. Using charm, guile and gifts for the guards, Chaloupka, who spoke fluent German, was able to acquire passes and valuable items for escapes, including railway timetables, hacksaw and radio parts, as well as food.

Champ, Jack W. K., Lieutenant, 6th Battalion Australian Imperial Force. Captured in 1941, arrived at Colditz in 1943. Champ had participated previously in a mass escape from Oflag VIB but was captured very soon after. One of the twenty Australian captives in Colditz, he later wrote a book about his experiences.

Champion, Ernest, Lieutenant, Royal Naval Reserves. Captured in 1940, arrived at Colditz in 1942.

Chrisp, John, Bosun, Royal Navy. Because of his experience rigging boats and laying buoys in the Navy, Chrisp was elected the official Colditz rope-maker, working with a team of eight, using needles and thread provided by the escape committee to convert bed sheets into ropes up to 100 feet in length.

Church of England Padre. There were a few Padres in Colditz, so it is unclear who wrote and delivered the tribute to Mike Sinclair at his funeral, as there is no signature. Ellison Platt later wrote a book about his experiences as Padre in Colditz, but the writing in this account is not his.

Cocksedge, A. R. A., Lieutenant, 2nd Regiment, Inniskillling Fusiliers. Captured in 1940, arrived at Colditz in 1943.

Colt, G. M., Lieutenant, 1ˢᵗ Battalion Tyneside Scottish (Black Watch). While being transferred between camps by train, Colt chose a dangerous method of escape: he jumped at night from a moving locomotive.

Courtenay, J. M., Lieutenant, Queen Victoria Rifles. Courtenay was a pre-war Divinity Student at Oxford until he joined the army. He was captured at Calais in 1940.

Crawford, D. A., Captain, Australian Imperial Force. Crawford was one of many Australians who took part in the Warburg Wire Job, a mass escape from Oflag VIIB before his transfer to Colditz.

Crawford, J. A., Lieutenant, Queens Own Cameron Highlanders.

Davies-Scourfield, Grismond, Lieutenant, 60ᵗʰ Rifles, Kings Royal Rifle Corps. Captured in 1940 after being left for dead after the street battle for Calais, he was sent to Laufen and then Posen. Considered by guards in Colditz to be a dangerous escaper, Davies-Scourfield worked as chief stooge (lookout) on the escape team after months on the run in Poland.

de Hamel, Max, 77305 Lieutenant, No.1 OCS, BOAR. One of the 'Prominente', de Hamel attempted an escape with four other Prominentes using a Dutch tunnel through eight feet of the castle wall, assisted by a Dutch Officer. The guards found them after an extensive search, which was made more urgent because Germany was about to capitulate, so the Prominente were to be transferred, used as bargaining chips and possibly executed.

Dickinson, J. P. 'Bag', Lieutenant, Royal Air Force. Dickinson escaped from Colditz in 1943 by jumping over the wall of the exercise yard in Colditz town jail. He stole a bicycle and rode forty miles south to Chemnitz where he was caught.

Donaldson, M. W. 'Don', Flight Lieutenant, Royal Air Force. Shot down in Norway in 1940 while attacking the cruiser Karlsruhe, Donaldson arrived in Colditz in 1941.

Drew, George S., (1918–2005): Lieutenant, 58ᵗʰ Royal Engineers, The Northamptonshire Regiment. Drew and Ferguson were responsible for producing a potent home brew from a mixture of yeast, water and turnip jam which contained sufficient sugar for fermentation. He escaped from Eichstätt with Ferguson and 65 prisoners after being part of a tunnelling team there.

Ecochard, Francois, Lieutenant, Corps France d'Afrique.

Ferguson, John Patrick, (1917-2004): Lieutenant, Royal Tank Corps. Part of Ferguson's contribution while in Colditz, was production of an unpleasant tasting but strongly alcoholic liquor from an illicit still, which he concocted with the help of Mike Edwards and George Drew.

Froger, Charles, Lieutenant, French Army.

Gee, Howard, Mr. A journalist and translator, Gee was one of only two civilian prisoners in Oflag IVC. After the war he wrote a book on Colditz.

Gilliat, W. J., (1913–1993): Captain, 60th Rifles. Gilliat went on to become an MBE and served as Private Secretary to the Queen Mother.

Green, Julius M., Captain, Army Dental Corps. Green exchanged information with London by writing coded letters to his mother so she could pass them on to the War Office at home.

Ha-Cohen, Simon, Lieutenant, Palestinian Royal Engineers. Born in Russia and raised in Palestine, Ha-Cohen was a Jewish officer who entered Colditz under special Gestapo guard because of his outspoken contempt for his Nazi oppressors. He had been a Sergeant Major in the British Army in the First World War.

Halfin, Solomon Dennis, Rifleman, King's Royal Rifle Corps. Captured in Crete in 1941, Halfin escaped and spent three months in the mountains with the partisans. After being recaptured and sent to Lamsdorf, he was about to be sent to another camp, but exchanged identities with Cordeau, who happened to be a dental technician. The authorities, needing dental care in Colditz, sent Halfin there, so he entered Colditz accidentally.

Hamilton-Baillie, John 'Jock' Robert Edward, (1919–2003): Lieutenant, 26th Field Company, Royal Engineers. A career soldier, Hamilton-Baillie was wounded while fighting on the Maginot Line. He was captured and detained in a prison camp at Peronne, from which he escaped. After being captured and attempting more escapes from various camps, Hamilton-Baillie escaped alone though the wire from Oflag VIID, walked 200 miles in ten days and nearly made it across the Swiss border. After more escape attempts, he saw the end of the war in Colditz and was awarded the Military Cross. Later he became Aide-de-Camp to the Queen.

Hamilton, D. K. 'Hamish', Lieutenant, Royal Artillery. Hamilton was sent after participating in a mass escape via tunnel from Oflag VIB and moving northwards for five days before being caught by Hitler Youth.

Harvey, L. W., (1913–1996): Lieutenant Commander, Royal Navy. A submarine commander captured early in the war, Harvey was a Colditz "ghost" who hid at all times, allowing the guards think he had escaped, while he acted as stand-in for actual escaped prisoners during roll calls.

Hawksworth, A., Captain, Royal Engineers. Moved from Banica concentration camp to Vienna, then Mathausen, from where instead of the gas chamber, Hawksworth was transferred to Colditz with Brigadier Davies and two others.

Herman, K. E., Captain, Durham Light Infantry. Arrived in Colditz in June 1943

Holroyd, Ralph, Lieutenant, Australian Imperial Force. Although he was an Australian soldier, his German mother was given permission to visit him in Colditz, much to the consternation of some other prisoners. Their fears were unfounded as he remained loyal to the allies. Because he had been a photographer in peacetime, he was assigned to taking photographs of all escapers in character before they left. He used a camera constructed by Anderson from a cigar box with a spectacle lens.

Hopetoun, Charles, The Earl of, (1912–1987): Captain, Lothian and Border Yeomanry. Charles, 9th Earl of Hopetoun, 3rd Marquess of Hopetoun and son of the Viceroy of India. Hopetoun was one of the 'Prominente', the prisoners with Royal connections.

Jones, L. A., 'Buckshie King', Sapper, Royal Engineers.

Jordan, A., Captain, ISAS Regiment, French Air Force.

Khelil, El Khemiri, Lieutenant, 4e Regiment de Fusiliers Francais. Captured on 19 June 1944 in Sienna (Mont Amiata Italy).

Lassalle-Astis, Jacques, Capitaine, Groupe Bombardeux.

Lee, J. Kenneth V., Lieutenant, Royal Signals. Working diligently for over three years as one of the chief forgers providing passports and other necessary papers for escapers, Lee's work was never discovered. He copied the German script in pencil and finished documents in indian ink.

Lochrane, F. A. J., Lieutenant, The Seaforth Highlanders. Lochrane was one of the unfortunate captives who were forced to march east across Europe after the fall of France, to begin incarceration in Germany.

MacAskie, Ian Bruce, Lieutenant, Royal West Kent Regiment. Captured in 1940 and transferred to Colditz in1943 after escaping from Eichstätt.

Mackenzie, Colin, Lieutenant, Seaforth Highlanders.

Marchand, A. R., Lieutenant, Fusiliers Mont Royal.

McColm, M. L., Squadron Leader, Royal Air Force. McColm was an Australian who joined the RAF before the war and was shot down in the early days of conflict.

McDonnell, James, Lieutenant, Royal Norfolk Regiment. In November 1942, McDonnell and four others disguised themselves as Frenchmen and marched out of the main gate of the prison before catching a train in a bid for freedom.

Merritt, C. C. I., (d. 2000): Lieutenant Colonel, South Saskatchewan Regiment. Originally a lawyer, Merritt was captured in 1942 at Dieppe and moved to Colditz in 1943 from Eichstätt. He was awarded the Victoria Cross.

Millar, (d. 1944?): Lieutenant William A. 'Dopey' Millar. Millar a Canadian engineer captured at Dieppe was instrumental in commencing the compilation of the *Wartime Log*. He slipped through a window and escaped from Colditz in January 1944, but was never heard of again, presumed killed at some point during his run.

Millett, John Robert 'Jack', (1919–1999): Lieutenant 2/11 Battalion. Australian Imperial Force. Jack Millett served in the Middle East before being captured in Crete in 1941. One of approximately twenty Australians in Colditz, he was renowned for producing high quality escape maps for fellow prisoners.

Milne, Keith, Flight Lieutenant, Royal Air Force. Milne worked with Norman Forbes in getting the wireless team in and out of the special hide in the rafters of Colditz. They opened and closed the hide and battened down the entrance while the operators were inside for two hours every night. Milne and Donald Middleton had escaped from Spangenberg in 1940 dressed as painters, complete with buckets of whitewash and a long ladder.

Moir, Douglas N., (1918-2008): Lieutenant, Royal Tank Regiment (Ch83)

Moody, R. F., Captain, New Zealand MC. (Ch42)

Moran, J. M., Pay Lieutenant, Royal Naval Reserves (Ch28). While on leave at his home in London, Moran had first-hand experience of German bombing raids on the city.

Morgan, Richard F., Lieutenant, No. 3 Commando (Ch52)

Morison, Walter McDonald, (1919–2009): Flight Lieutenant, Royal Air Force. Morison was imprisoned in Colditz in 1943 after escaping from Stalag Luft III and attempting to steal a German aircraft to fly to Sweden. His entry is the account of the night of 5 June 1942 when he was in a Wellington on a bombing mission to Essen. After colliding with another bomber, he was the only member of his crew to parachute to safety.

Nugent, D. M., Captain, The King's Royal Rifle Corps.

Pardoe, Phil, Lieutenant, 60th Rifles. Moved from Laufen prison camp to Posen, Pardoe was one of a group of prisoners transferred to harsher conditions in retaliation for complaints by German prisoners in Canada.

Parker, Vincent 'Bush', (1918–1946): Flight Lieutenant, Royal Air Force. An Australian who moved to England and joined the RAF, Parker was shot down over the English Channel but picked up by a German E-Boat. He was an expert lock-picker, and put his skills to good use in Colditz. He died just after the war in an RAF flying accident in England.

Pemberton-How, G. M., Captain, Royal Army Service Corps. A Territorial Officer from Oxford, Pemberton-How acted as Colditz Quartermaster, ensuring even distribution of black market goods.

Penman, J., Lieutenant, Argyll and Sutherland Highlanders.

Platt, Ellison, Captain the Reverend. Platt was a Methodist Chaplain who offered spiritual guidance throughout the war. Captured at Dunkirk in 1940 while attending to the wounded, Platt was one of the first to be sent to Colditz, and spent the next five years of the war as a prisoner. He kept a personal diary which he published later. He became an MBE.

Pringle, Jack, Major, 8th Hussars, (d. 1999). Captured in North Africa in 1941 and moved to Colditz in 1944, Pringle was a determined trouble-maker who arrived with David Stirling, the founder of the SAS.

Pumphrey, J. Laurence, (1916–2009): Second Lieutenant, Northumberland Hussars. Pumphrey was awarded the Greek Military Cross for bravery in battle. After the war he served in the Foreign Office as a diplomat and became ambassador to Pakistan. He was awarded a knighthood.

Purdon, Corran, Lieutenant, No.12 Commando. Captured at St. Nazaire, aged twenty, and labelled Deutschfeindlich (hostile), Purdon first met Campbell and Yule while in Spangenburg, awaiting transfer to Colditz. He made an escape attempt disguised as a Belgian.

Rash, E. L., Lieutenant Colonel, Royal Tank Regiment.

Redding, Claude, Lieutenant, General List. Redding arrived with five other British officers from Fresnes Jail in Paris in 1944 after parachuting into France as Special Operations Executive agents who worked with the French Resistance on sabotage operations. Caught by the Gestapo and sentenced to death in France, Redding, a wireless operator, waited two months in prison before being sent to Colditz instead.

Reid, Miles, Major, General Head Quarters Liaison. Miles Reid was the British Liaison officer to the French in 1940. He was captured in Greece in 1941.

Riviere, Michael, Lieutenant, Nottinghamshire Yeomanry.

Rogers, Douglas J., (d. 2000): Captain, Royal Engineers. Captured in France in 1940, Rogers arrived in Colditz in 1941. He was sent to Spangenberg in 1943 and back to Colditz the same year. He was one of the scribes who wrote down information gained by listening to the wireless set hidden in the rafters of the castle.

Rolfe, Gordon L., Major, Royal Canadian Signals. Rolfe joined the RCCS at the age of sixteen and was commissioned at the start of the war. He commanded the First Canadian Army Tank Brigade until his capture.

Roy, John H., Lieutenant, Les Fusiliers Mont Royal. Roy was captured at Dieppe. While incarcerated he learned Russian, German and Spanish.

Sandbach, C. E., Lieutenant, Cheshire Regiment. In 1943 Sandbach attempted to escape with two other officers by exchanging identities with French officers while in transit to Lübeck.

Schrire, Isidore, Captain, Royal Army Medical Corps, South Africa. Captured at Dunkirk, Shrire was a Jewish officer who became an MBE.

Scott, W. H. 'Bill', Lieutenant, Essex Scottish Regiment. Bill Scott led one of the few parties able to enter the town of Dieppe in the early part of the war.

Seni. Little is known of this artist, whose pen and wash illustrations are included. His name does not appear to match any of those on the lists of prisoners. However, January 1945 saw the arrival of a French Major General Arsene-Marie-Paul Vauthier (1885–1979), who could possibly have signed himself as Seni.

Silverwood-Cope, C. L., Lieutenant, Royal Artillery. After recovering from typhus in Poland with the help of a Jewish doctor and his daughter, Silverwood-Cope played a key role in running escape lines out of Poland, but the Gestapo infiltrated the organisation and he was arrested and sent to Pawiak civilian prison. The doctor and his daughter were sent to a concentration camp.

Storie-Pugh, Peter, (1919–2011): Lieutenant, Queen's Own Royal West Kent Regiment. Wounded and captured in France, Storie-Pugh made his first escape from a German military hospital, after which he was recaptured and sent to Oflag IX. There he cut through wires and swam away down the River, but was caught by German workers who treated him well, but he was badly beaten by German soldiers. Storie-Pugh, who became Colonel later, was awarded the Military Cross and an MBE. After the war he became President of the Royal College of Veterinary Surgeons.

Tine, Jean-Claude, Lieutenant, Regiment de Spahis Algerieus.

Tunstall, Peter D., (1920–2014): Flight Lieutenant, Royal Air Force. While in Colditz, Tunstall caused regular havoc during the frequent roll calls in order to confuse the guards, so that when an escape occurred, absences were not suspected. He was subjected to five courts martial and served 415 days in solitary confinement.

Van Rood, A., Flight Lieutenant, Royal Netherlands Army, RAFVR. Before the war, Van Rood was a medical student in England, married to an Englishwoman. When the war broke out he joined the Royal Netherlands Air Force, (Koninklijke Luchtmacht) and became a Spitfire pilot.

Ville, G., Captain, 1er Regiment Etranger de Cavalerie.

Vuillant, Sergeant, Free French Forces. An American citizen who signed up in New York for the Free French Forces, Vuillant was captured in the Middle East while on an operation with the Long Range Desert Group.

Walker, Stewart, Lieutenant, 9th Battalion, Durham Light Infantry. Walker was one of the officers dressed as 'frenchmen' who escaped from Eichstätt as recounted by Lieutenant James McDonnell.

Weldon, F. W. C., Captain, Royal Horse Artillery. A lawyer before the war. Weldon became one of the two chief engineers of the Eichstätt escape tunnel. On a previous escape, he cut through wires in daylight and was within yards of the Swiss frontier when recaptured.

Winton, Peter C., Lieutenant, Gordon Highlanders.

Wood, J. E. R. 'Jerry', Lieutenant, Royal Canadian Engineers (POW #4101). Taken prisoner in the 1942 Dieppe raid, Wood, a mining engineer by trade, studied German and worked on tunnels in Colditz. He was awarded the Military Cross. Wood acted as editor for Detour, the 1946 book from these accounts, and friendly references to 'Jerry' in some of the stories are to Wood.

Yule, James 'Jimmy' de Denne, (1916–2001): Captain, Royal Signals Regiment. While inside Colditz, Yule acted as wireless operator, sitting at nights with a scribe, Micky Burn as they listened for news on 'London Calling', with Alvar Liddell. The wireless, hidden high in the rafters, had been left by the French. In 1941 Yule had been captured near the Swiss border after escaping by jumping from a train with other prisoners.

Zafouk, Jack, Captain, Royal Air Force. Shot down in 1941 in a 311 Squadron Wellington. While being transported to Oflag VIB by train, several officers cut a hole in the floorboards and escaped. Zafouk, a Czech, and Roger Bushell hid in a Resistance safe house in Prague, but the SS executed over a thousand villagers there and Zafouk and Bushell were badly beaten by the Gestapo before being taken to Colditz.